D1291695

The Ozarks

AN EXPLORER'S GUIDE

The Ozarks

Includes Branson, Springfield & Northwest Arkansas

Ron W. Marr

photographs by the author

The Countryman Press ✳ Woodstock, Vermont

SECOND EDITION

This book is for Lori DeVita Hofman. If the journey of life is measured in friendship, rather than miles, we have traversed the universe.

"There is no path to happiness: happiness is the path."
—Siddhartha Gautama

"One's destination is never a place, but a new way of seeing things."
—Henry Miller

The author can be reached via his website at www.ronmarr.com

Copyright © 2012 by Ron W. Marr

Explorer's Guide The Ozarks
ISBN: 978-0-88150-962-5

Interior photographs by the author unless otherwise specified
Maps by Erin Greb Cartography, © The Countryman Press
Book design by Bodenweber Design
Composition by PerfecType, Nashville, TN

Published by The Countryman Press, P.O. Box 748, Woodstock, VT 05091

Distributed by W. W. Norton & Company, Inc., 500 Fifth Avenue, New York, NY 10110

Printed in the United States of America

10 9 8 7 6 5 4 3 2 1

EXPLORE WITH US!

Welcome to the second edition of *Explorer's Guide Ozarks*. Kick off your boots, pull up a chair, and set a spell. We hope that this latest version of the book continues to be the best and most comprehensive wanderer's bible of the hills, hollers, sights, and spectacles that make up the Missouri and Arkansas Ozarks. Within the pages to come you'll discover 50,000 square miles of sheer pretty, along with insights into the ways, traditions, history, and personalities of those who inhabit this ancient highland. In contrast to many such guides, this one is written by a local, someone who knows the hot spots and back roads. I've attempted to infuse every page not just with in-depth and opinionated descriptions, but also with a hefty and happily readable dollop of Ozark anecdotes, philosophy, and humor.

Before we get started, I do want to address a topic near and dear to the Ozarkian heart. We generally prefer squirrel rifles over elephant guns in these parts, but there's a big ol' pachyderm in the room and I figure we ought to blast it right off the bat. The subject of this brief discussion is the Ozark economy. I didn't really realize, until I got into the research for this second edition, just how bad the region had been financially smacked between the years 2006 and 2011.

What that means for the traveler, just to be blunt about it, is that restaurants and bed & breakfasts have dropped like flies from the Ozark landscape. Many of those places that were around five years ago have disappeared from sight. What's more, the money woes of this area have been severe enough that few new joints have cropped up to replace the old ones. That's not to say you won't find plenty· of places to stay and eat. It is to say that a number of the places you might have visited a few years back are no longer around. This is particularly true in the Missouri Ozarks (Arkansas seems to have fared better) and in many cases prices have remained fairly low.

Another sign of the times: Some towns and organizations have canceled long-cherished festivals. Two that come to mind—mostly because I used to attend—are the 50-year-old Hillbilly Days party in Lebanon, Mo., and the 25-year-old Ozark Hawg BBQ Championships in Batesville, Ark. Branson still seems to be booming, with a number of new and different shows, lodging options, and eatin' joints. One difference I've noted about Branson is that, when I wrote the first version of this book, kids were admitted free to quite a few of the Branson shows. That's no longer the case.

With all that said, we now return you to your regularly scheduled *Explore with Us* preview.

During your travels you'll trip across informed commentary on the shows, lodgings, restaurants, and attractions in Branson, Mo., Live Country Music Capital of the World. You'll discover unsuspected urbanity, wining, and dining in upscale and eclectic spots such as Springfield, Mo., and the ever-growing quad-cities region of Northwest Arkansas (known locally as "Arkansopolis"). That's just the beginning of the tale. You'll find tiny rib shacks and pie shops far off the beaten path, and learn of the best roads for soaking in the glorious colors inherent to an Ozark fall. Throughout the book are detailed listings for bed &

breakfasts and resorts, restaurants, and shopping; state, local, and federal parks; attractions and festivals galore; and more than a few spots frequented only by those in the know. Think of this book as a personal narrator, a guide whose services have been engaged to uncover the very best (and sometimes the very strangest) that the Ozarks region has to offer.

WHAT'S WHERE

The journey of 1,000 miles may begin with the first step, but in this case it also begins with the first page. At the beginning of this book is an A-to-Z listing of the basics, some highlights, and some tips that will be helpful while traveling the Ozarks. For a quick reference covering anything from apple festivals to float streams, BBQ joints to trout fishing, railroad trips to wineries, allow these pages to start you on your way.

LODGING

Most of the lodging options found in this guide are privately owned, with the lion's share of emphasis placed on bed & breakfasts, resorts, campgrounds, and private cabins (and one very cool, ultra-luxurious cave). Franchise or chain operations are not included here, nor should they be. My goal is to lead you to the roads less traveled, to respites often hidden by the bright lights and golden arches lining the main drag.

RESTAURANTS

As with all Explorer's Guides, each chapter of this book includes separate sections for *Eating Out* and *Dining Out*. The former is normally intended to specify a sense of the casual, while the latter implies the putting on of the dog. In the Ozarks, however, the line between casual and fancy-pants is blurry, if not wholly nonexistent. In 99.9 percent of cases you really don't have to worry about dress codes in these parts. Generally speaking, as long as you're a paying customer, Ozark restaurateurs don't give a hoot what you wear. As long as you've got on clothes and the folks at the next table don't start waving around a flyswatter or requesting a can of Lysol, you're fine.

PRICES AND TIMES

We're a happy bunch of capitalists in this great country, and therefore any of the prices and times listed in this Explorer's Guide are subject to change. Because this can happen so rapidly, most entries include present hours of operation and sample prices from current menus, rate cards, and attractions. This will give you a basic idea of what to expect, even if entrées, room charges, admission fees, or hours should suddenly change.

KEY TO SYMBOLS

⚭ **Weddings:** Listings including the wedding-ring symbol are a dandy place to get hitched. In the Ozarks that can include not only certain B&Bs, resorts, and hotels, but also caves and outdoor chapels.

✿ **Special Value:** The ✿ symbol represents spots that perform above and beyond the call of duty in terms of quality, service, or unique offerings. In many cases the ✿ symbol refers to free admission, which we all know is the very best kind.

🐾 **Pets:** If a listing is accompanied by a tiny dog paw, you are free to bring along Fido or Tabby. On the other hand, there will be leash restrictions (both in private and public campgrounds). Common sense is the rule, and obviously you won't be the most popular person on the block if your pooch howls at the moon from dusk 'til dawn. Few B&Bs accept pets, and some establishments accept them only with an extra charge. To date, no restaurants have been found that allow anything but Seeing Eye dogs . . . for that you have to go to either France or Montana. Seeing Eye cats, possums, and squirrels are also largely prohibited.

✎ **Kid-Friendly:** The crayon symbol identifies spots that allow and/or welcome the younger crowd. You should note that bed & breakfasts tend to have restrictions on your progeny. Some specify certain age limits, others ask you to call in advance, and some don't cotton to the younguns at all.

♿ **Handicapped Accessible:** The wheelchair symbol is intended to note locales that either meet Americans with Disabilities Act (ADA) standards, or at least have ramps or paved paths. This is the Ozarks, remember, so a number of sights and establishments may not yet be up-to-date. Others may be "partially" handicapped accessible. As with all things, if this is a concern, it is best to call ahead for detailed information.

❄ **Off-Season:** This symbol, the snowflake, is highly subjective in the Ozarks and subject to change. Shows and businesses in outdoor- and entertainment-oriented areas—such as Branson, Mo.; Eureka Springs, Ark.; and the Lake of the Ozarks—often close for vaguely specified periods during the winter months. This is due not to snow (we get very little) but to a lack of tourist trade. You should always call for information if traveling to such places between December and mid-March.

🍸 **Liquor:** The martini-glass icon is your key to John Barleycorn's World of Hydraulic Amusement. That said, lounges and bars are not as prevalent in the Ozarks as they are in most other regions. This stems in large part from the number of small towns and the accompanying local culture that doesn't promote getting a snoot-full. On the other hand, most little towns do have a bar hidden away someplace, and all the larger towns and cities are loaded (no pun intended) with restaurants offering award-winning wine lists and full bars. Areas such as Springfield, Mo., and Fayetteville, Ark., offer numerous clubs with outstanding live music.

The Ozarks

CONTENTS

List of Maps

ACKNOWLEDGMENTS

Compiling a book of this scope, length, and detail can at first glance be a bit daunting. At second glance it gets downright scary. Updating the tome for a new edition probably rates as some form of lunacy. Luckily I never experienced a drought in terms of folks who were ready, willing, and able to toss in hints, suggestions, tips, and advice. While it would be virtually impossible to list everyone who assisted with this guide—partially because of the sheer numbers and partially because I have a hard enough time remembering my own name—thanks are warranted nonetheless. Therefore, I send my heartfelt appreciation to each business, chamber of commerce, convention bureau, and state or federal agency that contributed information, offered assistance, and answered my frequently silly questions.

On a more personal note, a few people should be recognized for duty above and beyond the call. My profound thanks go to the good folks at Countryman Press, who have shown the good sense to release this book for a second go-round. Gratitude is also sent to my oldest friend, Edward T. Boys, for his incomparable insights into the location of the true Ozark borders and the inscrutable world of dandy rib shacks. Extra credit is awarded Edward T. for his encyclopedic knowledge of events involving horses, mules, steam-powered machinery, and generalized Ozark lore and gossip. Appreciation is happily sent to my parents, Bill and Ruth Marr, for providing me with their firsthand accounts of both the infinite sights of Branson and the equally infinite craft fairs of Northwest Arkansas. Of course, no acknowledgment page would be complete without recognition of the invaluable assistance of Fat Jack Rabinowitz and Hugo Bassaussie. These two pups are my constant companions and are well versed in the Ozark traditions of barking at river-giggers and informing their lazy human of the presence of trespassing armadillos.

The book would surely not have gone as smoothly as it did if not for a few other integral philosophical consultants. For starters, thanks to the late Mike Hibbard for vividly describing certain of his youthful days in Arkansas as "John Barleycorn's World of Hydraulic Amusement" (a phrase I stole at my first opportunity). Next would be former Beach Boys associate, traveling troubadour, and skateboarder extraordinaire Baron Stuart. Baron supplied a plethora of witty commentary throughout the writing process and helped me recall that I'm really,

12

ACKNOWLEDGMENTS

really glad I escaped the utterly awful town of Elk City, Idaho, with both skin and sanity partially intact.

And, as always, my eternal thanks to my best friend, Lori DeVita Hofman, for her loving support, research help, proofreading skills, and sense of humor. Lori consistently demonstrates incredible patience in putting up with my various moods, admittedly odd ways, and gratingly repetitious stories.

Thanks, y'all.

INTRODUCTION

When Herman Engelhardt immigrated to America in the late 1800s, it was with the prevailing illusion that the streets were paved with gold. Born in 1858 in Rubenau, Germany, a nail maker by trade, Herman's illusions were shaken when he first saw the 120 acres of government land he planned to homestead in Douglas County, Mo. Far from possessing glowing yellow pavement, this patch of Ozark ground near Ava, Mo., was covered with trees, rocks, snakes, and ravines. To Herman, however, the metaphorical gold was still there. He soon realized that superficial appearances are deceptive; to unearth a treasure, one must learn to dig.

And so he began, aided by his wife, Pertha, and their five children. During winters he felled trees and prepared the land for cultivation. Money could be made from the railroads in those days, at least by those who were accomplished with a broad-bladed ax, and the funds Herman acquired from hand-cutting railroad ties kept food on the table. A barn was built long before thoughts of a house were a glimmer in the eye, and the Engelhardts shared quarters with the precious livestock that meant the difference between survival and bankruptcy.

Time passed, and after nearly two decades of backbreaking labor, that entire 120 acres of trees, rocks, snakes, and ravines was under profitable cultivation. At least a small part of the Ozark wilderness had been tamed. Golden roads can appear in the most unexpected places.

I suppose I come by my love of the Ozarks naturally. My great-aunt Lena was born amid the cows, goats, and stacks of hay in that old barn. Framed photos of Herman and Pertha, my maternal great-grandparents, hang on a wall of the red Ozark cabin I call home. My grandmother Elsie taught me to fish, and gave me my love of dogs, woods, rainbows, and simplicity. I've no doubt she learned these things by osmosis at the knee of her own parents, acquiring via a harsh and happy rural life the skills inherent to mining humor from adversity and joy from the commonplace. Perhaps that's why she lived to nearly 102. Life is mostly about perception and approach, after all. My grandmother was still chopping down trees, making pies, and aging sauerkraut at 90 (though if I recall, she'd stopped cooking lye soap in the backyard some years earlier).

There are a thousand Ozark stories of similar vein. The personality of a rural region can usually be defined by observing the history of its settlers, and nowhere will you find a place with more personality (and personalities) than the Ozarks. Though modern culture is now a regular part of this hard and majestic place, modern amenities and conveniences share a lesser billing with well-established traditions and beliefs.

Quite simply, Ozarkers are a breed apart. To outsiders they often seem a contradiction, both shy and extroverted, quiet and boisterous, industrious and lazy. In truth, there are no contradictions at all. The Ozarker merely has a respect for priorities and a hefty dose of common sense. He rarely succumbs to the peer pressure or political correctness of the outside world (peer pressure within his own community is another story) and functions according to his own heart, rules, and genetically independent nature. Putting in the crops is important, but so is the first day of deer season. Fixing a leaky roof is vital, but if it's not raining, the roof doesn't leak (and if it is raining, it's too wet to fix the darn thing anyhow). Milking the cows, mowing the brush, and doing a fair day's work are essential; so are BBQ, fishing, and taking a nap.

Independence is the primary trait of the average Ozarker. That, and an outrageous sense of humor that encompasses the belly laugh, odd pun, practical joke, and graveyard genre. Both these characteristics were born of the population's predominant Scots-Irish ancestry, and a generations-long sequestering from society at large. The Ozarker knew he had to get by with the help of only family members or perhaps a few neighbors. He also knew that if he wanted to be amused, he'd best amuse himself.

Though the infusion of modern culture has to a great degree homogenized the almost Elizabethan language of yesteryear Ozarks, you'll still find a fair amount of colloquial expressions in everyday use. All these maxims, metaphors, and similes appear tailor-made to elicit a grin. An Ozarker might casually inform you that his house is so small he can't cuss the cat without getting hair in his mouth. He might say that a sleet-covered highway is slick as a wax snake on a glass floor. Those who contemplate purchase of a ridiculous item might be chastised with the wisdom that they "don't need that any more than a tomcat needs a

AN OZARKS MAILBOX

marriage license." Ozarkers know that some individuals would rather climb a ladder to tell a lie than stand on the ground and tell the truth. They realize that the world is chock-full of long-winded types who will talk your leg off and then cuss you for being crippled. They know that intelligence is not a given, and that a sizable percentage of the populace may well be duller than a pound of wet leather.

Independence and humor are key ingredients to the makeup of an Ozarker, but the hill folks share one additional attribute. Put bluntly, they have streak of stubborn a mile wide. Ozarkers can be so bullheaded that they'll not only disagree on how their homeland got its name, they'll even disagree on its borders. The former dispute is a bit easier to tackle than the latter. The word *Ozarks* is likely a corruption of the phrase *Bois d'Arcs,* meaning "wood of bows" and referring to the hedge trees from which the Osage Indians fashioned their archery gear. Then again, it may be a corruption of *Aux Arcs,* meaning "with bows," referring either to the Quapaw Indians or a French trading post located in northern Arkansas. The literal truth will never be known, which is just fine, as it gives us fodder for friendly arguments.

But a less convivial squabble involves the location of the actual borders of the Ozarks. Some say the region runs north and south between the Missouri and Arkansas Rivers. Others (myself included) say that such a claim is nuttier than a fruitcake. The eastern and western borders are even more dicey. You'll find people who say the Ozarks include parts of Kansas and Oklahoma (these people are typically either from Kansas or Oklahoma), and others who say the borders stop shy of Springfield, Mo. (long regarded as the Queen City of the Ozarks). A few deluded souls will go so far as to try to convince you that parts of the Ozarks lie in Illinois, which is a little like insisting parts of the Everglades are found in Wisconsin.

The only conclusion worth mentioning is that hardly anyone can agree on the borders and boundaries of the Ozarks. Ask a dozen different people—teachers, doctors, geologists, cartographers, fishing guides, or even your garden-variety hillbilly—and you'll get a dozen different answers. Some will define the borders by geological formations and topography, others by cultural standards and ethnic heritage. For the purposes of this book, I tend to integrate the two, with greater emphasis placed on the latter. After all, while the lay of the land can shape the attitudes and actions of people, it is the people who bring texture and character. They are the spice the keeps the stew interesting.

You can tell when you're in the Ozarks because the people act like Ozarkers. When they behave differently, you're someplace else. Roughly speaking, the area covered in this book places the northern border in a curvy line from Sullivan, Mo., on the east, around the Lake of the Ozarks, and down to Harry Truman's birthplace in Lamar, Mo., toward the southwest. The western border follows the natural western state lines of Missouri and Arkansas, south to a point somewhere near Crawford County, Ark. On the east the Black River serves as a delineating landmark in Missouri; the border then travels past Mammoth Springs, Ark., on an angle to Heber Springs, Ark., and Greers Ferry Lake. From there it takes a turn to the northwest and more or less makes a wobbling trek toward the western border of Arkansas.

OZARKS ARTIFACTS

The Ozarks are a real place, but in a sense they are also a state of mind. The pronouncements formed by those minds are wide and varied. There has not been (and never will be) any fast-and-firm method to assure that you're standing within the boundaries of the Ozarks. Unless, of course, you adopt our Hillbilly Zen attitude of "you either is . . . or you ain't."

Geologically, this is an ancient and enduring land; the rocks found around Taum Sauk Mountain and Elephant Rocks State Park in Missouri are a billion and a half years old. Scientists say that even millions of years ago, when seas still covered much of the Ozarks (and most of the rest of present-day America), this area formed a cluster of islands. The terrain of the Ozarks was shaped not by glaciers, but rather by volcanic activity, eons of erosion, and the uplift of the Ozark Plateau. For visitors (even if they're not rockhounds), ancient lands translate to ancient critters and ancient people. As a result, the ground is a treasure trove of minerals, fossils, and (thanks to a host of ancient tribes) arrowheads and primitive stone tools.

The Ozark Plateau is a highland region consisting of approximately 50,000 square miles, the only highland region between the Appalachians and the Rockies. In reality it is three plateaus: the Springfield Plateau, the Salem Plateau, and the Boston Mountains. The Bostons are the tallest and roughest of these areas (reaching more than 2,000 feet above sea level in spots) while the rest of the area is more rolling and deeply forested. It doesn't feel "rolling" if you're trying to walk it (the saying here is that while our mountains may not be that high, our valleys are mighty deep), so perhaps the allusion is more that of "rolling" down a steep hill than falling off a sheer cliff.

The Ozark topography is noted for its karst features, full of caves, springs, and sinkholes. To say there are a few caves and springs would be a gross understatement; we live among and above nearly 7,000 caves and at least that many springs. Big Spring, near Van Buren, Mo., and Mammoth Spring at Mammoth Springs, Ark., pump out 280 and 240 million gallons per day, respectively, and you can tour, ride, explore, dine, get married, or vacation in subterranean luxury in some our developed caverns. Also, the area is rich in minerals. The mining of lead, zinc, saltpeter and sulfur (for gunpowder), limestone, and charcoal have at one time or another all proven bonanzas in the Ozarks. The Joplin and Carthage, Mo., district at one time lived and died by mining, and the Missouri University of Science and Technology in Rolla is viewed as one of the country's finest schools for mining engineers. Timber also played a huge role in early industry. Today's visitors see our deep and mysterious forests and sometimes assume they are viewing stands of virgin growth. Nothing could be further from the truth. The Ozarks have been basically denuded (by humans) several times since the early 1700s. That's the nice thing about trees: They grow back. Such should prove a lesson to those who believe forestry is a destructive industry. When managed properly, this renewable resource springs to life time and time again.

And then there are our rivers. The Ozarks are ruled by rivers. From the days of the Bluff Dwellers and Osage to the days of satellite TV and the Internet, our spring-fed crystal waters have served as a source of food, transportation, commerce, and recreation. Travelers arrive from around the world to float and fish the legendary White River and Buffalo National River of Arkansas. In Missouri they seek out the Current and Jacks Fork, two streams that make up the Ozark National Scenic Riverways, or the stunningly beautiful North Fork of the White. The Army Corps of Engineers dammed many of our rivers over the past century, both for flood control and to harness hydroelectric energy. Lakes such as Table Rock, Bull Shoals, Norfork, Greers Ferry, Beaver, Taneycomo, and the world-renowned Lake of the Ozarks are sources of fun, functionality, and free enterprise not just for the souls who reside near their banks, but also for millions of visitors.

When viewed in their entirety, the Ozarks of today are a symbiotic relationship of new and old. The past is the present, and the present is the past. You will still find bluegrass, country, and gospel music played on many a town square on a summer's eve, just as they were 100 years ago. But you will also find them in the huge and luxurious theaters of Branson. The Live Country Music Capital of the World, Branson is now a first-tier vacation destination. The town welcomes more than 8 million visitors annually and boasts more than 57,000 theater seats (that's 12,000 more than Broadway). While the numbers seem to accelerate on a daily basis, you will also find 400 restaurants, 200 lodging facilities, 5,000 camping spaces, nine golf courses, 45 theaters offering 80 shows per day, and countless shops, stores, amusement parks, and attractions.

Other Ozark cities boast a similar level of growth and development. The northwest corner of Arkansas—holding the towns of Springdale, Rogers, Bentonville, and Fayetteville—is fast becoming a major metropolis. Universities, industry, restaurants, and entertainment that rivals the best of the coasts are found in this exploding region. Perhaps explanation enough arrives with the knowledge that Bentonville is home to the corporate headquarters of Walmart. Back in Missouri, Springfield has continued to live up to its moniker of Queen City of the Ozarks. Restaurants exist for any and all ethnic tastes; entertainment options range from baseball, major concerts, and collegiate athletics to opera, ballet, blues, live theater, and bluegrass. Springfield's growth is nothing short of astounding and can be attributed to wise planning, long-term vision, and excellent park and educational systems. This growing city is prosperous and clean, and more than a few residents have left major urban centers to spend their lives within its comparably idyllic boundaries.

The real draw, however, is that all the major Ozark cities have one thing in common: the attitude of the people. Even our larger cities still feel like small towns. On a busy street, drivers still allow you to pull ahead in traffic; residents wave and say hello. Again, it's the mesh of new and old; a 21st-century lifestyle combined with 19th-century values, convictions, and attitude.

When looking at the Ozarks, it seems to always come back to that word. It's an attitude. The people here are attached to their land, sometimes fiercely so. Get out in the country and you will find that nearly every hill, creek branch, or sharp curve has a name. Ask directions, and you might well be told to "drive up to where Jimmy Bob Taylor used to live, then turn right where the old church burned down in '84." We don't operate by street numbers or highway signs. We live by landmark and memory. What seems to make the Ozarker unique is that he'll generally define himself as an Ozarker (or, as many of us tend to say, "just a hillbilly") rather than as a resident of Missouri or Arkansas. Even when they are unacquainted, Ozarkers realize they have more in common with one another than they do with most who reside outside their region.

With that thought in mind, it should come as no surprise that things are a little different here. Things are fun and gorgeous and interesting, but they're different. For starters, you can rest assured that the Ozarker is a genial host to strangers, unless the stranger happens to be rude or nosy. In that case the local fellow will just appear genial, silently wondering how a body could get so far along in life without learning any civilized manners, and offer the drawling question, "You ain't from around here, are ya?"

The average Ozarker is also seriously fond of his church. If you're from one of the coasts, you may be surprised by just how many churches there are in these parts (not to mention the religious billboards found along major interstates). You'll see churches all over the place; they're thicker than June bugs on a new porch light. Quite a few may be denominations you never knew existed, and contrary to popular media conceptions, most of them don't endorse snake handling. Churches can be old or new, built of frame, brick, or cinder block. Lately, the church structure of choice seems to be the prefabricated steel building. In the warmer months you'll trip across a plethora of old-time tent revivals, which seem to magically transform into fireworks stands as Independence Day draws near.

That said, to clear up another erroneous media conception, residents of these hills are rarely pushy or overly evangelical about their religion. It's a private thing, as it should be. If you're interested and ask, the locals will gladly invite you to a service. If not, the subject will likely never arise. Hollywood portrayals and the malarkey of the evening news are far different from reality, and never the twain shall meet.

The goal of this Explorer's Guide to the Ozarks is to provide you, gentle reader, with a road map to many of the sights, sounds, tastes, and events of this quirky and beautiful hill country that so many of us love so deeply. The goal is not just to show you the popular high points and traditional tourist spots, but to take you down the patched blacktops and gravel paths, to give you directions on the road less traveled. Within these pages you'll find five-star restaurants, elegant spas, and a town whose claim to fame is albino squirrels. You'll find live performances by major stars, and drive far into the boondocks to a place where spectral balls of starlight (said to be the spirits of long-dead Indians) dance to and fro under a midnight sky. You'll see the cairns, cave dwellings, and artifacts of the first inhabitants, and follow your nose to the finest hickory-smoked ribs on the planet. You'll discover pie shops and Puccini, tour caves and castles, walk in the steps of Jesse James, Wyatt Earp, and Bill Hickok, and linger over the desk where Laura Ingalls Wilder wrote her Little House books. You'll ride at dude ranches, chase monster trout, and perhaps hunt a white-tailed deer (or even bag a buffalo, if such is your taste). You'll eat deep-fried catfish and hush puppies until you're fuller than a tick, then fall asleep in a Victorian bed & breakfast (no chain motels or restaurants are included in this guide; why go for carbon copies when you can have the real deal?). You'll paddle a canoe, ski behind a jet boat, and walk forest paths that seem untouched by time. You'll wander mills and museums and celebrate at festivals commemorating everything from frogs, sucker fish, and apple butter to kites, clowns, and hog calling.

And that's just the beginning. Welcome to the Ozarks.

The more they change, the more they stay the same.

ANTIQUES Nowhere in the world will you find more antiques shops than in the Ozarks. However, in this part of the world *antiques shop* is often synonymous with *junkyard*. A healthy sense of caveat emptor should be employed, for when it comes to dickering, the Ozarker will not tell you that the horse has only three legs; you'll have to count them for yourself. As a rule of thumb, antiques emporiums that appear too fancy are overpriced and full of reproductions. Those that appear too dumpy are loaded with rusty screwdrivers, broken can openers, and glass telephone insulators. Look for shops on the two-lane blacktops. For some reason, those sporting antiquated gas station signs and a preponderance of lounging dogs seem to hold the greatest treasures. On the other hand, trips to the massive **Heartland Antique Mall** (417-532-9350; www.heartland antiquemalllebanon.com) in Lebanon, Mo., have never disappointed. Plus, the **Russell Stover** candy store next door offers free samples.

APPLES Ozark residents will organize a festival at the drop of a hat, making merry over topics ranging from A to Z. At the start of that celebratory alphabet you will discover two excellent apple festivals. The **Old Tyme Apple Festival** in Versailles, Mo. (573-378-4401), is held the first Saturday of every October. Drawing an average of 35,000 people, it features 400 vendors, a parade, apple pie and fiddlers' contests, a tractor show, a car cruise, a demolition derby, and a gospel-singing extravaganza. In Mount Vernon, Mo., **Apple Butter Makin' Days** (417-466-7654), also held in October, attracts 50,000 people. Not only will you taste apple butter, apple dumplings, and apple pies, but you can also enjoy live bluegrass, a nail-driving competition, a turtle race, a gunfight, a bubble-gum-blowing contest, and 400 craft vendors.

BBQ Texans brag to high heaven about theirs. North Carolinians assume they serve up the ultimate. Down Memphis way the locals swear on a stack of Bibles that nothing can surpass their version. Of course, that's either a case of wishful thinking or delusions of grandeur. The only real BBQ is Ozark BBQ, and you'd be hard pressed to locate even the tiniest of towns that doesn't boast at least one purveyor of quality Q. We're talking hickory smoked, cooked slow, with sauce on the side. Though the dining possibilities are endless, you should strive mightily to visit **Homer's BBQ** (573-468-4393) in Sullivan, Mo. (he smokes over a hickory-and-sassafras mix), and the **Crosstown BBQ** (417-862-4646) in Springfield, Mo. If it gets any better than this, then you're up at the pearly gates, splitting a slab of ribs with St. Peter.

BLUEGRASS The heartbeat of the Ozarks is bluegrass. Mountain music is found on every corner in Branson, with the two oldest shows being the **Baldknobbers Jamboree Music**

Show (417-334-4528 or 1-800-998-8908; www.baldknobbers.com) and **Presleys' Country Jubilee** (417-334-4874 or 1-800-335-4874; www.presleys .com). Down in West Fork, Ark., you'll find the classic local venue known as the **Little O' Opry** (479-839-2992; www.littleoprey.org), and you won't want to miss the annual **Bluegrass Festival,** held in Harrison, Ark., in mid-May. An all-time classic festival, renowned from coast to coast, is **Bluegrass Pickin' Time** (573-759-7716; www.bluegrasspickintime.com) in Dixon, Mo. This party is so good they hold it twice each summer, on Memorial and Labor Day weekends.

BRIDGES Between the late 1800s and the 1930s more than two dozen swinging bridges were built in the Lake of the Ozarks region. Although most of these are long gone, either succumbing to time or disappearing beneath the waters of the lake, a couple still exist near the little town of **Brumley.** If you enjoy walking (or driving) across ancient, creaking, cracking suspension bridges, this is your cup of tea. North of Eureka Springs, Ark., on SR 187, the 1949 **Beaver Bridge** offers a suspension bridge measuring 554 feet long with a 312-foot span. Just keep in mind that it's a one-way road. You don't want to have to back up.

CATFISH In terms of both prevalence and popularity, catfish joints place a close second to BBQ joints in the Ozarks. These days, most places serve both. The favorite way to order catfish in the Ozarks is deep fried, and it usually arrives with hush puppies, french fries, coleslaw, and (at the really good places) a bowl of ham and beans. For a true catfish gorge-athon, simply visit either the **AQ Chicken House** (479-751-4633 or 479-443-7555; www.aqchicken.com) in Springdale, Ark., or **Gary's Dowd's Catfish House** (417-532-1777; www.dowds catfishandbbq.com) in Lebanon, Mo.

CAVES There are an estimated 5,500 caves in the Missouri Ozarks and another 2,000 in Arkansas. Not a people to look a gift horse in the mouth, the local folks have for years utilized these caverns to earn a living. You can explore, dine, walk, ride, and even get married in various Ozark caves. **War Eagle Cavern** on Beaver Lake (479-789-2909; www.wareaglecavern.com) has been open to the public since 1978, and the famous **Meramec Caverns** near Stanton, Mo. (573-468-3166; www.americascave.com) has drawn tourists since 1935. As a bonus, it's just one of the hundreds of spots where Jesse James allegedly hid out.

CIVIL WAR Missouri is in fact third (behind Virginia and Tennessee) in

numbers of Civil War actions fought on her soil, and blood flowed freely all over the Ozarks. One of the largest scrapes, which forced Missouri to remain in the Union, took place in Pea Ridge, Ark., in March 1862. The **Pea Ridge National Military Park** (479-451-8122; www.nps.gov/peri) is a 4,300-acre site that offers complete details of the day nearly 30,000 troops met in battle. Also, to the north in Republic, Mo., **Wilson's Creek National Battlefield** (417-732-2662; www.nps.gov/wicr) provides an in-depth look at the day in August 1861 when 2,300 combatants lost their lives.

DOGWOOD The dogwood tree is so beloved in the Ozarks that we have built entire festivals around it. (That said, we have also built entire festivals around frogs; a party is a party, after all.) In Siloam Springs, Ark., the **Dogwood Festival** draws 30,000 people annually on the last weekend in April. In Camdenton, Mo., the

Dogwood Festival (1-800-769-1004; www.camdentonchamber.com /DogwoodFestival.htm), also held in April, features more than 100 floats and a variety of events. Plus, the town hands out more than 1,500 free dogwood saplings.

DRIVE-IN MOVIES The drive-in theater is alive and well in the Ozarks, complete with movies, concession stands, and playgrounds up front for the kids. In Aurora, Mo., you'll find the **Sunset Drive-In Theater** (417-678-6609; www.sunsetdriveinaurora .com). In Cuba, Mo., there's the **Highway 19 Drive-In** (573-885-7752). And right on the trail of the hallowed Route 66, in Carthage, Mo., you'll find the **66 Drive-In Theater** (417-359-5959; www.comevisit.com /66drivein). The 60-year-old **Sunset Drive-In** (417-967-4142) in Houston, Mo. was completely restored in 2001, and the **Barco Drive-In** of Lamar, Mo. (417-682-2434; www.facebook .com/barcodrivein) accommodates 200 vehicles. Just pull in, park the car, and feel like a 1960s teenager again.

ELEPHANT ROCKS The massive boulders found at **Elephant Rocks State Park** (573-546-3454; www.mo stateparks.com/elephantrock.htm) are as much as 27 feet high and 680 tons. What's different about these hunks of stone is that they were not left by the glaciers. Rather, they are 1.5-billion-year-old pieces of granite that sheared off volcanic magma. The park itself is only 132 acres, but that's more than enough. Interactive in a prehistoric manner, Elephant Rocks offers a Braille Trail for the blind.

EQUESTRIANS It's an Ozark maxim that there's absolutely no reason you should walk when you can ride. With that thought in mind, you'll discover myriad parks, resorts, and dude ranches that can provide you with a well-behaved horse. Take a look in Eminence, Mo., at either **Coldwater Ranch** (573-226-3723; www.cold waterranch.com) or **Cross Country Trail Ride** (573-226-3492; www.cross countrytrailride.com), and you'll see why Eminence is known as the Trail Riding Capital of the United States. Another excellent resort for the horsey sort is the **Meramec Farm Cabins and Trail** (573-732-4765; www.meramecfarm.com) in Bourbon, Mo. Last but not least, if you wish to look rather than ride, don't miss the **Missouri Foxtrotting Horse Breed Association Show** (417-683-2468; www.mfthba.com) in Ava, Mo. Shows and sales take place in June and September.

FALL COLORS Fall in the Ozarks is no less than a riot of color, no matter your locale. The deep orange, red, and yellow hues are breathtaking. To see them up close and personal, one of the best drives you can take is the **Glade Top Trail.** In the third week of October, the **Glade Top Trail Flaming Fall Festival** (417-683-4594; www.avachamber.org) takes place in Ava, Mo. Not only can you look at the trees, but you also can enjoy square dancing, a sausage-and-pancake breakfast, and a BBQ chicken dinner on Sunday. As a side note, don't forget to drive this trail in spring. Our springtime colors are just as pretty as the fall version.

FESTIVALS As mentioned previously, in the Ozarks any excuse is reason enough for a festival. The options are nearly infinite, from **Frog Fest** in

Waynesville, Mo., to **Dixon Cow Days** in Dixon, Mo., to the **Crawdad Days Music Festival** in Harrison, Ark. This is but the smallest of samples and doesn't even consider the fairs that are held annually in nearly every county. For those who like their arts and crafts and wish to peruse the handmade goods of local artisans, few events compare to the **War Eagle Fair** in Rogers, Ark. (479-789-5398; www.wareaglefair.com). **Art at the Farm** (417-588-3768) is held the first weekend in June on Bill and Vera Harrill's 260-acre farm near Lebanon, Mo. The event is free and has been featured nationally by publications such as *American Profile.*

FISHING You're never far from water when you come to the Ozarks, which means you're never far from fine fishing on our innumerable lakes, creeks, ponds, and rivers. Most of us in these parts are handling a fishing pole by the time we can walk. A couple of personal recommendations here. If you're after bass, try the **Kings River** in Arkansas or the **Gasconade River** in Missouri. If you

want trout, there is no place better than either the **White River** of Arkansas or the **North Fork of the White** in Missouri. And for catfish, if you can find a local who is willing to share a few secrets, you can on occasion catch some honking-big catfish from Missouri's **Bryant Creek.** Of course you do need the proper licenses. The **Missouri Department of Conservation** (1-800-392-4115) provides all regulations and seasons, as well as online license purchase, at www.mo.wildlifelicense.com/start.php. **Arkansas Fish and Game** (1-800-364-4263) also offers complete information and online purchases at www.agfc.com/licenses/Pages/default.aspx.

FLOATING Many people simply think of the Ozarks as a land of rugged hills and deep forests. Thus it often comes as a surprise to learn that, more than anything, we are a region ruled by water. Visitors soon learn that our creeks and rivers are the paddler's version of Nirvana. Many travelers like to bring their own canoe, kayak, or raft—though it's hardly a necessity. The areas bordering nearly every Ozark river hold outfitters aplenty. Virtually all offer both canoe rental and shuttle service, with many also providing the option of campgrounds, cabins, or motel rooms.

GIGGING Since fishing is second nature to an Ozarker, there should be little surprise that we have come up with a wide variety of methods with which to send our piscine friends to their reward. Though it is no longer legal, for a brief time Missouri even offered a "noodling" season. This modified angling method requires participants to wade along riverbanks, blindly grope around under a hole or submerged log, tickle a catfish's belly to make him/her mellow, and then yank the sucker out bare-handed. Less painful, but no less unusual, is the sport of gigging. This is the practice of running a well-lit, flat-bottomed boat up a river at midnight and spearing fish with sharp sticks (and yup, there's a legal season for it). **Bird's Nest Lodge** (573-775-2606 or 1-877-707-7238; www.birdsnest lodge.com) in Steelville, Mo., is the only place I've ever heard of that offers gigging tours and provides gigging guides. The fine folks at Bird's Nest will also clean your catch, set you up on a float trip that doesn't involve impaling carp, rent you a campsite or cabin, and feed you. What more could a body want?

GOLF In an old episode of *The Beverly Hillbillies,* Jed and Jethro take to the golf course bearing rifles and shotguns. Their intention is to "shoot some golfs." Sadly, all they bag on their urban hunting trip are handfuls of little white "golf eggs." Times have changed; these days it seems the Ozarks have gone golf crazy. From

the championship courses at the **Lake of the Ozarks** and **Branson,** to the private golf community of **Bella Vista,** Ark., to the many 9- and 18-hole links found in virtually every town with more than 2,000 people, we can satisfy the inexplicable urge to drive, putt, and chip. Leave the shotgun at home. Golf eggs are mighty tough eating even after you boil them.

HARRY TRUMAN The 34th U.S. president, "Give 'Em Hell Harry," is one of but two Ozarkers who went on to become commander in chief (the other being some Arkansas fellow named Bill). Harry was born in an 1884, 560-square-foot home in Lamar, Mo., and the **Harry S Truman State Birthplace Historic Site** (417-682-2279; www.mostateparks .com/trumansite.htm) has been fully restored. The tour guides are especially friendly and knowledgeable here, and will show you everything from HST's baby bed to the outhouse. This home is actually something of a double-dip, as the Trumans sold it to relatives of **Wyatt Earp** (another Lamar native). The Earp clan ran the home as a memorial to the western lawman—of OK Corral fame—until the late 1950s.

HIKING You can hike just about any-where in the Ozarks. If you can handle the hungry ticks, chiggers, and mosquitoes that reside in the high weeds between late March and late October, then a hiking trail is normally no more than a stone's throw away. For those with stamina, perhaps the most interesting is the **Colosseum Trail** at **Ha Ha Tonka State Park** (573-346-2986; www.mostateparks .com/hahatonka.htm) near Camdenton, Mo. This trail can be as easy or as strenuous as you wish. If you decide to take the fork that ventures into **Whispering Dell Sink,** keep in mind that you'll encounter 300 wooden steps. It's a beautiful part of the world, of that there's no doubt, but you'll have to work to get there.

HILLBILLIES It's probably not such a good idea to walk up to a hillbilly and ask him if he's a hillbilly. We call ourselves that (and are proud of it), but we don't like it when others use it as a pejorative. That said, you can see plenty of reasonable facsimiles of hill-billies at the aptly named **Annual Hillbilly Fair** (573-374-5500; www .lakewestchamber.com) in Laurie,

Mo. This little town, located on the western side of the Lake of the Ozarks, throws a three-day, mid-September festival that includes tons of live music, crafts, games, a parade, and (of course) a beer garden. If you need more hillbilly infusions, simply go to Branson and enjoy a perform-ance of the **Baldknobbers.**

HOGS During football season it is not uncommon to see folks in Fayette-ville, Ark., walking around wearing red plastic pig snouts. That's because Fayetteville is home to the University of Arkansas and its cherished **Arkansas Razorbacks.** It's fitting and proper that an Ozark college team should be named for our friend the swine, for we have tendency to consume the little porkers with gusto (with sauce on the side, thank you very much). Though political pork has little to do with the real deal, Fayette-ville was also the home of newlyweds **President Bill** and **Secretary of State Hillary Clinton.**

HUNTING Tracking and smacking the wily woodland creatures— whether they be of fur or feather—is an Ozark tradition. The opening day of deer season is almost a national holiday for us, and you've never truly experienced tenacity and dedication until you've seen camo-clad folks heading out long before dawn to call in wild turkeys. We have hunting galore, and, as is true with fishing, you can find all the information you need in a couple of easily accessible locations. The **Missouri Department of Conservation** (1-800-392-4115) provides all regulations and seasons, as well as online license purchase, at www.mo.wildlifelicense .com/start.php. **Arkansas Fish and Game** (1-800-364-4263) also offers complete information and online purchases at www.agfc.com/licenses /Pages/default.aspx.

INNS By design and intent, this Explorer's Guide does not concentrate on motel lodging or franchises. Anyone can locate such places; they dot the American landscape like acne on a teenager. Luckily, if you're traveling in this part of the world, you will find a treasure trove of resorts, ranches, campgrounds, and especially bed & breakfasts. In addition to the numerous listings within each chapter, check out these locator sites for additional options. **Bed & Breakfast Inns of Missouri** (www.bbim.org) includes lengthy listings and descriptions of some of the best to be found in the Ozark region of the Show Me State. If seeking a B&B in Arkansas, the **Bed and Breakfast Association of Arkansas** (www.bedandbreakfast arkansas.com) will tell you everything you need to know.

IRISH WILDERNESS Located in the Missouri Ozarks' Oregon County, the 16,500-acre **Irish Wilderness**

(573-996-2153; www.fs.fed.us /recreation/map/state_list.shtml #Missouri) lies deep within the **Mark Twain National Forest.** A bit eerie, a bit mysterious, and more than a bit incredible, this deep-woods haven was home to a group of impoverished Irish immigrants prior to the Civil War. When the battles raged, the isolation of the area made the Irish Wilderness the perfect hideout for bushwhackers, thugs, and creeps of all shapes, sizes, colors, and denominations. What happened to the immigrants remains a mystery to this day. While you may not find that particular answer, you will find a wealth of streams, caves, sinkholes, and wildlife. And when the fog clings close to the ground in the morning, you may just hear the lilting songs of long-gone settlers from the Emerald Isle.

JAM SESSIONS Back in the days when highways were sparse and isolation a constant (in other words, from time immemorial until about the 1970s), Ozarkers found ways to entertain themselves. One of the most popular pastimes was music, and the free jam sessions live on today in a number of locales. Just drop by with an instrument or a lawn chair (depending on whether you want to play or listen) and have yourself a fine old time. **Pickin' in the Park** (479-636-8204; www.arkansas.com/calendar /details.aspx?id=26107) happens every Saturday night from April through October in Frisco Park, Rogers, Ark. During the summer months in the beautiful town of Neosho, Mo., you can drop by the **Gatherin' on the Square** any Thursday evening for a taste of bluegrass, country, and gospel. In Salem, Mo., **Ozark Country Music** (573-729-4811; www.salem

mo.com/community/artsculture
museums.asp) kicks into gear every
Friday 7–10 PM in the Salem City
Hall Auditorium.

JESSE JAMES Just a word of warning: 7 out of 10 attractions in the
Ozarks will likely make the claim that
Jesse James either slept there, hid
there, ate there, or robbed there.
Some of these tales are true, some are
not. Let's just say Jesse got around a
lot, and we're right proud of his fame.
Other than that, this guide makes no
comment on the veracity of any allegation regarding the sleeping, hiding,
eating, or robbing habits of the
renowned outlaw.

KEWPIE DOLLS If you want to know
the truth, they're scary-looking little
imps, reminiscent of a Depression-
era version of Chuckie the killer ven-
triloquist's dummy. Nonetheless,
Kewpie dolls were popular in their
time, and they originated in the heart
of the Ozarks. If you wish to see all
things Kewpie, visit the **Bonniebrook Historical Society and
Kewpie Museum** (1-800-539-7437;
www.roseoneill.org). The home was
the residence of Kewpie creator Rose
O'Neill. This "woman for all seasons"
was the most highly paid illustrator in
America, studied sculpture under
Rodin, became a millionaire and lost
it all, married a couple of times, and
was considered one of the five most
beautiful women in the world.

LAKES Thanks to the Army Corps of
Engineers, who get all giddy every
time they spy a creek with enough
water to dam, the Ozarks are full of
lakes. In Arkansas you have bodies of
water such as **Beaver Lake** and
Greers Ferry Lake, with **Bull**

Shoals and **Norfork Lakes** straddling the border with Missouri. Also
in Missouri are **Stockton, Pomme
de Terre, Taneycomo, Table Rock,
Clearwater,** and of course the massive **Lake of the Ozarks.** If water
sports are what you seek, you need
look no further.

LITTLE HOUSES Without doubt the
most famous "Little House" in the
world belonged to author Laura
Ingalls Wilder. You can tour her
Rocky Ridge Farm at the **Laura
Ingalls Wilder Museum and Home**
(417-924-3626 or 1-877-924-7126;
www.lauraingallswilderhome.com) in
Mansfield, Mo.

**MARK TWAIN NATIONAL
FOREST** Consisting of more than 1.5
million acres, the Mark Twain (www
.fs.fed.us/r9/marktwain) is a superb
wilderness dotted by rivers, streams,
and some of the largest natural
springs in America. Broken into nine
different ranger districts, the forest
includes hundreds of miles of hiking
trails, numerous scenic drives, seven
congressionally designated wilderness
areas, 40 campgrounds, and thousands of acres of primitive and semi-
primitive areas.

MILLS The gristmill was often the
center of life here, a place that not
only ground the grain but also served
as trading post and ground zero for
the telling of tall tales. The **War
Eagle Mill** (1-866-492-7324; www
.wareaglemill.com) in Rogers, Ark., is
one of the few that still work, dou-
bling as store and restaurant. Others,
such as the **Rainbow Trout and
Game Ranch** (417-679-3619; www
.rockbridgemo.com), **Zanoni Mill
Inn** (417-679-2181; www.zanoni

millinn.com) and **Dawt Mill** (417-284-3540 or 1-888-884-3298; www.dawtmill.com), have been transformed into bed & breakfasts and resorts.

MUSEUMS History and tradition rate highly in the Ozarks, and it's the rare small town that doesn't possess a local museum. The artifacts and subject matter encompassed by these bastions of the past are nearly infinite, but some of the best include the **Arkansas Air Museum** (479-521-4947; www.arkairmuseum.org) in Fayetteville, Ark., and the **Daisy Airgun Museum** (479-986-6873; www.daisymuseum.com) in Rogers, Ark. Those interested in the Civil War will want to check out the **Wilson's Creek Civil War Museum** (417-732-2662; www.nps.gov/wicr/index.htm) in Republic, Mo. However, perhaps the best museum in the Ozarks

is the **Ralph Foster Museum** (417-334-6411; www.rfostermuseum.com), located in Lookout, Mo., on the campus of the College of the Ozarks. It features 40,000 square feet and three stories of displays, where you'll find everything from prehistoric Indian artifacts to the truck owned by Jed Clampett of *Beverly Hillbillies* fame.

NUTS Natives of this region will freely speculate that most urban folks likely think them a bit nuts. However, the festival held each year in Stockton, Mo., refers to a type of nut grown on trees, not the type of nut who braves subfreezing weather to spear fish from a jon boat. The **Black Walnut Festival** (417-276-5161; www.stocktonlake.com) is a four-day event held in late September that draws thousands of visitors from far and wide. Not so coincidentally, Stockton, Mo., is also the home of the **Hammons Products Company,** largest processor of black walnuts in the world.

OPERA Contrary to popular belief, not all opera in the Ozarks is of the horse or Grand Ole variety. At **Opera in the Ozarks at Inspiration Point** (479-253-8595; www.opera.org), located in Eureka Springs, Ark., you can soak up all the Rossini, Verdi, or Puccini you'd like. And then of course you'll want to go have some catfish and catch a screaming bluegrass band.

OZARK NATIONAL FOREST Consisting of 1.2 million acres in Arkansas, the **Ozark National Forest** (479-964-7200; www.fs.fed.us/oonf/ozark) offers anything the outdoors person could desire. From hiking, biking, and horseback riding to floating, kayaking, picnicking, and camping, this sprawling and rugged forest is a cavalcade of bluffs, mountains, rivers, and trees.

PASSION PLAY The world's number one attended outdoor dramatic presentation (viewed by more than 7 million people and counting) is **The Great Passion Play** (1-800-882-7529; www.greatpassionplay.com) held in Eureka Springs, Ark. Chronicling the last week of Jesus Christ, performances are held from April through October. It goes without saying that this just wouldn't be the Ozarks if the venue for this performance wasn't also home to the **Top of the Mountain Gospel Music Dinner Theater.**

PIE Homemade pies are a staple in this part of the world, but the best of the best can be found in the tiny establishment known as **A Slice of Pie** (573-364-6203), located in Rolla, Mo. You can eat there, or pick up pies, cakes, and even slices to go. Just a tiny sample of choices includes apple and blackberry crumb, chocolate chip mint, and Tahitian cream. There's a "Toll House" pie, and of course such favorites as pecan, strawberry rhubarb, mincemeat, and mudslide. A favorite cheesecake is the white chocolate cappuccino. This place is so addictive it should sport warning labels on the doors. Quite simply . . . there's none better.

QUILTS It's only when an Ozarker moves from the Ozarks that he learns not all womenfolk are expert quilters. It's the rare home indeed that doesn't have at least one or two quilts passed down from mothers and grandmothers. For those from parts yonder who sadly remain quiltless, a trip to **Ozark**

Quilts and More (417-336-6364) in Branson, Mo., is in order. Virtually everything in this store is handmade, and many of the intricate designs rate as true works of art.

RAILROADS For many years the only way to travel the Ozarks (with the exception of mule, foot, and canoe) was by railroad. You can still view the deep forest and rugged hills from restored passenger cars if you climb aboard the **Arkansas & Missouri Railroad** (479-751-8600 or 1-800-687-8600; www.amrailroad.com) or the **Eureka Springs & North Arkansas Railway** (479-253-9263; www.esnarailway.com) in Eureka Springs, Ark. Both trains offer a variety of trips, historical narration, and food. The latter in particular is known for its fine dinners on the Eurekan Dining Car.

RELIGION When it comes to churchgoing, the Ozarks is a bit like Baskin-Robbins. The only difference is that we have far more than 31 flavors. This strong faith is exemplified by the giant **Christ of the Ozarks** (1-866-566-3565; www.greatpassion

play.com), located on the site of *The Great Passion Play* in Eureka Springs, Ark. The sculpture is more than 250 feet tall and weighs more than 2 million pounds. When we say religion is big in these parts, we're not just whistlin' Dixie.

RIVERS If bluegrass is the heartbeat of the Ozarks, then our amazing rivers are the lifeblood. Many visitors choose to float the crystal-clear **Current** and **Jacks Fork,** the two streams protected under the auspices of the **Ozark National Scenic Riverways** (573-323-4236; www.nps .gov/ozar). Pretty as they are, however, that duo is but the tip of the proverbial iceberg. In Arkansas you can hook the massive trout that reside in the legendary **White,** or take a trip back in time and float the awe-inspiring **Buffalo.** For bass fishing it's hard to beat the **Kings River;** for a leisurely float there is always **War Eagle Creek.** In Missouri it quickly becomes clear why so many settlers traveled via water and why so many visitors continue to explore or rivers and creeks today. The **Niangua,** the **Meramec,** the **Big Piney,** and the **Gasconade** are all favorites of fishermen and floaters, as are smaller tributaries such as **Bryant Creek, Courtois Creek, Huzzah Creek,** and the **Bourbeuse River.** The choices just go on and on—**Elk River, Beaver Creek, Big** and **Little Sugar Creeks,** the **James River**—but there's one stretch of water that everyone agrees is the best. That would be the **North Fork of the White River.** The North Fork has Missouri's largest population of wild rainbow and trophy-sized brown trout, and words simply do not do justice to the scenery you'll experience

during a float. To enjoy the North Fork up close and personal, stay on its banks in one of the luxurious treehouse cabins at **River of Life Farm** (417-261-7777; www.riveroflifefarm .com). Located on the North Fork in the heart of the Mark Twain National Forest, River of Life has been featured by NBC's *Today* show, *The Wall Street Journal,* the *St. Louis Post-Dispatch,* and *Missouri Life* magazine.

SPOOKY LIGHTS It is the understatement of the millennia to say that the Ozarks are a bit long in the tooth. Traveling back to the dawn of time itself, this country was high and dry when much of the rest of the continent was nothing but a deep puddle. When a place is that old, it should come as no surprise that inexplicable phenomena are a regular part of life. For one of the most popular unexplained mysteries, head south of Joplin, Mo., to the road known as the **Devil's Promenade** (any local will give you directions). If you're lucky, you'll be visited by the **Hornet Spook Lights.** These glowing, darting, and diving balls of orange and yellow flame (investigated but never explained by the Army Corps of Engineers) are thought by many to be either the disembodied spirits of a star-crossed Quapaw Indian couple or the ghost of a miner searching for his missing head. Tales abound, including the legend that many who see the lights discover only the next morning that their head is pounding and the back of their pickup truck is full of empty Budweiser cans. Amazing!

SPRINGS If you wonder why so many Ozark streams are icy cold and crystal clear, it's because many of them are fed by natural springs. Counting the springs found in the Ozarks would be a tall order (the numbers run into the thousands), so just appreciate how pretty they are as you take a gander at the deep-blue waters. The biggest spring in the Ozarks (in fact, the biggest in the world) is creatively named **Big Spring** (573-323-4236; www.nps.gov /ozar). This giant, found in Carter County, Mo., pours forth 286 million gallons per day. Not far behind, just across the border in Arkansas, the average flow at **Mammoth Spring** (870-625-7364; www.arkansasstate parks.com/mammothspring) is nearly 240 million gallons per day. Many other springs push out nearly as much water; **Greer Spring,** which doubles the flow of Missouri's Eleven Point River, comes in at 220 million gallons per day. For high ratings on the Richter scale of drop-dead gorgeous, don't miss **Alley Spring** (314-323-4236; www.nps.gov/ozar) on the Jacks Fork River or **Blue Spring** (314-323-4236; www.nps.gov/ozar) on the Current. The latter sports one of the deepest blue colors imaginable.

SYMPHONIES The classics are alive and well in the Ozarks. Two symphonies demonstrate melodious proficiency: The **Symphony of Northwest Arkansas** (479-521-4166; www.sonamusic.org) has interpreted and performed the finest in musical interludes for more than half a century. Equal in expertise is the **Springfield Symphony,** which offers everything from Broadway's best to jazz jams to chamber groups. For more information on the Springfield Symphony, it is best to contact the **Juanita K. Hammons Hall for the Performing Arts** (417-836-7678 or

1-888-476-7849; www.hammons hall.com).

TROLLEYS The trolley still goes clang, clang, clang in Eureka Springs, Ark. The **Eureka Springs Transit System** (479-253-9572; www.eureka trolley.org) will take you to every location in this most hilly of towns, saving time and preventing wear and tear on shoe leather, legs, and lungs. The Eureka Springs Trolley is the past made modern, and an adult's all-day pass is just $5.

TROUT In a nationwide Trout Unlimited survey taken in 1998, the **White River** of Arkansas was named the 11th best trout stream in the nation. This is no small accomplishment, as it places the White in close proximity to such world-class streams as the Madison and Upper Yellowstone Rivers in Montana and the Henry's Fork of the Snake River in Idaho. This river is particularly known for its rainbow and brown trout, and excellent fishing can be had below **Beaver Dam,** in **Lake Taneycomo,** and below **Bull Shoals Dam.** The last choice alone provides close to 100 miles of trout water.

Brown trout of more than 40 pounds have been taken from the White and its tributaries. One of these, the **North Fork of the White in Missouri, is esteemed for not only its great** fishing but for its stunning scenery as well. The trout-fishing possibilities abound in the Ozarks. On March 1 of each year at **Bennett Spring State Park** north of Lebanon, Mo. (417-532-4338 or 417-532-4307; www.mostateparks.com /bennett.htm), more than 3,000 anglers line up shoulder-to-shoulder in anticipation of the bell that signals the start of the season.

UNDERGROUND WEDDINGS
You've heard of underground newspapers and underground railroads, but near Camdenton, Mo., the underground wedding has been all the rage since 1948. **Bridal Cave** (573-346-2676; www.bridalcave.com) has been the site of more than 2,000 weddings, and varied packages offer such perks as recorded pipe-organ music and a lifetime pass to the cave. The cost to get hitched beneath the earth is in the $500 range, though an adult can tour the cave for a mere $15.

VERMIN Not the most pleasant of categories, granted, but in this case forewarned is forearmed. If you plan to do some hiking in the Ozarks between early spring and late fall, you should know that an army of hungry little critters wish to tag along. Our hot temperatures and high humidity are the perfect climate for ticks, chiggers, mosquitoes, and snakes (cottonmouths, copperheads, and the occasional rattler being the ones to watch out for). Make sure to bring along the Off, Cutter, Skin So Soft, and a big stick. Also, you would be

well served to do just a bit of prehiking research into how to deal with tick bites. Lyme disease isn't a big fear factor here, but ticks can carry all sorts of crazy stuff, and more than a few people have skin reactions to the bite itself. If you know you're even somewhat allergic to chomping bugs, you might consider hiking during the colder months. The weather is generally quite mild, and you'll avoid all that pesky swatting, itching, and cursing.

VICTORIAN HOMES Some of the finest examples of Victorian architecture can be found in Carthage, Mo. At one time the home of more millionaires per capita than anywhere else in America, Carthage is loaded with well-preserved residences in the Classical Revival, Queen Anne, Georgian, Italianate, and Romanesque styles. Free maps to a **Victorian Home Driving Tour** are available from the Carthage Convention & Visitors Bureau (417-359-8181; www .visit-carthage.com). Some other homes—such as **Leggett House** and **Phelps House**—offer public tours. Either way you'll come in contact with domiciles exemplifying just how high on the hog some of the other half used to live.

WALMART It's the world's largest retailer, but its humble beginnings go back to Sam Walton's five-and-dime in downtown Bentonville, Ark. The international headquarters of Walmart is still located here, as is the newly remodeled and expanded **Walmart Visitor Center** (479-273-1329; www .walmartstores.com/AboutUs/287.aspx). The center is found in that original shop from which Sam built an empire, and you'll receive a detailed history of both past and present. Best of all, admission is free.

WILDLIFE Drive down any two-lane blacktop or gravel road in the Ozarks and you'll see plenty of wildlife. In fall white-tailed deer tend to get a little more up close and personal than you'd prefer, often jumping in front of your car. That said, either a simple drive off the beaten path or a trip to any state park or conservation area would be rewarded with abundant wildlife sightings. We seem to have a lot of armadillos these days; most can be viewed in a squashed state on the aforementioned two-lane blacktops.

WINERIES Prior to Prohibition, the wine industry of Missouri ranked second behind only New York. Many wineries still exist today, perfecting and selling award-winning vintages. Some of the more famous of the more than 50 Ozark-region vineyards include **Ferrigno Winery** (573-265-7742; www.missouriwinecountry.com /wineries/winery.php?wineryID=19& regionID=3), **Heinrichshaus Vineyard and Winery** (573-265-5000; www.heinrichshaus.com), **Meramec Vineyards** (573-265-7847 or 1-877-216-9463; www.meramecvineyards .com), **Stone Hill Winery** (417-334-1897 or 1-888-926-9463; www.stone hillwinery.com), and the **Peaceful Bend Vineyard** (573-775-3000; www.peacefulbendvineyard.com). And here you thought we were all about moonshine.

X FILES If little green men are your thing, you need to sign up for the annual **Ozark UFO Conference** (www.ozarkufo.com) held in Eureka Springs, Ark., every April. Three days of speakers, discussions, and presentations on all things otherworldly should provide plenty of fodder at the next meeting of your local alien abductee club.

ZOOS At the **Turpentine Creek Exotic Wildlife Refuge** (479-253-

5841; www.turpentinecreek.org), near Eureka Springs, Ark., you can observe more than 100 lions and tigers that have been rescued from mistreatment. There are also plenty of bears, monkeys, deer, and birds on hand, and you may opt to rent a room or tree-house cabin on the refuge grounds. The **Dickerson Park Zoo** (417-864-1800; www.dickersonpark zoo.org) in Springfield, Mo., is a first-class operation featuring more than 500 animals representing better than 170 species.

BALDKNOBBERS
JAMBOREE SHOW

SEASON PASSES

WELCOME
NEXT SHOW
MONDAY 8PM
PRE SHOW 7PM

BRANSON, MISSOURI

In the Ozarks they look at things a little differently. What happens in Vegas may very well stay in Vegas, but what happens in Branson . . . now, that's something you're not ashamed to talk about in church.

In an era when flash, shock, and gratuitous thrills inundate the national entertainment scene, Branson, Mo., hit upon a lucrative formula for which the public was apparently starved. You will not find slot machines or scantily clad showgirls in Branson. You will find Andy Williams and Ann-Margret singing standards of yesterday. You do not go to Branson to rave pretentious over Christo's latest surreal rendition of modern art. You go to laugh at corny jokes and visit the Ripley's Believe It or Not Museum. You do not go to Branson to wax eloquent over a tiny overpriced entrée that would fail to sate the appetite of a baby bird. Instead you belly up to the trough and gorge yourself silly on catfish and BBQ.

Simply put, people do not visit Branson to impress their friends, neighbors, and co-workers. They visit for the pure pleasure of simple fun. The town is the antithesis of highbrow and tony, and the visitor who expects quiet refinement will be sorely disappointed. Urban chic and Ozark humor are at least 1,000 light-years apart and, at least in Branson, never the twain shall meet.

Branson is admittedly something of an anomaly in a region whose main claim to fame is outdoor beauty; even locals seem a tad baffled by the town's rise to prominence. Ask native Ozarkers their opinion of Branson, and at first you'll notice a regional pride in the vein of "local boy makes good." That this once tiny village in the Ozark boonies has transformed itself into the Live Country Music Capital of the World is no small source of bragging rights.

Welcoming more than 8 million visitors annually and boasting more than 57,000 theater seats (that's about 12,000 more than Broadway), the lofty designation is not without merit. Branson's 242 restaurants (37,000 seats), 207 lodging facilities (22,000 rooms), 5,000 camping spaces, 12 golf courses, 50 theaters offering 102 shows per day, and countless shops, stores, amusement parks, and attractions have made it a first-tier vacation destination.

On the other hand, those same native Ozarkers will shake their heads and display the mildest trace of a frown over the bright lights and crowds that intrude upon the solitude of their beloved Ozark hills, rivers, and forests. The glitter and fame of Branson slightly rubs against the grain of rural locals who

Branson

Lake Taneycomo

Point of Interest
Visitor Center

© The Countryman Press

enjoy their isolation, folks who are genetically disposed to embarrassment by copious amounts of hoopla. The natives respect Branson for taking the national stage—they just wish it didn't carry on so.

Nevertheless, Branson is here to stay. To no small degree, the area's ever-growing popularity can be attributed to that fierce dedication to providing wholesome family entertainment. As suggested earlier, Branson is the "anti-Vegas," a place where Mom, apple pie, and a celebration of the "good ol' USA" reign supreme. Perhaps 15 years ago the town risked stereotyping itself as catering mostly to Grandpa and Grandma, NASCAR fans, and members of the Tea Party. Such is no longer the case, though such folks are still welcomed with open arms.

Branson has adapted with the times, constantly expanding its selection of shows and attractions, all of which retain a squeaky-clean aura. It's now a top destination for people of all ages, and the Florida mouse should be very afraid: Branson is marketing heavily for younger families with small children. Branson Landing, which was not quite open when the first edition of this book came out in 2006, is a $420 million, 95-acre development located along the Lake Taney-comon shorefront in downtown Branson. It features shopping, dining, luxury lodging, condos, two marinas, a town square, and one of the finest convention centers in the Midwest. The town square itself can hold 5,000 people, and stretches for a mile and a half next to Taneycomo. In the midst of the square is a $7.5 million fountain that puts most of the Vegas fountains to shame. The Landing, which is anchored by a Bass Pro Shops and a Belk department store, makes

THE STARLITE THEATRE

those who view Branson as merely a "hick" town in the Ozarks shake their head in wonder.

Though it has only received international prominence as a country music Mecca since the late 1980s, Branson's evolution as an entertainment center stretches back nearly a century. Rueben Branson opened his general store and post office near White River in the early 1880s. Though the first industry of the area revolved around timber and logging (homesteaders could purchase 160 acres for approximately $14), whispers of tourism were heard as early as 1907. In that year Harold Bell Wright published his novel, *The Shepherd of the Hills.*

Wright, afflicted with tuberculosis, spent seven years enamored with the peace and serenity of the Ozarks. From his notes about real-life people and events (mixed with hefty side orders of fiction) he penned a book that became a publishing phenomenon, spawning eight movies and more than a dozen TV productions. In modern terms, think *Bridges of Madison County,* a simplistic tome that somehow caught the collective imagination and achieved household-name status. As the years went by, thousands traveled to the Ozarks to view the land described by Wright.

But prior to Wright's book, fame of the long-lasting sort was already trickling from a hole in the ground. Before long that trickle would become a torrent.

The hole in question—originally called Marble Cave—was located roughly 6 miles from Branson and thought to contain a huge cache of Carthage marble. The Marble Cave Mining and Manufacturing Company was certain it had struck the mother lode at the onset of 1884 operations. It was only half wrong.

The bad news was that the "marble" turned out to be subpar. The good news was that the cave contained a treasure trove of bat guano, used as nitrate for gunpowder and fertilizer. While not as exotic sounding as marble in terms of dinner conversation, guano still fetched the princely sum (in mid-1880s prices) of $700 a ton.

Of course, all good things must come to an end. The guano train ran out of steam in 1899, and since the bats refused to make more, the company sold Marble Cave to Canadian William Lynch. Lynch began developing the cave for tourism (changing the name to Marvel Cave), and though he died in 1927, his daughters kept the operation running until 1950.

In that year Marvel Cave was leased to frequent visitors Hugo and Mary Herschend of Wilmette, Illinois. The couple, along with sons Jack and Pete, took over and expanded the cave tours, drawing 8,000 visitors in their first summer. Over the next few years they constructed an authentic 1880s Ozark village, initially to entertain and occupy those waiting to tour the cave. In 1960 Silver Dollar City was born, drawing 125,000 visitors in its inaugural season.

The expansion has been nonstop ever since. Today Silver Dollar City remains the primary draw of Branson—one of many entertainment properties owned by the Herschends.

Like smoking licks from a bluegrass banjo, things started happening fast. Hot on the heels of Silver Dollar City came the music and shows. The Baldknobbers Hillbilly Jamboree opened in 1959. In 1960 the Old Mill Theater began "organized" *Shepherd of the Hills* performances. In 1963 Table Rock Dam was completed, with Table Rock Lake joining Bull Shoals and Lake Taneycomo as a huge draw for boaters and fishermen. In 1967, the Presley family (who has been performing in area caves and from the back of flatbed trucks for at least a decade) opened the first theater on what would come to be the legendary Branson Strip (the Presleys are still there today, but in much nicer quarters).

In 1969 *The Beverly Hillbillies* filmed five episodes at Silver Dollar City, with Jed, Granny, and the rest of the Clampett clan giving Branson a priceless amount of national publicity. In the 1980s country stars such as Roy Clark, Boxcar Willie, and the Sons of the Pioneers rolled into town.

In 1991 *Time, People, The Wall Street Journal,* the *Los Angeles Times,* and *60 Minutes* all discovered Branson. Since then the area has virtually exploded, suffering some of the pangs of extreme growth but for the most part retaining a hometown atmosphere and a reputation for down-home fun and clean entertainment.

It's not Manhattan. It's not Chicago. It's not San Francisco.

It's just Branson . . . and proud of it.

AREA CODES The area code for Branson and surrounding communities is **417.**

GUIDANCE Branson/Lakes Area Chamber of Commerce (417-334-4084 or 1-800-214-3661; www.bransonchamber.com or www.explorebranson.com), 269 SR 248, Branson, Mo. This is the most complete source you will find for all things Branson. That said, a trip through the Internet, phone book, or tourist magazines will garner hundreds of spots willing to sell tickets for Branson shows, offer package deals for lodging, or inundate you with promotional legerdemain. Prices vary, and a little research could save you a few dollars here and there. Just make sure your "bargain" doesn't involve a three-hour presentation for the poor little time-share nobody wanted. An afternoon with a boring time-share salesman will not only put a damper on your trip, but recovering from it might require alcohol abuse or years of intensive therapy.

By the same token, I doubt you could stop at a single chamber of commerce office or visitors center in the state of Missouri and not find a 7-foot-tall carousel loaded with Branson pamphlets. Such being the case, you might as well go to the source and speak with the Branson chamber. The folks here are extremely helpful (it's a well-funded outfit) and truly do offer a wealth of knowledge.

For the Table Rock Lake area, contact **Table Rock Lake Chamber of Commerce** (1-800-595-0393; www.visittablerocklake.org), P.O. Box 495, Kimberling City, MO 65686.

GETTING THERE *By car:* US 65 connects from Springfield, Mo., to the north, and from Harrison, Ark., to the south. Stretches of this road were in a state of perpetual construction when I wrote the first edition of this book, a result of ever-increasing traffic, but thankfully that's a thing of the past. US 65 is four-lane these days, and driving is right speedy. If you're arriving from either the east or west via I-44, simply watch for the US 65 exit at Springfield. Branson is a mere 35 miles south.

By air: **Branson Airport** (1-888-359-2541; http://flybranson.com), 4000 Branson Airport Blvd., Hollister, Mo., opened in May 2009; it holds the distinction of being the only privately owned, privately operated, commercial service airport in the United States. The airport offers direct, nonstop flights to a number of cities, and is serviced by AirTran, Frontier, and Branson Air Express. **Springfield-Branson National Airport** (417-868-0500; www.sgf-branson-airport.com), 2300 N. Airport Blvd., Springfield, Mo., located 40 miles north of Branson, is served by American Airlines, Allegiant, United, and Delta. The airport offers facilities for buses, vans, rental cars, and hotel and hospitality limousines for groups en route to Branson (or other Ozark locations). The airport underwent a multimillion-dollar expansion between 2006 and 2009, resulting in a new, midfield terminal and expanded services. A little more than 100 miles to the southwest of Branson is **Northwest Arkansas Regional Airport** (479-205-1000; www.nwara .com), 1 Airport Blvd., Bentonville, Ark. This airport, in operation since 1998, is serviced by American Airlines, American Eagle, Continental, Allegiant Express, Delta, US Airways Express, and United.

MEDICAL EMERGENCIES All of the following hospitals operate satellite clinics in surrounding counties.

Skaggs Community Health Center (417-335-7000; www.skaggs.net), 1150 SR 248, Branson, Mo., has been a part of the Branson community since 1950. The facility has 165 rooms, numerous specialties, 24-hour emergency care, and helicopter service. A staff of 1,000 physicians, nurses, and support personnel are required to operate the hospital and its numerous clinics. **Cox Medical Center North** (417-269-3000; www.coxhealth.com), 1423 N. Jefferson Ave., Springfield, Mo., and **Cox Medical Center South** (417-269-6000; www.coxhealth.com), 3801 S. National Ave., Springfield, Mo., are part of the massive Cox network and include 770 beds. **Mercy St. John's** (417-820-2000; www.stjohns.net), 1235 E. Cherokee St., Springfield, Mo., is an 866-bed center. **Ozarks Community Hospital** (417-837-4000; www.ochonline.com), 2828 N. National, Springfield, Mo., formerly known as Doctor's Hospital, consists of two hospitals, 14 clinics, and more than 800 employees. **Lakeland Regional Hospital** (417-865-5581 or 1-800-432-1210; www.lakeland-hospital.com), 440 S. Market St., Springfield, Mo., has served Springfield for more than 100 years. It now provides psychiatric services for children, adolescents, and their families.

✳ Wandering Around

EXPLORING BY CAR Once you arrive in Branson, expect to slow down and enjoy the scenery. For years SR 76 (aka **the Strip:** go west for all the theaters, eateries, shows, and motels; go east or take US Bus. 65 South to visit downtown Branson itself) was not only the main drag, it was the only drag. Traffic would become so backed up that many visitors referred to the Strip as the "5-mile parking lot." Things are better now. City fathers realized that traffic snarls had to be eliminated, and an ambitious highway project was instituted in 1992. The first third of the time-saving loop around Branson opened in 2003. Drivers can now bypass much of the Strip if they so choose by taking SR 465 (the **Ozark Moun-**

OZARKLAND SOUVENIRS

tain Highroad) off US 65. It will pop you out right around the Shepherd of the Hills attraction and Silver Dollar City. You'll eventually want to cruise the Strip, but if it's your first trip to Branson, you might not want to tackle it right off. Be advised that the traffic, from folks coming from or going to shows, is worst in the early evening.

EXPLORING BY FOOT **Table Rock Lakeshore Trail** (417-334-4101), 4600 SR 165, Branson, Mo. A 2.2-mile trail (that would be one-way), this is a beautiful hike that runs from the Dewey Short Visitor Center to the Table Rock State Park Marina. If you should happen to visit in spring, you'll see an amazing array of wildflowers in bloom, not to mention redbud and serviceberry trees. If you come in fall, your jaw will drop open at foliage as multicolored as an earth-toned rainbow. At either time bring your camera, for there are also some great views out over Table Rock Lake itself. This is a smooth and easy trail, an easy trek for those who want to stop and smell the roses (or, more likely, the dogwood).

✳ To See

🐾 ✎ ♿ **Dewey Short Visitor Center** (417-334-4104), 4600 SR 165, Branson, Mo. Open Apr. 1–Oct. 31, daily 9–5. Located just south of the Table Rock Dam, the Dewey Short Visitor Center is a cut above your usual informative stopover. The center features several films that will give travelers a true sense of the Ozarks in all their glory (with sight and sound, but alas no olfactory nuances), and displays chronicling how life was in the hill country of olden days. Various presentations are provided on Table Rock itself and the surrounding areas in the facility's 176-seat theater. Admission is free.

🐾 ✎ **Table Rock Dam Tour** (417-266-7261; www.tablerockdamtours.com), 4600 SR 165, Branson, Mo. While at the Dewey Short Visitor Center, don't miss the chance to visit the Table Rock Dam and Powerhouse. Tours are conducted daily at a price of $14.50 for adults and $8 for children ages 6–11. You will travel to the depths of the dam and see how electricity is produced. Seriously, it's a lot more interesting than it sounds on paper. Call for reservations.

🦫 ✂ ♿ **Shepherd of the Hills Trout Hatchery** (417-334-4865; www.mdc.mo .gov/areas/hatchery/shepherd), 483 Hatchery Rd., Branson, Mo. This hatchery, a massive facility with open-air tanks, is the largest in the state of Missouri. More than 400,000 trout are raised here each year, with 80 percent of them released into nearby Lake Taneycomo. There is a free visitors center and trails, but should you visit in winter you'll encounter a little-seen natural attraction: For whatever reason—likely the sight of all those tasty fish—the area around the hatchery has turned into a winter roost for a huge number of turkey buzzards, great blue herons, bluebirds, blackbirds, and seagulls. The hatchery is 6 miles south of Branson, occupying 211 acres and hosting a quarter-million visitors annually. The grounds include four hiking trails, and guided hatchery tours are a tourist favorite. The free tours are held Memorial Day–Labor Day, weekdays at 10 AM, 11 AM, 1 PM, and 2 PM.

SCENIC TOURS ✂ ♿ **Branson Scenic Railway** (417-334-6110 or 1-800-287-2462; www.bransontrain.com), 206 E. Main St., Branson, Mo. For a unique look at the Ozarks, climb aboard the Branson Scenic Railway. Departing Mar.–early Dec. several times a day (closed most Sundays), the 1¾-hour narrated trip takes visitors to places deep in the hills that are inaccessible via car. A regular boarding pass is $25.25 for adults and $14.75 for kids 3–12. Apr.–early Nov., a dinner train departs the station (the historic old depot in downtown Branson) each Saturday at 5. For the price of $55 you will receive not only the full tour, but also an elegant four-course candlelight dinner.

✂ ♿ **Ride the Ducks** (1-877-887-8225; www.bransonducks.com), 2320 W. SR 76, Branson, Mo. Departing Mar.–Dec., approximately every 15 or 20 minutes 8–5, these modified, World War II–era, amphibious vehicles take visitors down SR 76 and SR 165, past Table Rock Dam and the Shepherd of the Hills Fish Hatchery, and then cruise the waters of Table Rock itself. A trip on the Ducks is something of a Branson tradition, possibly because all riders receive a "wacky quacker." The yellow plastic noisemakers lose their adult appeal after about two minutes, but they will provide your kids with endless hours of amusement as the grating, pseudo-quacking sounds send you on a premature excursion to the insane asylum. A Duck tour takes about 70 minutes. $21 adults, $12 ages 3–12. A second tour travels Lake Taneycomo and departs from Branson

THE BRANSON SCENIC RAILWAY
AT BRANSON LANDING

Landing. The price is the same, but Taneycomo tours take place only between Mar.–Sept.

MUSEUMS 🐚 ♿ **Titanic: The World's Largest Museum Attraction** (417-334-9500 or 1-800-381-7670; www.titanicbranson.com), 3235 76 Country Blvd. and SR 165, Branson, Mo. Open June–Dec. daily at 9 AM; closing hours vary during the summer months. Jan.–May hours vary depending on special events. Admission is $23 adults, $11 ages 5–12; free for children 4 and younger. Everyone who saw the much-ballyhooed movie with Leonardo DiCaprio knows how this show ends (the boat sank). However, as one of Branson's largest attractions, the Titanic museum takes you behind the scenes and inside the hull of history's most celebrated shipwreck. More than 400 personal and private artifacts from the disaster are on display, and visitor tickets resemble the actual boarding pass given to passengers on the White Star Line. The exhibit includes an interactive area along with authentic renditions of staterooms, the bridge, and the Grand Staircase. For history buffs, Titanic aficionados, or simply those who want a slightly waterlogged trip back in time, this promises to be a novel experience.

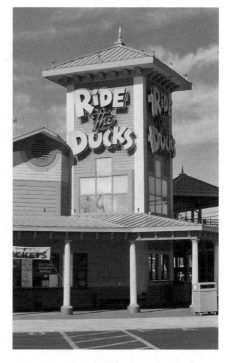

TOUR BRANSON ON THE AMPHIBIOUS DUCKS

BRANSON'S TITANIC IS THE WORLD'S LARGEST MUSEUM ATTRACTION

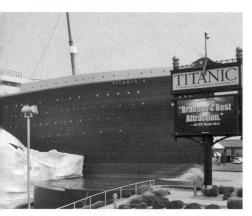

🐚 ♿ **Ripley's Believe It or Not Museum** (417-337-5300; www.ripleys branson.com), 3326 W. SR 76, Branson, Mo. Open Sun.–Thurs. 9:30 AM–7 PM, Fri.–Sat. 9:30 AM–9 PM. $17.99 adults, $8.99 ages 4–12. Kids under 4 are admitted free. You might as well go ahead and take a picture of it; everyone else does. The cracked, split, and broken-front facade (not to mention the foyer) of the Ripley's museum is designed to resemble the aftermath of the great New Madrid, Mo., earthquake of 1812 (the worst earthquake in recorded history, making those California temblors pale in comparison,

RIPLEY'S BELIEVE IT OR NOT MUSEUM

"believe it or not"). Here, you've got your two-headed calves, shrunken heads, and unicorn men. You've got your model of the USS Forrestal built out of 48,000 matchsticks, not to mention a miniature Roman Colosseum constructed of 1,971 playing cards. Such are just a sample of the oddities you will find in this latest cavalcade of the bizarre in the Ripley's franchise. Take the self-guided tour through seven separate galleries and prepare to experience shock and awe.

♂ ♿ **World's Largest Toy Museum** (417-332-1499; www.worldslargesttoy museum.com), 3609 W. SR 76, Branson, Mo. Open Mon.–Sat. at 9 AM. $13.95 adults, $10.95 ages 7–16, free for kids 6 and younger. If you're feeling nostalgic

THE WORLD'S LARGEST TOY MUSEUM

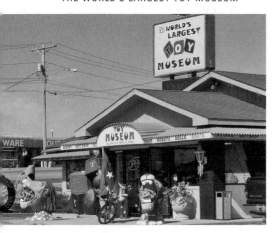

for a cherished toy, you will no doubt find it here. The range runs from toys of the 1800s to Shirley Temple and Tom Mix memorabilia to Spider-Man and Star Wars. Of course there's an on-site gift shop where you can purchase (what else?) toys. Also located within the museum is the **Harold Bell Wright Museum,** devoted to the acclaimed author of *The Shepherd of the Hills.* Visitors can view Wright's original manuscript, his gun collection, numerous artifacts, and a half-hour movie.

♂ ♿ **Veterans Memorial Museum** (417-336-2300; www.veteransmemorial

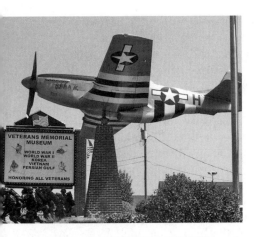

THE VETERANS MEMORIAL MUSEUM

branson.com), 1250 W. 76 Country Blvd., Branson, Mo. Open Aug.–Dec., daily 9–7. $14.95 adults, $13 veterans, $10 students 13–17, $5 kids 5–12. Fred Hoppe has pulled off a major accomplishment in creating his Veterans Memorial Museum, geared toward honoring those who fought and died in both world wars, Korea, Vietnam, and the Persian Gulf. Inside, you'll find the walls covered with more than half a million names of veterans who have given their lives in time of war, as well as the world's largest war memorial bronze sculpture. More than 70 feet long and weighing 15 tons, the piece features 50 life-sized soldiers storming a beach. Each soldier's face was modeled after an actual combat veteran; Hoppe's father, a World War II hero, was the basis for the lead soldier. There are more than 2,000 military artifacts in this museum (Hoppe personally wrote the description for each one), and in front of the museum sits a full-sized P-51 Mustang fighter plane. Ten great halls cover the wars and conflicts fought during the 20th century. Circulation and viewing starts in the World War I Hall, progressing through World War II, Korea, Vietnam, Desert Storm, and more.

⚓ ♿ **Hollywood Wax Museum** (417-337-8277; www.hollywoodwax.com), 3030 W. SR 76, Branson, Mo. Open year-round, but hours vary; May 19–Oct. 31, daily 8 AM–midnight. $17.95 adults, $15.95 seniors, $8.95 ages 4–11. I like to keep this guide honest, so before describing the Hollywood Wax Museum, let me offer a disclaimer. I've always found celebrities to be a bit fake, and thus have little desire to look at their wax counterparts. Frankly, it's my opinion that the personalities and intellect of the real and the tallow are pretty similar. That said, if you want to spend $18 to view the visage of your favorite talk-show host, professional wrestler, or movie star du jour in wax, then go right ahead. You'll find about a zillion of them here. Some people like such stuff—different strokes for different folks and all that. Still, if you really want wax, for $18 you can probably find a place in Branson to buy a couple of really nice scented candles.

⚓ **Bonniebrook Historical Society and Kewpie Museum** (1-800-539-7437; www.roseoneill.org), 485 Rose O'Neill Rd., Walnut Shade, Mo. Apr. 1–Nov. 30, Tues.–Sat. 9–4. $8 adults; $3 students; kids under 12 free. Born in the 1870s, Rose O'Neill was way ahead of her time. At one time the most highly paid illustrator in the U.S. (accomplishing this goal while still a teenager), she studied sculpture under Rodin, became a millionaire, lost her entire fortune, was divorced twice, and had homes across America and in Europe. She was called "the Queen of the Bohemians" and considered one of the world's most beautiful women. Her greatest claim to fame, however, was the creation of the legendary Kewpie doll. Rose's most cherished residence, and the home in which she died, was Bonniebrook, located 10 miles north of Branson in the little town of Walnut Shade. Today visitors can not only tour the restored mansion (it burned to the ground in 1947), but also view original drawings and personal letters, photographs, copies of Rose's artwork, and various Kewpie items. On-site is a gift shop where you can purchase Bonniebrook trinkets and some of the Kewpie items that are still being manufactured today.

✿ ✍ ♿ **Ralph Foster Museum** (417-334-6411; www.rfostermuseum.com), 685 Graham Clark Dr., Point Lookout, Mo. Mon.–Sat. 9–4:30. $6 adults; $5 ages 62-plus; free for high-school-aged students and younger. Located just 2 miles south of Branson in Point Lookout, on the College of the Ozarks campus, the Ralph Foster Museum is a stop that should not be missed. This is the mini Smithsonian of the Ozarks. Originating in the 1920s as a way to collect, preserve, and exhibit the history of the region, the museum really took off when radio pioneer Ralph Foster of Springfield took an interest during the 1960s. Contributing extensive collections of western and Native American artifacts, as well as a huge gun collection and financial assistance, Foster was instrumental in helping the facility thrive. Today it consists of three stories of exhibits, a total of 40,000 square feet of displays, and another 20,000 square feet dedicated to research areas and offices. Gallery topics within the structure include African and North American animals, firearms through the ages, Ozark history, natural history, and the minerals, birds, butterflies, and rocks of the Ozarks. As well, there are clocks, primitives, an area devoted to Kewpie doll creator Rose O'Neill, and the huge Ralph Foster gun collection. Last but not least, be sure to look over the original Clampett family truck featured on *The Beverly Hillbillies.*

GIANT BANJO ✿ ✍ ♿ **The World's Largest Banjo** (1-888-505-4096; www.grandcountry.com), Grand Country Square, 1945 SR 76, Branson, Mo. This giant re-creation of a collectible Gibson banjo, weighing in at more than 3,000

GRAND COUNTRY FUN SPOT, HOME OF THE WORLD'S LARGEST BANJO

pounds and more than 47 feet long, can be found in the Grand Country Market, part of the Grand Country Square complex. The neck holds five fiber-optic strings, and many visitors think it's right cool to have their photo taken next to it. I'm not sure of the reason for this, though the site is admittedly more interesting than the World's Largest Ball of Twine or the World's Largest Frying Pan.

✷ To Do

THEME PARKS & ATTRACTIONS 🦐 ✎ ♿ **Silver Dollar City** (1-800-475-9370; www.silverdollarcity.com), 399 Indian Point Rd., Branson, Mo. The original Branson theme park and without question the biggest draw in town, Silver Dollar City originally arose in 1960 as a small 1880s Ozark village. Its purpose was to entertain travelers while they waited to tour Marvel Cave, the tourist attraction leased and operated by the Herschend family. You have to wonder if the Herschends ever suspected that Silver Dollar City would develop into one of America's favorite theme parks, or that they would expand and develop their company into a national entertainment powerhouse. Today the 61-acre Silver Dollar City complex includes five huge festivals, 30 state-of-the-art thrill rides, 60 specialty shops featuring handcrafted goods, live entertainment (more than 40 shows daily), literally hundreds of old-time craftsmen demonstrating skills and arts from eras past, and more than a dozen restaurants. For the kids, the rides include roller coasters such as Wildfire (five inversions and a 15-story drop at 66 mph), the Powder Keg (0–53 mph in 2.8 seconds), and the Lost River of the Ozarks (you will get very wet on this one). Parents may more enjoy the **Frisco Silver Dollar Line Steam Train** or the guided tour through **Marvel Cave.** The latter is a one-hour jaunt that descends 300 feet underground to the Cathedral Room, one of the largest cave entrance rooms in the U.Ss. The tour continues downward for another 200 feet, where visitors can hop a cable train back to the surface. The trip encompasses 600 stairs, so you best be in decent shape before attempting the descent.

The restaurants at Silver Dollar City are geared toward leaving you full, sometimes too much so, but there is a much-appreciated twist here: In contrast to many theme parks, the food is very good. The Herschend family has long prided itself on first-class operations, and whether you are indulging in fried chicken, BBQ, or one of the famous buffets, you will be surprised at the quality. The favorite here is **Molly's Mill restaurant.** This is the original eatery in the park, offering an all-you-can-eat buffet and its famous fried chicken. The Lumbercamp Falls Skillet is a pretty amusing place for those who like to see their food

SILVER DOLLAR CITY

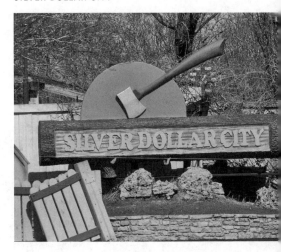

cooked in a giant pan, and the Riverside Ribhouse offers a host of hickory-smoked delights. Those who wish to imbibe should keep in mind that alcohol is neither served nor permitted in any Silver Dollar City property. Smoking is allowed, but only in 14 designated smoking areas.

The craftsmen at Silver Dollar City tend to be native Ozarkers, folk who have learned their trades from birth. You'll find glassblowers, basket makers, black-smiths, candy makers, wood-carvers, gun and knife experts, log hewers, lye soap makers, and much more. Most of these artisans sell their works in the Silver Dollar City stores, and again, the quality of the goods is what you would expect in fine city boutiques.

Music shows run the gamut from outdoor shoot-outs to Cajun singers, bluegrass experts, hillbilly singers, street comedians, and at least one pack of trained dogs. The Silver Dollar City festivals are large-scale productions, not gimmicks just thrown together to make a few extra bucks. Few visitors ever go away dissatisfied.

A one-day pass to Silver Dollar City, which includes all rides and shows, runs $59.11 for those over 12, $56.96 for those over 62, and $48.36 for ages 4–11. Kids 3 and younger are admitted free. The park is open from late March until the end of December. Hours vary depending on the month. Call for current times, but as a general rule you're safe if you assume 10–6 for rides, shops, and attractions. Music shows and dining run later in the evening.

If you're planning a longer trip, packages and three-day passes offer some good values.

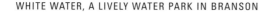 **White Water** (1-800-475-9370; www.bransonwhitewater.com), 3505 W. SR 76, Branson, Mo. Open May–Sept., daily 10–6. Open later during specific nights and weeks during the height of summer. White Water at Branson (owned by Silver Dollar City) offers ample opportunity to get soaking wet. The attrac-

WHITE WATER, A LIVELY WATER PARK IN BRANSON

tions include an 800-foot river adventure through a Polynesian forest, the Raging River Rapids, and the Pipeline Plunge. In 2011, Aloha River at Hula Hula Bay joined the lineup. The Surf's Up Wave Pool holds 500,000 gallons of water and allows for tube riding and bodysurfing. Throughout the park are dining spots featuring the expected ice cream, funnel cakes, and hamburgers. You might opt for a Domino's pizza or enjoy a larger selection of eats at the Big Island Marketplace. Alcohol is neither sold nor permitted, as is true with all Silver Dollar City properties, and revealing swimsuits or thongs are forbidden. One admission fee covers all the rides: $42.41 adults, $35.71 ages 4–11. Seniors (over 62) can buy a one-day pass for $30.13. If you're planning a longer trip, some good values can be found in packages and three-day passes.

🦐 ⌀ ♿ **The Shepherd of the Hills** (417-334-4191 or 1-800-653-6288; www.old matt.com), 5586 W. SR 76, Branson, Mo. Author Harold Bell Wright completed *The Shepherd of the Hills* in 1907, and the publishing world has never been the same. This blockbuster, fictionally based upon the authentic characters Wright came to know and love in the Ozark hills, became the fourth most read book in history (no small feat when you consider that the number one spot is held by the Bible). The book still offers a relevant topic today, comparing the social structure of urban areas—with their anonymity and technology— against the unspoiled and regenerative purity of nature and those who reside there. A basic theme lies in the concept that having less equates to actually having more.

INSPIRATION TOWER AT THE SHEPHERD OF THE HILLS, HOME OF THE VIGILANTE EXTREME ZIPRIDER

The original homestead of John and Anna Ross (the couple known in the book as Old Matt and Aunt Mollie), who allowed Wright to stay in their home during the eight summers it took to complete his tome, is now the site of tours, shows, and the famous dramatic performance of *The Shepherd of the Hills*. The Ross cabin has been completely restored, and the 1901 Morgan County Church, which was moved to its current location, is a popular spot for weddings (417-332-4971). You can enjoy shops on the grounds, a homestead tour by Jeep, a climb to the top of the 230-foot **Inspiration Tower,** the **Rockin' S Chuckwagon** music show and brunch, and a campfire dinner with the legendary **Sons of the Pioneers.**

Ticket prices for the outdoor drama (May–Oct.) are $37 for adults and $18 for kids 4–16. This production involves a cast of more than 80 actors, 40 horses, a flock of sheep, several firearms, and the actual burning of a log cabin (you should note that the show is canceled should it happen to rain). Prices for the Sons of the Pioneers (May–Oct.) run $39 for adults and $19 for children 4–12. The admission fee includes both the dinner and the show. The "Christmas on the Trail" dinner (Nov.–Dec.), which includes a lighted trek through the park, costs $39 for adults, $18 for kids. A trip to the top of Inspiration Tower is $10 for adults, $5 for kids (Apr.–Dec.). Those 7 and older may also take a horseback trail ride (Memorial Day–Labor Day) for $25. A guided Homestead Tour covering all the park's major attractions (visitors are transported in Jeeps) costs $22 for adults and $10 for kids (May–Oct.).

From Nov.–early Jan., a special **Trail of Lights** tour is offered when the park is decked out for Christmas. Call for prices.

✐ ☃ ❋ **Vigilante Extreme ZipRider** (417-334-4191 or 1-800-653-6288; www .oldmatt.com), 5586 W. SR 76, Branson, Mo. One of the largest ziplines in the U.S., the Vigilante is part of the Shepherd of the Hills complex. Riders are strapped into chair harnesses at a height of 170 feet (actually, from the observation deck of Inspiration Tower). They then zip a half-mile over the Ozark hills at a speed of 50 mph. Open Apr.–Dec. Tickets average $9.50 per ride for adults, $6.50 per kids. Also on site is the Heavy Metal High Rise, a steel and concrete go-cart track that reaches four stories into the air.

✐ **Branson Ballknocker** (417-335-3958; www.ballknocker.com), 3320. W. Harvey Ln., Branson, Mo. Open Mar.–Oct. $29.95. If you feel the urge to crawl inside a 12-foot-tall plastic ball and go rolling down a 550-foot track, then this is

THE HEAVY METAL HIGH RISE AT ONE OF THE TRACK FAMILY FUN PARKS IN BRANSON

HANNAH'S MAZE OF MIRRORS AND
THE CASTLE OF CHAOS

the ride for you. Inside the clear ball is a 6-foot passenger chamber, cushioning, and harnesses. Up to three people can ride in the ball at once, and if you prefer a soaking wet trek, the management will load the ball with up to 5 gallons of water.

◈ **Branson Zipline Canopy Tours at Wolf Creek Preserve** (417-561-2500 or 1-800-712-4654; www.branson zipline.com), 2399 US 65, Walnut Shade, Mo. Open Mar. 1–Dec. 31. Usually open daily by 9 AM, but you'll need to book your ride in advance. Billed as an "eco-adventure," these zipline canopy tours traverse the trees of the Wolf Creek Preserve. The setup cost about $4 million to build, and the tours are generally of the scenic variety. The Flying Prospector Canopy Tour ($69.99 for adults, $66.99 for kids) takes 90 minutes, while the Ozarks Xplorer Canopy Tour ($99.99 for adults, $89.99 for kids) requires 2 hours. Those feeling the need for speed might opt for the Blue Streak Fast Line and Freefall Xpress $39.99 for adults, $38.99 for kids). Options also exist to go zipping around at night.

◈ ♿ ❈ **Castle of Chaos** (417-337-8700; www.castleofchaosbranson.com), 3030 W. SR 76, Branson, Mo. Open daily 8 AM–midnight. $14.95 for adults and $7.95 for kids. It's not 3D or 4D . . . it's 5D. I'm not sure what that means, but if you apply Einstein's theory to this attraction, then you perhaps go back in time. At any rate, visitors to this state-of-the-art attraction view a 3D horror film that is billed as including "heart-pounding motion, special effects, animatronics, and an all-out shooting battle against evil." In short, everyone gets a light-emitting gun and gets to blast away at the critters on the screen. It's a good time, and unlike skeet shooting, you don't need any earplugs.

◈ ♿ ❈ **Castle Rock Resort and Waterpark** (417-336-6000 or 1-888-273-3919; www.castlerockbranson.com), 3001 Green Mountain Dr., Branson, Mo. Located within the Castle Rock Resort, the water park features 30,000 square feet of splashing indoors and 15,000 more outdoors. You'll find a river, a couple of three-story thrill rides, and a 2,500-gallon tipping bucket. Both the resort and water park are open year-round. Hours vary, but you need not be a guest of the resort to go soak your head. Admission is $15 a day for ages 3 and up.

✍ ♿ ❋ **Dolly Parton's Dixie Stampede** (417-336-300 or 1-800-520-5544; www.dixiestampede.com/branson.php), 1525 W. SR 76, Branson, Mo. Open Feb.–Dec. Showtimes, which vary by month, are either 3, 5:30, or 8 PM at the Dixie Stampede building. Admission is $47 for adults and $26 for kids 4–11. Quite simply, the Dixie Stampede defines Branson. Dolly Parton is not known for doing things in a small way, and this extravaganza fits her image like a glove. Those in attendance at this show should be prepared for a good nap afterward, for the meal alone will leave you fat and happy. Where else will you be served not only a whole rotisserie chicken, but also a BBQ pork loin, soup, biscuit, corn on the cob, baked potato, dessert, and unlimited soft drinks, tea, or coffee? Always covering the bases, the show does offer a vegetarian meal, even though the sight of a vegetarian in Branson is on a par with seeing Mick Jagger at a Baptist picnic. The show itself is on an equally grand scale. Think of a full-scale re-creation of the Civil War, complete with buffalo stampedes, nearly two score of horses, pyrotechnics, and a huge cast. The Dixie Stampede is something you have to see in Branson, if for no other reason than to brag to your friends how much you ate. The stampede also offers a Christmas extravaganza in Nov.–Dec.

✍ ♿ ❋ **Grand Country Fun Spot** (417-334-2454; www.grandcountry.com), 1945 SR 76, Branson, Mo. $7.50 for adults, $6.50 for kids. The Grand Country complex features family-friendly lodging, not to mention a water park, numerous shows, four restaurants (one of which is the ubiquitous Branson all-you-can-eat buffet), and games galore. The Fun Spot offers kids and their parents endless opportunities for black-light mini-golf, mini-bowling, bumper cars, a laser maze, and a fully loaded video-arcade area.

DOLLY PARTON'S DIXIE STAMPEDE

WILD WOODY AT ONE OF THE TRACK FAMILY FUN PARKS IN BRANSON

⚔ ♿ **Greatest Adventures Miniature Golf** (417-332-0888; www.minigolfin branson.com), 4800 Gretna Road, Branson, Mo. Open from mid-Mar.–mid-Nov., daily 10 AM-11 PM. $7.50. If you're into hitting a golf ball through windmills and such, this is your ultimate locale. Greatest Adventures was the site of the 2011 U.S. Open Miniature Golf Tournament. The 36-hole course was built in 2008, and features a couple of different themed courses. Putt through greens featuring fountains, bridges, dragons, a waterfall cave, a gorilla, and a host of Egyptian-type artifacts. The facility includes a snack bar with a giant-screen TV in case your golfing endeavors plum wear you out.

⚔ ♿ ✻ **Hannah's Maze of Mirrors** (417-337-8700; www.mazeofmirrors branson.com), 3030 W. SR 76, Branson, Mo. Open daily year-round; hours vary depending on the season. Hours from May–Sept. are 8 AM–midnight. An unlimited, one-day pass costs $9.95 for adults, $6.95 for kids. Not the place to go if you have a bad self-image or are a vampire. You'll wander through a mirrored maze containing 288 potential turns. Participants meander through mirrored hallways in an attempt to save Princess Hannah of Savannah (you just know they wanted to say "Montana"). The animated storyline should keep young adventurers satisfied.

⚔ **The Track Family Fun Parks** (417-334-1612; www.bransontracks.com), locations at 2911 Green Mountain Dr., 2505 W. SR 76, 3345 W. SR 76, and 3525 W. SR 76, Branson, Mo. Open May–Dec., but call ahead for details. Most tracks open daily at 10 AM June–Oct. This is go-kart Nirvana! You'll find kiddie go-karts ($6), rookie go-carts ($6.50), a heavy-metal high-rise track ($9.50), classic wooden tracks ($9.50) and much more. The parks also offer skycoasters, laser tag, bumper cars, and game arcades.

GOLF Branson Creek Golf Club (417-339-4653; www.bransoncreekgolf.com), 1001 Branson Creek Dr., Hollister, Mo. Designed by Tom Fazio, this 18-hole course has been rated the number one public course in Missouri. Fees, which include cart, bag tag, and range balls, are $48 in Jan.–Feb.; $60 in Mar.; $76 in Apr.; $90 (Sun.–Thurs.) and $99 (Fri.–Sat.) May–Oct.; and $60 in Nov.–Dec. T-shirts or denim are not allowed, personal coolers are forbidden, and all food and beverages must be purchased on the property.

Holiday Hills Resort and Golf Club (417-334-4838; www.holidayhills.com), 238 E. SR 76, Branson, Mo. This course, originally built in 1938, was completely overhauled in 1997. Not nearly as tough as Branson Creek, it is the perfect choice for those who prefer relaxation over fierce competition. Golf carts are equipped with a GPS system that provides a real-time view of the course, displays distance from your ball to the green, and allows you to order food and beverages. Open year-round. $59 7–noon, $45 noon–3, and $34.50 after 3.

Thousand Hills Golf Resort (1-800-864-4145; www.thousandhills.com), 245 S. Wildwood Dr., Branson, Mo. A local favorite, the 18-hole Thousand Hills offers a par-64 course. Small things matter, and if you tend to lose balls (as I do), you'll appreciate the fact that this facility provides a GPS free on every cart. As for awards, *Golf Digest* gave Thousand Hills a four-star rating in 2009. Greens fees are in the $30–$60, range depending on day and time.

Payne Stewart Golf Club of Branson Hills (417-337-2963; www.paynestewart golfclub.com), 100 N. Payne Stewart Dr., Branson, Mo. In 2011, *Golfweek* magazine called this course the third-best in the state of Missouri. The par-72 course (which just opened in 2009) features 18 holes comprising 7,234 yards. Fees are $59 in Jan.–Feb, $72 in Mar., $86 in Apr., $75–$99 May–Oct, and $69 in Nov.

LedgeStone Golf Course and Country Club (417-335-8187; www.ledgestone golf.com), 1600 LedgeStone Way, Branson West, Mo. *Golf Digest* has described LedgeStone as "a masterpiece of mountain golf architecture." After one visit you'll see what that means: This is a stunningly beautiful course. Water comes into play on 10 of the 18 holes, but the par-3 hole 15 may bring your biggest challenge. From a cliffside tee box, you shoot straight down into a valley. This one will test both your control and your distance perspective. Greens fees and cart are $89 for 18 holes during peak months. Winter rates (Oct.–Feb.) are $74.

Pointe Royale Golf Course (417-334-0624 or 1-866-334-4477; www.pointe royale.com), 1000 Point Royale Dr., Branson, Mo. If you play Pointe Royale, keep an eye out for some of the country music stars who live alongside the course. Also, keep an eye out for the water hazards on 12 of the 18 holes. This is a challenging facility with narrow fairways, usually considered the original championship course of Branson. Greens fees are $39–$49 Apr.–Oct., and $39 Nov.–Mar.

Murder Rock Country Club (417-332-3259; www.murderrock.com), 1250 Golf Club Dr., Hollister, Mo. Possibly the best name for a golf course in the U.S., Murder Rock opened for business in 2007. The 18-hole, par 71, 6,700-yard course is open to the public and serves many of the communities and suburbs that have sprung up around Branson. The course was lauded by *Golfweek* magazine in both 2010 and 2011. Greens fees from May–Oct. are $72 for weekdays and $80 for weekends. Rates vary from $40–$72 in the off-season.

✳ Wild Places

Table Rock State Park (417-334-4704; www.mostateparks.com/tablerock.htm), 5722 SR 165, Branson, Mo. Created in 1959 and spanning 356 acres, Table Rock State Park is a very busy little place encompassing numerous campsites, a marina, store, dive shop, and trails. The marina itself is a major rental center for WaveRunners, pontoon boats, ski boats, and fishing boats, and it also includes a well-stocked scuba shop. The store has all the supplies you could desire for a day messing around the lake or hanging out at the campsite, and visitors can even try their hand at parasailing.

Ruth and Paul Henning State Conservation Area (417-895-6680; http://mdc4 .mdc.mo.gov/Applications/MOATLAS/AreaSummaryPage.aspx?txtAreaID=8208), Missouri Department of Conservation, Branson Forestry Office, US 65 North, Branson, Mo. Just past the end of the twinkling lights of the Branson Strip (SR 76) you'll come across a 1,534-acre area of steep hills and hickory trees. Paul Henning (producer of *The Beverly Hillbillies*) and his wife, Ruth, donated this land to the Missouri Conservation Department, thus protecting for perpetuity many of the areas described in Harold Bell Wright's *The Shepherd of the Hills*. Locales such as Mutton Hollow, Little Pete's Cave, and Sammy Lane's Lookout can all be viewed by visitors. Within the Henning Conservation Area (which is a nice break from Branson's nonstop shows and buffets) are trails, great views of the White River hills, and a blessed silence. The area is open 8 AM–dark, and neither fires nor camping is permitted.

Hercules Glades Wilderness Area (417-683-4428; www.fs.fed.us/r9/forests /marktwain/ranger_districts/ava), Mark Twain National Forest, Ava/Cassville /Willow Springs District Office, 1103 S. Jefferson St., Ava, Mo. Located 20 miles

HENNING STATE CONSERVATION AREA

east of Branson, the 12,3413-acre Hercules Glades is one of the seven wilderness areas falling within the Mark Twain National Forest. Loaded with springs, creeks, bald hills, and glades, the area's only access is via foot or astride a horse. Spring and fall are the best times to visit due to the array of colors, but in summer you will likely see critters normally assumed to live primarily in the Southwestern deserts (armadillos, lizards, and roadrunners, for example). Keep in mind that spring and summer in the Ozarks also feature a proliferation of ticks, mosquitoes, and all those other fun vermin that lead to itchy skin. You can camp anywhere in Hercules Glades, as long as you move 100 feet or more off a trail. Make sure your fire is dead-out before you leave.

🐾 ♿ **Dogwood Canyon Nature Park** (417-779-5983; www.dogwoodcanyon .com), 2038 W. SR 86, Lampe, Mo. A 2,200-acre private preserve, Dogwood Canyon was developed by Johnny Morris, founder of Bass Pro Shops, and is full of ridges, forests, and creeks. Visitors can view elk, buffalo, and Texas longhorn cattle. There is also a Civil War museum, an old lead mine, and a working general store. Located south of Branson (and 16 miles west of Big Cedar Lodge), Dogwood offers a 6-mile paved trail that visitors can hike for $8.95 adults, $4.95 ages 3–11. Bicyclists share this trail, and bikes can be rented for $17.95 adults, $8.95 kids. This is just the beginning. Although some activities are weather dependent, options are many. An open-air tram provides a two-hour wildlife tour ($25.95 adults, $11.95 kids) through the depths of the Ozarks. Self-guided catch-and-release trout fishing runs $25 adults, $15 kids (for the first hour); guided half-day fishing trips are $225 per person. Horseback riding fees are $30 per person.

LAKES Table Rock Lake (417-334-4101; www.swl.usace.army.mil/parks/table rock), Army Corps of Engineers, 4600 SR 165, Branson, Mo. The Table Rock Dam, one of the four dams used to control flooding on the White River and provide hydroelectric power, was completed in 1958. At 252 feet high and nearly 6,500 feet long, the dam holds in a reservoir comprising some 43,000 acres with 745 miles of shoreline. Located 6 miles south of Branson, this Army Corps of Engineers project offers all the amenities and activities you would imagine on most lakes and is also home to the 350-acre Table Rock State Park. For fishermen, much of the lake is suited to the pursuit of bass, crappie, and channel catfish. However, the tailwaters of Table Rock (which are also the headwaters of Lake Taneycomo) are very cold and provide some lunker brown and rainbow trout. If you want to have some fun, fish for largemouth bass after dark during mid to late summer. Hit the banks south of the dam in the wee hours of the morning and try for smallmouth bass.

Lake Taneycomo (417-334-4101; www.swl.usace.army.mil/parks/tablerock), Army Corps of Engineers, 4600 SR 165, Branson, Mo. A trout fisherman's heaven, the cold waters of Taneycomo (at places they average 48 degrees) came about thanks to the building of Table Rock Dam 22 miles upstream. When Taneycomo was first constructed in 1913 it was a warm-water lake, but Table Rock gave it a physical southern boundary in 1958 and the waters cooled dramatically. This was bad for such early resort towns as Rockaway Beach (who wants to swim in 48-degree water?), but good for those who wish to catch record-breaking brown and rainbow trout. At 2,080 acres, Taneycomo is the home of both the Shepherd of the Hills Trout Hatchery and the Powersite hydroelectric dam. If you stick your toe in the water you'll get a chill, but if you toss a line you'll likely get a trout.

CAVES Talking Rocks Cavern (417-272-3366 or 1-800-600-2283; www.talking rockscavern.com), 423 Fairy Cave Ln., Branson, Mo. Found 5 miles to the west of Branson, this cavern offers 45-minute tours daily 9:30–6. For cavers the crystal formations, stalactites, soda straws, and curtains offer innumerable photo opportunities. The tours are $17.95 for those 13 and up, $9.95 ages 4–12.

✳ Lodging

BED & BREAKFASTS For those who would prefer a bed & breakfast over one of the infinite numbers of franchise hotel rooms in town, you might check out the **Branson Bed & Breakfast Service** (1-800-933-8529; www.ozarkbedandbreakfast .com). Its website provides many lodging options, complete with numerous pictures and prices.

Finding a room isn't tough in Branson; hotels and motels are thicker than cats at a fish fry, and vacancies are usually available even if you don't have reservations. Both the Strip and the entire surrounding area are lined with hotels and motels of varying price and quality. Almost all will have their prices shining from a huge, lighted sign, along with the omnipresent non-teaser in the genre of FREE HBO or CONTINENTAL BREAKFAST. In this guide I'm avoiding comment on the vast majority of the franchised Super 8/Comfort Inn/Best Western offerings and their clones. You can find those on your own. Below are selected establishments that offer a bit more for your money.

♿ ✳ **Abbe Chimes Bed and Breakfast** (417-779-1630; www.abbechimes .com), 464 Pokeberry Ln., Lampe, Mo. Located to the south of Silver Dollar City, the Abbe Chimes is a 2003 contemporary home set on 46 acres above Table Rock Lake. The home features central air, an indoor swimming pool, and exceptionally large rooms with cable TV, VHS and DVD player, fireplace, microwave, refrigerator, dataport-equipped phones, and double whirlpool bath. The three suites range in decor from contemporary to 19th century to South Pacific. A gourmet breakfast is served every morning at 9. Rates begin at $125 a night. Pets, kids, and smoking are not permitted, but a boarding kennel is nearby for the first. Boarding kennels have not yet been invented for kids or smokers.

🐾 ✳ **Aunt Sadie's Bed and Breakfast** (417-335-4063 or 1-800-944-4250; www.auntsadies.com), 163 Fountain St., Branson, Mo. Aunt Sadie's was voted one of the four most romantic inns in the U.S. by *Redbook* magazine. The four private cabins and two guest rooms offer amenities such as hot tub or whirlpool bath, TV/VCR, microwave, small refrigerator, and fireplace. It's a lovely setting, back in the midst of 7 acres of timber and only a few minutes from Branson. A huge country breakfast is included in the price, and on-site you'll find not only a day spa with three massage therapists, but also a beautiful wedding chapel. Rates begin at $120 for a room and $135 for a cabin. Children are not permitted, but smoking is OK on the outside decks. Dogs are accepted with innkeeper approval and an extra charge of $20 per night. The dog must be housebroken and not have fleas or be filthy. Presumably that same stipulation applies for two-legged guests.

✔ ❋ **Bear Creek Lodge** (1-866-443-0030; www.bearcreekbedandbreakfast .com), 1320 Keithley Rd., Walnut Shade, Mo. Offering four suites and three cabins, Bear Creek Lodge sits high on a hill overlooking Bear Hollow. Guests enjoy climate-controlled accommodations, king or queen beds, a fireplace or parlor stove, microwaves, satellite TV, and free WiFi. Breakfast is included in the price of the stay, and activities range from horseback riding and fishing to zipping down a zipline. The Bear's Den master suite runs $139 per night for two people, or $200 per night for six people. Cabins begin at $125 per night for two people, and Bear Creek offers an extensive wine list. Kids are welcome here, but pets are not. As usual, smoking is allowed outdoors only.

♿ ❋ **Bradford House** (1-888-488-4445; www.bradfordhouse.us), 296 Blue Meadows Rd., Branson, Mo. A gorgeous Victorian home built in 1994, the Bradford House borders on majestic. Guests are welcomed by a two-story spiral staircase, common room with 25-foot ceilings, and panorama of windows. One of several Bradford properties located in Branson, the home is more of a cross between hotel and inn than the typi-

cal B&B. However, it does a good job of holding on to a sense of class. Rates run from $89–$169. A full breakfast is served, and amenities include an outdoor pool, Jacuzzi rooms, a 400-movie video library, free wireless Internet, and private hot tub or whirlpool bath. Pets and smoking are not permitted, but children are considered on a case-by-case basis.

✔ **Cameron's Crag** (417-334-4720 or 1-800-933-8529; www.camerons-crag .com), 738 Acadia Club Rd., Hollister, Mo. If you want to enjoy the best views of both Lake Taneycomo and Branson, stay at Cameron's Crag. Perched high on a bluff above the lake, the contemporary home's four suites offer king-sized bed, private entrance and bath, cable and VCR/DVD, microwave, coffee bar, and refrigerator. A private hot tub overlooking the lake is a perfect spot from which to enjoy the panoramic vista. Rooms run $125–165, and school-aged kids are accepted. As is the standard, smoking is allowed only outdoors and pets are not welcome.

Crystal Cove Bed and Breakfast (417-338-2715 or 1-888-699-0444; www.crystalcovebranson.com), 635 Compton Ridge Rd., Branson, Mo. Crystal Cove offers seven luxury suites situated on a hillside above Tablerock Lake. The main lodge provides a sort of rustic elegance, and each of the suites features a different them. This is an extremely comfortable place, and each room comes with a log-hewn, king-sized bed, extra-large Jacuzzi, fireplace, 37-inch flat-screen TV, and mini-kitchenette. Rates are $139–149, and a variety of packages are available. Breakfast is a big deal here, and might include such items as apple cinnamon stuffed

French toast, maple sausage, biscuits and sausage gravy, eggs Benedict, scrambled eggs, bacon and hash browns, a variety of stratas, fresh fruit, muffins, cinnamon rolls, and biscuits. Smoking is not allowed, and they're right serious about it. Call to inquire about kids and pets.

🐾 ♨ ❋ **Emory Creek Victorian Bed and Breakfast** (417-334-3805 or 1-800-362-7404; www.emorycreek bnb.com), 143 Arizona Dr., Branson, Mo. There's a reason Emory Creek is considered the most elegant bed & breakfast in Branson. The luxurious blue and white Victorian, built in 1993 and owned by Sammy and Beverly Gray Pagna, features five suites and a host of amenities. Breakfast is a four-course affair, with live music coming from Sammy on the piano. Fresh cookies are in your room upon arrival, and plush terry-cloth robes are in the bathrooms. A wildlife trail wanders through 7.5 acres, with a garden gazebo suspended over the forest floor. Furnishings inside are Victorian to the core, and a shining grand staircase rises from the home's main salon to the second story. Should you wish to read, a library offers both the classics and best-sellers. Rates run $99–159 a night, and lunch and dinner can be arranged for an additional fee. Kids over 13 are permitted, and pets are welcome in the specially designed "Dogwood Room" ($99 per night).

❀ ❋ **Falls on the Lake Bed & Breakfast** (417-334-3833 or 1-866-448-9760; www.fallsonthelake.com), 417 Dale Ave., Hollister, Mo. Just minutes from Branson, this getaway on Table Rock Lake offers peace and quiet. The landscaping is impeccable, complete with flowing waterfall, and

rates for the three suites range $105–180 per night. Amenities can include TV and VCR, central air, private spas, outdoor hot tub, private entrance, fireplace, and free WiFi. For breakfast make sure to sample (or more than sample . . . this stuff is good) the caramel walnut French toast. Kids of all ages are accepted at the Falls, but smoking is outside only and pets are a no-no.

♨ ❀ ❋ **Gaines Landing** (417-334-2280 or 1-800-825-3145; www.gaines landing.com), 521 W. Atlantic St., Branson, Mo. Each of the three suites at Gaines Landing features a private hot tub right outside your door, but such is just the beginning of the nice touches provided by this small establishment located in "old" downtown Branson. The rooms feature a king-sized bed, TV/VCR with free popcorn and movies, microwave, and a small refrigerator with complimentary refreshments. One has a wood-burning fireplace. Gaines is close to everything, but also situated back in a small stretch of woods. It's the best of both worlds, with restaurants and shows very close, but peace and quiet awaiting back at your room. $110–159. Smoking and pets are out, but kids are accepted without restriction. Rates include a buffet breakfast.

♨ ❀ ❋ **Lakeshore Bed and Breakfast** (417-338-2698 or 1-800-285-9739; www.lakeshorebandb.com), 47 Elm Ln., Branson, Mo. Located right on Table Rock Lake and just 2 miles south of Silver Dollar City, Lakeshore offers three rooms (one is a two-bedroom suite) that are close to all the attractions but also allow for the fun of splashing around in the water. Kids are welcome here, and at $65–95 per night, the lodgings are some of the most economical in Branson. You can bring your boat and moor it at Lakeshore's dock, pedal around in their boat, do a bit of fishing, or simply sit outside and watch the sunset. Rooms come with queen beds, a full kitchen, and private bath; the suite also includes TV, DVD/VCR, refrigerator, coffee bar, and whirlpool tub and shower. A large breakfast is provided each morning. Pets are prohibited, and smoking is allowed outside only.

🦆 ✍ ❄ **Red Bud Cove** (417-334-7144 or 1-800-677-5525; www.redbud cove.com), 162 Lakewood Dr., Hollister, Mo. This is a nice place to visit in spring if you enjoy a gorgeous garden of flowers and the purple blossoms of the trees that are this inn's namesake. A renovated barn, Red Bud features eight suites (queens, kings, honeymoon, and family). Located right on Table Rock Lake and only about 15 minutes from the Branson Strip, Red Bud's suites feature private entrances, a living room (some have a working fireplace), private bath, kitchenette, TV, and phone. Rates, which include breakfast, run $118–168 per night, and kids are accepted. Pets are not allowed, and if you wish to smoke, you will have to do it in the great outdoors.

RESORTS ✍ ♿ ❄ 🍸 **Big Cedar Lodge** (1-800-225-6343; www.big cedar.com), 612 Devil's Pool Rd., Ridgedale, Mo. For sheer beauty and luxury and the feel of the best lodge you could ever discover in either the Adirondacks or the Rockies, Big Cedar Lodge wins hands-down. Purchased in 1987 by John Morris (owner of Bass Pro Shops), the facility included and expanded greatly upon the palatial homes and grounds of several

wealthy Missourians from generations past. Just 10 miles south of Branson, the 800-acre lodge offers accommodations in the form of 81 log cabins, each with a fully equipped kitchen, gas grill, deck, fireplace, and whirlpool bath. The Falls Lodge contains 65 rooms, with whirlpool baths, king-sized beds, balconies, and a fireplace. Nine "knotty pine" cabins remain from the days when Big Cedar was a dude ranch, and the SpringView lodge features 17 rooms offering a view of Table Rock Lake. Fifty-one more rooms are available in the Valley View Lodge, and cabins also can be rented in the Dogwood Canyon Nature Park. The size and available amenities on all the cabins, rooms, cottages, and suites vary by day, week, and season. Big Cedar seems a bit reluctant to give out a general range of rates to a travel writer, so all I can give you is information from friends who have stayed there. They tell me it's as nice as advertised, if not better, but far from inexpensive. In other words, you're going to drop a bundle. Check the lodge's website for availability and pricing if you have an exact travel date in mind. Value, Deluxe, Premier, and even a Governor's Suite are available, as are one and two-bedroom cabins with or without lofts.

This resort lives up to its lofty reputation by providing a full-service marina on Table Rock, trails, fishing, horseback riding, a spa, massage, carriage rides, campfire chuckwagon tours, and much more. As for dining, the **Devil's Pool** restaurant (see *Dining Out*) is known for its lunch and breakfast buffets, prime rib, and champagne Sunday brunch. The **Truman Coffee and Café** offers sandwiches, salads, and accompaniments. The

Worman House restaurant provides its own champagne Sunday brunch. For casual dining there is the **Buzzard Bar** and the **Top of the Rock.** Big Cedar is popular for groups, meetings, and weddings.

♂ ఉ ❋ ⅌ **Chateau on the Lake Resort, Spa, and Convention Center** (417-334-1161 or 1-888-333-5253; www.chateauonthelakebranson.com), 415 N. SR 265, Branson, Mo. A John Q. Hammons hotel, the Chateau prides itself on Old World charm and service. Given a Four Diamond rating by AAA, this "Castle in the Ozarks" is situated on the peak of a forested hill overlooking Table Rock Lake. The hotel includes 301 rooms divided into Standard, Traditional, Deluxe, over-sized Chateau Kings, and 57 elaborate suites. A 10-story lobby atrium greets visitors, who will enjoy a level of professionalism and courteous service more commonly associated with renowned urban establishments. Accommodations include such touches as tiled stone baths, hand-tooled iron lamps, and cherrywood beds. All rooms come standard with two phone lines with voice mail and dataports, iron and ironing board, wireless web TV, feather pillows, triple sheets, hair dryers, and lighted make-up mirrors. Lake-view Ambassador Suites, a Vice Presidential Suite, and a 1,000-square-foot Presidential Suite (one of two) offer every perk imaginable. The Chateau folks aren't big on giving out a range of prices either–it must be a trend in the crummy economy of 2011–so call them with the exact date of your stay for more info. Quotes are also available off the website.

In terms of amenities and recreation, guests can enjoy indoor and outdoor pools, a 24-hour fitness area and salon, hot tubs, tennis courts, hiking and biking, and a full-service marina. For those who wish to be pampered in style, the **Spa Chateau** has a lengthy menu of both spa and beauty treatments. The Chateau is also an increasingly popular wedding spot, boasting a 32,000-square-foot ballroom capable of hosting from 50 to 1,500 guests. For outdoor weddings, both the Greenbelt and Garden Terraces can easily handle 50 to 250 guests, and full catering (small or large) is a regular service.

The Chateau Grille (see *Dining Out*) features accomplished chefs and is a Wine Spectator award-winning eatery, while the **Atrium Café and Wine Bar** and **Downstairs Deli** allow for more casual meals. You would also be remiss if you failed to stop in the **Sweete Shoppe,** with its pastries, ice cream, and classic soda fountain.

CAMPING Private campgrounds and RV parks in Branson are as prevalent as fleas on a fat dog. With more than 50 sites from which to choose, visitors can take their pick from simple tent spaces to full-service accommodations capable of handling the largest RVs. Public campgrounds at Table Rock Lake are largely managed by the Army Corps of Engineers.

♦ ♂ ఉ ❋ 🐾 **Compton Ridge Campground** (417-338-2911; www.comptonridge.com), 5040 SR 265, Branson, Mo. The best time to hang your hat at Compton Ridge is in early September, when fiddle players from across the country descend for the annual Ozarks Fiddler's Convention. Tent sites at the main campground begin at $29 (with water and electric); full RV hook-ups are

$33–43. At the smaller, north campground, hook-ups run $33–39.50. Amenities include restrooms, laundry facilities, WiFi, three pools, a game room, hiking trails, tennis courts, basketball courts, and playgrounds. Shuttles are available to Silver Dollar City (free) and to Branson Landing (there's a small fee). There are kitchen and pavilion shelters on the grounds, a 650- seat convention building, church services, and a store. The on-site Whistle Stop Café is open Thurs.–Sun. for breakfast and dinner in-season. The Compton Ridge lodge and motel features motel rooms beginning at $62.95. Cabins can be rented for $130–229 per night. Pets are welcome as long as they're kept on a leash and don't bark loudly enough to wake the dead.

🦌 ✿ 🐾 ♿ **Table Rock Lake** (417-334-4101; www.swl.usace.army.mil/parks/tablerock), 4600 SR 165, Suite A, Branson, Mo. With more than 1,200 individual campsites, the Army Corps of Engineers offers camping in 13 different campgrounds. Most of the areas are open from spring (generally Mar. or Apr.) until Sept. or Oct. Fees are $14–18 for a basic site, $18–22 for a site with electricity, $19–23 for sites with electricity and water, and $20–24 for sites with electricity, water, and sewer. It should be noted that only two of the sites (Big M Park and Eagle Rock Park) have the full facilities. Sites can be reserved by phone at 1-877-444-6777, or online at www.recreation.gov. Most come with a picnic table, shower, toilet, fire ring, and parking space.

🦌 🐾 ♿ ✳ **The Wilderness at Silver Dollar City** (1-800-477-5164; www.thewildernesslogcabins.com), 5125 SR 265, Branson, Mo. Located just a few minutes from all the theaters, the Wilderness offers cabins, 50-amp RV spots, rental RVs, and campsites. Though right in the thick of things, this lovely spot will make you feel you are out in the woods. Cabins come in various sizes (sleeping four comfortably or six if you don't mind a bit of crowding) and run $65–188 per night. RV trailer rentals begin at $112 per night; if you bring your own rig, 30-amp and 50-amp sites are $32 and $35, respectively. A basic tent site is $19–21, or $26 if you opt for water and electricity. As to amenities, all cabins (with the exception of the "pioneer cabin," which lacks a bathroom and most other amenities) come with heat, air, table and chairs, ceiling fans, bathroom, shower, microwave, cable TV, coffeepot, refrigerator, gas grill, and rocking chairs. Cabins with kitchens also include a sink, two-burner stovetop, linens, and towels. The RV rental trailers include heat and air, TV, refrigerator, stove, microwave, coffeepot, shower, toilet, and fire ring. Pets are not accepted.

✳ Where to Eat

EATING OUT The main thing you need to know about dining in Branson, at least for lunch and breakfast, is that quantity is almost always viewed as more important than quality. This town is the epicenter of the all-you-can-eat buffet, no matter if you're talking about French toast, bacon, pancakes, fried chicken, or catfish and hushpuppies. It's not that the food is bad, and in fact some of it is pretty good. It's about timing.

The trick to all-you-can-eat dining lies in trying to arrive during a time when everybody else in town isn't also trying to eat all they can eat. Though

Branson is drawing a younger crowd than in years past, the percentage of middle-aged and retired folks is still pretty high. This translates to the fact that lunch is going to be going strong right at noon, and that the dinner crowd will start flocking in at about 4 (and be gone by 7). If you see a lot of tour buses in the parking lot, you might want to wait an hour or try a different restaurant. That last piece of chicken sitting on the steam table is sometimes a bit tough.

♦ ⌀ ⌖ **McFarlain's** (417-336-4680), 3562 Shepherd of the Hills Expy. Sun.–Thurs. 7:30 AM–8:30 PM, Fri.–Sat. 7:30 AM–9:15 PM. Located in the Branson IMAX, McFarlain's has become one busy place due to good food that is also inexpensive. The emphasis is on quality. Breakfast might be as simple as the $3.49 biscuits and gravy, or as decadent as the $8.49 crabcakes Benedict. There are also numerous skillets and omelets in the $6–9 range. Appetizers for lunch or dinner could be either fried green tomatoes or fried sweet potatoes at $6.99, and a host of burgers and sandwiches for $6–8. Dinner entrées encompass deep-fried catfish (the only way it should be cooked) at $12.99, chicken-fried steak ($9.49), and a 10-ounce rib-eye steak for $15.99. If you've got some time after the meal (and don't forget to order pie), catch the IMAX film *Ozark Legacy and Legend.* It chronicles six generations of the native Ozark McFarlain family and will give you a clear view of what the Ozarks both were and are.

♦ ⌀ ⌖ ⌘ **The Plantation** (417-334-7800; www.bransonsbestrestaurant .com/Plantation_Branson.html), 3460 SR 76. Mon.–Thurs. 7 AM–10 PM, Fri.–Sat. 7 AM–midnight, Sun. 9–9. The name alone will tell you what it looks like. This is a big, long eatery right on the Strip, and it's been voted Best Buffet in Town more times than I can count. Inside, you will find plants everywhere, as well as copious amounts of food. Many chickens gave their lives in the quest to make The Plantation a Branson icon, and diners show their appreciation by eating 'til they burst. With a drink, the daily lunch buffet (11–3:30) costs $7.99. The dinner buffet is a buck cheaper if you eat after 7 PM. While chicken is the claim to fame (well-battered and tasty), you'll also find such regional favorites as catfish (usually prepared in your choice of baked, breaded, or

MCFARLAIN'S FAMILY RESTAURANT

THE PLANTATION RESTAURANT

Cajun), hush puppies, and fried okra. An all-you-can-eat chicken meal is $10.99. The same deal is available for catfish and hush puppies at a price of $11.99.

🦐 🍽 ♿ **Fall Creek Steak and Catfish House** (417-336-5060; www .bransonsbestrestaurant.com/Fall _Creek_Branson.html), 997 SR 165, Branson, Mo. This is one of those restaurants where the management instructs the staff to toss hot rolls to the customers. That trick was perfected long ago by a famous Ozark restaurant (Lambert's Cafe), so I wasn't really impressed by the imitation and lack of creativity. Nonetheless, Fall Creek does put out some good catfish, not to mention fine steaks cooked over hickory wood. An all-you-can-eat catfish dinner is $15.99, and an 18-ounce porterhouse steak is $23.99. Burgers are in the $7 range, and a brisket and rib platter runs $16.99.

🦐 🍽 ♿ **Grand Country Buffet** (417-335-2434; www.grandcountry.com), 1945 W. SR 76, Branson, Mo. Yup . . . it's another buffet. This is a big one, with a full spread laid out for breakfast, lunch, and dinner. The restaurant can hold nearly 500 people, so be advised that Grand Country is a tour bus favorite. Dinner here features five food bars loaded with a variety of meats, fruits, vegetables, salads, fresh-baked breads, bakery desserts, and even an ice cream sundae bar. Ham and roast beef are most always being carved, just in case you've overdosed on chicken and catfish. Grand Country is open every day, year-round. Prices average between $7 and $13.

🦐 🍽 ♿ **Whipper Snappers** (417-334-3282), 2421 W. SR 76, Branson, Mo. Open for dinner daily 4–8. I once knew a fellow in Butte, Montana, name of Scott, with a severe crustacean addiction. With his black hole of an appetite, Scott actually ran a Red Lobster out of lobster during one of its "all-you-can-eat" specials. I look forward to the day he stumbles into Whipper Snappers. For $33 this restaurant offers an all-you-can-eat lobster, crab leg, and seafood buffet. For those who don't feel like a gorge-a-thon, there are plenty of regular menu items. Fried chicken and country-fried steak are $10.99, and the 8-ounce rib eye is $12.99. Whipper Snappers is very casual, totally nonsmoking, and does not serve alcohol of any kind. A children's menu is available.

✐ 🍴 ♿ **Sadie's Sideboard** (417-334-3619; www.sadiessideboard.com), 2830 W. SR 76, Branson, Mo. Open daily for breakfast 7–11, lunch 11–4, and dinner 4–8. If I was going to send a Branson visitor someplace for a casual breakfast or BBQ, I'd probably send him to Sadie's. Yes, it's another buffet; however, Sadie's is a notch or two above most of the others. Breakfast features grits, griddle-cooked pancakes (with warn maple syrup), ham, bacon, fried taters, sausage gravy that actually contains sausage, and home-baked bread and rolls. It's a steal at $5.99 for adults and $3.99 for kids. The lunch buffet is loaded with BBQ ribs, fried chicken, fried chicken livers, catfish, and ham-and-beans with cornbread. It's $8.99 for adults

and $5.99 for kids. Lunch sandwiches are good here as well. A prime rib sandwich, served with peppers and onions, is $7.99. Numerous burgers and sandwiches are offered in the $6.99–$7.99 range. Just a suggestion here, but you might ask your waitress to serve the sauce on the side; for some reason the kitchen seems to enjoying dousing every BBQ sandwich with KC Masterpiece. The dinner buffet is much like the lunch version, but with more choices, including brisket. It runs $12.99 for adults and $6.99 for kids. Ribs, BBQ platters, steaks, and individual entrées are also available.

DINING OUT Unless otherwise noted, all listings are in Branson, Mo.

✐ ♿ 🍸 **Buckingham's** (417-337-7777; www.clarionhotelbranson.com), 2820 W. SR 76. Daily 1–11 PM, with dinner served after 4:30. You could call the decor of Buckingham's, located in the Clarion Hotel, "early American African veld." This place is amusing,

SADIE'S SIDEBOARD AND SMOKEHOUSE

and not only is the food good, but the outside patio is the perfect spot for a drink or three. There's a full lounge at Buckingham's, and at last count it served 20-plus types of martinis. The bartenders also invite you to make up your own. No matter how strange, they'll take a shot at creating it. In the realm of food, start with the Ozark-smoked trout ($7.95) or the crab au gratin ($8.95). The list of appetizers is lengthy, but not as long as the entrées. The Ozark staples are available; a 16-ounce fried catfish is $16.95. Or you could order seafood pasta served tableside for $32.50. The restaurant offers numerous pasta, seafood, pork, and beef selections (the 16-ounce T-bone is $25.95); unique desserts; and more than a few dishes prepared tableside. A free kids' menu is offered for children under 10. It's not fancy, with its grilled cheese, chicken fingers, and spaghetti with marinara sauce, but just that the restaurant thought to provide such a service shows impressive forethought and a dedication to customer service.

♂ ქ ▽ **Candlestick Inn Restaurant & Lounge** (417-334-3633; www .candlestickinn.com), 127 Taney St. Dinner served Tues.–Sun. beginning at 5. With its ambience of linen and candlelight, and its romantic view of Lake Taneycomo, the Candlestick Inn is regarded as one of the finest dining establishments in Branson. True to the Branson atmosphere, Candlestick manages to offer well-prepared dishes and great service without coming off as snobbish. Some diners, those accustomed to the "fine-dining" offerings and rather snooty demeanor of chic urban restaurants, might be a bit disappointed. That would be a mistake. What seems formal in Branson

would be defined as casual in other venues, but that's part of the beauty of the region. The Candlestick strives to make patrons comfortable, and those patrons can range from an elderly couple out for an anniversary dinner to a family with a passel of kids. Comfort is the byword here, something provided by the view over Taneycomo, the wood-burning fireplace, and the non-hovering service that makes you feel at ease. Appetizers include such tried-and-true favorites as wild boar sausage served with mixed peppers and toast points ($15) or escargot presented with fresh Shiitake mushrooms, garlic butter, Ban Gough cheese and toast points ($13). As for entrées, the 14-ounce frenched elk rack, served with a ground mustard beurre blanc, runs $54. A 10-ounce Australian lobster tail is $49. Desserts are creative and plentiful. The restaurant has smoking and nonsmoking sections and a full bar. Reservations are requested. You might get in without one, but better safe than sorry.

♂ ქ ▽ **The Chateau Grille** (417-334-1161 or 1-888-333-5253; www .chateauonthelakebranson.com), 415 N. SR 265. Open daily for breakfast 6:30–10, lunch 11–2, and dinner 5–10. Located within the Chateau on the Lake, this restaurant offers a more formal dining atmosphere without being stuffy. Continuing the Old World look for which the Chateau is renowned and featuring views of Table Rock Lake, the Grille specializes in American selections for breakfast, lunch, teatime, and dinner. The Sunday brunch, with more than 50 entrées, is a perennial favorite. Also, the Chateau Grille was named a 2008 Award of Excellence winner by *Wine*

Spectator magazine (check out their six-page wine list). A children's menu is available (no need to leave the kids in the room), and guests may even reserve the Chef's Table, enjoying their meal deep within the Grille kitchen and discussing techniques of preparation with the chef himself. For lunch, try the braised, acorn-fed Iberico bacon for $12. Or, go elegantly southern with the grilled shrimp and pepper-jack grits for $14. Dinner offers such selections as the Humboldt-fog, goat-cheese crusted, 12-ounce, milk-fed veal chop for $65. Or, go a bit more simple and try the roasted Amish chicken for $26. Dress is casual and smoking is not allowed. The restaurant features a full bar; reservations are recommended.

✔ ✆ �Y **The Devil's Pool** (417-335-5141; www.bigcedarlodge.com), 612 Devil's Pool Rd., Ridgedale, Mo. Open daily for breakfast 7–11, lunch 11–2, and dinner 5–9:30. Sunday brunch ($21.95 for adults, $10.95 for kids under 12) is held 10–2. Located in the luxurious Big Cedar Lodge, Devil's Pool offers "contemporary Ozark cuisine." In English, that means the servings are large and the flavor exceptional. For an appetizer, try the BBQ pork nachos at $10 or the buttermilk fried chicken livers at $10. Popular entrées include the hardwood-smoked prime rib ($36 for a 16-ounce serving) and BBQ-glazed country-style meat loaf ($16). A country-fried rib-eye steak is $17 (I endorse this highly), or you can opt for a locally grown, grilled Rockbridge trout for $19. The Devil's Pool has a full bar and is entirely nonsmoking except on the patios. Reservations are recommended for dinner.

✳ **Entertainment**

BRANSON SHOWS All listings are located in Branson proper unless otherwise noted. Showtimes change on a regular basis and vary greatly from month to month. More than a few of the entertainers tend to move from theater to theater. For a further note on prices, please be aware that the figures listed below are guidelines. Admission fees can vary by several dollars depending upon where and when you purchase. I advise you to check the websites of performers for the exact schedules. Quite a few of these groups perform in venues across the country, and at least for the lesser-known performers, show dates are rarely the same from week to week.

This is not an inclusive list, but I have included the shows and theaters that have the most staying power. Branson is full of "tribute" shows (ranging from Neil Diamond to John Denver to George Strait imitators . . . and more than a couple of Elvis acts), and often it seems like just about every diner, restaurant, bowling alley, or shopping mall has a stage. Some of these gigs come and go, so my intent is to provide you with the productions that have a proven track record, the ones that are going to be around for a long time. To check out current shows year by year, complete with ticket prices and descriptions, there are two websites you should keep in mind. The first is **The Branson Tourism Center** (1-800-689-3969; www .bransontourismcenter.com). The second is the official website of the **Branson Lakes Area** (1-800-296-0463; www.explorebranson.com). Both of these organizations list show info on an annual basis.

Acrobats of China Featuring the New Shanghai Circus (1-877-212-4462; www.acrobatsofchina.com), 645 SR 165. Open year-round. Shows at 3 and 8 PM daily during season. $35 adults, $18 ages 13–17, $11 ages 6–12. If you want to see the definition of grace, art, and true athleticism, do not miss this show. Held in the New Shanghai Theater, this is the sort of performance that will leave you shaking your head in wonder. The acrobats, ranging in age from 13 to 45, have trained since they were young children, and many of the feats they demonstrate simply do not seem possible.

Amazing Pets (417-335-2484; www.grandcountry.com), 1945 W. SR 76. Showtime is at 10 AM on selected days year-round at the Grand Country Music Hall. $26 adults, $15 ages 4–17. Ringmaster Sean Paul, along with a monkey named Frankie, has trained a collection of dogs and cats to assist him in a number of odd and unusual tricks. The show was huge in Vegas, and you may have seen it on both Jay Leno and David Letterman. If you're traveling with kids, don't miss this stop on your Branson vacation. They'll be talking about it for months.

Andy Williams Moon River Theater (417-334-1800; www.andywilliams.com), 2500 SR 76. Open Mar.–Dec. and features a variety of performers when Andy isn't on-site. Most shows are either at 2 or 7. Kids under 17 admitted free. Andy Williams is getting up there in years (we're talking the mid to late octogenarian realm), and times and shows change depending on his throat, schedule, and stamina. At the time of this writing his main performance is a

7 PM show in Sept.–Oct. ($43) that co-stars Ann-Margret. It would behoove the visitor to call ahead and check exact performers, performances, and ticket availability. The Moon River Theater itself is a warm and charming venue, shooting for sophistication via woodwork and selected pieces of fine art. The hall does offer a reasonable facsimile of Moon River in the form of a koi-stocked pond that runs along the side of the building itself. Of course the legendary entertainer still sings his trademark song. Despite his age, you receive the impression that Andy truly enjoys putting on a show, and his voice has held up surprisingly well. The typical presentation will include trademark hits, with comedy and dancing thrown in to offer a well-rounded performance reminiscent of Andy's TV variety show. The 11-member orchestra—featuring musicians from all over the world—is an extremely talented group that provides excellent backup. The annual Christmas Show (also $43) starts at 7 PM Mon.–Sat. during Nov. and early Dec. (Andy returns to the theater and

ANDY WILLIAMS MOON RIVER THEATRE

performs for this one). You'll need reservations, as the production sells out early.

Baldknobbers Jamboree Show (417-334-4528; www.baldknobbers .com), 2835 W. SR 76. One show per day is offered Mon.–Sat. at 8 PM, Mar.–Oct. $33.50 adults, $18 children. Check the website for specific dates and an exact schedule. The Baldknobbers are Branson's original country music act, having been in town since 1959. Their theater complex encompasses a motel, restaurant (which seats 230 and offers inexpensive meals and a country buffet), and theater. The entertainment here is pure country—this troupe was doing *Hee Haw* long before *Hee Haw* was a glimmer in the eye of network TV programmers. Expect lots of country, gospel, and patriotic music interspersed with rapid-fire jokes and an abundance of slapstick comedy.

Righteous Brothers' Bill Medley (417-337-9333 or 1-866-991-8445; www.starlitetheatre.com), 3115 W. SR 76. Showtimes are Mon.–Sat. at either 3 or 8 PM during selected months. Call the theater for exact appearance dates. Adults $35, kids under 16 admitted free. The former Righteous Brother and Grammy Award–winning singer of "Unchained Melody" and "Lovin' Feelin'" performs his greatest hits during this popular show. Bill is joined on stage by his daughter, McKenna, who seems to have inherited the old man's vocal abilities.

Breakfast with Mark Twain (417-336-2112 or 1-800-358-4795; www .bransonsuperstars.com), 206 S. Commercial St. Showtimes are Apr.–Dec. at 10 PM (breakfast served at 9 AM) on selected Mon., Tues., and Wed. $28.75 for adults, $8.75 for children.

Mark Twain is practically synonymous with Missouri, and Norman Rockwell with the hometown values espoused by Branson. In this one-man show by Clem Samuels, held at the Owens Theater in "old" downtown Branson, you'll get plenty of both in a nice little show. The Twain character will regale you with the wit and wisdom for which the classic American author was noted, while the backdrop consists of more than 100 of Rockwell's best-known prints.

Brett Family Morning Show (417-336-4222 or 1-877-252-7388; www .brettfamily.com), 3600 W. SR 76. Showtime is 10 AM on selected days, Apr.–Dec., at Dick Clark's American Bandstand Theater. $34 adults, $13 ages 4–16. A variety show in the old-fashioned sense, the Brett Family Morning Show has consistently been voted one of the best in Branson. Singing, dancing, comedy, and patriotic music (with some magic thrown in for good measure) are all a part of this fast-paced production. There is some major talent to be enjoyed at this event, especially the well-blended harmonies and a cappella solos.

DICK CLARK'S AMERICAN BANDSTAND THEATER

Buck Trent Morning Show (1-800-764-9324; www.bucktrent.com), 3216 W. SR 76. Showtimes are Apr.–Dec., sometimes at 10 AM and sometimes at 2 PM, depending on the day and month. All performances take place at the Clay Cooper Theater. $27 adults, $14 for kids 6–16. For 20 years Buck Trent's screaming five-string banjo has served as a wake-up call for Branson visitors. Buck is an all-around entertainer—tossing plenty of country comedy into his act—and is accompanied by a troupe of first-tier vocalists and fiddle players.

Christmas on the Trail Dinner Show (417-334-4191; www.oldmatt .com), 5586 W. SR 76. Nov. 1–Dec. 31, showtime and dinner is Mon.–Sat. at 5:30 PM at the Pavilion Theatre. $41 adults, $19 for kids 4–16. Santa meets John Wayne at Christmas on the trail. Guests first receive dinner from an 1800s chuckwagon—the menu consisting of trail stew, corn bread, taters with honey, and a campfire cobbler—and then are invited to join in for cowboy Christmas carols. Later on comes a stop at the holiday gift shop, complete with a St. Nick

who is waiting to review Christmas lists from the kids. The finale of the event is a trip up the legendary Shepherd of the Hills Trail of Lights, which ends with an ascent of the 230-foot-tall Inspiration Tower.

Cirque Montage (417-337-9333 or 1-866-991-8445; www.starlitetheatre .com), 3115 W SR 76. May–Aug., shows Tues.–Sun. at 3 and 8 PM at the Starlite Theatre. Tickets are $37 for adults, free for kids under 15. Many of the members of Cirque Montage are former members of the renowned Cirque du Soleil. You'll see juggling, aerial feats, contortionists, pole climbers, and a host of amazing acts. No elephants or tigers at this circus, but lots of acrobatics, pageantry, and fancy costumes.

Clay Cooper's Music Express (417-332-2529 or 1-888-222-8910; clay coopertheatre.com), 3216 W. SR 76. Open Mar.–Dec. with shows on selected days at 10 AM and 8 PM. $34 adults, $17 ages 6–16. Clay Cooper leads a cast of 20 in this country music variety show. Also on stage is New York cowboy Jonny Lonestar. The terms *New York* and *cowboy*

THE CLAY COOPER THEATRE

THE GRAND COUNTRY MUSIC HALL AND BUFFET

would generally strike most in these parts as something of an oxymoron, but Johnny puts on one heck of a show with his trick roping and gun shootin'. Also joining the show are Clay's wife, Tina Cooper, and his young son, Colt.

Comedy Jamboree (1-888-505-4096; www.grandcountry.com), 1945 W. SR 76. Shows year-round at 3 PM on selected days at the Grand Country Music Hall. $30 adults, $15 ages 4–17. If you don't like being yanked from the audience and pulled on stage to participate, this might not be the show for you. On the other hand, *Comedy Jamboree* offers machine-gun jokes, lots of music and dance, and the virtuosity of pianist Tracy Heaston. It's good for more than a few laughs, particularly if you're not the shy type.

Dalena Ditto Country Variety Show (1-888-335-2080; www.dalena ditto.com), 3090 Shepherd of the Hills Expy. Shows are Apr.–Dec., Tues.–Thurs. at 2, with additional days and 10 PM showtimes in Nov. and early Dec. at the Hamner Barber Theater. $31 for adults; $19 for kids 13–17; $10 for ages 4–12. Dalena Ditto grew up in the world of country music and has performed all over the country with the likes of Willie Nel-

son and Faith Hill. She appears with her six-piece band, The Boys.

Doug Gabriel Show (1-800-954-8554; www.douggabriel.com), 1835 W. SR 76. Shows Mar.–Dec. on selected days at 10 AM or 8 PM at the Music City Centre. $30 adults, $5 kids ages 3–16. Doug is a superb piano and guitar player (he occasionally brings out the guitar he built from the muffler of an old Thunderbird); the show consists of not only music, but also comedy and dancing. Also on stage are the Gabriel family, performing everything from gospel standards to the best of Elvis.

Dutton Family (417-332-2772 or 1-888-388-8661; www.theduttons.com), 3454 W. SR 76. Showtimes are Feb.–Dec., Tues.–Sat. at 10 AM, 2, 5, and 8 PM in the Dutton Family Theater. $33.50 adults; $15 ages 13–18; $10 ages 4–12. If you want proof of the power of genetics, just take a gander at the Dutton family. There, up on the stage, are about 20 Duttons of various ages. All are playing different instruments, singing, and entertaining the crowd. From classical to bluegrass and country to swing, with plenty of rock thrown in for good measure, the family offers a fully loaded buffet of musical entertainment. Small wonder that Dutton performances are one of

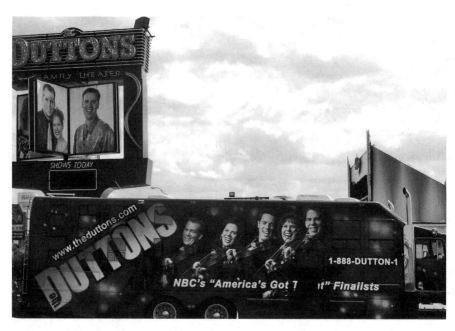

THE DUTTON FAMILY THEATER

the favorites of Branson locals. You may have caught this mega-talented clan on America's Got Talent a few years back.

Grand Jubilee (417-335-2484; www .grandcountry.com), 1945 W. SR 76. Shows year-round, Mon.–Sat. at 7:30 PM. $34 adults, $17 ages 4–17. A music and comedy show with a wide range. Visitors can enjoy the sounds of the jubilee's headliner band, New South. Both country hits and some excellent quartet vocals are the primary draw. Comedian Jamie Haage joins in with his own brand of hillbilly humor.

Grand Old Gospel Hour (417-337-8888; www.gospelhour.org), 1600 W. SR 76 at Dick Clark's American Bandstand Theater. Year-round, every Sun. at 10 AM at the Grand Palace Theater. Free. This honestly isn't a show, but more of a very large church service. On the other hand, there is

plenty of gospel music. It's a bit fire-and-brimstony for my tastes, but some folks like their religion on the caffeinated side. A second show is held Wed. nights at 6.

Hamner Barber Variety Show (417-334-4363 or 1-888-335-2080; www.hamnerbarber.com), 3090 Shepherd of the Hills Expy. Feb.–Dec., showtimes are Tues.–Sat. at 8 PM, Sun. 3 PM in the Hamner Barber Variety Theatre. Call for exact days and times. $33 adults; $18 ages 13–17; $10 ages 4–12. A bit of author bias here: I never met a magician or ventriloquist I didn't like (if you exclude that stupid "Waylon and Madame" act). That said, the Hamner Barber show offers some great comedy and some right dandy illusions. The duo of Dave and Denise Hamner seem to have a thing for birds, and you'll be amazed by the appearance of these trained avians. Ventriloquist Jim Barber enjoys his work, judging by his grin, and manages to perform several different voices at virtually the same time. To top it all off, the show ends with an extravagant tribute to veterans.

Hank Williams Revisited (417-335-4832 or 1-800-422-0076; www.branson imax.com), 3562 Shepherd of the Hills Expy. Shows Fri.–Sat. at 2 PM, Sun.–Mon. at 8 PM at the Little Opry Theatre. $26 adults; kids 12 and younger admitted free. In this venue the venerable Mr. Williams (he sure gets around a lot for a dead guy) is portrayed by Nashville recording artist Tim Hadler. If you saw the classic George Clooney movie *O Brother, Where Art Thou* and loved the Ry Cooder soundtrack, this show is for you. Hadler has the old Hank tunes down pat and offers up his own tribute to June Carter and Johnny Cash as well.

The Haygoods (417-339-4663 or 1-866-343-7469; www.haygoods.com), 12905 W SR 76. Shows Feb.–Dec. Tues.–Sat. at 8 PM in the Americana Theater. $33 adults, $15 kids 4–12. Forget the Partridge Family; those clowns were nothing compared to the Haygoods. The eight Haygood siblings (seven brothers and one sister ranging in age from 12 to 28) bounce back and forth between playing fiddle, sax, guitar, drums, harp, and piano. They sing, they dance, they tell jokes. This is a truly talented bunch, and for pure technical prowess, wait until they start belting out their a cappella numbers. Small wonder they have been in Branson for nearly 20 years and entertained nearly 4 million visitors.

Hughes Brothers (417-334-0076 or 1-800-422-0076; www.hughes -brothers.com), 3425 W. SR 76. Open Feb.–Dec. with showtimes varying between 10 AM, 2, and 8 PM, usually weekdays, in the Hughes Brothers Theater. $36 adults, kids 17 and younger admitted free. If Branson ever goes the way of reality TV, the first act would no doubt be a wrestling match between the Haygoods and the Hughes Brothers. These five guys, who own their own theater, are known for singing in near-perfect harmony and for dancing like screamin' demons. Their repertoire is massive, covering everything from old

THE HUGHES BROTHERS THEATRE

western standards to Broadway show tunes to gospel.

The Jim Owen Show (417-334-5412; www.jimowenmusic.net), 2206 W. SR 76. Shows Apr.–Dec. (no shows in July) at 10 AM on selected days in the Branson Mall Theater. $22.50 for adults, $10 for kids. Jim Owen is known in country music circles as not only a performer, but as an acclaimed songwriter (one of his biggest hits was "Louisiana Woman, Mississippi Man," recorded by Loretta Lynn and Conway Twitty). He has also portrayed Hank Williams Sr. in two TV movies. In Branson, Jim offers up a pure country show with lots of comedy and tributes to the likes of Williams and Grand Ole Opry legend Ernest Tubb.

THE JIM STAFFORD THEATRE

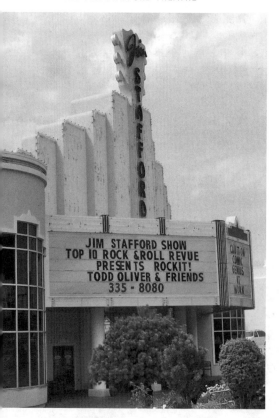

The Jim Stafford Show (417-335-8080 or 1-800-667-8533; www.jimstafford.com), 3440 W. SR 76. Open Feb.–Sept. with shows Sat.–Thurs. at 3 and 8 PM. Special Christmas shows in Nov.–Dec. $35 adults, $13 kids 7–12; $5.50 kids 4–6. They call Jim Stafford the "Victor Borge of the Guitar," which is pretty appropriate since the multitalented musician is best known for his hit songs, "Spiders and Snakes," "My Girl Bill," and "Cow Patti." Jim was a huge hit when he had his nationally televised TV show back in the 1970s, and he still commands a legion of diehard fans. As is the case with many Branson theaters, this one is shared by multiple performers. When Jim is on tour you can catch musician/ventriloquist Todd Oliver and his talking dogs, or the high-energy rock and roll tribute known as Rockit.

Joey Riley Comedy and Music (417-334-3219 or 1-877-750-5639; www.joeyriley.net), 3455 W. SR 76. Open Apr.–Dec. Showtimes are at 2 PM in the Mickey Gilley Theatre. $29 adults, $6 children 12 and younger. Joey Riley was a popular comic in Branson for many years, usually opening for, or appearing onstage with, a number of headline acts. It was only a matter of time before he got his own gig. Aside from making you laugh, Joey is seriously wicked on the fiddle and steel guitar. Again, a number of acts appear at the Mickey Gilley Theatre depending upon the time of year. Other productions include The Rankin Brothers, the Roy Rogers Jr. show, and of course Mickey Gilley his own bad self.

The Kirby VanBurch Show (417-337-7140 or 1-877-223-7959; www.kirbyvanburch.com), 2353 SR 248.

THE THEATER OF MAGICIAN KIRBY VANBURCH

Open Mar.–Dec., with showtimes Tues.–Sun. at 3 and 8 PM. $36 for adults, $19 for ages 13–17, $11 for ages 4–10. The Travel Channel has called Kirby's act "one of America's best magic shows." I can't really disagree with that estimation. He performs tricks ranging from up-close sleight of hand to massive illusions. Moreover, he still enjoys performing with lions and white tigers. Don't be fooled into thinking this is a slow-paced magic show. The illusions are nonstop, interspersed with a host of musical acts, comedy skits, and major production numbers. Oh, and did I mention that Kirby was named Entertainer of the Year and Magician of the Year by the International Magician's Society, or that he won the title of World's Best Illusionist from the World Magic Awards? This is some first-rate trickery from a first-rate trickster.

Legends in Concert (417-335-7827 or 1-800-374-7469; www.legendsin concert.com), 1600 W. SR 76. Feb.– Dec., 3 and 8 PM in Dick Clark's American Bandstand Theater; call ahead for exact days. $35 adults, $12 ages 4–12. They call this the "World's Greatest Tribute Show," and the impersonators at Legends will make you think that the likes of Buddy Holly and Frank Sinatra have returned for one more performance. The list of stars imitated by the troupe includes Patsy Cline, Roy Orbison, the Blues Brothers, Elvis, Marilyn Monroe, Judy Garland, Johnny Mathis, Shania Twain, and many more. You'll leave the theater wondering, was it live or was it Memorex?

The Mansion Theater (417-239-1333; www.themansiontheatre.com), 189 Expressway Ln. The Mansion is a bit different than most of the venues in Branson. It tends to bring in big-name performers for brief periods of time. Check the Mansion's website for specific shows. Those appearing in 2011 included the likes of Tim Conway, the Gatlin Brothers and Debbie Boone, the Liverpool Legends (a show produced by Louise Harrison, brother of the late Beatle George Harrison), Johnny Mathis, Michael Bolton, Vicki Lawrence (reprising her beloved Mama's Family character), and the Three Redneck Tenors. Some or all of these shows are likely to change year to year, but you can generally count on high-caliber entertainment at the Mansion.

Mickey Gilley (417-334-3210 or 1-800-334-1936; www.gilleys.com), 3446 W. SR 76. Shows Apr.–Dec., Sat.–Wed at 8 PM, in the Mickey Gilley Theatre. $32 adults, $6 ages 5–12. Mickey Gilley's nearly 40 major hits (17 of those went to number one) and honky-tonk piano fill the air as the country legend is backed by an eight-piece band. Mickey tells plenty of amusing stories in between tunes, many about his childhood in Louisiana and youthful adventures with his cousins, Jerry Lee Lewis and TV preacher Jimmy Swaggart.

#1 Hits of the 60's (417-339-1960; www.1hitsofthe60s.com), 3446 W. SR 76. Apr.–Dec., generally at 2 PM, though there are some 8 PM shows, at the Caravelle Theater. $30 adults, $9 kids 6–12. While there was some absolutely great music that came out of the 1960s, those who made the music weren't exactly the epitome of squeaky clean or all-American. Frankly, it's a little surreal watching a show that portrays the 1960s as such a happy and peaceful era. No matter; the large cast of this show does perform more than 100 of the best '60s hits (such as tunes from Ray Charles, the Beatles, the Beach Boys, Sonny and Cher, the Supremes, and the Mamas and the Papas). Just enjoy the music, and try and not to take a psychological detour into the fact that

THE MANSION THEATRE

most of it was the result of a twisted youth culture that thrived on protests, drugs, and flag burning.

Ozark Mountain Jubilee (417-335-2484; www.grandcountry.com), 1945 W. SR 76. Feb.–Dec., 7 PM Sun. only, in the Grand Country Music Hall. $33 adults; $17 for kids 4–17. The show is pure country, both old and new, as performed by local entertainers and the Max Bacon family.

Pierce Arrow Theater (417-336-8742 or 1-877-687-4241; www.pierce arrowtheater.com), 3069 Shepherd of the Hills Expy. Feb.–Dec., 3 and 7:30 PM. $33 adults, $17 kids up to age 17. Listen to patriotic medleys and gospel with a rock overtone from one of Branson's most popular male singing groups. Equal opportunity for vocal skills comes via Kim Boyce (a former Miss Florida with 11 number one gospel hits) and Desta. Comedy is provided by Jarret Dougherty.

Presleys' Country Jubilee (417-334-4874; www.presleys.com), 2920 W. SR 76. Mar.–Dec., Mon.–Sat. 8 PM in the Presleys' Theater. $31 adults, $15 ages 4–12. The Presley family was the first Branson act to have a theater on the SR 76 Strip, this arriving after numerous years performing their musical comedy in any venue where people would pay to listen, including more than a few dripping Ozark caves. As the town of Branson exploded, the Presleys were right in the thick of the action, and their show continues today. You'll hear gospel (one of the family's patriarchs was a Pentecostal preacher), listen to hill-billy comedy (the blacked-out teeth are a must), and enjoy country standards and the hits of today. All this accompanied by finger picking, strumming, and fiddle playing as can

only be done by those who have grown up with a guitar, banjo, or bow in their hand. The piano expertise is amazing and the vocals are always spot-on. I admit I'm a bit biased here, since the Presleys are friends of mine, but even if they weren't I'm pretty certain I'd rate this the best show in Branson. I've never seen a family that can play so many instruments so well. The patriarch and matriarch of the Presley clan, Lloyd and Bessie Mae, have sadly passed away since the first edition of this book was printed, but the legacy and musical expertise of the Presley family lives on.

Red, Hot and Blue (417-339-4663 or 1-866-343-7469; www.theamericana theater.com), 2095 W. SR 76. Mar.–Dec., shows at 10 AM or 2 PM, but days and times vary throughout the year. $29 adults; $14 ages 4–12. With a cast of eight high-energy performers, Red, Hot and Blue is a nostalgic musical tour. This is a longtime Branson favorite, now in its 16th year. You'll enjoy a variety of well-known tunes that span a range from the 1940s to the 1970s.

THE PIERCE ARROW THEATER

RFD-TV Theatre (417-332-2282; www.rfdtvthetheatre.com), 4080 W. SR 76. Open Mar.–Dec., showtimes at 2 and 7 PM. RFD-TV, billing itself as the network for rural America, is seen via satellite and cable networks such as DirecTV, the Dish Network, Comcast, Mediacom, Cox, Verizon, and Time Warner. The company airs a huge amount of programming, with one segment of the network geared solely toward music (for instance, you can see weekly episodes of Presleys' Country Jubilee). The theater itself brings in a revolving selection of top-name acts. Some of those appearing in 2011 were Bill Anderson, Brulé, and Marty Stuart. Contact the theater directly for show dates and prices, as both vary depending on the artist and season.

Red Skelton: A Tribute by Tom Mullica (417-239-1333; www.skelton tribute.com), 189 Expressway Ln. Apr.–Aug., Tues.–Sat. at 10 AM in the Mansion Theater. $25 adults, $13.50 ages 13–17, $11.50 ages 4–12. Red Skelton was the gentle giant of comedy, making people laugh without the need for shock, obscenity, or vulgarity. In this tribute his admirer and friend, Tom Mullica, re-creates all of Red's great characters, such as Freddy the Freeloader, Clem Kadiddlehopper, Gertrude & Heathcliff, the Mean Widdle Kid, and George Applebee.

The Shepherd of the Hills Outdoor Drama (417-334-4191 or 1-800-653-6288; www.oldmatt.com), 5586 W. SR 76. May–Oct., Mon.–Sat. at 8:30 PM (7:30 PM after Aug. 23) at The Shepherd of the Hills Outdoor Theater. $39 adults, $19 ages 4–16. *The Shepherd of the Hills* has been performed at this theater thousands of times since 1960, making it the longest-running outdoor drama in history. The story, based on the 1906 book of the same name by Harold Bell Wright (the fourth most widely read book in publishing history), brought the Ozarks to the attention of the world and predated the entertainment phenomenon that would

THE BRANSON HEADQUARTERS OF RFD-TV

THE SHOJI TABUCHI THEATRE

only picked up steam. He's a virtuoso fiddle player who incorporates fantastic vocalists, dancers, and elaborate production numbers. The last are choreographed by Shoji's wife, Dorothy. He is also joined on stage by his daughter, Christina. This is one of Branson's "don't miss" theaters.

Showboat Branson Belle (417-336-7171 or 1-800-775-2628; www.show boatbransonbelle.com), 4800 SR 165. Mar.–Dec., noon, 4, and 8 PM; call ahead for exact days. $55 adults, $27 ages 4–11. More than just a show, the *Branson Belle* offers a three-course meal and more than two hours of entertainment as you cruise slowly around Table Rock Lake. The boat itself is an 1890s-style paddle-wheeler, 78 feet wide, 265 feet long, and capable of handling more than 700 guests per cruise. Entertainment varies depending upon whether you take a noon, afternoon, or evening jaunt on the water, but the possibilities include everything from full-scale Vegas-style productions—musicals with all the special effects—to fiddling aerialist Janice Martin, to the comedy and magic of Christopher James. The meals are very good on the *Belle*—likely on a par with, if not above, anything you'd find at the restaurants in town, with children's meals, vegetarian offerings, and restricted diet requests gladly provided. This attraction is part of the Silver Dollar City family (the heaviest of the heavy hitters responsible for much of Branson's rise to fame), and they don't skimp on the quality.

become Branson by more than half a century. The tale, based partially on residents Wright met when he came to live in the Ozarks, is a broad-strokes epic centering on collective human traits—love, loss, power, and the meaning of life. No small production, each performance requires 80 actors, 40 horses, a flock of sheep, several guns and rifles, and the actual burning of a log cabin.

Shoji Tabuchi Show (417-334-7469; www.shoji.com), 3260 Shepherd of the Hills Expy. Shows at 7:30 PM on selected days, mid-Apr.–mid.-Aug.; 10:30 AM, 3, and 7:30 PM on selected days, mid-Sept.–mid-Dec. $53 adults, $34 ages 12–18, $23 ages 11 and younger. Springfield's *417 Magazine* named Shoji the Best Branson Entertainer in 2010. This is on the heels of *The Wall Street Journal*, which reviewed the show by saying "The audience gasp quotient is high, as is fan loyalty." Shoji has been wowing the crowds in Branson for many years, and the draw of his production has

Smoke on the Mountain (417-335-4832 or 1-800-419-4832; www.branson imax.com), 3562 Shepherd of the Hills Expy. Apr.–Dec., Tues.–Sat. at 8 PM at the Little Opry Theatre. $27

adults; free for kids under 12. A musical comedy that is drawing great reviews, the story is set in 1938 at the fictional Mount Pleasant Church. The event is the church's first Saturday Night Sing. The audience is treated to such old-time gospel favorites as "Church in the Wildwood" and "I'll Fly Away." These are the gospel tunes of yesteryear that moved on to become folk classics.

The Magic and Comedy of Taylor Reed (417-332-3232; www.taylor reed.com), 1835 W. SR 76. Mar.–Dec., with showtimes Tues.–Sat. at 2 PM in the Music City Centre. $33.50 adults, $18 ages 3–15. Taylor is not only an amazing illusionist and performer, he's also the designer and builder for many of the magic devices used by some of the most renowned names in the industry. The show com-

ENTRY TO THE YAKOV SMIRNOFF THEATER

bines illusion with a bit of comedy, and is fast paced to say the least. There's quite a bit of audience participation in one of Taylor's shows, something that the crowds seem to love.

Tony Roi's Elvis Experience (417-334-4500 or 1-800-666-6094; www .andywilliams.com), 2500 W. SR 76. Mar.–Sept., Mon.–Sat. at 7 PM at the Andy Williams Moon River Theater. $33 adults, free for kids 2–17. Cuban-born Tony Roi does look an awful lot like the King of Rock and Roll, and his singing and dancing prowess is self-evident. Though the Elvis imitation business has been overworked to the hilt, Tony's version is far better than most. For Graceland devotees, this is a well-done and genuine tribute.

Yakov Smirnoff (417-332-1234 or 1-866-559-2568; www.yakov.com), 470 SR 248. Sept.–Dec. with limited dates Apr.–May, 2 PM in the Yakov Smirnoff Theater; call ahead for exact dates. $39 adults, $19 ages 4–16. Yakov Smirnoff defines Branson when he says, "Only in America can a Russian and a Japanese own theaters in the middle of the Ozarks." Yakov, who has starred in movies with Robin

THE LITTLE OPRY THEATRE

Williams, Tom Hanks, and Jack Nicholson (to name a few), has been pulling in crowds for years. As always, he performs at a high energy level, tells tales of his immigration to America, and lets everyone know without question that he loves his adopted country. The man is also very accessible to visitors, taking photos with many patrons after the show.

✳ Selective Shopping

MALLS AND COMPLEXES Branson Landing (417-239-3002; www .bransonlanding.com), 100 Branson Landing, Branson, Mo. Branson Landing, which was not quite open when the first edition of this book came out in 2006, is a $420 million, 95-acre development located along the Lake Taneycomo shorefront in downtown Branson. It features shopping, dining, luxury lodging, condos, two marinas, a town square, a 1,500-seat amphitheater, and one of the finest convention centers in the Midwest. The town square itself can hold 5,000 people, and stretches for a mile and a half next to Taneycomo. In the midst of the square is $7.5 million fountain that puts most of the Vegas fountains to shame. The Landing is anchored by a Bass Pro Shops and a Belk department store. You'll find two Hilton Hotels, a boardwalk along the lake, and the type of nightlife that is far removed from the theaters and stages dotting the Strip (think pub atmosphere). Just a few of the many shops are an Ann Taylor Loft, Finish Line, and Victoria's Secret. Galleries and specialty shops abound. Familiar restaurants include Liberty Tavern at the Promenade Hilton, Ernie Biggs Chicago Style Dueling Piano Bar, Garfield's Restaurant & Pub, The

White River Fish House, Waxy O'Shea's Pub, Famous Dave's BBQ, Cantina Loredo, Charlie's Grilled Subs, and Romano's Macaroni Grill.

The Branson Mall (417-334-5412; www.bransonmallonline.com), 2206 W. SR 76, Branson, Mo. Also known as the home of Branson's original **Walmart,** this mall features roughly 25 shops. You'll find a Ruby Tuesday restaurant, Hard Rock Ice Cream parlor, and a plethora of specialty stores geared toward hair, nails, clothing, and jewelry. What makes the Branson Mall a bit different is that it attempts

THE HILTON HOTEL AT BRANSON LANDING

to mix live shows with the shopping experience. Almost 20 different acts share the stage at the Branson Mall Theater. Most of these are tribute bands or revues.

Factory Merchants of Branson (417-335-6686; www.bransonoutlets .com), 1000 Pat Nash Dr., Branson, Mo. Just look for the big red roof with the white lettering reading 90 STORES. Though the number is actually one or two above 90, this two-level outlet facility features such names as Bon Worth, Dressbarn Woman, Izod, Jones New York, Koret, L'eggs Hanes Bali Playtex, Lane Bryant Outlet, Limited Editions for Her, Motherhood Maternity, Pendleton, Reebok, and Van Heusen. You can spend a few hours wandering around here, and munch on hot pretzels to boot. Prices here are approximately 25 to 65 percent off normal retail.

The Shoppes at Branson Meadows (417-339-2580; www.branson-discount .com/branson-shopping.asp), 4562 Gretna Rd., Branson, Mo. Built in a Victorian design, The Shoppes are anchored by an 11-screen theater complex and a 30,000-square-foot factory outlet store. Names represented include Spiegel, Westpoint Stevens, Sunbeam, Duck Head, Bugle Boy, Easy Spirit, and Totes, as well as shops covering the gamut of jewelry and home decor.

Grand Village (1-888-505-4096; www.grandcountry.com), 1945 W. SR 76, Branson, Mo. I've never quite known how to define Grand Country. It's part water park, part hotel, part arcade (with an indoor miniature golf course), part live country theater, part restaurant, and part shopping center. If you add all these together, the whole is greater than the sum of the

parts. The Grand Country Shoppes are interspersed between cobblestone walkways, fountains, flowers, and trees. Gifts and novelties are endless, with items ranging from handmade jewelry to books, toys, and tacky souvenirs. Stores include Thomas Kinkade's Signature Art Gallery, Katherine's, Abbey Rose, and Kringle's Village Shop, the largest Christmas store in Missouri. **The Gift Shop** is tourist central, carrying Branson-themed T-shirts, mugs, key chains, magnets, shot glasses, and ashtrays. Grand Village is admittedly sort of an odd place, but odd in a good way. If you get tired you can drop into the **Grand Country Buffet** and consume enough food to feed the entire population of a small Third World country.

Tanger Factory Outlet (417-337-9328 or 1-800-407-2762; www.tanger outlet.com), 300 Tanger Blvd., Branson, Mo. Another mega complex with nearly 100 shops, this outlet establishment includes Ralph Lauren, Tommy Hilfiger, Gap, Old Navy, Fossil, and Factory Brand Shoes. There are more of the currently popular brand names here than at some of the other spots in town (Nike and Eddie Bauer, to name two), and the shopping possibilities aren't confined to clothing. A Bath & Body Works, Mick's Nut Shack, Disney Store, Zales Diamond Outlet, and Yankee Candle are representative of what is available at Tanger. After all the buffets and deep-fried catfish you've consumed on your trip, you might even drop by Vitamin World for some omega-3 fish oil. A trip to the Ozarks lowers the blood pressure, but it can play havoc with the cholesterol.

Branson Mill Craft Village (417-334-8436; www.bransonmill.com),

3300 N. Gretna Rd., Branson, Mo. It was a sad day for Branson when the **Engler Block** shut down in 2009. That venerable institution had been the town's major center for authentic Ozark crafts and demonstrations by working artisans. Luckily, the Branson Mill Craft Village arose to take its place. Quite a few of the folks formerly located at the Engler can now be found at the Craft Village. What you have here is a 60,000-square-foot complex in Branson Meadows that features glassblowers, leather and wood carvers, china and oil painters, stained glass workers, silversmiths, scrimshaw experts, potters, copper colorists, etched glass artists, custom sign and musical instrument makers, and much more. The Village contains 150 showrooms and is anchored in part by Mountain Mama's General Store, The Leather Trading Company, and Bandana's Bar-B-Q. The Village is open 362 days a year, and is one of the places you really shouldn't miss.

SPECIAL SHOPS Alaska Down South (417-339-2800 or 1-885-754-2770; www.alaskadownsouth.com), 1150 W. SR 76, Branson, Mo. In Branson for more than 15 years, Alaska Down South started by focusing on bringing all things Alaska to the Ozarks. Since that time it has expanded to include art and decor from the northern U.S., Canada, and Africa. Shop for antler and ivory carvings, scrimshaw, and a wide variety of unique home decor.

Dick's Oldtime 5 and 10 (417-334-2410; www.dicksoldtime5and10.com), 103 W. Main St., Branson, Mo. Dick's is almost as well known in Branson as the Baldknobbers or Silver Dollar City. In business since 1959, this store in the original part of town carries a bit of everything imaginable. It holds true to what it always was, a five-and-dime store, and in a lot of ways it feels like a museum. From A to Z, you'll no doubt find something you can't live without among Dick's infinite number of items. The original

THE CRAFT VILLAGE AT BRANSON MILL

DICK'S 5 & 10 HAS BEEN DOING BUSINESS IN DOWNTOWN BRANSON FOR MORE THAN 50 YEARS

owner, Dick Hartley, passed away in 2006, but the store is still run by his son and son-in-law. One of the big draws of Dick's is that it features a wide array of collections. You'll find whole areas devoted to aviation prints, sports memorabilia, trains, arrowheads, and more. On the other hand you can buy gifts, sewing notions, housewares, embroidery supplies, crafts, linens, gadgets, and just about everything else under the sun. Check out the massive selection of nostalgic toys and family board games. Even the candy assortment is a step back in time. I really don't know of any other place where you'll find BB Bats, Slo-Pokes, candy cigarettes, or horehound lozenges.

Frontier Flags (417-334-1776 or 1-800-658-0413; www.frontierflags .com), 212 S. Commercial, Branson, Mo. No matter what kind of flag you seek, chances are you can find it here. U.S. flags, military flags, state flags, Confederate flags, and religious flags are just a few of the offerings. You can also find wind socks, decals, magnetic ribbons, and flagpoles of all sizes.

Ozark Quilts and More (417-336-6364), 4320 Gretna Rd., and (417-334-6375), 121 Main St. There are several quilt stores in Branson, but this shop has the widest selection and features the most shapes, sizes, designs, and colors (more than 200 styles in total). Almost everything here is handcrafted, in contrast to the machine-made items found in chain stores. If you want a quilt that looks like it was painstakingly sewn by your great-grandmother, this is the place. Quilts and More has been in Branson for more than a decade, and with good reason.

✳ Special Events

March **Branson Tri-Lakes Building and Home Show** (417-239-1042; ww.bransonhomeshow.com), Branson Convention Center, 200 W. Main St., Branson, Mo. Show hours are typically Fri. 2–8, Sat. 9–5, and Sun. 11–5. The Vacation Channel sponsors this huge event, which has taken place annually for the past 15 years. Generally occurring the first weekend in March, the show features vendors and exhibits that run the gamut from kitchens and cabinets to fencing to custom homebuilders. Literally hundreds of booths and displays cover the entire spectrum of building, sprucing up, or remodeling your home. This one draws thousands of attendees from visitors over a four-state area.

April–May **World Fest** (1-800-475-9370; www.silverdollarcity.com), 399 Silver Dollar City Pkwy., Branson, Mo. It's billed as the largest international festival in America. That just might be true, seeing as how more than 100 performers and entertainers from across the world descend on Sil-ver Dollar City to take part. You'll see everything from Irish dancers to Kenyan dancer to steel drummers from Trinidad, not to mention a showcase of food that represents nearly any culture you could imagine. This is a month-long affair that runs from mid-April to early May. A regular admission price ($55 for adults and $45 for kids under 12) gains you entrance, though you can expect extra fees for food and some of the shows.

May–June **Bluegrass and BBQ Festival** (1-800-475-9370; www.silver dollarcity.com), 399 Silver Dollar City Pkwy., Branson, Mo. Throughout the second half of May, Silver Dollar City begins to reflect the Ozarks the way they're meant to be. The Bluegrass and BBQ Festival brings in top bluegrass groups and solo acts from around the nation, and the BBQ buffet served up in the Frisco barn will leave you feeling fat and happy. All styles of Q are on hand, from the vinegar-based sauce ladled on a smoked North Carolina pulled-pork sandwich, to Memphis dry rub, to an

THE BRANSON CONVENTION CENTER AT BRANSON LANDING

ultraslow-cooked Texas brisket. When you combine those delectables with smoking bluegrass, there is simply no way to go wrong. This shindig has become so popular that the International Bluegrass Music Association nominated it as the bluegrass event of the year.

June–July ♪ **National KidsFest** (1-800-475-9370; www.silverdollarcity .com), 399 Silver Dollar City Pkwy., Branson, Mo. Running from early June through late July, National Kids-Fest provides more than 100 hands-on activities. There's music, food, street entertainers, and a variety of special shows geared specifically to the younger set.

September **Compton Ridge Camp-ground Fiddler's Convention** (417-338-2911; www.comptonridge.com), 5040 SR 265, Branson, Mo. For three straight days (usually Thurs.–Sat.) in early September, fiddlers from around America take the stage at Compton Ridge and compete for top honors. The jam sessions are nonstop during this annual celebration, taking place on an impromptu basis all over the park. You can't listen to fiddle music on an empty stomach, so there's a cat-fish fry Friday night and a pig roast on Saturday. Talk about cheap eats: Call Compton Ridge for up-to-date pricing, as it tends to vary year to year.

September–October **National Har-vest Festival** (1-800-475-9370; www .silverdollarcity.com), 399 Silver Dollar City Pkwy., Branson, Mo. This is the festival that made Silver Dollar City famous, a shindig that has taken place since the park's inception. It used to be known as the **Festival of Ameri-can Music and Craftsmanship;** however, the change in moniker

doesn't mean that the event itself has been watered down. From early September until the end of October, craftsmen from all over the country are on hand to show, sell, and demon-strate how they make their fine hand-crafted goods. There are juried art shows, a food fair, and more than 400 musicians who fill the air with the sounds of gospel, bluegrass, folk, country, western, swing, and big band music. If you're going to make plans to hit only one major festival in Bran-son, this should be your first choice. You might even want to hang around for the biggest barn dance in Missouri.

November–December **Veterans Homecoming Week** (417-337-8387; www.explorebranson.com/veterans). Takes place all over town. Most peo-ple probably don't know this, but Branson is far and away the top spot in the country for military reunions and events that are geared toward honoring our brave military veterans. The Veterans Homecoming takes place every year from Nov. 5–11. It's probably the largest Veterans Day cel-ebration in the world, drawing thou-sands of veterans and currently enlisted military personnel from all over the country. The outpouring of appreciation is amazing to see. Events designed especially for veterans are far too numerous to list (and they change a bit from year to year), but suffice to say that most are free for vets and their families. This is more than just lip service or a way to draw some extra income to the town. Bran-son has earned national recognition as the most patriotic city in the nation, and was awarded the first Stewards of Freedom Award by the National Flag Foundation. It's also been recognized by the World War II Memorial Campaign as the only city in the nation collecting funds as a city for the World War II Memorial. On Memorial Day 2000, Branson was asked by the White House to serve as a template city for the National Moment of Remembrance. That ain't small potatoes.

An Old Time Christmas (417-266-7300 or 1-800-475-9370; www.silver dollarcity.com), 399 Silver Dollar City Pkwy., Branson, Mo. According to Good Morning America, this is one of the top five holiday events in the country. Christmas comes early to Silver Dollar City—the park starts getting decked out in early November (we're talking about more than 4 million lights) and stays that way until the end of Christmas. Offerings include a Dickens Christmas Show, a Holiday Lights Parade (Santa's sleigh alone boasts more than 3,000 lights), the tree-lighting celebration, carolers, and all the good feelings of the holidays. Weather permitting, certain rides and attractions are open during this celebration of yuletide joy.

The Northern Border

2

ROUTE 66 COUNTRY

THE LAKE OF THE OZARKS

THE OSAGE LAKES DISTRICT

ROUTE 66 COUNTRY

T hough most people feel the need for speed, the desire to reach their destination as quickly as possible, such an approach is unsuited for the Ozarks. Forget the normal expectations of modern life, and realize that you are traveling through a land older than time itself. The Ozarks are for dawdling, for wandering around, for taking the time to smell roses, wade creeks, and allow the mystical feel of this ancient region to seep into your soul. Remember that the joy is in the journey.

As with most parts of the country, the interstate highway system has taken all the fun out of travel here. You zip along with the stampede, avoiding the big rigs as they blow past, viewing scenery that is hardly dramatic (unless you consider golden arches to be stunning or powerful). Highway designers are to travel what fast-food cooks are to eating. Their entrées will fill you up, and they might even keep you alive. But did you really enjoy it?

The northern border of the Missouri Ozarks is no different in this respect. I-44 stretches from St. Louis to Texas, a seemingly unbroken path of franchise operations and rolling countryside. In the northern Ozarks, what would later become I-44 was originally an Indian trail, later becoming a wagon path for settlers and freighters. For a time it was known as the Wire Road, a bumpy and muddy track running alongside newfangled telegraph poles. During the Civil War both the Blue and the Gray used the thoroughfare to shuttle troops. Finally, the earth that once felt only the hooves of spotted ponies and the step of tanned moccasins became "the Mother Road," the legendary Route 66 running 2,448 miles from Chicago to Santa Monica, California. Built between 1927 and 1938, Route 66 was not a straight stretch of asphalt. Intentionally, it wandered and veered and connected the heartbeat of the small towns that dotted its entire length. Roadside attractions of every type, shape, color, and description became the rule of the day, unique stopping points that gave moments of lighthearted joy to travelers weary from the Depression and those heading west in the hope of a better life.

This section of the northern Ozark border (as is true for the Ozarks as a whole) has no definitive boundaries. Technically, a geologist would tell you that Sullivan, Mo., is included within the region. Then again, there are also those who claim that tomatoes are a fruit and that dogs can't smile. In short, to use the

Route 66 Country

THE NORTHERN BORDER

© The Countryman Press

Lake of the Ozarks

Osage R.

Gasconade R.

Bourbouse R.

Meramec R.

Meramec Caverns

Oak Grove

Sullivan

Bourbon

Onondaga Cave State Park

Steelville

Cuba

HIST 66

Meramec Spring Park

St. James

University of Missouri-Rolla

Rolla

Belle

Vienna

Dixon

Onyx Mtn. Caverns

HIST 66

Crocker

Waynesville

Richland

Tuscumbia

Osage Beach

Lake of the Ozarks State Park

Camdenton

Ha-Ha Tonka State Park

Lebanon

HIST 66

Rolla Nat'l Airport

MARK TWAIN NATIONAL FOREST

Red Bluff

Dillard Mill State Historical Site

Indian Trail State Forest

Salem

Mill Creek

FORT LEONARD WOOD

MARK TWAIN NATIONAL FOREST

Population Center of U.S.

N

Miles

0   5   10

Point of Interest

Campground

8
49
72
32
19
19
68
72
63
32
17
5
7
7
17
42
42
28
28
63
63
19
52
54
5
44
44
88
63

Ozark vernacular, what's true in theory "ain't necessarily so" in reality. The closer you get to St. Louis, the farther away you are from the real Ozarks. The speech is different; the attitudes and approach to life are different. Life is quicker and less traditional. The independent spirit that makes the Ozarks unique succumbs to the group-thought and influence of pop culture. Frankly, many of those living in the north and northeast border country would not identify themselves as Ozarkers (and neither would those of us who live in the midst of the real deal). They would prefer to be viewed as more urban and mainstream.

However, in deference to the geologists, and because of the fine examples of karst features (caves and sinkholes), state parks, fine rivers, and at least one BBQ joint in Sullivan, I'm blurring the lines and stretching the border to the northeast. Again, it's a rather subjective call. Sullivan doesn't feel like the Ozarks, but just down the road, St. James and Cuba do. It's a matter of perspective and attitude.

AREA CODES There are two area codes over the Route 66 region. The Lebanon area to the southwest is covered by the **417** code. The rest of the region falls under **573**.

GUIDANCE Pulaksi County Tourism Bureau (573-336-6355 or 1-877-858-8687; www.visitpulaskicounty.org), 137 St. Robert Blvd., St. Robert, Mo. This bureau is extremely helpful and covers a wide area. It is your best source of information for not only the Waynesville/St. Roberts/Fort Leonard Wood vicinity, but for regional lodging, dining, and various driving tours as well.

Lebanon Area Chamber of Commerce (417-588-3256; www.lebanonmissouri .com or www.lebanondowntown.com), 186 N. Adams, Lebanon, Mo. The folks at the Lebanon chamber offer an excellent package, well worth ordering before beginning your trip. Just ask and they'll provide everything from phone books, brochures, and maps to directions and events calendars.

Two other chambers that offer helpful literature and information are the **Cuba Chamber of Commerce** (573-885-2531 or 1-877-212-8429; www.cubamo chamber.com), 71 SR P; and the **Rolla Area Chamber of Commerce** (573-364-3577 or 1-888-809-3817; www.rollachamber.org), 1311 Kingshighway, Rolla, Mo.

GETTING THERE As pointed out elsewhere in this Explorer's Guide, the Ozarks are not known for a plethora of major airports. Most travel is best accomplished by car, although there are options aplenty if you consider boat, canoe, foot, horse, or mule to be viable conveyance.

By car: From Sullivan to Lebanon, the most efficient path is I-44. However, the most efficient is not always the best or most scenic. If you're not in a tremendous rush, do your best to follow the historic road signs and wander the back roads on old Route 66.

By air: **Lambert–St. Louis International Airport** (314-426-8000; www .lambert-stlouis.com), 10701 Lambert International Blvd., St. Louis, Mo., is the

THIS AREA OF THE OZARKS IS KNOWN FOR ITS SCENIC BACK ROADS

closest major terminal to Route 66 country. Try to avoid taking I-270 South between 4 and 6 PM weekdays, or you may find yourself in a traffic jam.

When leaving the terminal, head toward the airport exit on Lambert International Blvd. You will travel 0.2 mile, at which point Lambert International Blvd. becomes Natural Bridge Rd. Drive 1 mile on Natural Bridge Rd. and turn left onto I-70 West. Travel 2.9 miles and take Exit 232 onto I-270 South. (toward Memphis). After 14.4 miles, take Exit 5B onto I-44 West toward Tulsa. Sullivan, Mo., the eastern edge of the Route 66 Ozark journey, is 71 miles west on I-44.

You can also fly into **Springfield-Branson National Airport** (417-869-0300; www.sgf-branson-airport.com), 2300 N. Airport Blvd., Springfield, Mo. The multimillion-dollar expansion of this airport between 2006 and 2009 was extremely well done. Travel through this facility is low stress. Traffic is light, with easy access and convenient parking. By and large the staff (including TSA agents) are very friendly.

MEDICAL EMERGENCIES Both these small regional hospitals offer a wide range of surgical and medical specialties, as well as 24/7 emergency room services: **Phelps County Regional Medical Center** (573-458-8899; www.pcrmc .com), 1000 W. 10th St., Rolla, Mo.; and **St. John's Hospital–Lebanon** (417-533-6100; www.stjohns.com/lebanon), 100 Hospital Dr., Lebanon, Mo.

✳ Wandering Around

EXPLORING BY CAR The construction of I-44 began in the late 1950s and lasted until the 1970s. By 1985 **Route 66** had been decommissioned, its meandering trek tossed to the wayside in the name of expediency. The Ozarks are a rugged country, even the northern border, but you couldn't really tell it if you stayed on the big highways. From Sullivan to Lebanon they were more or less created in the gentle drainage dividing the Meramec, Bourbeuse, and Gasconade Rivers.

It is possible to take historic Route 66 southwest across the entire Ozarks. Just follow the small signs, generally located on the outer roads paralleling I-44. For a true taste of what this renowned thoroughfare used to be, however, leave the interstate at Exit 169. Turn left onto CR J, cross over I-44, and immediately turn right onto CR Z. This portion of Route 66 was paved in 1943 and was one of the few stretches of the famous road that was four lanes. Proceeding ahead, you will pass through **Hooker Cut,** immortalized on many period postcards and at one time considered the deepest highway cut in the U.S. Watch for the very first crossroads (the only indicator is a yellow house on your left) and turn left onto Teardrop Rd. Drive 0.25 mile and you will notice a bar and BBQ pit on your right. This is the **Elbow Inn,** a popular hangout (catering to locals, soldiers from Fort Leonard Wood, and motorcycle enthusiasts) that serves tasty BBQ on the outdoor deck during the summer months. Originally known as the Munger-Moss sandwich shop, this spot has been in business on and off since the 1930s.

Just past the Elbow Inn turn left onto the gravel road with the street sign reading Temporal Road. This scenic 5-mile drive takes you deep in the hills following the Big Piney River. Peering through foliage (which in spring or summer is thicker than cats at a fish fry), you will notice that the river bends in a sharp U. This is **Devil's Elbow,** for which the community in the vicinity of the Elbow Inn was named. Travel a few miles farther and you will drive underneath a 40-foot-high wooden railroad trestle bridge. It makes a fantastic photo opportunity, and you'll feel like you just stepped onto the set of an old John Wayne movie.

THE ELBOW INN, JUST OFF ROUTE 66

Turn around in the driveway of the first house on your left (it is at the foot of a steep grade) and return the way you came. Take a left at the intersection of Teardrop and Temporal Roads (at the Elbow Inn) and cross the 1923 steel bridge over the Big Piney. You will now head toward the community of Devil's Elbow.

Pass through Devil's Elbow, with its many breathtaking views, and you'll arrive back on CR Z, the four-lane section of Route 66. You'll notice a "half curb" on this length that was originally designed to keep the cars on the highway (though quite often drivers ran up on it and tipped over). Continue straight ahead at the CR Z and SR 28 intersection. At the stoplight, the entrance to **Fort Leonard Wood,** home to several army museums, Stone Mill Spring, and Miller Cave, will be 2 miles to your left. To continue on Route 66, drive straight ahead and down the hill into the town of Waynesville. Here there is a historic square containing an old stagecoach stop and courthouse museum. If you proceed straight ahead, watch for Superior Road on your left. A 0.25-mile drive down Superior will bring you to the small parking lot of Roubidoux Spring, which pumps out 30 million gallons of water per day. Trout can be caught in this creek as it flows 2 miles to the Gasconade River. Also, note a large pasture across from the spring. This was a resting spot for Cherokee Indians on the infamous forced march known as the Trail of Tears.

EXPLORING BY FOOT Those who enjoy hiking should keep in mind that the Ozarks tend to become hotter than a pistol during the summer months. And of course, at least in this part of the world, you can't have heat without skyrocketing humidity. In other words, the deep forests and trails provide the perfect breeding conditions for creepy crawlies such as ticks, mosquitoes, and chiggers, not to mention a very healthy population of copperheads, cottonmouths, and the occa-

WAYNESVILLE'S HISTORIC STAGECOACH STOP

THE COLORFUL HISTORY OF HOOKER AND DEVIL'S ELBOW
In the 1890s, the now barely existing hamlets of Hooker and Devil's Elbow were the home of sporting clubs for the wealthy. These hunters and fishermen, who were primarily businessmen from St. Louis, converged upon the stretches of the Big Piney and Gasconade Rivers in search of near-guaranteed hauls of fish and wild game. More than that, though, the sportsmen's clubs were the site of major bragging sessions. It's easy to imagine the air was heavily scented with the acrid smell of Cuban stogies, and more than a few potent potables no doubt added detail to the tales of the "ones that got away." The most popular of the clubs—long since gone—was Hooker's Camp, named for local woodsman and guide John Hooker.

sional rattlesnake. This information is not meant to deter the hiker, but rather to advise that bringing bug repellent is just as important as sturdy and comfortable shoes. Some readers of this book's first edition have claimed that my opinions and advice regarding Ozark bugs and reptiles might be a bit exaggerated; it's not. Personally, I don't take to the woods in the summer without snake boots, a big can of DEET, and a shotgun pistol (the Taurus "Judge" model is a good choice for a .410-caliber snake gun). To each his own.

Walking the Ozarks is much more fun in the cooler months than at the height of summer, and during fall the colors are beyond vibrant. Still, a spring or summer hike has its own rewards. The woods are full of life, a symphony of sight, sound, and scent. Just remember your Boy Scout training and "be prepared."

All of the state parks feature a number of fine hikes with varying degrees of difficulty.

Bennett Spring State Park has numerous trails that provide views of hardwood forests, crystal-clear streams, the spring itself, and the spring branch. All trails are limited to foot traffic and average a 7 percent grade. **Natural Tunnel Trail** is a 7.5-mile hike (allow four hours for the round-trip) extending south along Spring Hollow to the Natural Tunnel. Follow the blue arrows on either the east or west side of Spring Hollow, then take the single trail to Natural Tunnel. This unique geological feature is 15 feet wide and takes an S-shaped curve before ending 296 feet later. When you first notice the opening of Natural Tunnel, you may think it's a cave. Upon stepping in, you will see the exit and realize you are in a huge natural tube. Reliable sources claim that, at various times in the past century, one end of Natural Tunnel was boarded up and used as a cattle pen.

At **Meramec State Park** the only trail designated for anything other than hiking is the **Wilderness Trail,** which may also be used for overnight backpacking. It comprises a 6-mile southern loop and a 4-mile northern loop, the latter of which winds through the Meramec Upland Forest Natural Area and heads to Copper Hollow, where lead and copper were once mined. Copper Hollow Spring is a scenic flow that cascades down cliffs into the valley below; behind the

BENNETT SPRING STATE PARK

spring you can find a conical sinkhole. Eight backpack camps are located along the trail; overnighters must register near the trailhead. It's been reported in recent years that black bears have been spotted along the Wilderness Trail. Sightings have been very infrequent, but the black bear population of the Ozarks is definitely on the increase. If you do encounter a black bear, it is good to remember that "playing dead" is not a wise idea; that technique only works on grizzlies (and, thankfully, the Ozarks are grizzly-free).

If a more urban hike is to your liking (and if the convenience of being able to fish within the city limits is appealing), you'll enjoy the **Waynesville Walking Trail,** located right in the middle of Waynesville, Mo. This 1-mile trail winds along Roubidoux Creek from the Waynesville Park to Laughlin Park. Follow the path down a slight incline and you will come to the Roubidoux Bridge. Continue and you'll soon wind up in Laughlin Park. Here you will find **Roubidoux Spring,** home of an underwater cave that draws scuba divers from around the country. A deck overlooks the spring, and Laughlin Park offers picnic tables, a large playing field, and easy-access fishing even for the handicapped. If you have a fishing license and remembered to bring your gear, you may cast a line into the Roubidoux.

EXPLORING BY RIVER The **Niangua River** is a slow and scenic stream that begins near the town of Marshfield in Webster County, Mo., and dumps into the Osage Arm of the Lake of the Ozarks. The river flows from south to north-northeast, and 114 miles of it are navigable by canoe. It's popular in fishing circles for brown and rainbow trout, bass, catfish, and a variety of panfish; much of the land surrounding it is undeveloped. Access is good, and outfitters become plentiful as floaters approach the Bennett Spring State Park vicinity. The best time to float is spring to fall (Apr.–Sept. is prime season), when the river is consistently at navigable levels via both rains and numerous springs.

The **Big Piney River** begins in the south-central Missouri Ozarks (Texas County), flows northward through the Mark Twain National Forest in Phelps and Pulaski Counties, and empties into the Gasconade River near St. Robert. Like most rivers in this region, it is a slow and tranquil stream, though floaters should note that deadfall can accumulate around bends during the higher water flows of spring. The Big Piney is almost always navigable and, thanks to the lack of development in surrounding areas, offers numerous photo opportunities.

The **Gasconade River** is reminiscent of the day Dolly Parton visited a pretzel factory: You've never seen so many curves in your life. At 265 miles, this is the longest river lying wholly within the state of Missouri, and it's arguably in the competition for most crooked stretch of water in the world (by air, the length from end to end is only 120 miles). The Gasconade begins in Wright County near Hartville, Mo., finally flowing into the Missouri River near the town of Gasconade. The river is generally slow, except during high water, and flows to the northeast. That is to say, the Gasconade eventually ends northeast of where it started, and canoeists traveling this stream will literally find themselves, at one time or another, hitting every point on the compass. Don't let the curves discourage you; the Gasconade may be the best-kept secret in the Ozarks. The river runs through isolated areas—much of it ranchland and the Mark Twain National Forest—and floaters should not forget a camera. The tree-covered bluffs are stunning, pocked with caves both small and large, and wildlife is prevalent. The Gasconade is an excellent fishing river for smallmouth bass, goggle-eye (a member of the bass family), bluegill, crappie, and a variety of sucker fish (right tasty if deep fried, but then again what isn't?).

The **Meramec River** receives an awful lot of press, primarily because there are so many things along the northern Ozark border named Meramec. The river first rises near Salem, Mo., in Dent County, and pours into the Mississippi about 20 miles south of St. Louis. The entire river can be paddled year-round, but the most popular stretch is between Maramec Spring Park and Meramec State Park. There is a little more whitewater on this river than on the other streams in this region—some stretches can hit a Class II status—but it's all still easily handled by novice floaters. The Meramec offers good fishing and is very pretty unless you plan on going all the way to the Mississippi. The closer you get to St. Louis, the more development you'll see. As far as scenery, there is very little reason to proceed past the towns of St. Clair or Pacific. But, at 207 miles in length, the Meramec does provide plenty of awesome sights. The numerous outfitters that service the Meramec, and the proximity to the recreational possibilities of larger towns and cities, consistently make it a tourist favorite.

Courtois Creek, a very fun, 21-mile length of water, has its headwaters in the Mark Twain National Forest of Washington County. The stream terminates when it flows into the Meramec River near the CR E bridge in Crawford County. The forests along the banks are dense, and wildlife viewing is plentiful. Floaters on the Courtois will feel they have traveled back in time, as most of the river is remote and secluded. Normally the Courtois is a shallow, flat water river with very little current. Take note of the word normally. During high water the current can increase dramatically, resulting in crosscurrents and eddies. Plus, due to the proximity of overhanging limbs, floaters unaccustomed to hairpin turns can suddenly find themselves wet. That said, if you are a paddler of even intermediate skill, I strongly recommend the Courtois at high water; it's perhaps my favorite Ozark float. While not dangerous in the least, the Courtois can offer some mild thrills when it runs swift.

Last, but not least, don't try to pronounce Courtois with a French accent. If you do, the locals will look at you funny. It's pronounced COTE-a-way or sometimes CODE-way.

Huzzah Creek, like the Courtois, is another tributary of the Meramec; its 23 miles both begin and end in Crawford County. Anyone can normally float the Huzzah; 9 days out of 10 it will be slow and tranquil. However, caution should be exercised on the 10th day. At high water this is a curvy stream that can become a nudge dangerous for the novice. One of the best things about the Huzzah (although this situation is changing due to St. Louis weekend traffic) is that it's uncrowded. Go on a weekday and you may well have the creek to yourself. The water is clear, the fishing is good, and outfitters are plentiful.

Yet another tributary of the Meramec, the **Bourbeuse River** gives the Gasconade a run for its money in terms of curves. The river itself measures 138 miles total, but that means nothing on the Bourbeuse. For example, the 107-mile stretch through Franklin County measures only 27 air miles! Still, that is no reason to avoid the Bourbeuse. Yes, you can travel long distances between access points (count on a minimum of 8 miles), but the bass fishing is excellent and the scenery will distract you. The water isn't as clear as on some of the other Ozark rivers, but a plus of the Bourbeuse is that there are a few ripples here and there. Nobody in their right mind could call these "rapids," but it's still fun to see and hear some splashes of whitewater from time to time. You'll feel like you're going a heck of a lot faster than you really are.

✳ Villages

Bourbon, Mo. Bourbon prides itself on a small-town atmosphere and being a community full of "plain folks." The 1,415 residents have little desire to be part of the big city and wisely enjoy their slower pace.

Although populated since the early 1800s, settlers didn't really begin arriving in the area until after the 1860 completion of the southern branch of the Frisco (then Pacific) Railroad to Rolla. Land was plentiful and cheap thanks to railroad right-of-way offerings and land grants promised to veterans of the War of 1812. The town was supposed to be called St. Cloud, and then Richard Turner set up a general store.

Turner was no fool, and he began selling a newfangled type of whiskey to the primarily Irish laborers who spent long days at work on the railroad. On the porch of his store, at all times, sat a large barrel of bourbon.

The rest is history.

Crocker, Mo. In the late 1800s the Crocker depot was the heart of the Frisco Railroad line. Today the Crocker Festival of Railroad Days occurs each year the weekend before Labor Day.

Cuba, Mo. Considered one of the fastest-growing small towns in the Ozarks, Cuba boasts 3,555 residents, two industrial parks, and a small municipal airport. Incorporated in 1857, scenic Cuba is often referred to as the City of Murals. The town is dotted with many wall-sized paintings celebrating both the town's island namesake and local history. In 1928, for instance, mechanical problems once forced famed pilot Amelia Earhart to land outside town. Yes, there is a mural celebrating that event.

Dixon, Mo. The famous Bart Simpson line, "Don't have a cow, man," is wholly inappropriate in Dixon. This is perhaps the only village in America where you can win your own bovine during the annual Dixon Cow Days, held the third weekend in September. A trip back in time, Dixon also offers visitors the chance to pick fresh fruits and vegetables from a variety of local berry, tree, and pumpkin farms. Not last and certainly not least, fishermen shouldn't miss an inexpensive (and usually productive) day of angling at the well-stocked Cardin's Lake.

Leasburg, Mo. A hamlet of but 337 people, Leasburg is graced with some exceptional natural wonders. Both Onondaga Cave and Huzzah State Forest are just a few miles from town; still, the most unusual attraction of the area is Snake Pit Cave, a 50-foot-wide sinkhole. You can peer over the rim and see an underground lake. A word of warning: They don't call it Snake Pit Cave for nothing. During the warmer months, watch out for slithering reptiles that might well be working on their tans.

A MURAL IN DOWNTOWN CUBA

Lebanon, Mo. A jewel of a town, Lebanon's location halfway between Rolla and Springfield has led economic prognosticators to label it a "micropolis." Numerous predictions state that phenomenal growth is a certainty over the next decade.

Lebanon is lucky, for if appearances are any indicator, the 14,292 residents appear to have the sort of civic pride that will permit such an explosion to occur in a beneficial manner. In 1998 Lebanon opened the 120,000-square-foot Kenneth E. Cowan Civic Center, an unusual addition to a town of this size, and a variety of "clean" manufacturing industries have proven a huge boon to the local economy. Known as the Aluminum Boat Capital of the World, the town features a number of major watercraft manufacturers as well as the Independent Stave Company, the world's largest producer of wooden barrels for the aging of fine wines and bourbon. Floating and fishing are nearby on the Gasconade and Osage Fork Rivers, and nearby Bennett Spring State Park draws trout fishermen by the thousands.

Rolla, Mo. No one is quite sure how Rolla got its name. One theory points to the suggestion that southern settlers meant to honor Raleigh, N.C., but lacked the spelling skills to appropriately complete the task. Yet another theory is that it was named by disgruntled citizens who had been ignored in picking the town site. As payback, or so the legend goes, they chose to name the town for a very homely stray dog named Rollo who thrived on harassing the locals and creating general mischief.

No matter. Rolla is these days an eclectic town of 19,559 souls and home to the Missouri University of Science and Technology (also known as MST, and formerly the University of Missouri–Rolla). The college was initially founded in 1871 as the University of Missouri School of Mines and Metallurgy, but was elevated to a higher status in 1964. The campus's primary focus is still engineering and mining, although full-course majors covering the spectrum of other fields are also offered.

St. James, Mo. There is an intangible something about St. James that personifies charm. The town of 3,994 is clean, well kept, and friendly. Visitors can enjoy the beautiful, 1,800-acre Maramec Spring Park, which not only pumps out more than 100 million gallons of water per day, but also holds the remains of the fascinating Maramec Iron Works. If that's not enough, visitors can fish for trout; float nearby rivers such as the Courtois, Huzzah, and Meramec; or enjoy the fruits of five local wineries.

St. Robert, Mo. The "Gateway to Fort Leonard Wood," St. Robert is a modern boomtown. Though the official population stands at 3,642, the daily transit work population is estimated to be 30,000 to 40,000. Within the town itself are more than 500 businesses and 1,200 hotel rooms. Until 1951, St. Robert was known as Gospel Ridge; its location at the intersection of the legendary Route 66 and Fort Leonard Wood was famous for bars and other "personal services" popular among the troops. These days the town has calmed considerably, a well-kept and extremely busy bedroom community that continues to grow by leaps and bounds.

HOMER'S: IT DOESN'T GET ANY BETTER THAN THIS

Steelville, Mo. Billing itself as the Floating Capital of the United States, Steelville's claim to fame can be found not only via the recreation of surrounding rivers, but also from its quaint and picturesque Main Street. Founded in 1835, Steelville is called home by an estimated 1,490 residents.

Sullivan, Mo. Though I really don't consider the Sullivan area as being in the Ozarks proper, a trip is more than worth your time. The reason would be Meramec State Park. Also, located in nearby Stanton, Mo.—and promoted by the billboards you've no doubt seen for 100 miles in either direction—is Meramec Caverns. The caverns opened as a tourist attraction in 1935 and were one of the infinite oddities found on old Route 66 during its glory days. Meramec is the most popular commercial cave in Missouri.

The best thing about Sullivan, however, is that it is the home of Homer's BBQ, a simple and simply incredible little eatery that should never be missed.

Waynesville, Mo. With more than 4,287 residents, Waynesville was named for Revolutionary War hero General "Mad Anthony" Wayne. The oldest town in Pulaski County, founded in 1833, it is also home to the U.S. Army's 65,000-acre Fort Leonard Wood Maneuver Support Center. Waynesville, Pulaski's county seat, is a town that likes its festivals, with Paw Paw Daze and Frog Fest being two area favorites.

✳ To See

MUSEUMS ⊛ ✿ ᕬ **The Mineral Museum** (573-341-4616), 125 McNutt Hall, MST campus, Rolla, Mo. Open year-round, Mon.–Fri. 9–5. Free. Featuring many displays from both the 1893 Chicago and 1904 St. Louis World's Fairs, the museum boasts of more than 3,500 specimens of rocks and minerals from 47 states and 92 countries.

Memoryville, USA (573-364-1810; www.missouriozarks.org/memory.html), 2220 N. Bishop Ave., Rolla, Mo. If vehicular nostalgia is your thing, then this collection of automobiles from yesteryear and scenes from the early 1900s is well worth a stop. Memoryville is easy to find, located on US 63 North off I-44 at Exit 186.

🦌 ✿ ⅙ **Route 66 Museum and Research Center** (417-532-2148; www.llroute 66society.bravehost.com/Museum.html), 915 S. Jefferson, Lebanon, Mo. Mon.– Thurs. 8–8, Fri.–Sat. 8–5. Free. Loaded with one-of-a-kind memorabilia from the heyday of "the Mother Road," this tribute to Route 66 is the result of thousands of hours of volunteer labor. Located in the same building as the **Lebanon–Laclede County Library,** the museum boasts of possessing the collection of renowned historian Jim Powell, founder and former president of the Missouri Route 66 Society. On-site is a themed diner and gift shop, the latter just because no one should ever be lacking a replica US 66 highway sign in their office, den, or bedroom.

CULTURAL SITES 🦌 ✿ ⅙ **Stonehenge** (573-341-4111 or 1-800-522-0938; http://rockmech.mst.edu/stonehenge), 14th St. and Bishop Ave., Rolla, Mo. Open year-round. Free. The famous English megalith of the Salisbury Plain, or at least a reasonable facsimile thereof, can be found on the northwest edge of the MST campus. As is appropriate for a town with a renowned engineering and mining school, the structure determines equinoxes, solstices, and dates, and allows for a correct astronomical viewing of the North Star.

🦌 ✿ **Stoney Acres** (417-668-5560; www.stoneyacres.biz), 11399 Claxton Rd., Competition, Mo. Stoney Acres is Missouri's first licensed sheep/dairy farm. You will definitely want to call ahead before heading 13 miles south of Lebanon on

ROLLA'S VERSION OF STONEHENGE

Flying J Travel Plaza (573-860-8880), 825 N. Church St., Exit 226 off I-44, Sullivan, Mo. There is absolutely no logical reason why a truck stop was included in the first edition of this Explorer's Guide. It's even less logical that it be included in the second edition. I would fully adhere to such a sensible premise if it wasn't for the fact that I highly admire the brazen kitschiness of the Flying J. This outfit merged with Pilot Travel Centers in 2010, so now the crazy things are all over the county. It's one of those strange places that tries to sell everything under the sun . . . and actually succeeds. Feel free to buy loads of interesting, amusing, and largely useless odds and ends, and eat like there's no tomorrow. Last time I was there they were serving Mexican food and fried chicken gizzards . . . at 6 AM!

THE FLYING J TRUCK STOP

SR 5. This is partly because Stoney's is very hard to find, and partly because the owner/operators might be busy. Stoney's gives tours and lessons in sheep milking by appointment. They also offer sheep's milk, cheese, soap, and Smudge (sheep's milk fudge).

WINERIES If popular media conceptions are to believed, the garden-variety Ozarker is far more likely to take a tug off a jug of white lightning than to daintily sip a glass of white wine. A steaming still full of moonshine is a more common depiction than a lovingly tended vineyard.

The truth, however, is that the Missouri Ozarks have specialized in the art of growing grapes and making wine for more than a century. Prior to the Volstead Act of 1919, Missouri's wine industry ranked second behind New York. Though production fell during the Depression and post-Depression years, in the 1960s many of the original wineries and vineyards experienced a renaissance.

Today Missouri has 51 wineries that rack up $26 million per year in wine sales. The rocky soil, sunny days, and a long growing season result in consistent bumper crops. In the St. James and Steelville area, six different wineries offer tours, samples, and sales.

Three Squirrels Winery (573-265-7442; www.threesquirrelswinery.com), 17301 SR B, St. James, Mo. Three Squirrels is both a winery and an art gallery, and should not be missed if for no other reason than its name. Wines, cheeses, salami, and gifts are all available for sale; some of the winery's specialty labels include Acorn Red, Acorn White, Red Squirrel, White Squirrel, Nutty Red, Nutty White, and Norton. Tastings are provided Fri. 1–5:30, Sat. 11–6, and Sun. noon–5. Three Squirrels is located 4.5 miles north of I-44 at the St. James exit (Exit 195) and 12 miles east of Rolla.

Heinrichshaus Vineyard and Winery (573-265-5000; www.heinrichshaus .com), 18500 SR U, St. James, Mo. Open most weekdays and Sat. 10–6, Sun. noon–6. Closed Wed. Call ahead. Heinrichshaus specializes in dry white wines produced from French hybrid and native American grapes. The winery also offers a very pretty terraced picnic area and sells a variety of wine accessories.

Meramec Vineyards (573-265-7847 or 1-877-216-9463; www.meramecvineyards .com), 600 SR B, St. James, Mo. Open year-round, Mon.–Sat. 10–5, Sun. noon–5. One of the more well-known and well-visited vineyards, this facility's main lobby contains both the works of local artists and a gourmet gift shop stocked with food and wine-related items. The staff is friendly, full of information, and always willing to answer questions. Meramec's **Bistro d'Vine** serves light lunches and has even been mentioned in Southern Living magazine. Lunch is served Mon.–Sat. 11–2, Sun. 11–3. The covered courtyard, gardens, and **Bocce Court** (now there's something you don't often find in the Ozarks) make Meramec Vineyards well worth the stop. It's easily reached by taking Exit 195 off I-44 and driving 0.75 mile east on the north outer road.

St. James Winery (573-265-7912 or 1-800-280-9463; www.stjameswinery.com), 540 Sydney St., St. James, Mo. Open Mon.–Sat. 8–6, Sun. 9–6. Since 1970 St. James has been producing wines (23 varieties) that have been award winners in both national and international categories. Justifiably proud of their operation, the folks here offer an extensive tour of the facilities and feature gourmet foods, wine accessories, and glassware in their gift shop. St. James currently makes 200,000 cases annually, and in 2009 was named the top winery in the eastern U.S. The winery is visible when taking the St. James exit off I-44.

Peaceful Bend Vineyard (573-775-3000; www.peacefulbendvineyard.com), 1942 SR T, Steelville, Mo. Open Tues.–Fri. 10–5, Sat. 10–6, Sun. noon–5. Take Exit 208 off I-44 and drive south 8 miles on SR 19. Turn right onto SR 8 and drive 2 miles, turning right onto SR T. Peaceful Bend is 2 miles ahead on your left. This beautiful vineyard and cellar set on 72 acres is one of those well-kept secrets that is no longer a secret. Visitors can take a gentle stroll through the vineyards or walk along the banks of the Meramec River. Peaceful Bend features 14 wines, and is open daily 11–6. Local and regional musicians perform live Sat. from 1:30–4:30, Apr.–Nov. In most cases admission is free.

✳ To Do

🦐 🐾 🔟 **Meramec Farm Cabins and Trail** (573-732-4765; www.meramecfarm .com), 208 Thickety Ford Rd., Bourbon, Mo. It's been a bed & breakfast since 1982, but a working family farm since 1811 (10 years before Missouri was granted statehood). This is a full-scale farming and ranching operation, raising hay, cattle, horses, and a bit of anything else you could name. But it also makes for a unique vacation, one that has been touted in such magazines as *Travel and Leisure* and *American Cowboy*. Guests may stay in one of two well-equipped log cabins (rates begin at $80 per night) and are encouraged to help around the ranch (or not), relax, enjoy the river, or hike about the 470 acres. The big draw here, however, is horses. Even the tenderfoot guest will enjoy sitting high in the saddle on one of the famed, smooth-riding, gaited Missouri Foxtrotters. A variety of different riding/lodging packages are offered. A three-day/two-night package for two is $450 and includes cabin, riding guide, and picnic. There are also weekday specials, a kayaking and riding special, or even rides by the hour ($25 per hour). Those who really want to get out and see the Ozarks up close can take part in a no-frills, 100-mile trek. Prices are $1,400 for two people.

🦐 🐾 🔟 **Clifty Creek Natural Bridge** is also located north of Dixon. Drive north on SR 28 for 4 miles, turning onto SR W. After 3.9 miles you will see a CONSERVATION DEPARTMENT sign. The hike to this unique formation will take more than an hour, and because it involves wading through creeks and traversing rocks, heavy footwear is strongly recommended. If you make the hike in summer, also bring mosquito repellent. Tuck your pants legs into your boots and check for ticks after your trek.

🦐 🔟 ♿ **Fort Leonard Wood** (573-596-0131; www.wood.army.mil/wood_cms), Nebraska St. and E. Dakota St. Mon.–Sat. 10–4; closed Sun., Christmas, and New Year's. Covering more than 100 square miles of territory, Fort Leonard Wood is larger than some eastern states. The home of the military police school, chemical school, and Army engineer school, the complex is also the Maneuver Support Center for the Army. The base's **John B. Mahaffey Museum Complex** represents the contributions of the Military Police, Chemical Warfare, and Engineering Divisions to the armed forces throughout history. There are both static and interactive displays.

Having been carved out of rugged Ozark terrain, Fort Leonard Wood is home to more than a few natural wonders. **Stone Mill Spring,** with a flow of 18 million gallons of water a day, is stocked with more than 3,000 pounds of rainbow trout per year and offers some very good fishing. Caves abound in the area, with **Miller Cave** being the largest. Archaeological evidence from the cave has proven that the area was inhabited from 8000 B.C. to A.D. 1300. The mouth of the cave overlooks a scenic view of the valley and Big Piney River, and it can be reached via a difficult hiking trail.

✳ Wild Places

PARKS AND PRESERVES Mark Twain National Forest (573-364-4621; www.fs.fed.us/r9/marktwain). Comprising more than 1.5 million acres, the Mark

Twain is a superb wilderness dotted by rivers, streams, and some of the largest natural springs in America. Broken into nine different ranger districts, the forest includes hundreds of miles of hiking trails, numerous scenic drives, seven congressionally designated wilderness areas, 40 campgrounds, and thousands of acres of primitive and semi-primitive areas. The Mark Twain is a true playground for hunters, fishermen, hikers, equestrians, and campers.

✐ 🏕 ♿ ❄ **Bennett Spring State Park** (417-532-4338 or 417-532-4307; www .mostateparks.com/bennett.htm), 26250 SR 64A, Lebanon, Mo. Open daily, sunrise to one hour past sunset. General admission is free. Each year, on the first day of March, upward of 3,000 fishermen will line the banks of the 1.5-mile spring branch creek of Bennett Spring State Park. In that there is little surprise, because in the weeks leading up to opening day of trout season more than 8,000 trout will have been stocked in the meandering spring branch. Missouri fishing licenses and a daily trout tag can be purchased at the park store.

Pumping out more than 100 million gallons of water per day, Bennett is Missouri's third largest spring. The park itself consists of more than 3,200 acres and offers a nature center, swimming pool, dining lodge, trout hatchery, seven different trails, rental cabins, float trips, fly-fishing lessons, picnic areas, and playgrounds. Five different campgrounds provide a total of 189 individual sites. Campground 1 is open year-round, with running water available Apr. 15–Oct. 15. Campgrounds 2 and 3 are open Apr. 15–Oct. 31. Campgrounds 4 and 5 are available to the public Feb. 25–Oct. 31. Reservations can be made for campgrounds 1 through 4; campground 5 operates on a first-come, first-served basis.

Lodging and camping is plentiful in commercial concerns adjacent to and near the park. Many of these have access to the Niangua River, into which the spring branch flows. The Niangua, only 1.5 miles downstream, is a slow river of the Class I genre serviced by numerous outfitters.

A word of advice to prospective floaters: The Niangua is a very pretty river, but lately it seems to attract a younger crowd. On fine summer weekends those out for laid-back paddling or bird-watching might note a number of boisterous 20-somethings on the river, performing with the hyperactivity for which 20-somethings are known. While this is a good thing in and of itself, it should be noted that those with small children (or old fogies, a category in which I voluntarily accept membership) might better enjoy a calmer float.

🐾 🏕 ✐ ♿ ❄ **Maramec Spring Park** (573-265-7124 or 573-265-7387; www .maramecspringpark.com), 21880 Maramec Spring Dr., St. James, Mo. Open morning to dusk (usually until 9 PM in summer). $5 per car, $25 per bus. Unlimited season pass for $35. This gem is one of the most peaceful, gorgeous, and well-kept parks you will ever find. Located just 6 miles southeast of St. James on SR 8, the park is privately owned and operated by the not-for-profit James Foundation.

More than 96 million gallons of water per day burst forth from the spring. However, that's just the beginning of the sights in this off-the-beaten-path discovery. More than 200,000 trout are stocked annually into the Meramec River, which seems a bit odd since *meramec* is the Algonquian word for "catfish." Also on the subject of names, sharp-eyed readers will notice that Maramec Spring Park insists on spelling its name differently from either the Meramec River or Meramec State Park. The reason is that the privately owned Maramec Spring Park retains the original Algonquian spelling, while Meramec State Park and Meramec River do not.

Maramec Spring Park contains 1,860 acres of forest and fields, and the public-use portions include amenities such as a café, store, campsites, fish feeding, picnicking, shelters, and fishing. You can even get married in Maramec, assuming you want to and somebody has asked.

Several trails are located within Maramec, with the prettiest being the **Spring Branch Trail.** This 1.5-mile trek meanders around both the spring and spring branch. Visitors will also wish to visit the fascinating and imposing remains of the old **Maramec Iron Works.** Founded by the James Family in the early 1800s (that would be the James family whose foundation owns the park and for whom the town of St. James is named, not the Jesse James family), Maramec was the first successful ironworks west of the Mississippi. The Meramec River, a clear, calm Ozark stream, flows through the park, providing excellent fishing and floating. You just don't find a better day trip than this park.

🐾 🎿 ⚓ ♿ ❄ **Meramec State Park** (573-468-6072 or 573-468-6519; http://mo stateparks.com/park/meramec-state-park), 115 Meramec Park Dr., Sullivan, Mo. Open Apr.–Oct., daily 7–10; Nov.–Mar., daily 7–9. Its proximity to the greater metropolitan St. Louis area makes Meramec State Park a busy place. If you seek a quiet trip, I suggest you try to hit this spot on a weekday rather than a height-of-summer weekend. On the other hand, should your timing not be so precise, Meramec's 6,896 acres will normally allow you to find a corner away from the madding crowd. Open since 1927, the park has more than 40 caves. Tours of

THE SPRING BRANCH AT MARAMEC SPRING PARK

Fisher Cave, the largest, are offered for a nominal charge on a seasonal basis. Most caves in Missouri's state park system are closed for touring as of 2011 in order to halt the spread of a fungus disease in bats. Fisher is one of only four tour caves in the system–the others are Onondaga Cave and Cathedral Cave at Onondaga Cave State Park, and Ozark Caverns at Lake of the Ozarks State Park–that remain open to the public. Swimming, fishing, rafting, and canoeing in the Meramec River are the major appeals of this very popular area. The park store offers raft and canoe rentals, campsites (including three group sites), rental cabins, motel rooms, and a conference center. A rustic dining lodge provides hearty and decent food, but don't expect anything too fancy (if you're looking for Wolfgang Puck, you took a wrong turn at Los Angeles).

LAKE ✿ ✎ **Cardin's Lake** (573-759-6664), 14200 Colorado Rd., Dixon, Mo. You'll need to pick up a Missouri fishing license, but this local lake stocked with perch, catfish, and crappie is an area favorite. Take Exit 163 off I-44 and travel 10 miles north on SR 28 to SR D. Turn right onto SR D for 0.25 mile, then take another right onto Colorado Rd. Cardin's Lake is 0.75 mile ahead. The lake is stocked well enough that the fish generally bite with enthusiasm.

CAVES ✿ ✿ ✎ ♿ ❄ **Onondaga Cave** (573-245-6576; www.mostateparks.com /onondaga/geninfo.htm), 7556 CR H, Leasburg, Mo. In addition to the Show-Me State, Missouri is also known as the Cave State. More than 5,500 caves go far to prove that beauty is more than skin deep. One of the most popular of these underground wonders is Onondaga Cave, located in **Onondaga Cave State Park** on SR H in Crawford County, 7 miles southeast of the I-44 Leasburg exit.

From Mar.–Oct., a 75-minute, 1-mile cave tour is led by a naturalist over concrete walkways (with lights and handrails). Onondaga is a highly scenic cave, with many stalactites, stalagmites, cave corals, and massive draperies. Fees are $12 for adults, $7 for children ages 6–12. A more strenuous. 0.25-mile tour can also be had on weekends between Memorial Day and Labor Day (or by special arrangement) in **Cathedral Cave,** the park's other cavern. Fees for this trek are $8 for adults and $6 for children ages 6–12.

However, the attractions of this park are not merely subterranean; you'll also find plenty of activity on the surface. The park's campground offers both basic and electric/water campsites, and **Vilander Bluff Natural Area** provides a panoramic view of the Meramec River. The river valley offers many opportunities for fishing, canoeing, or a relaxed picnic, and a park visitors center is loaded with historical tidbits and exhibits.

✎ ♿ **Meramec Caverns** (573-468-2283; www.americascave.com), I-44 and SR W, Exit 230, Stanton, Mo. Open every day except Thanksgiving and Christmas. Opens at 9 AM most months. $9.50–$14. Wheelchair accessible. Consisting of seven levels and 26 miles of underground passages, Meramec Caverns was opened as a tourist attraction in 1935. Now, topside, visitors can enjoy a motel, campgrounds, canoe floats, riverboat rides, a gift shop, restaurant, and a mid-1800s mining village. The largest commercial cave in Missouri, Meramec also wins the award for the most billboards on I-44. It features an amazing array of stalactites, fossils, limestone formations, and an underground river, and over the years it has played host to Indians, European miners, ballroom dances, and Civil War engagements. A Confederate gang once blew up a federal powder mill here, and local legend insists that Jesse James and his gang later used the caverns as a hideout during their outlaw days. As you'll quickly learn in the Ozarks, Jesse James is still a drawing card. In eastern states, hotels and inns like to boast that "Washington slept here." In the Ozarks, it's "Jesse James and his gang hid here." That kind of tells you where we Ozarkers place our priorities.

✳ Lodging

BED & BREAKFASTS

Bourbon, Mo.

🦴 🐾 ✎ **Meramec Farm Cabins and Trail** (573-732-4765; www.meramec farm.com), 208 Thickety Ford Rd. See *To Do.*

Steelville, Mo.

🐾 ✎ **The Cottage at Peaceful Bend** (573-775-3000; www.peaceful bendvineyard.com), 1942 SR T. Those seeking privacy or the perfect site for a romantic getaway will not be disappointed with the Cottage at Peaceful Bend. The original cottage is being fully remodeled at the time of this writing (2011) but will be available for rental in 2012. Found on the grounds of the Peaceful Bend Vineyard, the single, simple cottage includes a kitchen, full bath, two bedrooms, laundry facilities, and a small living room. There is easy access to the Meramec River right there on the property, and with 72 acres of ground there are plenty of opportunities for hiking, birding, or a sunset picnic. The owners of Peaceful Bend don't provide meals (guests are given a basket of treats and wine upon arrival), but they do stock the fridge. Rates are anticipated to be $200 per night. Smoking is permitted; pets must fork over an additional $10-per-night charge.

St. James, Mo.

Crutiques Bed and Breakfast (573-265-7931), 18790 CR 3480. Located 2 miles south of St. James on SR 3480, Crutiques is a relatively new home (built in 1981 and owned by Sharon and Bob Wilson) that makes up in amenities what it lacks in age. The wraparound porch and patio are relaxing (the latter even has a woodstove should the morning be chilly), and the screened porch features a 7-foot wicker porch swing. The small touches are what make Crutiques special. Primitive antiques are everywhere, and cut flowers and freshly baked cookies are present upon arrival. The home overlooks the Meramec River Valley, and a lake (complete with jon boat) is available for use by guests. A full breakfast is served on china, crystal, and linen. Right next to the kitchen and dining room is a hearth room with a homey brick fireplace. Three guest rooms are available, all of which contain feather beds and ceiling fans; rates range from $90–120 per night. The inn is open year-round (closed Thanksgiving and Christmas), and neither children nor pets are allowed. Smoking is not permitted inside the home itself.

✎ **The Painted Lady Bed and Breakfast and Guest House** (573-265-5008 or 1-877-563-4720; www

THE PAINTED LADY B&B

.paintedladybandb.com), 1127 S. Jefferson. Luxurious amenities such as turndown services and chocolates on the pillow are the standard here, and the goal of innkeepers Sandy and Wanda Ziff is that guests finish their stay feeling pampered and relaxed. Built in 1990 and opened in 1995, the Painted Lady features six guest rooms with showers or tubs (one has a Jacuzzi); the iron and brass beds range from double to queen to king. An all-you-can-eat breakfast is served, and guests may dine either in a formal dining room, at the informal harvest table, or on an outside deck—or receive a "breakfast in a basket." The grounds surrounding the home comprise 60 acres of grass and woods.

Accommodations run $85–175 per night. Reservations are recommended, and smoking is permitted only in designated areas. Pets are not allowed. The Painted Lady welcomes children, but prefers that families with children younger than 12 stay in the property's detached guest house. The Painted Lady also welcomes both honeymooners and those who wish to hold their wedding on the grounds. The latest addition to the property is a small private cottage named Little Tara adjacent to the main home, perfect for those seeking a bit more privacy.

Rolla, Mo.

🖋️ 🌹 **A Miner Indulgence Bed & Breakfast** (573-364-0680; www .minerinn.com), 13750 Martin Spring Dr. A large, modern, brick Colonial home, A Miner Indulgence offers elegance, spacious rooms, and a unique antique decor (as in a corn shucker, invalid chair, and newspaper delivery wagon, to name just a few items). Guests can enjoy an in-ground heated pool, hot tub, and well-stocked library, but they will especially enjoy the food. The attention some B&Bs afford to dining places a distant second to appearance and physical surroundings. Not this one. The menu varies, but guests are guaranteed a full country breakfast typically consisting of fresh orange juice, a fruit cup, an egg dish, waffles, French toast, or pancakes. Each has a flavor unique to A Miner Indulgence. Bacon or sausage complements the meal, along with a never-ending supply of coffee, tea, or milk. Let's put it this way: You won't start the day hungry.

Set on 4 acres that were once a Civil War campground, the inn offers two spacious rooms. Both have a private bath and sitting area, and both come complete with a coffeemaker and a variety of teas, coffees, and hot chocolate. Those acquainted with the heat and humidity of an Ozark summer will be happy to hear that A Miner Indulgence has central air-conditioning. Rates are currently $85 per night (double occupancy, with a $10 charge for each additional person). Special meals are available, and dietary restrictions can be accommodated. Children over age 12 are welcome; critters, smoking, and smoking critters are not (smoking is allowed on the porches or in the pool area). As an aside, there is a meaning behind the name A Miner Indulgence: The inn is owned by Barb and Ron Kohser, and Ron is a professor and chairman of the Metallurgical Department at the Missouri University of Science and Technology.

Dixon, Mo.

🦌 🐾 🛶 **Rock Eddy Bluff Farm**
(573-759-6081; www.rockeddy.com), 10245 Maries Rd. 511. *National Geographic Adventure Magazine* said that Rock Eddy Bluff Farm is "a perfect antidote to work or holiday (or any) stress." There's a reason for such an accolade. When Tom and Kathy

Corey decided to forgo city life and move back to the Ozarks, they did so with a firm philosophy in mind. They sought to escape the frenzy of racing rats. More than that, they wished to share what they love with guests. As those who stay at their Rock Eddy Bluff Farm will attest, the Coreys have not faltered in that goal. A small, scenic inn surrounded by 150 acres of lush Ozark landscape, Rock Eddy looks down upon the one-of-a-kind Gasconade River Valley. Visitors can hike, canoe (canoes are provided for guest use), fish, swim, or take an Amish wagon tour. The point of this retreat, however, is simple relaxation. Accommodations include the Treehouse Suite, with three delightfully furnished rooms and an outdoor hot tub. The Turkey Ridge Cottage is but a brief stroll from the river and has three bedrooms and a foldout couch. Those who want to rough it can choose the Line Camp Cabin, with heat from a woodstove, lights from oil lamps, and water from a pitcher pump. Rates at Rock Eddy run $100–155 per night, and it's open all year (except when the Coreys take a vacation themselves). Smoking is only permitted outdoors or on porches. Children are welcome, as are well-behaved pets. A full country breakfast is part of the Treehouse Suite's package (in the cabins, the fixin's for breakfast are provided, and guests do their own cooking). Also, the farm hosts small, intimate weddings.

🐾 🛶 **Blue Jay Farm** (573-759-2400; www.bluejayfarm.net), 10500 Circle Dr. Situated on 360 acres, complete with a 7-acre, spring-fed lake, Blue Jay Farm was established in the early 1900s by Frank Wielandy, one of the original founders of the Missouri

Department of Conservation. The current owners, the Goodman family, have lived on the property for five decades. At this relaxing and tranquil escape, with lovingly restored log cabins, guests have the option of either taking part in numerous activities or doing nothing at all. Five cabins and one group facility are found at Blue Jay Farm, and guests will not be disappointed by any of them. Rates run $80–210 per night (double occupancy, with a $10 charge for each additional adult), and weekly rates are available. Smoking is not permitted, but (one of the rare places that really boasts of this) the farm is extremely pet-friendly.

CANOE OUTFITTERS AND CAMPING

Even the less popular rivers of the Ozarks are serviced by numerous outfitters, most of which offer their own campgrounds and shuttles. Prices for canoe rentals run approximately $25–40 per day. Camping can range from the primitive (some outfitters offer free tent camping; most charge a minimum of $5) to RV hook-ups to cabins and motel-style rooms. Canoe rental rates quoted in the following listings generally refer to a single craft for one or two people, and rates often drop a bit if several canoes are rented. Most outfitters also rent kayaks, rafts, jon boats, and float tubes. Camping and accommodation rates listed are for adults (across the board, the charge is lower for children), usually per person per day.

The following firms have all exhibited staying power (smaller outfitters come and go) and offer something a bit different from the standard campground. Because many of the outfitters advertise floats on several rivers,

I've listed them under the primary area to which they provide service. Travelers should call the individual establishments or check websites prior to embarking. Reservations are heavily recommended, and in most cases a deposit is required. Outfitters and campgrounds more times than not accept pets with the provision that the pet is leashed (and no, you can't take Fido along in the canoe or raft). Also, by very wise Missouri law, no glass containers are allowed on the river.

Niangua River

🐾 🛶 **Adventures Float Trips and Campground** (417-588-7238; www.mo-adventures.org), 1667 SR 64, Lebanon, Mo. Tent camping $2.50 per person per night, RV sites $7.50 per two people per night. Canoe rentals begin at $40 per day, and decrease with the number of canoes rented.

🐾 🛶 ⚲ **Bennett Spring State Park** (417-532-4338 or 417-532-4307; www.mostateparks.com/bennett.htm), 26250 SR 64A, Lebanon, Mo. Cabins include a kitchen and one or two bedrooms and begin at $117 per night. Motel rooms start at $72. Visitors who enjoy a smoke should know that the park no longer allows smoking in any of its rooms. This is either a positive or a negative, depending upon your opinion of the devil weed. Campsite fees begin at $11 per night. A single canoe rental is $40.

🐾 🛶 **Circle J Campground Canoe Rental and Cafe** (417-532-4430; www.circlejcampground.com), 10221 SR 64, Lebanon, Mo. RV spots start at $20; cabins, $50. Canoe rental starts at $40 and raft rental at $80. Guided fishing trips are available. A nice touch at Circle J is the hand-dipped ice cream at the campground café. You'll also want to try the meringue coconut cream pie. It's killer.

Fort Niangua River Resort (417-532-4377 or 1-877-588-7066; www .fortniangua.com), 84 Cat Hollow Trail, Lebanon, Mo. Fort Niangua offers a choice of air-conditioned and heated cabins, trailers, an RV park, and primitive campgrounds. Recreational facilities include a lighted basketball court, volleyball court, swimming pool, and fully equipped game room. A convenience store, laundry, and showers are located in the main building. Cabins begin at $59, RV hook-ups start at $22, and tent camping is $5.50 per person per night. Canoe rental begins at $39 a day.

Maggard's Canoe & Corkery Camp (417-532-7616 or 1-888-546-9788; www.nianguariver.com), 15750 SR 64, Lebanon, Mo. Most of the campsites are shaded, with picnic tables and flush toilets close by. Two days of camping are free year-round (Sun.–Thurs. nights, holidays not included) with canoe or raft rental. Camping without a rental runs $7 per night per person, and canoe rental starts at $34–42. Pets are not allowed.

Niangua River Oasis Canoe Rental (417-532-6333 or 1-800-748-7249; www.nrocanoe.com), 171 NRO Rd., Lebanon, Mo. Canoes are $40. Eleven cabins and guests houses range in price from $65–325 per night. Smoking, tents, and pets are not permitted in the guest house and cabin area. Two nights of tent camping are provided (when available) with canoe rental. This campground has security personnel, and loud noise isn't tolerated after 11 PM. Dogs are permitted only on a leash and only in the campground.

Redbeard's Ranch (417-588-7337; www.redbeardsranch.com), 30075 Marigold Dr., Lebanon, Mo. Owned and operated by Jane and Bud Meador, Redbeard's is located on 295 acres with more than a mile of Niangua River frontage. In winter, open most weekends from 6 PM Fri. to 3 PM Sun. Open daily Apr.–Sept., and during the fall and winter season by advance reservations only. This is a very family-oriented environment, and the owners do not tolerate wild parties or foul language. Visitors can take advantage of guided trail rides, kiddie rides, bow hunting, and hayrides. Though cabins are expected to be built in the future, at present only primitive camping spots (there are showers and flush toilets) are available. The cost is $6 per person per night. Canoe rental starts at $38. "Glamping," which translates into glamorous camping in a spacious wall tent, begins at $95 per night for two people.

Riverfront Campground & Canoe Rental (417-588-3386 or 1-888-673-7668; www.riverfrontcamp canoe.com), 13 Riverfront Trail, Lebanon, Mo. A family-owned facility, the premises consist of 200 acres fronting the Niangua. Primitive campsites are $5.50 per person per night; RV sites are $20 per night for two people. Security is provided on the grounds, and breakfast and lunch can be purchased at the camp cookshack. For groups of more than 30, dinners can be catered on request. Riverfront enforces a quiet environment after 11 PM, and a convenience store is stocked with minor provisions. Canoe rental starts at $38.

✔ **Sand Spring Resort** (417-532-5857; www.riverfrontcampcanoe.com), 1996 SR 64, Lebanon, Mo. Reservations only. This is a more upscale facility with above-average accommodations; it is owned by the same family that operates **Riverfront Campground.** Prices run from $44 for a single sleeper to $95 for a suite. Canoe rental starts at $35. A full-service restaurant with weekend and breakfast buffet is located within the confines of the resort, and fly-fishing tips and seminars are regularly available.

Big Piney and Gasconade Rivers
✔ ✿ **Boiling Spring Campground** (573-759-7294; www.dixoncamping.com), 18700 Cliff Rd., Dixon, Mo. Floats are available on both the Big Piney and Gasconade Rivers, with the campground open year-round. Camping begins at $6 for a primitive site and $25 for an RV spot. RV lodges are available for $69 per day. Canoe rental starts at $50. This is a simple campground, but one that is kept up. The facilities include tent camping sites, RV hook-ups, restrooms and showers, a lighted boat ramp, camp grills, picnic tables, volleyball nets, and horseshoe pits.

🐾 ✿ ✔ **Rich's Last Resort** (573-435-6669; www.richslastresort.com), 3401 Windsor Ln., Duke, Mo. Rich's has provided camping, canoes, and cabins since 1972. It's been a home to so many campers and floaters that the owners are actually compiling a book from the memories and anecdotes of the regulars. The campground offers tent sites beginning at $7 per person, with electrical hook-up for RVs costing an additional $7 per night. For scout, church, and youth groups, tent sites are $5 per night. Cabins begin at

$60, and while pets are allowed, there is a $5 nightly charge for dogs. Canoe rental for Big Piney floats runs in the $42 vicinity, and rafts and kayaks are available. Rich's is open from around the beginning of turkey season in April until the end of deer season in November.

🐾 ✔ **Lay Z Day Canoes and Camping** (573-336-8639; www.layzday.com), 23455 Teak Ln., St. Robert, Mo. Located 3 miles south of I-44 off Exit 163, the Lay Z Day offers several **Full Moon Floats** on the Big Piney each summer (whenever there is a full moon, more or less). The trip begins at 7:30 PM and ends at midnight. It features a hot dog and marshmallow roast underneath an old railroad trestle bridge. Prices for this trip should be obtained by calling in advance. Regular canoe rental starts at $45, and campsites begin at $8 for a primitive site or $25 for an RV site.

🐾 ✿ ✔ **Gasconade Hills Resort** (573-765-3044 or 1-800-869-6861; www.canoemissouri.com), 28425 Spring Rd., Richland, Mo. Gasconade Hills offers 14 cabins, cottages, and a lodge for nightly or weekly rental. Two cabins front the river, and six allow dogs inside. Charges run from $95 (for cabins) to $250 (for the lodge) per night. Canoes, kayaks, jon boats (nice on the Gasconade), rafts, and tubes are available, with canoe rental beginning at $42. Primitive campsites start at $7; RV sites, $22. Hot showers, a swimming pool, and a store are on the premises, and for a small charge the resort holds a fantastic Saturday night BBQ. This is a true family retreat, situated in a drop-dead gorgeous location on the Gasconade. No boom boxes, loud music, foul language, or obnoxious behavior is permitted, and public intoxication results in expulsion from the premises with no refund. Gasconade Hills is the place for campers with kids, or simply those who don't wish to put up with screaming yahoos.

Courtois Creek, Huzzah Creek, Meramec River

🐾 🛶 Ozark Outdoors (573-245-6437 or 1-800-888-0023; www.ozarkout doors.net), 200 Ozark Outdoor Ln., Leasburg, Mo. The amenities offered by outfitters tend to increase when you move up to the Meramec River and its tributaries. Ozark Outdoors is no exception, offering floating, camping, and cabins on the Meramec, Huzzah, and Courtois. There are many options here for trips and groups, but daily canoe rental starts at $23 on weekends ($17.50 weekdays). No children under 12 are allowed without parental supervision. Campsites are either on or near the banks of the Meramec River; most are shaded and include picnic tables and grills. Amenities at the campground include a 30-by-50-foot swimming pool, full-service shower house, fishing, swimming, children's area, hiking trails, volleyball, and horseshoes. Campsites start at $10 per night for adults, $7 for children 8–12. Full hook-ups are $11 per night for RVs, plus the general campground fee. For those who don't feel like truly roughing it or seek a bit more privacy, Ozark Outdoors has a number of small log cabins. They come complete with kitchenette, refrigerator, microwave, air-conditioning/heat, restroom, shower, and one bedroom with bunk beds and a full-sized bed. Weekend rates start at $75 per night. A 10-unit motel is also on the premises.

🐾 🛶 Bass' River Resort (1-800-392-3700; www.bassresort.com), P.O. Box BB, Steelville, MO 65565. This resort offers everything from canoeing and rafting to steak dinners and log cabins. Numerous trip plans to fit most needs are offered on the Meramec, Huzzah, and Courtois. Primitive campsites, cabins, A-frames, a "hideaway house," and more are the lodging options at Bass' River Resort. Prices run from $8.50 for a campsite to $59 for a cabin to nearly $369 per night for a house. Canoe rental starts at $38 per canoe (or $19 per person). A nice touch here is that the resort can provide a number of different horseback adventures, most in the $20–40 range.

🛶 Huzzah Valley Resort (573-786-8412 or 1-800-367-4516; www.huzzah valley.com), 970 E. Hwy. 8, Steelville, Mo. Huzzah Valley Resort has been outfitting trips on the Huzzah, Courtois, and Meramec Rivers since 1979, and this operation makes a considerable effort to provide a large variety of options and services. Lodging at Huzzah comes in a number of forms. Weekend campsites start at $10.65 and come with an outdoor table and fire ring with BBQ grill. All the campsites are near the beaches, swimming, and playgrounds. RV enthusiasts can get full hook-ups, including 30- or 50-amp electric, and never fret about hitting slideouts with their neighbors. Pull-through sites are also available for big rigs. A motel room starts at $63.83, and cabins start at $93.70. If you have a large group, you can rent one of several renovated farmhouses for $1,150 per two nights' lodging. That sounds steep until you realize there is a 20-person minimum and the houses have six bedrooms capable of sleeping four to six people each. Keep in mind that neither smoking nor pets are permitted in the cabins or farmhouses. Canoe rental starts at $19, and one of several horseback excursions begins at $23 (a "kiddie ride" is offered for around $6). Huzzah also provides hiking trails, volleyball, hayrides, and a well-stocked store. Best of all—and more campgrounds should do this—there is an area for families and a "loud" area.

♘ ♥ ♪ **Garrison's Canoe Rental RV Park and Resort** (573-775-2410 or 1-800-367-8945; www.garrisons resort.com), P.O. Box 1069, Steelville, MO 65565. Garrison's is yet another one of the resorts offering a massive menu. Floats are available on the Meramec, Huzzah, and Courtois, with canoe rental beginning at $38. Horseback trail rides come in a gamut of packages and choices. The campgrounds focus on families and groups, and lodging choices are infinite. You can rent a $7.70 tent site, or spring for a $660-per-night river bluff lodge. In between is every size and shape of cabin, ranch house, RV spot, and cottage imaginable. You can even rent a tent in the event you left yours lying in the driveway back home. All services are available between Memorial Day and Labor Day; if you're vacationing in winter, call to see what is available and open. Garrison's holds a number of festivals throughout the year. Independence Day is big, as is the annual bluegrass festival. The resort has a store on-site, as well as a rustic diner serving weekend meals cafeteria-style.

♥ ♪ **Bird's Nest Lodge** (573-775-2606 or 1-877-707-7238; www.birds nestlodge.com), P.O. Box 898, Birds Nest Rd., Steelville, MO 65565. Bird's Nest Lodge is the only place I've ever seen that offers gigging tours and provides gigging guides. Gigging, if you've never done it or heard of it (and most people haven't if they aren't from the Ozarks), basically involves killing fish with sharp sticks. In short, you spear the little devils from boats. It's pretty popular in these parts—so popular, in fact, that it has its own legal season. The staff at Bird's Nest will not only take you out for a day of gigging, but also clean and cook your catch later on. It's doubtful you will find this service anywhere else in the country. For more traditional fun (but seriously, you should go gigging sometime just to say you've done it), float trips begin at $40 per canoe. Lodging starts at $10 for a campsite and runs up to $55 for a modern cabin. Premier cabins feature hot tubs. Many package plans are offered on these 29 acres of riverfront. The lodge's dining hall is rustic but good, with a large outdoor deck (with tables) overlooking the Meramec River.

✸ Where to Eat

EATING OUT A Slice of Pie (573-364-6203), 601 Kingshighway, Rolla, Mo. It's a little cubbyhole of a place, marked with a small sign and painted arrow next to a Laundromat. The parking lot holds only a few cars, but it probably sees more auto traffic than I-44. The comings and goings at A Slice of Pie are nonstop. This little shop is a local tradition sure to please, whether you're eating in or grabbing pie to go. Its excellent reputation is justified, for the pies, cakes, and cheesecakes offered here will remind you of the kind Grandma used to make (assuming, of course, that

Grandma came from the Ozarks and made pies with crusts as tasty as their filling). The choices are endless, from apple and blackberry crumb to chocolate chip mint to Tahitian cream. There is a "Toll House" pie, pecan pie, strawberry rhubarb, mincemeat, and mudslide. A favorite cheesecake is the white chocolate cappuccino, and the apple walnut cake is a work of art. It should be noted that not all pies are offered on all days—the current menu is on a blackboard behind the counter—but at any given moment you'll have enough selections that decision making will become difficult. Prices vary, but are in the $5 a slice range. Whole and half-pies are available, as are cakes, quiches, pot pies, and sandwiches. Hours are 10–10 daily. There's always a pie of the month, and special orders can be provided with a couple days' notice.

The Missouri Hick Bar-B-Q (573-885-6791), 913 E. Washington St., Cuba, Mo. Open Mon.–Thurs. 11–8, Sat.–Sun. 11–9. The most basic rule of thumb when seeking out a BBQ joint is this: You should smell it long before you see it. If the scent of hick-ory reaches you inside the car, the place is usually worth a try. The Missouri Hick Bar-B-Q passes this initial litmus test with flying colors. The restaurant is housed in a relatively new, two-story building purposefully rustic in appearance, and the staff is very friendly and happy. Smoking all the meat over wood (as is the only true way to BBQ), the Hick features brisket, ribs (pork), chicken, and sausage. Combo platters, a large number of side dishes, family packs, and catering are also available. Prices run from $5.49 for a pulled-pork sandwich to $16.95 for a full slab and all the fixin's. There is a children's menu, and for those who really want something different, Ory's Spud is a house specialty. This is a monster-sized baked potato full of baked beans and pulled pork, covered with cheddar and Monterey Jack cheese ($6.99). The ribs are first-rate here; the pitmaster at the Hick applies a dry rub prior to cooking that is tasty without being overpowering. It seems to hold traces of pepper and paprika, but there is also a slight sweetness. No matter the ingredients, the rub creates a light

THE MISSOURI HICK BAR-B-Q

crust that adds character without numbing the taste buds.

Ⴒ **Zeno's Steakhouse** (573-364-1301; www.zenos.biz), 1621 Martin Springs Dr., Rolla, Mo. Serving the Rolla area for more than 40 years, Zeno's has long been a local tradition for breakfast, lunch, and dinner. Located at the 184 exit off I-44 (a quick 0.25-mile drive down Martin Springs Dr.), the entire facility encompasses not only the restaurant itself, but also a motel and **Scheffer's Lounge.** For an appetizer, many people choose the "Madisonion"—a giant, blooming onion served with a special sauce ($7.95). "Center of the Plate" steaks are this restaurant's primary claim to fame, with prices ranging upward from $20.50. "Zeno's Pride," a 20-ounce slab of prime beef, is $29.50. A number of traditional Italian dishes are on the menu, and seafood offerings include an entire channel catfish ($11.90), walleye ($19.95), and either broiled or batter-fried lobster (market price). If you've never had a batter-fried lobster, you should try it. In the Ozarks deep frying is considered a fine art, and this is one tasty crustacean.

Johnny's Hickory Pit BBQ (573-364-4838), 201 W. SR 72, Rolla, Mo. Johnny's Hickory Pit used to be known as Johnny's Smokestack. The local rumor mill states that the original owners are once again holding the reins, which might explain a higher quality fare than was present when this book was first written in 2006. According to many folks, Johnny's is the *only* place in the northern Ozarks for BBQ. It's been a consistent winner in the *Rural Missouri* magazine readers' poll, and its BBQ buffet (daily 11–2; Fri.–Sat. 5–8; closed Mon.) draws a huge crowd. A full-slab rib

dinner, burnt ends, steaks, and catfish are also on the menu. Although I wouldn't give this restaurant nearly the accolades others do—the sauce is a little bit too sweet and tomato-heavy for my taste—it is a good choice while in the Rolla area. The interior is comfortable and the portions are hearty. Johnny's also offers beer and wine.

🦐 🍴 ♿ **Gary's Dowd's Catfish House** (417-532-1777; http://dowds catfishandbbq.com), 1710 W. Elm (old Route 66), Lebanon, Mo. Open daily at 11 AM. Reservations are recommended on Friday and Saturday nights, and for Sunday lunch. Located at Exit 127 off I-44 on old Route 66, Dowd's is another local favorite that has changed hands since the first edition of this book. It was good before, but it has now evolved into one of my all-time favorite places. As the name says, the specialty is catfish. These fillets are all boneless and come either deep fried or broiled. The batter on the deep-fried version is light, and the consistently high quality of this eatery rates at 100 percent. The four-fillet meal (the smallest) goes for $9.15 and comes with hush puppies; choice of potato, a side salad, or pinto beans; tomato relish; and coleslaw. If you think you could eat all that and still be ravenous, you'll be happy to know that Dowd's is famous for its all-you-can-eat dinners. Catfish, of course, serves as the basis for all of them. At $13.99, the all-you-can-eat catfish dinner features the same sides as the regular dinner, but with the addition of fried okra after 4 PM. From there, though, the choices multiply. You can get an all-you-can-eat catfish, shrimp, or ribs meal for $15.39 (or get all three—ribs, shrimp, and catfish for $16.49). The catfish, shrimp, and crab legs selection is $24.99. Even children get an all-you-can-eat option. The prices start at $1.50 for each year up to 11 years of age. Dowd's is also a fine BBQ smokehouse, and (as if you didn't expect this) all-you-can-eat BBQ entrées (brisket, ribs, or chicken) begin at $10.99.

The Cave Restaurant and Resort (573-765-4554; www.thecaverestaurant andresort.com), 26880 Rochester Rd., Richland, Mo. Open daily 11:30–8:30 during the spring and summer. Winter hours begin on Oct. 1. Formerly known as the Caveman BBQ and Steak House, more than 160 tons of rock were smashed, drilled, shoveled, and carted to create this unique establishment. The resulting cave is located on a bluff 100 feet above the Gasconade River. Nearly 20 years after the excavation was finished, the restaurant remains a huge hit not only with locals, but with patrons from around the world. That's not a surprise, as the current owner is Gary Dyer (who formerly owned Dowd's Catfish House in Lebanon). Full of waterfalls, fish ponds, and fountains— and sporting a carpeted floor (easier on the feet than rocks)—the Cave's humidifiers remove 9 pounds of water from the air per hour. The resulting atmosphere is comfortable, with the temperature remaining a constant 69 degrees. Visitors park in a gravel lot, are driven to an elevator, and then are lifted the 100 feet to the restaurant by elevator.

Visitors first come to see this most unusual of restaurants, but they return for the food. The Cave is known for its hickory-smoked ribs, steaks, seafood, cheesecake, home-made pies, and a huge salad bar. This is just part of the story. A 36-ounce

rib eye is available for $49.99, but you can also order Italian dishes (Gary's specialty) or a wide variety of other items from the lengthy menu. Prices for appetizers begin at $5.99.

The establishment has expanded since 2006, and now offers canoe rental, rustic cabins, and outdoor picnics complete with bluegrass bands.

♪ ℗ ♿ **Bennett Spring Dining Lodge** (417-532-4547), 26250 SR 64A, Lebanon, Mo. The Bennett Spring Dining Lodge was built by Franklin Roosevelt's Civilian Conservation Corps in 1933. Costing $14,000 at that time, it still reflects that great rustic look with plenty of stone and dark wood. Today the dining lodge remains a favorite with the thousands of visitors who descend upon Bennett Spring each year. Open daily from 7 AM to one hour past the whistle (during trout season it signifies the end of the day's fishing), the lodge is open for breakfast, lunch, and dinner. Breakfast and dinner buffets are offered Saturday and Sunday mornings and Friday and Saturday nights. While not a fancy place, Bennett Spring Dining Lodge does offer a few twists along with traditional favorites. You can order sandwiches from a long list, and prices are generally in the $6–$15 range. The lodge will cook your fresh trout to order (you have to catch it and clean it), and the meal comes with soup, salad bar, and two side dishes. Children 10 and younger can eat at the buffet for half price.

✳ **Entertainment**

♪ ♿ **Meramec Music Theater** (573-775-5999; www.mmt.misn.com), SR 8 West, Steelville, Mo. Live performances take place from Mar.–Dec. Prices for most shows are $18 for adults, $17 for senior citizens, and $9 for kids 12 and younger. A truly excellent facility for such a small town, the Meramec Music Theater's Christmas show is considered a very big deal. Still, quality entertainment can be found in this venue every month save January and February (not because awful music is performed in January and February, but rather because the theater is closed). Shows generally take place once per week, and the normal starting time is 2 or 7. Performances tend to be in the genre of classic country, gospel, bluegrass, or cowboy music, but you'll occasionally find a headliner out of Branson.

🐟 𝒶 ⛟ **Highway 19 Drive-In** (573-885-7752) 5853 SR 19, Cuba, Mo. The drive-in movie is often thought of as a thing of the past, but somehow the legacy of Route 66 has allowed a few of these American treasures to hang on. In Cuba, Mo., it seems the drive-in is alive and well. For more than 50 years the Highway 19's solo silver screen has stood tall over a grassy parking lot. Holding 250 cars, this bit of nostalgia even still has some of the old-style car speakers (though radio sound is available, too). This memory of simpler times can be found just north of the I-44 and SR 19 intersection. Ticket prices are $8 for adults and $2 for children.

SPECTATOR SPORTS 𝒶 ⛟
Lebanon I-44 Speedway (417-532-2060; www.i44speedway.net), 24069 SR 66, Lebanon, Mo. Auto racing has moved into the first tier of spectator sports, and nowhere is this trend more evident than at the I-44 Speedway. A new, high-banked, asphalt oval track was built in 2009, and races take place every Saturday, May 7–Oct. 1. Divisions include late models, modi-

fieds, factory stocks, and bombers. The gates open at 5 PM, and admission is $10 for adults, $7 for children 11–15, and free for those under 10.

✴ Selective Shopping

Heartland Antique Mall (417-532-9350; www.heartlandantiquemall lebanon), 2500 Industrial Dr., Lebanon, Mo. Open daily 8–8. With 40,000 square feet and 250 individual dealers, Heartland is an antique lover's dream come true. There are countless aisles of antiques, and the staff is both knowledgeable and courteous. Found inside the mall is **Knife Country,** which features a nice selection of blades, and a **Wisconsin Cheese** outlet boasting 130 varieties. Next door (and this place is worth it just for the free samples) is a 5,000-square-foot **Russell Stover** candy outlet. The complex is located off I-44 at Exit 127.

Lebanon Books (417-532-2500), 1116 Lynn Ave., Lebanon, Mo. You'll find a bit of everything in Lebanon Books, the largest bookstore in town. Aside from the latest best-selling tomes, the store carries magazines, toys, games, gifts, and even some sporting goods.

Shepherd Hills Factory Outlet (417-532-7000 or 1-800-727-4643; www.shephills.com), 1900 W. Elm St. Lebanon, Mo. Open daily 8–8. Most factory outlets are pretty much the same, offering little of unique value. Such cannot be said of the Shepherd Hills Factory Outlet. It's ranked as the world's largest dealer of Case pocketknives, but wandering the aisles of this huge store will result in even greater finds. There is Mikasa china, Denby pottery, Hummel figurines, and a large selection of walnut bowls and carvings. You will find massive amounts of pictures, candles, baskets, artificial flowers, and wind chimes. Best of all is an unbelievable number of Zippo lighters and Swiss Army knives. Until you've seen some of the ones for sale here, you wouldn't have believed so many blades and tools could fit into a single implement.

Nancy Ballhagen's Puzzles (417-286-3837; www.missouripuzzle.com), 25211 Garden Crest Rd., Lebanon, Mo. (Exit 135 off I-44 east of Lebanon). Open daily 11–4; call first if you wish to visit on Sun. Closed most major holidays. Nancy Ballhagen likes her puzzles. She likes them so much that she keeps more than 3,200 different jigsaw puzzles in stock at her store. Obtained from more than 50 American and European companies, the puzzles range in size from 100 to 18,000 pieces. From clown puzzles and Civil War puzzles to covered bridge puzzles and Colorado ski resort puzzles, the puzzling topics run from A to Z (obviously, I stopped looking at C). They might be constructed of wood or metal. They might be two dimensional or three dimensional (the four-dimensional puzzle, which allows you to travel through time, is not yet on the market). When completed, they might appear in holograph form or as a photomosaic. The store does a booming online business, too.

The Book Addict (573-265-5665), 116 N. Jefferson St., Saint James, Mo. Those who enjoy the written word should make a point of stopping into the Book Addict, a nice little store on the main drag of St. James. Not only does this surprising shop have more than 20,000 used volumes for sale (surely you can find something to read with this many choices), but it also features locally made stained-glass art pieces.

✳ Special Events

May **Frog Fest** (www.frogfest.info), Waynesville, Mo. Held annually on the first weekend in May, Waynesville's two-day Frog Fest offers bluegrass, food vendors, frog jumping, frog kissing, and a three-legged race (for humans, not frogs). The festival began when the Missouri Department of Transportation was widening the road into Waynesville. An outcropping seemed to have a familiar shape, and enterprising locals painted it into the likeness of a frog. That the rock only kinda/sorta looks like a frog is not really important.

Bluegrass Pickin' Time (573-759-7716; www.bluegrasspickintime.com), Carol's Memorial Bluegrass Park, N. SR 133, Dixon, Mo. For nearly three decades, the Jones family has played host to one of the best bluegrass festivals in the country on their farm just north of Dixon. Though the event takes place twice per summer— on Memorial Day and Labor Day weekends—it is usually best to arrive a couple of days before the actual performances start. There is parking for more than 1,000 cars and electricity for 400 RVs, and most of the folks camping out will have their own impromptu concerts. Everyone is welcome (bring an instrument, no matter what it may be)—this is a real family event. Drugs and alcohol are forbidden. There's an admission charge ($10 for Thurs., $20 for Fri. and Sat.) or three- and four-day passes for $35 and $45, respectively), but you'll more than get your money's worth.

June **Pulaski County Regional Fair**
(816-261-6051; www.pulaskicounty
regionalfair.com), St. Robert City
Park, St. Robert, Mo. Taking place
each year in early June, Pulaski County
puts on a fair featuring crafts, a carnival, a livestock show, and bull riding.
If you want to see a real fair, this is a
good one. Admission is free, but you'll
have to buy tickets for the carnival
rides or ATV rodeo.

July **Laclede County Fair** (417-322-
5349), Laclede County Fairgrounds,
Lebanon, Mo. Laclede County's fair
has been a tradition since 1910. Livestock displays are numerous, and
evenings feature a demolition derby,
horse pulls, and truck pulls. A full
midway lights up the grounds with
the sights and sounds of carnie games
(and carnie workers, of course).

August **Central Missouri Regional
Fair** (573-578-3314), Regional Fairgrounds, US 63 South, Rolla, Mo.
Drawing nearly 15,000 people, Rolla's
fair is a four-day event that occurs in
early August. It's a large-scale version
of the smaller county fairs—you can
easily spend several days at this event
and not feel you've seen it all. There's
a $15 admission fee, but that includes
carnival rides and entertainment.

September **Dixon Cow Days** (573-
759-3980), Dixon City Park, SR 133,
Dixon, Mo. In 1929, Dixon merchants
hoped to attract Depression-era shoppers to town. For several months the
hook was a drawing for a free cow.
Not only did thousands of people
come to town, but they stayed for
dancing, dining, and discounted retail
items. The tradition soon died off, but
Dixon merchants of the 1980s rein-
carnated it. Thus was born Cow Days,
a two-day event held annually on the
third weekend in September. You can
enter the drawing to win your own
cow, as well as enjoy crafts, street
dances, live music, parades, and a
beauty pageant. Really, who could
pass up the chance to play Cow Patty
Bingo? Admission is free.

Paw Paw Daze (573-774-5368),
Waynesville City Park, Waynesville,
Mo. Waynesville Planter's Club
spends a Saturday in late September
celebrating the pawpaw tree. This
annual event offers a chance to dig
into some pawpaw pie and pawpaw
jam. Craftsmen and vendors are
always on hand with examples of
wood carving, basket weaving, and
other traditional arts.

Bluegrass Pickin' Time (see May).

THE LAKE OF THE OZARKS

As is true with many rural residents of south Missouri, I have mixed feelings about the Lake of the Ozarks. On the one hand, there are fond childhood memories of family visits to our cousin Junior's primitive fishing resort and marina near Gravois Mills. On the other, crossing to the east side of the lake and viewing the perpetual development on US 54, I am reminded of the frenzy for dollars that transformed Florida from bucolic wonderland to a close encounter of the hyped kind. Progress has its price, and the bargain struck by the Lake of the Ozarks included trading a bucket of tradition for a barrel of tourism. The frenzy of building has not slowed in the five years since this book was first published. It's increased, despite times of economic trouble.

But beauty is in the eye. For many, the lake—which covers 57,000 acres and includes 1,375 miles of shoreline—is known as the Midwest Coast. The entire area is a cross between upscale trendy and downscale day trip, with only a lingering hint of the old-time Ozarks remaining. Nationally regarded golf courses, luxurious resorts, and restaurants with $500 bottles of wine share space with go-cart tracks, burger joints, water parks, and T-shirt shacks. The pace (as well as the shopping possibilities) is literally nonstop. Boats by the thousands cruise the 129-mile main channel and its tributaries, and those seeking an outdoor vacation with an urban flair will not be disappointed.

The Lake of the Ozarks originally sought to distance itself from its locale. Union Electric Light and Power of St. Louis, the firm that built Bagnell Dam, first called it the Osage Reservoir. In 1931, when the lake was bank-full, members of the Missouri Congress thought it deserved more respect. After all, at the time this was the largest human-made lake in the world. Their idea was to honor a famous (and long-dead) Missouri politician. For a brief time the Lake of the Ozarks was known as Lake Benton. But ad executives and promoters usually win the day in these matters, and by 1932 virtually every piece of ad copy to reach the public extolled the virtues of Lake of the Ozarks. It sounded better, in a build-it-and-they-will-come sort of way.

The history of the lake reaches back to the Osage Indians, who traditionally wintered in the area. French fur trappers may have been the first white residents (leading to communities such as Gravois Mills and Versailles), and Zebulon Pike and his gang of intrepid explorers passed close by. It is known that just after

The Lake of the Ozarks

1800 both Daniel Boone and his son Nathan trapped beaver on Ha Ha Tonka Lake. By the early 1800s white settlers were moving in, and in 1825 the Osage ceded all their lands and were moved west. Up until the early 1900s the lake region was just like the rest of the Ozarks. Those who settled here were fond of isolation and independence (though the majority were of German descent, in contrast with the Scots-Irish who adopted the Ozark lands to the south). The Civil War brought regional conflicts, bushwhackers, and outlaws. People lived off the land, making the necessities themselves and making money from outside sources as required.

The idea of damming the Osage River, and by extension the tributaries of Gravois Creek, the Grand Auglaize River, and the Niangua River, came about shortly after the turn of the 20th century. When Union Electric picked up the reins of the project, the idea became a reality. Construction of Bagnell Dam began in 1929, privately financed to the tune of $30 million (the last privately financed dam in America). More than 20,000 workers flocked to the massive undertaking, hungry for the Depression-era jobs. Not so happy were those who lived in towns such as Linn Creek, which was to be inundated. Providing the luxury of electric lights to St. Louis city folks didn't strike the insular locals as a particularly rational or convincing reason for the bum's rush, but the end result was predictable. More than 500 Linn Creek residents were dislodged from the simple farmsteads they had treasured for generations (the government had given Union Electric the power to condemn homes and farms), 32 cemeteries were relocated, countless buildings were destroyed, and 30,000 acres of timber were cleared. Bagnell Dam, 2,500 feet long and 150 feet high, was completed in record time. By May 1931, there was boat traffic on the lake; production of electricity began the following December.

Today the production of power shares prominence with the tourist industry. The Lake of the Ozarks falls into the category of prepackaged fun in that you will not find any unpleasant surprises here. You can enjoy a fine meal, hear popular music, hire a guide, spend the day waterskiing, shop 'til you drop, and retire in a sumptuous suite featuring turndown service and chocolates on your pillow. The bad news is that such homogenized and utterly safe conformity makes for few happy surprises. I'm not saying it isn't fun; for millions the lake is the epitome of a good time. I am saying it is fun in the amusement park fashion, with sensory overload and a predictable plot being a given. Many folks refer to the Lake region as "Little St. Louis." As the years progress, that moniker is becoming more and more apt.

After 75 years, natives of the predominantly rural Ozarks will still freely expound that the big lake and its environs don't reflect their heritage or lifestyle. In the geographic sense they are wrong, but in the cultural sense they could not be more on the money. Perhaps better stated, the lake region resides in a type of Ozarks that's different from what "real" Ozarkers know and love.

AREA CODES The Lake of the Ozarks is a huge body of water, and if taken in its entirety (with connecting lakes and river tributaries to the north and west included), it would encompass several area codes. All the towns and attractions covered in this chapter, however, are found in the **573** area code.

GUIDANCE Long known as the Midwest's summer playground, the Lake of the Ozarks is adept at promoting its infinite recreational opportunities, events, and businesses. Six different chambers and visitors bureaus offer extensive websites and will gladly answer questions and mail vacation guides.

Lake of the Ozarks Convention and Visitor Bureau (1-800-386-5253; www .funlake.com), 5815 US 54, Osage Beach, Mo. This should be your first stop, as it will tell you everything you ever wanted to know about the Lake of the Ozarks but were afraid to ask. Contact the bureau via phone or website and request its free guide, which runs more than 150 pages and is packed with details pertaining to lodging, dining, boating, golf, and area history.

The Lake of the Ozarks West Chamber of Commerce (573-374-5500; www.lakewestchamber.com), 125 Oddo Dr., Sunrise Beach, Mo. This chamber includes the towns of Gravois Mills, Laurie, Sunrise Beach, and Greenview. The visitors center can be found on SR 5 in Sunrise Beach.

Camdenton Chamber of Commerce (573-346-2227 or 1-800-769-1004; www .camdentonchamber.com), 73 W. US 54, Camdenton, Mo. Serving the communities of Camdenton and Linn Creek, the Camdenton Chamber also provides data on both the Big and Little Arms of the Niangua River.

Lake Area Chamber of Commerce (573-964-1008 or 1-800-451-4117; www .lakeareachamber.com), 1 Willmore Ln., Lake Ozark, Mo. Specializing in the east side of the lake, this chamber can provide you with details on Lake Ozark, Osage Beach, Horseshoe Bend, North Shore, Linn Creek, and Kaiser. It's located in the historic Willmore Lodge just north of Bagnell Dam.

Eldon Chamber of Commerce (573-392-3752; www.eldonchamber.com), 203 E. First St., Eldon, Mo. To the north and east of the lake proper, Eldon offers a respite from the heaviest of the tourist traffic.

Versailles Chamber of Commerce (573-378-4401; www.versailleschamber .com), 109 N. Monroe, Versailles, Mo. Versailles is a historic town that predates the building of the lake. Its chamber can provide guidance on water activities, dining, and the local Mennonite community.

GETTING THERE *By car:* Whether driving in from Springfield or St. Louis, the simplest way to the Lake of the Ozarks is via I-44. Take the 130 exit at Lebanon, Mo., and head north on SR 5 for 25 miles to Camdenton. From there, either continue on SR 5 to visit the western side of the lake or turn right onto US 54 to reach the eastern. If traveling from Kansas City, Mo., take I-70 East to Columbia, Mo., and turn right onto US 63 South. At Jefferson City, Mo., turn onto US 54 South, which will take you directly to the lake.

Navigating the Lake of the Ozarks is a bit easier than it was when the first edition of this book came out in 2006. Traffic flows much more smoothly since the completion of the **US 54 Expressway Project.** The old section of US 54 is now known as Osage Beach Boulevard; it has limited access to the new highway. Bagnell Dam Boulevard will give you access to Bagnell Dam, Horseshoe Bend Parkway, and the Community Bridge. The new expressway bypasses all these areas.

By air: The closest major airports to the lake itself are **Lambert–St. Louis International Airport** (314-426-8000; www.lambert-stlouis.com), 10701 Lambert International Blvd. , St. Louis, Mo., **Kansas City International** (816-243-5237; www.flykci.com), One International Square, Kansas City, Mo., and **Springfield-Branson National Airport** (417-868-0500; www.sgf-branson -airport.com), 2300 N. Airport Blvd., Springfield, Mo. Of these, the last is the most convenient, only 75 miles southwest of Camdenton, Mo. Prices are likely the cheapest if flying to or from Kansas City or St. Louis. The lake region does offer five commuter airports for those who might be arriving by small plane.

Lee C. Fine Airport (573-348-5251) offers a 6,500-by-100-foot asphalt runway. It is located on SR 134 in Osage Beach.

Grand Glaize Airport (573-348-4469) is also located in Osage Beach, at the intersection of US 54 and SR KK. Its asphalt runway is 3,205 feet by 60 feet.

Camdenton Memorial Airport (573-346-3600) is on SR 5 South in Camdenton. The airport's asphalt runway is 4,000 feet by 75 feet.

Eldon Model Airpark (573-392-2291) is situated at Airport Rd. and US 54 in Eldon. The runway is concrete and measures 3,330 feet by 75 feet.

Roy Otten Memorial Airfield (573-378-6373) in Versailles, Mo., has a concrete runway of 2,800 feet by 40 feet. The address is 10998 SR 52.

MEDICAL EMERGENCIES Lake Regional Hospital (573-348-8000; www .lakeregional.com), 54 Hospital Dr., Osage Beach, Mo. Lake Regional is a 300,000-square-foot, 116-bed hospital offering comprehensive services such as cardiac, oncology, orthopedic, and ob-gyn care. The facility is state of the art, with 75 doctors and more than 1,300 total employees on staff. The emergency department is first rate, having been designated a Level III Trauma Center by the Bureau of Emergency Medical Services. The Lake Regional System provides services in seven primary care clinics, one urgent care clinic, and 14 specialty clinics over a five-county area.

✳ Wandering Around

EXPLORING BY CAR When you wish to escape the frenzy of the Osage Beach area and have a relaxing picnic, don't forget the "other dam" on the Lake of the Ozarks. **Tunnel Dam,** located 20 miles west of Camdenton, crosses the **Big Niangua River.** The drive to Tunnel Dam is outstanding, running through hills and deep forests, crossing low water and one-lane bridges. Many times you will find yourself on old gravel roads that will make you feel as if you've slipped 50 years back in time.

Take US 54 west out of Camdenton for 8.4 miles to the junction of SR J and SR U. Turn left onto SR U, then immediately turn right, heading 2.5 miles to Edith.

TUNNEL DAM

Turn right onto Whistle Rd. (gravel), travel 1 mile, and cross the small bridge. This is **Tunnel Dam Road** (in local lingo, the area is known as "the Whistle"). You will probably find no better place for a picnic in the Lake of the Ozarks vicinity. The water is cool, clear, and shallow enough that kids can wade and play to their hearts' content. This is not a speedboat place (you'll understand when you see it), but it could be the ultimate spot to splash around in an inner tube, canoe, or kayak.

Past the Whistle, you can travel on up (and up, and up, and up) Tunnel Dam Rd. to the top of some very large hills. Make sure to stop and look around, for the scenic vista brings meaning to the term *photo opportunity*. You will be looking down on the dam and powerhouse, not to mention green-forested hills. This area has neither the urban pace nor the dining/dancing/shopping experiences prevalent on the Bagnell Dam Strip, but it is one of the few places in the Lake of the Ozarks region that will remind you that you're in the Ozarks. This drive offers the perfect contrast between old and new, what is and what was.

EXPLORING BY FOOT Colosseum Trail/Ha Ha Tonka State Park (573-346-2986; www.mostateparks.com/hahatonka.htm), 1491 SR D, Camdenton, Mo. If you want a relatively short (half-mile) hike with splendid sights, Colosseum Trail will gladly fill the bill. Beginning at the Natural Bridge parking lot, you will pass underneath the 70-foot-wide, 60-foot-long, 100-foot-high natural bridge. Continue following the trail and you may venture to the Colosseum, a sinkhole 500 feet long and 300 feet wide. The history and legend behind this area is unsurpassed. Within the Colosseum is Whispering Dell Sink—more than 150 foot deep—and both Counterfeiter's and Robber's Caves. These shelters were

"THE WHISTLE"

used by outlaws in the 1830s (true to the name, one of the caves held the printing press of a gang of counterfeiters). It should be noted that while parts of the Colosseum Trail are ranked as moderately difficult, the trek down Whispering Dell Sink to the spring should only be attempted by those in very good shape. There are more than 300 steep wooden steps, enough to test the calves, knees, and lungs of seasoned hikers (it about killed me).

EXPLORING BY WATER The Missouri Department of Natural Resources came up with a novel twist when it floated the idea (pun intended) of creating the **Aquatic Trail** at **Lake of the Ozarks State Park.** It's a 9-mile trek (requiring about two hours) running between Grand Glaize Beach on the northwest and Public Beach #1 at the lake's east end. A total of 14 stops, each brightly marked with an orange and white buoy, highlight unique geological features, plant life, shelters used by Indians, caves, and glades. One of the best sights is the **Lumberman's Logging Chute.** Before the lake was created (covering Grand Glaize Creek), hill residents often made money by hand-cutting railroad ties and floating them to market. The bluff shown on the tour is where—well over a century ago—these pioneers pushed the ties down into the creek's current. You'll need to bring a boat (or rent one) to take this trip, but a detailed map and booklet of the tour is available at the park office (573-348-2694).

✳ Towns and Villages

Camdenton, Mo. Camdenton is one of the newest county seats in the state of Missouri, established in 1931. When Union Electric Light and Power Company of St. Louis dammed the Osage River, the body of water held captive by Bagnell Dam forced the relocation of more than a few towns. One of these was Linn Creek, the original Camden County seat. Some residents moved to a "new" Linn Creek while others moved to the freshly minted Camdenton, being platted at the intersection of SR 5 and US 54. Camdenton is home to Bridal Cave, which holds the world's record for most underground weddings (to my knowledge there are no records kept for underground divorces). During the third week of April the famous Dogwood Festival brings visitors from around the world. Just a few miles outside town you'll find the not-to-be-missed Ha Ha Tonka State Park and the ruins of what was to have been the opulent 20th-century castle and estate of a wealthy Kansas City businessman.

Gravois Mills, Mo. Before the town was platted in 1884, early Missourians had congregated around a local gristmill, built in approximately 1835. These days the economy of this village of 226 souls centers on the lake. As is true with its neighbor Versailles, Gravois Mills steers clear of the fancy-sounding French pronunciation (the local name is pronounced *grav-OYS* or sometimes *grav-OY*). A few miles north of Gravois Mills is Jacob's Cave. The largest commercialized cave in the lake area, Jacob's boasts of possessing the world's largest geode. It's also the only walk-through cave in Missouri completely accessible to the disabled.

Lake Ozark, Mo. Located on what locals often call the "St. Louis side of the lake," Lake Ozark will never be accused of ignoring the tourists. It's a cornucopia of T-shirt joints, arcades, psychics, tattoo parlors, boutiques, restaurants, and shops, not to mention high-end resorts, homes, golf courses, and condos. This first mile or so of US 54 (south of Bagnell Dam) is referred to as "the Strip," and those seeking go-cart rides (a novelty here are "bumper boats"—basically motorized inner tubes) or ashtrays boasting hillbilly caricatures won't be disappointed. Neither, however, will those seeking world-class dining or in-hotel Pilates classes. Bagnell Dam Blvd. (US Bus. 54) turns off US 54 and winds into the aforementioned upscale district of eating and lodging. Because the Lake of the Ozarks was privately financed (not an Army Corps of Engineers lake, as are most in the Ozarks), homes can be built right down to the waterfront. Many visitors love Lake Ozark, which offers the traditional tourist venues and infinite preplanned vacation packages. Two events are truly noteworthy. Eagle Days takes place in early January, when thousands come to view the bald eagles that winter around the lake. And on the third weekend of September, the three-day annual Osage Mountain Man Rendezvous is a fantastic chance to see buckskin-clad, latter-day Jeremiah Johnsons test their frontier skills.

Laurie, Mo. The town of Laurie didn't officially come into existence until after the state began construction of SR 5 in the mid-1920s, at which time area residents built a general store, gas station, and church (Laurie was the surname of the store's original owners). Though today it is full of resorts, marinas, restaurants, and stores, Laurie still manages to hold on to its unique and friendly personality. A worthwhile stop in Laurie is St. Patrick's Church, Cemetery, and Museum, which dates from 1868. Also, mid-September brings the annual Hillbilly Fair, featuring carnival rides, music, food, a beer garden, and a hillbilly dress contest.

Osage Beach, Mo. Immediately south of Lake Ozark on US 54 is Osage Beach, the tourism epicenter for the Lake of the Ozarks. The community stretches for 8 miles, a testament to consumerism on steroids. You'll find malls and shops of all shapes, creeds, colors, and descriptions. The largest of these is the Osage Beach Premium Outlet, which alone holds 110 top-name manufacturers. You'll also find more golf courses, resorts, restaurants, and nightclubs than you can shake a platinum card at; each year the options seem to become larger and more luxurious. The majority of these venues are well planned and well staffed, offering fine fare and anything your heart desires. Osage Beach is also the main entry to the massive Lake of the Ozarks State Park. The powers that be hold numerous festivals and regionally oriented extravaganzas here; in mid-July, the Midwestcoast Summerfest offers bands, a BMX bicycle stunt team, and more than 100 competing wakeboarders.

Versailles, Mo. The Morgan County seat, Versailles was named for either (a) the palace in France, or (b) a town in Kentucky. Conventional wisdom points to the latter, and those who insist upon pronouncing the town as *ver-SIGH* will immediately be pegged as pretentious tourists. The name is *ver-SALES*. With a population of 2,663, Versailles is an old town (platted in 1835) that seems a laid-back rural contrast to the hectic and increasingly upscale west side of the lake. Numerous Mennonite farms are located in the surrounding area, and drivers should be aware of horse-drawn buggies traveling down the road. Versailles is also the home of the Morgan County Museum, a pre–Civil War hotel that allegedly played host to the likes of Jesse James (one of the 10,000 places Jesse slept) and P. T. Barnum. Not to be outdone in terms of townwide celebrations, the Old Tyme Apple Festival is held the first Saturday of each October.

✳ To See

MUSEUMS 🐾 ✍ ♿ **Old St. Patrick's Church, Cemetery, and Museum** (573-374-6279; www.mothersshrine.org), 176 Marian Dr., Laurie, Mo. French traders were the first non-native people to settle in this area, and by 1822 several of the Osage chiefs had converted to Catholicism, in large part because the first priest allowed the Indians to inject aspects of their culture into traditional rituals. The original St. Patrick's Church was completed in 1868, and much of the original look and feel remains intact. Thanks to a massive renovation, St. Pat's was placed on the National Register of Historic Places in 1979. Inside the church is a museum that was once the living quarters of the circuit-riding priest. Tours of the church and grounds take place Memorial Day–Labor Day, Sun. 10–noon.

🐾 ✍ ♿ **Mothers' Wall of Life** (573-374-6279; www.mothersshrine.org), 176 Marian Dr., Laurie, Mo. Open to the public 24 hours a day. Paying tribute to all mothers and the Virgin Mary, this shrine features 25,000 flowers, a waterfall, fountains, and a 14-foot-tall stainless-steel rendition of Mary. A black granite wall contains the inscribed names of more than 2,300 mothers (the first person to place his mother's name on the wall was the late Pope John Paul II), and 102 flags set off this 80 acres of peace and tranquility. At Christmas, thousands of lights replace the flowers. Anyone can have a name inscribed on the shrine—all that is required is that you have a mother and $350.

THE MOTHERS' WALL OF LIFE

🐾 ✆ **Camden County Museum** (573-346-7191; www.camdencountymuseum .com), 206 S. Locust, Linn Creek, Mo. Mar.–Oct., open Mon.–Fri. 10–4; open on a limited basis or by appointment Nov.–Feb. The Camden County Museum can be found on SR V (just off US 54) in Linn Creek, the former county seat that was relocated upon the construction of Bagnell Dam. The building is in fact the old Linn Creek school, and each classroom revolves around a different historical theme. One of the best exhibits is the weaving room, where local residents create rugs that are available for purchase. The museum is known for hosting dinner theater productions; ballroom dancing with live, big band music; luncheons; garage sales; and children's theater groups. The list of events at this small but enthusiastic museum is endless (you can even have dinner with Santa).

🐾 ✆ **Miller County Museum** (573-793-6998; www.millercountymuseum.org), 2005 SR 52, Tuscumbia, Mo. Generally open mid-May–mid-Sept., Mon., Wed., and Fri. 10–4. You sort of take your chances on hours here, so the wise traveler will call ahead. This museum is of the "folk life" variety and contains all sorts of antique machinery and crafts. Its main goal is to offer a glimpse into the Miller County lifestyle of yesteryear, and it also concentrates on the area's Indian heritage. Located on West SR 52 outside Tuscumbia, the museum is situated in the old Anchor Mill building.

🐾 ✆ **Morgan County Historical Museum** (573-378-5530; www.morganco history.org), 118 N. Monroe St., Versailles, Mo. Open May–Oct., Mon.–Fri. 9–4. The best-known landmark in Versailles is the Martin Hotel, which predates the Civil War and was regularly used by troops of both sides (legend has it that both Old Glory and the Stars and Bars were on the hotel's flagpole, depending upon who was in residence). Now the home of the Morgan County Historical Museum, the hotel's 28 rooms have each been decorated with a different historical theme. When walking into the main lobby, be sure to note the eight-day Seth Thomas wall clock, as well as the original hotel desk. Also take a gander at the square grand piano that was first displayed at the 1904 St. Louis World's Fair.

MORGAN COUNTY HISTORICAL MUSEUM

HISTORIC SITES 🐾 ✆ ♿ **Willmore Lodge** (573-964-1008 or 1-800-451-4117; www.willmorelodge.com), 1 Willmore Ln., Lake Ozark, Mo. Open year-round, Mon.–Fri. 9–4:30, Sat. 9–3. This one-time lodge is home to the Lake Area Chamber Visitor Center and Museum. Upon its completion in 1930, it was known as Egan Lodge, allegedly an administrative building named for the president of Union Electric. Of course, things are not always as they seem, and the 6,500-

square-foot, 29-room Adirondack log building included an oil-burning furnace, the 1930 version of an air conditioner, a huge kitchen, servant quarters, a bar with an ice-making machine, and a primitive intercom system wired to each guest room. In other words, it was a party pad.

But there was a scandal involving Egan Lodge (what a surprise), and in 1945 the lodge was sold to Cyrus Willmore, a prominent St. Louis developer who saw that the lake was going to be a major destination for wealthy St. Louisans. He paid $320,000 for not just the lodge, but also a Union Electric–owned hotel, pleasure boats, 40,000 acres of lakefront property, and 800 miles of shoreline. Union Electric reacquired the building and adjoining property in 1996, purchasing the lodge and 30 acres of undeveloped shorefront property for $1.06 million. During that same year Union Electric offered use of the building—now listed on the National Register of Historic Places—to the Lake Area Chamber of Commerce for its offices, a visitors center, and a museum of lake history.

The Swinging Bridges. Between the late 1800s and the 1930s, more than two dozen swinging bridges were built in the Lake of the Ozarks region. Although most of these are long since gone, either succumbing to time or disappearing beneath the waters of the lake, a couple of examples still exist near the little town of Brumley. Locals still drive over these bridges, but both appear as if they could collapse in a strong wind. The smaller, metal-floored bridge has holes and cracks. The wood-planked bridge crossing Auglaize Creek has many loose boards that bounce and squeal. (If you're walking across it, watch for gaps between the old boards. You could easily break a leg or ankle if you're not careful.)

From Osage Beach, take SR 42 for 11 miles to the southeast. If you go past the CITY LIMITS sign, you've gone too far—the turnoff is just before the sign. Take a left onto Swinging Bridges Rd., and you will soon come to the smaller of the swinging bridges, now part of the Lake of the Ozarks State Park. Cross over, take

BRUMLEY SWINGING BRIDGE

DAMMED IF YOU DO, DAMMED IF YOU DON'T

The Great Osage River Project, started in 1929, provided jobs for thousands during the Great Depression. The price tag was $30 million (a heap of coin in modern terms, a fortune of inconceivable proportions in Depression-era economics), and Bagnell was the last and largest major dam to be built in the U.S. entirely with private capital. It's 2,543 feet long and supports a 20-foot-wide roadway (about wide enough for two Model T's) and a 3-foot-wide sidewalk. The power station is 511 feet long; the flood-control spillway section, 520 feet. Most of the power plant's 215,000 kilowatts goes to eastern Missouri, particularly the St. Louis area. The dam was what led to the creation of the Lake of the Ozarks, which covers 57,000 acres, stretches 92 miles, and encompasses more coastline (1,375 miles) than the state of California. For further historical information, or to inquire about scenic overlooks or tour possibilities of Bagnell, stop by the Lake Area Chamber Visitor Center and Museum at the Willmore Lodge.

BAGNELL DAM IS 2,543 FEET LONG

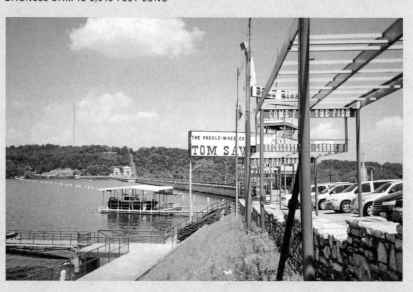

a right, and you will be met by the 400-foot plank bridge. It was built in 1930 by Union Electric after the waters backed up by Bagnell Dam covered the roads. There are few better picnic spots than along the banks of this creek (the fishing is pretty good when the water is up), and fires are allowed in specified areas. Also, camping is permitted (an honor box on a post will accept the small charge), and there are outdoor restrooms on-site. The bridges are a bit off-the-beaten-path, but a side trip to see them is well worth your time.

GOLF Golf has always been a drawing card at the Lake of the Ozarks, but over the past 20 years the region has gone crazy over the addictive allure inherent in whacking the little white ball. With all the waterfront resorts, amenities, and championship courses from which to choose, you might think you took the wrong exit at St. Louis and wandered down to south Florida. More than 15 golf clubs with designs by the likes of Robert Trent Jones, Arnold Palmer, and Tom Weiskopf make the lake region a golfer's paradise.

The rates provided here are for greens fee, cart, and a round of 18 holes, and represent weekday and weekend costs in-season. In most cases off-season rates run $10–15 less per round. Also, many of the lake's hotels and resorts provide "golf-a-round" packages via which you can sample a variety of area links. The most comprehensive list of participating resorts and details on each particular course can be found at **www.golfingmissouri.com.** Most courses accept reservations for tee times far in advance of daily play, and tee time reservations are recommended.

Bear Creek Valley Golf Club (573-302-1000; www.bearcreekvalley.com), 910 SR 42, Lake Ozark, Mo. Bear Creek opened in 2001 and is known for its beautiful scenery. An 18-hole, par-72 public course, its facilities include a full-service bar and restaurant. $48–50.

The Golf Club at Deer Chase (573-346-6117; www.deerchasegolf.com), 770 Deer Chase Rd., Linn Creek, Mo. Deer Chase is an 18-hole, par-71 public course that is open year-round. Both duffers and experienced golfers will appreciate the scenery, as the fairways wind through the hills surrounding the Auxglaize River Valley. Tee times are accepted up to 30 days in advance. $46–55.

Dogwood Hills Golf Club (573-348-3153; www.dogwoodhillsresort.com), 1252 SR KK, Osage Beach, Mo. One of the original courses in the region, Dogwood Hills has been around since 1962. Open year-round, this 18-hole, par-70 public course (part of the Dogwood Hills Resort Inn) is a local favorite. $32–49.

Eldon Country Club (573-392-4172; www.eldongolfclub.com), 35 Golf Course Rd., Eldon, Mo. Heading north from Osage Beach on US 54, you will come to the small town of Eldon. Here, the Eldon Country Club features an 18-hole, par-70 semiprivate course. In 2001 the zoysia fairways and bunker system were upgraded. For $39–44 per round, this course offers fewer crowds and a good value.

Indian Rock Golf Club (573-372-3023; www.indianrockgolfclub.com), 100 Indian Lake Ave., Gravois Mills, Mo. Hole 17 at Indian Rock, a par 3, is known for a deep lake in front and a large rock outcrop in the rear. The 18-hole, par-72 semiprivate course is set among the homes that are a part of this golf/retirement community.

Lake Valley Country Club (573-346-7218; www.lakevalleygolf.com), Lake Rd. 54-79, Camdenton, Mo. With six par 3s, six par 4s, and six par 5s, Lake Valley features large and fast greens. Open year-round, the course is an 18-hole, par-72 challenge. Greens fees are $54 for both weekdays and weekends.

Lodge of the Four Seasons (573-365-3000; www.4seasonsresort.com), 2733 Horseshoe Bend Pkwy. Lake Ozark, Mo. Located 3 miles down SR HH (Horseshoe Bend Pkwy.) off US Bus. 54. One of the most prestigious resorts at the Lake of the Ozarks, the Lodge of the Four Seasons has long been known for its golf possibilities. The 18-hole, par-71 **Cove** course was built in 1971 and was designed by Robert Trent Jones. The course was recently redesigned, with the front nine becoming the back nine (and vice versa). Beware the 65 bunkers and the extremely difficult fourth hole. $75–90.

The Ridge Course opened in 1991 and consists of 18 holes at par 72. In 1996 *Golf Digest* ranked it one of Missouri's top 10. As is true with the courses at the Four Seasons, scenic features such as rock outcrops, spring-fed lakes, and considerable elevation changes are a given. $70–80.

For seriously devoted golf aficionados (with deep pockets), Four Seasons offers the **Private Quarter's Club,** a luxury villa time-share option that includes membership at the **Club at Porta Cima Jack Nicholas Signature Course.** This is the only 18-hole, waterfront Jack Nicklaus Signature Course in Missouri.

Old Kinderhook (573-317-3500; www.oldkinderhook.com), SR 54-80, Camdenton, Mo. The 18-hole, par-71 semiprivate Tom Weiskopf course is nicely set off by rolling fairways, flowering trees, and rock waterfalls. $69–85.

Osage National Golf Club (1-866-365-1950; www.osagenational.com), 400 Osage Hills Rd., Lake Ozark, Mo. The original 18 holes at Osage National were designed in 1992 by golfing legend Arnold Palmer. Since then another nine holes have been added, leading to three different 18-hole combinations, all of which are par 72 and public. The motto of Osage National is "The must-play course at the lake." $75–89.

Rolling Hills Country Club (573-378-5109; www.playrollinghills.com), 13986 Country Club Rd., Versailles, Mo. The oldest course in the lake area, Rolling Hills was established in 1957. A member-owned course, it is far enough away from the lake proper to allow a sense of quiet and tranquility. The 18-hole, par-71 course is open year-round and costs a mere $20–35. This is the best golfing value to be found at the lake.

Sycamore Creek Golf Club (573-348-9593; www.sycamorecreekgolfclub.com), 1270 Nichols Rd., Osage Beach, Mo. Sycamore Creek may be the only golf course in the U.S. that is built around an operating fish hatchery. It is an 18-hole, par-72 public course known for exquisitely manicured greens and fairways. According to surveys by local media, Sycamore Creek has been the favorite of area residents for the past seven years. See the fish and whack the ball for $46–54.

Tan-Tar-A (1-800-822-8272; www.tan-tar-a.com), SR KK, Osage Beach, Mo. Along with Lodge of the Four Seasons, Tan-Tar-A is arguably the most famous resort at the Lake of the Ozarks. **The Oaks** course, a public, 18-hole par 71, features water hazards on 11 holes and more than 60 white-sand bunkers. This was the site for the 1994 PGA Club Pro Championship, and fees are $50–69. The nine-hole, par-35 **Hidden Lakes** course is also part of Tan-Tar-A's offerings. Play nine holes for $29 or 18 holes for $39.

PARKS ☸ ✿ ♿ ❊ **Lake of the Ozarks State Park** (573-348-2694; marina 573-348-1233; stables 573-348-6670; www.mostateparks.com/lakeozark.htm), 403 SR 134, Kaiser, Mo. Open from sunrise to half an hour after sunset. The park office is open Mon.–Fri. 8–4:30; the visitors center, Apr.–Oct. daily 9–5. With 17,441 acres and 85 miles of shoreline, Lake of the Ozarks is the largest state park in Missouri. Though the main roads can become very crowded in summer (as can side roads), its size alone makes it a fine respite from the nonstop pace of the area's commercial frenzy. There are 12 different trails stretching a total of nearly 52 miles, all of which are open to hikers. Backpackers are permitted on the **Woodland Trail,** and all-terrain bicycling and horseback riding are popular on **Trail of the Four Winds** and **Squaw's Revenge Trail.**

Within the park are 230 campsites (ranging from the primitive to those with electric hook-ups) and eight rustic cabins and yurts. Also, guided cave tours are available at the wheelchair-accessible **Ozark Caverns,** which features the well-known Angels Showers. This formation, a combination of stalactites and water-falls that drip into a natural basin, is a visitor favorite. Two swimming beaches are provided (Public Beach #1 is the most popular with locals and tourists alike), and marinas offer boat rentals.

Perhaps among the most unusual aspect of this park is the **Ozark Homestead Stables,** open daily from 9–5. Both experts and novices can rent horses that suit their fancy; 1-hour and 2½-hour rides for $30 and $60, respectively. Pony rides are offered for $20. All are staff guided, and reservations are strongly suggested. The stables also give lessons, and by special arrangement will set up hayrides and overnight trips.

CAVES ✿ ♿ **Jacob's Cave** (573-378-4374; www.jacobscave.com), 23114 SR TT, Versailles, Mo. Located between Versailles and Gravois Mills on SR TT (off SR 5), the cave is open daily 9–5 from Memorial Day through Labor Day, 9–4 the rest of the year. $15 adults, $7 ages 4–12. Open to the public in 1932, Jacob's Cave was the first "show cave" at the Lake of the Ozarks. Taking the guided tour through the cavern (which holds a constant temperature of 53 degrees), you'll find pools, the obligatory stalactite columns and "soda straw" formations, the bones of mastodons and bears, and the much-advertised "world's largest geode." Also within the operation is a large rock shop where you can purchase any number of souvenirs or pieces of handcrafted silver jewelry.

✿ ♿ ❊ **Bridal Cave** (573-346-2676; www.bridalcave.com), 526 Bridal Cave Rd., Camdenton, Mo. Winter, daily 9–4; spring and fall, 9–5; summer, 9–6. $15 adults, $7 ages 5–12. The Lake of the Ozarks' answer to the wedding chapels of Las Vegas has to be Bridal Cave, located just north of Camdenton, Mo., on SR 5 and open to the public since 1948. More than 2,150 weddings have been performed in the underground bridal chapel. Two different packages are offered for the prospective bride and groom ($400 and $550), and both come standard with minister, recorded pipe-organ music, and of course a lifetime pass to the cave for the happy couple. Other options are available, and those wishing to get hitched in subterranean style may call the wedding reservations department at 573-346-

LAUGHING WATERS GET THE LAST LAUGH

🐾 ✎ ♿ ❄ Ha Ha Tonka State Park (573-346-2986; www.mo stateparks.com/hahatonka.htm), 1491 SR D, Camdenton, Mo. Nov.–Mar., open at 8 AM; Apr.–Oct., open at 9 AM. Park gates close at sunset. Park office open Mon.–Fri. 8:30–3 in winter, 9–5 in summer. Visitors center area open 8–sunset. Ha Ha Tonka was proposed as Missouri's first state park in 1909. But government moves slowly, and 69 years later that proposal became reality. This is one of the most unusual parks not only in the Ozarks, but in the entire

THE VIEW FROM SNYDER CASTLE

United States. It's in keeping with the odd history of the place that it's not better known. Full of caves, springs, sinkholes, natural bridges, and creeks, Ha Ha Tonka even features its own haunted castle.

The name is said to mean "laughing waters," although the etymology is fairly dubious. Somehow it seems an inside settlers' joke that the Osage Indians would use the phrase *ha ha* for laughter. No matter; it does seem true that the Osage used the huge open areas and natural amphitheaters (the result of collapsed cave systems) as meeting places. There is no doubt at all that Daniel Boone and son Nathan trapped here around 1801, or that Meriwether Lewis wrote to Thomas Jefferson of the spot in 1805, or that the area was a favorite of a notorious band of robbers and counterfeiters (who minted fake Mexican dollars in one of the caves) in the 1830s.

But what most people want to know about is the castle. Wealthy Kansas City businessman Robert Snyder was enamored with the area, which he first encountered on a 1903 hunting trip. Buying up 2,500 acres (in 60 different tracts), he imported stonemasons from Scotland and began work on a 9,000-square-foot castle (not including stable houses, greenhouses, or the 80-foot water tower). Alas, Snyder would never see the structure completed. He was not only one of the first automobile owners in Kansas City, but also one of the first people killed in an car accident in Kansas City. Sometimes being a trendsetter is painful, and by 1906 Robert Snyder had shed this mortal coil.

Snyder's sons finished the castle, though not with the grandeur their father intended, and used it as a summer home. When Bagnell Dam was built by Union Electric in 1931, the lake waters backed into the Niangua River's spring branch and flooded some of the most beautiful parts of Ha Ha Tonka. The sons sued the power company; after a long fight, Union Electric eventually settled out of court.

The Snyder boys used the castle less and less; eventually, as changing times and the Great Depression shrank the family fortune, they leased it out as a hotel. It was supposedly unburnable, and yet, in 1942, the wooden shingles caught fire and the entire interior was gutted by flame. Over the next 35 years numerous private owners acquired the property. Most had great designs for commercial success, with success remaining consistently elusive. In 1978 the state of Missouri acquired the land. Thanks to a grant from the Federal Land and Water Conservation Fund, and the desire of the 1978 owners to acquire a tax write-off on a white-elephant property, the sale price of Ha Ha Tonka was only $160,000. Ironically, that was the same amount Governor Herbert Hadley had requested that the 1909 legislature provide for the acquisition (the expenditure failed to carry by a single vote).

Now consisting of more than 3,600 acres, Ha Ha Tonka offers a number of trails, courtesy docks for those who arrive by boat, picnic areas, and a deep and mysterious spring that spews out 49 million gallons of water per day. It's a beautiful place, full of wonders uncounted, a Hearst-like monument to fleeting wealth, and the only partially quiet ghosts of Indians, trappers, heroes, villains, and time.

THE SNYDER CASTLE RUINS AT HA HA TONKA STATE PARK

2676. Fortunately, you aren't required to pledge undying love in order to experience the formations and interesting lake here: Tours leave every few minutes. On the surface are a 2,400-square-foot rock and gift shop, snack center, nature trails, and a boat dock (you can reach Bridal Cave by water; just dock up at Mile Marker 10 on the Big Niangua River).

⚓ ♿ **Ozark Caverns.** See Lake of the Ozarks State Park, above.

✳ Lodging

If you're looking for a place to stay at the Lake of the Ozarks, you'll have plenty of options. In the immediate vicinity (I'm not counting outlying areas here) you'll discover more than 20 bed & breakfasts, 28 campgrounds and RV parks containing more than 1,500 campsites, and 165 resorts, condos, and motels. In addition, there are 26 marinas, many of which offer boat rentals, and one featuring houseboat rentals. However, the plethora of choices does not mean you can safely wait until the last minute to make your decision. The lake is a very busy place between Memorial Day and Labor Day, and the wise traveler books a reservation early. This is particularly important in regard to the larger, upscale resorts, which have traditionally enjoyed a huge amount of repeat business. Keep in mind that the lake is the preferred summer weekend escape of St. Louis residents, and they flock in droves to their favored spots.

The selections provided are intended to represent the western, northern, and eastern (Osage Beach) sections of the lake, and are establishments offering something a bit above and beyond—golf courses, marinas with boat rental, restaurants and lounges on-site, or full handicapped access. Prices are per night and reflect summer rates. Most of these operations are open year-round, and off-season rates are considerably less.

BED & BREAKFASTS Bass & Baskets Bed and Breakfast (573-964-5028; www.bassandbaskets.com), 269 Dogwood Rd., Lake Ozark, Mo. Ed Franko is happily addicted to bass fishing. His wife, Debbie, collects and sells **Longaberger Baskets.** Integrating their hobbies into the decor of their home, in 2001 the Frankos opened Bass & Baskets Bed and Breakfast (try saying that five times fast). From a boat hanging from the ceiling to fishing lures, from family portraits to Debbie's mother's wedding dress, personal touches are everywhere. Each of four guest rooms comes with a Jacuzzi tub, fireplace, satellite HDTV, and DVD/CD players, not to mention views of the lake. A full breakfast is served each morning. As is true with the majority of B&Bs these days, smoking, pets, and young children are not permitted. Prices range from $149–159 per night for both single and double occupancy. You should note that Bass & Baskets is located at the bottom of a very steep hill. Proceed slowly while heading down the driveway.

Blackhawk Inn (573-480-6597; www.blackhawkinn.com), 25 Blackhawk Estates, Lake Ozark, Mo. According to the prestigious *Missouri Life* magazine, "Blackhawk Inn is so much more than a bed and breakfast. Really, it is a resort and breakfast." Many who have spent a few days at the 5,500-square-foot home, situated atop a bluff looking out over the lake, seem to agree. A three-level home with three outdoor decks, Blackhawk features three suites, all with private bath and lakeside views, private balcony, TV/DVD, and WiFi. Some include a fireplace, and a large hot tub is available on the main deck. Kids, pets, and smoking are not allowed. Rates run $135–165 per night.

Buck Creek Bed & Breakfast (573-372-1212; www.buckcreekbb.com), 32907 Buck Creek Acres Rd., Gravois Mills, Mo. Over on the quiet side of the lake in Gravois Mill, Buck Creek is a peaceful B&B with a great front porch. Breakfast is a major attraction here, and though the menu varies, guests can count on homemade biscuits and gravy, eggs and sausage, fruit, and homemade pastries. Four guest rooms, most warm and homey with dark paneling and plush carpet, run $77–120 per night, making it one of the better values on the lake. Buck Creek does not allow inside smoking or pets.

✻ **Castleview Bed & Breakfast** (573-346-9818 or 1-877-346-9818; www.castleviewbedandbreakfast.com), SR D, Camdenton, Mo. Though most B&Bs tend to name their individual suites, Castleview's names—the Hunter, the Sweetheart, the New Orleans, and the Vintage—truly reflect the intended theme. All in all, this is the type of enterprise that allows you to feel at home. Better yet, this informal retreat is right next to Ha Ha Tonka State Park. The home's large living room features a fireplace, cable TV, and stereo, and all rooms include private bath, satellite TV, ceiling fan, and queen-sized bed. Smoking, children under 12, and pets are

not permitted; you'll be charged a $200 service fee is you're caught smoking inside. Normal rates are $99–109. Castleview offers a number of specials, a corporate rate, and a military rate.

✻ **Cliff House Inn** (573-348-9726), 2183 Carlson Ct., Osage Beach, Mo. You begin your day at Cliff House (which does sit high on a cliff; no false advertising here) with a full breakfast delivered to your room. Next, you look out over the main channel of the lake from your private deck. Serving visitors for more than a decade, the B&B's landscaping is extensive, featuring flowers, trees, a goldfish pond, and a gazebo with hot tub. The four guest suites come complete with cable TV, DVD player, clock radio, hair dryer, iron, and ironing board. Rates begin at $137 per night, and weekends and holidays require a two-night minimum. A popular lodging choice at Cliff House is the Garden House: With its fireplace, Queen Anne canopy bed, and location just a few steps from the outdoor hot tub, this is a favorite for a romantic weekend. The normal restrictions apply as to smoking, children, and pets.

🐾 🏠 ✐ ♿ **Inn at Harbour Ridge** (573-302-0411 or 1-877-744-6020; www.harbourridgeinn.com), 6334 Red Barn Rd., Osage Beach, Mo. Built in 1999, Harbour Ridge is designed for couples of any age. The romantic getaway is the house specialty (you can even get married, with up to 25 guests in attendance, at the wedding gazebo), and the innkeepers thrive on filling personal requests. They are more than happy to pick up flowers or champagne for your room, set your tee time for golf, or assist in discovering any of myriad lake activities. Four guest rooms are rented at $119–189 per night. The Inn at Harbour Ridge will accept children and pets, but accommodations are limited. Pets must be crated, not left alone in rooms (there is a $50 deposit and $10-per-night fee), and leashed when in common areas. Kids do not need their own crate, though it would best if they were older and housebroken. You'd be wise to call ahead and discuss the matter with the innkeepers prior to making a reservation. Don't smoke in your room unless you want an extra $250 on your bill.

HOUSEBOATS Lake of the Ozarks Marina (573-873-3705 or 1-800-255-5561; www.lakeoftheozarks marina.com), SR 5 North, Camdenton, Mo. You needn't stay in a resort, hotel, or B&B when visiting the Lake of the Ozarks. If you have a large family or group of friends, you can spend your entire vacation on the water. Lake of the Ozarks Marina rents houseboats ranging in length from 56 to 59 feet, sleeping 10 to 12. These luxurious cruisers come complete with everything from electronics (both personal and aquatic) to sheets, silverware, dishware, gas grills, microwaves, and much, much more. Rates vary depending on the date, but during the height of the summer season expect to pay from $775–995 per day.

RESORTS AND LODGES

Lake of the Ozarks West
❦ ✎ ♿ ❀ **Lakeview Resort** (573-374-5555 or 1-800-936-5655; www .lakeview-resort.com), HCR 69, Box 505-L5, Sunrise Beach, Mo. It's fitting that a family-oriented resort is still owned by the family who founded it.

St. Louis butcher Jake Drake first saw the Lake of the Ozarks in 1946. Today Lakeview, with its three peninsulas and more than a mile of shoreline, is owned and operated by son Dan and grandson Jake Jr. The resort offers 75 cottages or condos, each containing one to six bedrooms, priced in the $99–350 range. Items that are not furnished by Lakeview include towels, washcloths, dish towels, maid service, soap, coffee filters, salt and pepper shakers, and in-room phones. Otherwise, all accommodations are fully equipped. On-site are indoor and outdoor swimming pools, swim docks, pebble beaches, a boat ramp, covered docks, tennis courts, a Laundromat, and a marina with boat rentals. The only thing you can't bring to Lakeview are pets.

❦ 🐾 ✎ **Rock Harbor Resort** (573-374-5586 or 1-877-203-4186; www .rockharborresort.com), 973 Rock Harbor Rd., Sunrise Beach, Mo. Located in a quiet cove, Rock Harbor is another family-owned and family-operated establishment with one-, two-, three-, and four-bedroom units. The choices range from a simple motel room to cottages, duplexes, and fourplexes. With the exception of the motel rooms, all accommodations come with living and dining areas and a furnished kitchen, and both daily and weekly rates are available ($65–230 per night; $350–1,610 per week). Pets are accepted here with prior approval and an extra fee, but the resort really prefers you leave Lassie in a kennel or with friends. Activities are plentiful, with a pool, playground, launch ramp, and boat rentals. Canoes, fishing boats, bass boats, and pontoon boats are available for rent.

North Lake

♠ ♨ ✆ ⛬ ❄ ⍾ **Alhonna Resort** (573-365-2634; www.alhonna.com), 1237 Outer Dr., Lake Ozark, Mo. Those who enjoy boating will not be disappointed with Alhonna, built in the 1950s by Al and Honna Vilmin. The resort offers 30 different boat rentals, with choices ranging 16–28 feet. Rates vary, with a 16-foot fishing boat renting for $77 for two hours, a 22-foot ski boat costing $130 for two hours, and a 24-foot pontoon boat going for $119 for two hours. Skis and ski tubes can also be rented. The resort, which started out as eight cabins with rustic knotty-pine interiors, now boasts of 60 lakefront and lakeview units. There are motel rooms, deluxe four-bedroom condos, and even a private house, with prices stretching $77–254 per night. All accommodations (with the exception of the motel) are equipped with a BBQ grill and picnic table, basic kitchen supplies, microwave, coffeepot, and toaster. Small pets are accepted, with an extra charge of $9 per night and a $25 deposit. Other amenities include an indoor pool with sauna and hot tubs, a heated outdoor pool, and a full-service gas dock at the marina, which also sells bait and licenses.

Also at Alhonna is **Bobber's Restaurant and Lounge,** featuring breakfast and lunch on Fri., Sat., and Sun. Bobbers serves breakfast until noon, and hours vary during the week and off-season. The lounge is usually open until 9 PM.

✆ ⛬ ❄ ⍾ **The Resort at Port Arrowhead** (573-365-2334 or 1-800-532-3575; www.theresortatportarrowhead.com), US Bus. 54 (2 miles south of Bagnell Dam), Lake Ozark, Mo.

The Resort at Port Arrowhead went through a major renovation in 2002; it features 209 rooms and suites, not to mention a full-service restaurant and lounge. It is as renowned for weekend vacations and family trips as it is for being a conference center. The renovation led to the creation of 12 conference rooms with a total of 17,000 square feet. The facility includes two outdoor pools (one heated), one indoor pool, a children's wading pool with a waterfall, two hot tubs, miniature golf, seasonal supervised children's activities, a playground, fitness room, arcade, shuffleboard, boat slips, boat ramp, and gift shop. Your vacation becomes more pricey on this side of the lake: A standard room in-season begins in the $163 area.

✆ ⛬ ❄ ⍾ **Country Club Hotel and Spa** (573-964-2200 or 1-800-964-6698; www.countryclubhotel.com), 301 Carol Rd., Lake Ozark, Mo. With 12 outdoor and four indoor tennis courts, racquetball courts, indoor and outdoor swimming pools, a fitness center, exercise classes, and proximity to area golf courses, the Country Club Hotel is aimed at those who enjoy physical activity. However, thanks to health spa services, spa treatments, and personal training, it also caters to the guest who enjoys a degree of pampering. The variety of accommodations includes deluxe rooms, suites, and villas, with nightly rates averaging from $109–250. The **Country Club Restaurant and Lounge** serves breakfast, lunch, and dinner. Last but not least, the resort is adept at weddings and wedding receptions, and has a skilled staff of professional event planners.

✆ ⛬ ❄ ⍾ **The Lodge of the Four Seasons Resort and Spa** (573-365-

3000 or 1-800-THE-LAKE; www .4seasonsresort.com), 315 Lodge of Four Seasons Dr., Lake Ozark, Mo. Arguably the most famous resort at the lake, Four Seasons' nearly 400 rooms are both spacious and luxurious. Rates at the height of the season run anywhere from $144 to $364 per night. The resort is the home of the lake's largest and most complete marina, and golf is a huge draw here. The Ridge and Cove courses are regularly named as two of the best in the state. As well, the lodge houses one of the Midwest's largest resort spas, **Spa Shiki,** which has been recognized by NBC's *Today* show and *Self* magazine. The 15,000-square-foot facility offers massages, body treatments, facials, and salon treatments, as well as a fully equipped Pilates studio, steam, sauna, and whirlpool.

The dining options at this resort are numerous. Included are **Breeze's Restaurant, Soleil Café** (for breakfast and lunch), and **Baxter's Lakeside Grill.** For dinner, **HK's** restaurant (named for Four Seasons founder Harold Koplar) is a lake tradition. In terms of thirst quenching, **The Ridge Bar and Grill** and **The Cove Bar and Grill** provide a casual and laid-back atmosphere.

Osage Beach

🦐 🐟 ♿ ❄ 🍸 **The Inn at Grand Glaize** (1-800-348-4731; www.innat grandglaize.com), 5142 US 54, Osage Beach, Mo. If you want something that is right in the thick of things but offers good value as well, the Inn at Grand Glaize is a fine choice. The renovated facility is located 0.25 mile west of the Grand Glaize Bridge on a secluded cove. Rooms (147 standard rooms, three parlor suites, and one junior suite) run $89–219. On-site are

two restaurants and bars, a marina with boat and WaveRunner rental, an outdoor pool, fitness room, outdoor volleyball court, and game room.

🦐 🐟 ♿ ❄ 🍸 **Tan-Tar-A Resort, Golf Club and Spa** (573-348-3131 or 1-800-826-8272; www.tan-tar-a.com), 494 Tan-Tar-A Dr., Osage Beach, Mo. This is the big kahuna of all the lake resorts, the only one more famous than Lodge of the Four Seasons. A AAA Three Diamond establishment, Tan-Tar-A was ranked one of the three Midwestern resorts "families would love most" by Midwest Living magazine. A huge facility situated on 420 acres, it offers 27 holes of championship-level golf, one indoor and two outdoor pools, bowling, tennis, horseback riding, a health club, a spa and salon, an arcade, and the (three-stories tall) **Timber Falls Indoor Waterpark.** Also on-site is a full-service marina with boat rental and fishing guides. Food and drink are plentiful here. The **Black Bear Lodge** features casual fare and a rustic decor, while **Windrose on the Water** provides fine dining with a lake view. The **Oaks** bar and grill overlooks the golf course of the same name, and for the kids there is also a **Burger King** and **Sbarro** pizza.

Accommodations are a bit different here, and there are a number of options amid the 970 rooms and suites. The complex consists of five interconnecting buildings, all of which are within walking distance of restaurants and activities. A few minutes away is Tan-Tar-A's **Estates Complex.** These buildings, set on 200 acres surrounding a nine-hole golf course, appear from the outside to be private homes. In reality, they contain two to four guest rooms or full suites.

Midsummer prices range from $154–250, but a multitude of packages and reservation options are available. Tan-Tar-A is also known for its weddings; a very quaint stone chapel is on the grounds. A full staff of wedding planners can put together an affair for anywhere from 10 to 200 guests.

CAMPGROUNDS 🏕 🐾 🐾 Cross Creek RV Park and Campground (573-365-1211 or 1-888-250-3885; www.crosscreekrvpark.com), Lake Ozark, Mo. Located 3.5 miles north of the dam and then another mile off SR W, the 40 acres of Cross Creek make for a natural lake vacation. Open Apr.–Nov., the 40-acre campground features a stocked, 10-acre fishing lake, petting zoo, playground, store, showers, Laundromat, miniature golf course, and paddle boat rental. Moreover, pets are welcome here for a minimal extra charge. Lodging includes tent sites from $25, RV sites from $28 for full hook-up, and either rustic, deluxe, or treehouse cabins from $49–139. For something different, you can even cross the water and sleep on your own small island. For $39 you achieve privacy, and the site includes electricity, water, toilet, and BBQ grill.

🏕 🐾 🐾 Ⴤ Deer Valley RV Park and Campground (573-374-5277; www.frankyandlouies.com/campground.html), Lake Rd. 5-41, Sunrise Beach, Mo. Sunrise Beach, on the west side of the lake, is not known for having a beach. The Deer Valley Campground changes that each year between Apr. 15 and Nov. 1, when the 100 tons of sand it hauls in sports palm trees and happy campers. The 221-campsite park offers both tent camping and full

RV hook-ups beginning at $20 and $30, respectively. **Franky and Louie's Bar and Grill** faces the beach, and is considered one of the best (if not the best) bar and grills at the lake by locals and insiders. Live entertainment is frequent. Pets are welcome at Deer Valley as long as they are on a leash.

🐾 🐾 **Osage Beach RV Park** (573-348-3445 or 1-800-562-7343; www.osagebeachrvpark.net), 3949 Campground Ln., Osage Beach, Mo. This park includes five air-conditioned cabins and 74 cable TV, full hook-up RV sites. Tents are not permitted. Summer rates for cabins (one to four people) are $39.95, and the fee for hook-ups is $29.95. Pets on leash (maximum of two dogs) are allowed at the RV sites, but neither pets nor smoking are permitted in the cabins. Open Mar. 24–Nov. 1. Note that the cabins do not have kitchens. All have TVs and some have restrooms. The park has showers on-site, as well as a swimming pool, playground, meeting room and pavilion, shuffleboard, Sunday church services, and free WiFi.

✳ Where to Eat

EATING OUT 🐾 ♿ Ⴤ On the Rise Bakery & Bistro (573-348-4224; www.ontherisebakery.com), 5439 US 54, Osage Beach, Mo. Open Wed.–Sun., 7 AM–3 PM for lunch. Owner-chef Mike Castle knows the Lake of the Ozarks better than most. He spent summers working at area restaurants in his high school days, prior to attending the Culinary Institute of America. After graduation he returned, first working as a sous chef at the near-legendary Blue Heron and later managing the Heron's sister restaurant, the Potted Steer. In 1995 he and his wife, Cheryl, struck out on their own, the result being the On the Rise Bakery & Bistro. The establishment was named a "Top 10 Taste" in 1999 by *Southern Living* magazine. The interior has sort of a courtyard style, complete with striped awnings, bronze tables, wicker chairs, and clouds painted on the ceiling. There is also a small outdoor courtyard should you want the real thing. The array of breads, muffins, cookies, pastries, and flatbreads will convince even the most hard-core Atkins dieter to fall off the wagon. Lunch offers specialty soups, salads, and sandwiches, with all meats smoked over dried applewood. The menu is a cross between American and European with a definite French emphasis. Semipotent potables are offered, and choices range from wine to beer to Kahlua. The bakery prepares pies, cakes, and other delights for take-away service.

✔ Y ❀ **The Fish and Co.** (573-873-0022; www.thefishandcompany.com), 268 Wego Fish (Mile Marker 31; Lake Rd. 5-89U), Camdenton, Mo. Open daily from 11 AM. You get the impression, upon walking into Fish and Co., that this is truly a local place. You're half right. Lots of locals do congregate here, but there's also a fair number of visitors who arrive both by land and water. What the heck, a place that still has an air hockey table in the game room has to be OK. The menu has the usual burgers and tenderloins, but fried dill pickles ($5.99), baked potato soup ($4.99), and a catfish dinner ($14.99) are also available. Live entertainment is provided most weekend nights during summer months, with karaoke on Thurs. and Sun. The bar serves beer, wine, and mixed drinks.

✔ ❤ Y **The Ozark Bar-B-Que** (573-374-7769; www.ozarkbar-b-que.com), 608 Wings Circle (Mile Marker 10.5 by water), Sunrise Beach, Mo. Is it a BBQ joint, a marina, or a gift shop? Truth be known, it's all three. From swimwear to kids' toys to wakeboards to skis and ski ropes, the boutique, marine store, and marine market (where you can purchase food, soda, and packaged liquor and beer) has quite an impressive selection. There are gas pumps at the dock and the smell of hickory smoke in the air. The Ozark features hickory-smoked meats, as well as salads, sandwiches, and burgers. A slab of ribs runs $19.99, but those who wish to make a gastronomic statement might choose the $12.99 Ozark Burger. This is the ultimate cheeseburger in paradise, and it weighs in at a full pound. Aside from some tasty BBQ, the signature item here seems to be the onion rings. For $14.99 you receive a huge pile (feeding several people), all hand-breaded and made to order. Open Thurs.–Sat. 11–8, Sun. 11–3, the Ozark is a nice, casual diversion after a hard afternoon of water sports. Enjoy the Q, look at the goldfish in the pond, or view the numerous carp that congregate at the dock (hoping for a free meal, no doubt).

DINING OUT ✔ ❤ Y **The Duck Restaurant** (573-365-9973; www.the duckrestaurant.com), 67 Cherokee Court, Lake Ozark, Mo. Open Apr.–Dec. Dinner is served after 5 PM Wed.–Sun.; Sunday brunch is 10–1. As is true with a number of eateries at the lake, the Duck is a recipient of *Wine Spectator* magazine's Award of Excellence. A wide variety of wines are available, but connoisseurs will appreciate the selection of vintage ports. The Duck is appropriately located right on the water. The front balcony is inviting, the perfect spot for a cocktail and a relaxing view of the lake. Prices range from $24–40, and though the menu is not huge, it seems to go for quality over quantity. Diners might enjoy the seafood ravioli or the chicken jeaeger schnitzel. Dessert should not be forgotten: The name molten chocolate cake says it all. A final reason to appreciate the Duck is that it's serious about its embargo on cell phone usage. The place should get a medal just for that.

♦ ⅙ ℆ **The Blue Heron** (573-365-4646; www.blueheronpottedsteer .com), 180 Heron Hill Ln., Lake Ozark, Mo. Located high on a bluff overlooking the lake (it's the first driveway on your left after you turn onto SR HH off US 54); open Tues.–Sat. 5–10 PM. The Blue Heron is, well, blue. Diners can enjoy cocktails at the outdoor gazebo (yup, it's blue too) and soak in some spectacu-lar views. The Heron has held a *Wine Spectator* magazine Award of Excellence almost since its opening in 1984. With more than 350 selections and many limited vintages, this is no surprise. Prices run $30–13,000 per bottle (the latter is for a very rare, boxed cognac). The Heron offers Kobe beef, which comes from Wagyu cattle in the Kobe province of Japan. Free of antibiotics and hormones, these cattle are fed beer and massaged by a geisha and are no doubt the envy of overly hormonal cattle raised in the American West, who chug tetracycline at the first sniffle, drink too much whiskey, and rarely get a date. The menu here is as long as your arm, loaded with excellent lamb, veal, seafood, poultry, and beef entrées. Don't miss the batter-fried lobster tail for around $45, the fresh Dover sole walewska, or the Alsace-Lorraine stuffed pork tenderloin. In addition, some of the appetizers provide a unique taste. For something different, order Missouri golden

THE BLUE HERON RESTAURANT

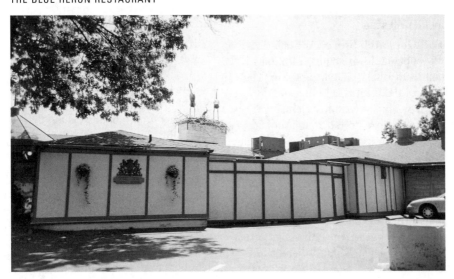

spoonbill caviar (in the $65 range) or a lobster bisque supreme soup ($15.95).

✴ Selective Shopping

Osage Beach Premium Outlet (573-348-2065; www.premiumoutlets .com), 4540 US 54, Osage Beach, Mo. Mon.–Sat. 9–9, Sun. 9–6. A regional draw that attracts shoppers from far beyond the Lake of the Ozarks, the Osage Beach Premium Outlet features more than 110 shops and stores in the vein of Brooks Brothers, Ann Taylor, Banana Republic, Ralph Lauren, and Reebok. More than just clothing, the center also offers ample selections of housewares, home furnishings, gifts, and specialty items.

Wood'n Ya Wanit and Art Gallery (573-348-6300), 5497 US 54, Osage Beach, Mo. With two locations in Osage Beach (a second one is found at the Tan-Tar-A Resort), this gallery represents more than 140 American artists. The good thing is that it's not your typical gallery. Yes, there are the obligatory limited-edition prints, but what you should really check out are the wood carvings, glass fish, and metal wall scenes.

The Dogpatch Store (573-365-6344; www.dogpatchstore.com), 1482 Bagnell Dam Blvd., Lake Ozark, Mo. The Lake of the Ozarks is built around tourists. Thus it is almost demanded that you take a stroll through the oldest tourist shop around. The Dogpatch Store, located right on the Strip, has been here since 1947. You've got your magnets and T-shirts, your Route 66 stuff, your water pistols, your live hermit crabs, and your saltwater taffy. When it comes to souvenir shops at the lake, Dogpatch stands head and shoulders above the rest.

✴ Special Events

January **Eagle Days** (573-526-5545 or 573-964-1008; mdc.mo.gov/discover -nature/programs/eagle-days), Willmore Lodge, 1 Willmore Ln., Lake Ozark, Mo. The American bald eagle is a regular at the Lake of the Ozarks—Missouri has become one of the leading states where the big birds winter—and eagle-watching has become the thing to do when the water is too cold for water-skiing, swimming, or fishing. High-powered telescopes are provided on the deck of the Willmore Lodge; however, the eagles can be viewed all the way from the lodge down the Osage River to the town of Tuscumbia. The World Bird Sanctuary in St. Louis provides naturalists to answer questions, brings live eagles in captivity, and offers interactive displays. The event is free and open to everyone.

February **Polar Bear Plunge** (573-230-1894), Osage Beach, Mo. Some things are admittedly more fun to watch than they are to do. Still, if you want to brave the elements and help raise money for the Special Olympics, the Polar Bear Plunge might be your cup of iced tea. In late February at Public Beach #2 in Lake of the Ozarks State Park, hundreds of participants don odd costumes, hold a parade, and go splashing neck-deep into the 38-degree water. For those who aren't crazy about freezing themselves silly, a 3.1-mile Polar Bear Strut (walk/run) is also available. Afterward, a huge party is held at the Tan-Tar-A Resort. It's free for the plungers, but anyone can join the fun for a low admission price.

April **Annual Dogwood Festival** (1-800-769-1004; www.camdenton chamber.com), Camdenton, Mo. The flowering dogwood is the state tree of Missouri, and nowhere do they celebrate this white-blossomed beauty more than in Camdenton. Having taken place in mid-April for more than 50 years, the Dogwood Festival begins on a Thursday evening with a ham-and-bean dinner, carnival, and live music. On Friday evening you can enjoy an art show, fish fry, talent show, and the Miss Dogwood Pageant. Saturday brings the famed Dogwood Parade, featuring more than 100 floats (more than 1,500 dogwood saplings are given away to those in attendance). Hammered dulcimer music, an art show, and a lawn tractor pull are all part of the fun. Live music can be heard noon–10 PM. A dogwood festival just wouldn't be complete without dog contests, and you can enter yours in a variety of categories ranging from cutest to ugliest (as if there were any ugly dogs).

June **Osage River Pow Wow** (573-392-3752; www.osageriverpowwow.com), Miller County Fairgrounds, Eldon, Mo. For a celebration of all things Native American, the annual Osage River Pow Wow features authentic dances, arts, period and ceremonial dress, and food (lots of it). The drummers and dancers are the big draw here, though you will also find many booths and activities for both kids and adults. The pow wow kicks off in mid-June and runs for three days.

July **Miller County Fair** (573-480-0375; www.millercountyfair.com), Miller County Fairgrounds, Eldon, Mo. Held the third weekend in July, the Miller County Fair is a major event featuring carnival rides, a midway, entertainment, tons of food, and livestock displays and competition.

Thankfully, the fair has reinstituted the greased pig race that was canceled a few years back, partially due to political correctness and partially due to a lack of willing pigs. A demo derby, antique tractor show, numerous pageants, and a parade are long-standing traditions at this traditional hoedown.

August **Lake Rescue "Shoot Out" Benefit** (573-216-6363; www.lakeof theozarksshootout.org), Mile Marker 34.5, Captain Ron's Bar and Grill at the Lake, Sunrise Beach, Mo. This is the largest unsanctioned boat race in the U.S., and it's been taking place for nearly two decades. Some of the fastest boats in the world compete in a variety of classes for the fastest 1-mile time (some top 208 mph!). The event is sponsored in part by all the fire departments in and around the Lake of the Ozarks (not to mention such folks as *Powerboat Magazine,* Pepsi, and Budweiser); all proceeds benefit local fire and rescue teams.

Laurie Hillbilly BBQ Cook-Off (573-374-8776), Laurie Fairgrounds, 269 Fairgrounds Dr., Laurie, Mo. This two-day BBQ extravaganza, sanctioned by the Kansas City BBQ Society, just gets bigger and better each year. It's now expanded to offer a "Kid's Q," a separate competition for those ages 5–15. The winner of the cook-off instantly earns an invitation to one of the greatest of all BBQ events: the American Royal Livestock, Horse Show and Rodeo in Kansas City. In Laurie itself, however, the cash prize for first place is a cool $1,500. Make sure to get in on the free BBQ chicken wing samples that are provided at certain hours. And don't miss touring the grounds and looking at the competitors and their rigs. As you might imagine, the food is great. On-site, as is only fitting and proper at a BBQ competition, there is live music, dancing, and a beer garden.

September **Hillbilly Fair** (573-374-8776), Laurie Fairgrounds, Laurie, Mo. Held over three days in mid-September, locals and visitors dress in hillbilly attire, hold a parade, and enjoy all the carnival rides and food that make any fair a raging success (and this one has been going on for more than 40 years). Friday and Saturday nights offer dancing, live music, a beer garden, and bingo. Of course, this just wouldn't be the Ozarks unless, come Sunday morning, worship services were offered. The arts and crafts booths offer a good chance to view and buy some unique items.

Osage River Rendezvous and Mountain Man Festival (1-800-451-4117), Silver Star Campground, Lake Ozark, Mo. Always taking place the third weekend in September, the Mountain Man Rendezvous is without doubt one of the best times to be had in the lake region. It's a three-day affair held at the foot of Bagnell Dam (open to the public Fri.–Sat. 9–5, Sun. 9–3), with a theme of pre-1840 Ozark life. Although little discussed in popular fiction, the Ozarks were heavily influenced by the fur trade from the 1600s up to the mid-1800s. This modern shindig is a re-creation of the same festivals held by the early pioneers, who would meet on occasion to socialize, barter, trade, and restock on provisions. You'll see living history via black powder and anvil shoots, tomahawk and knife throwing, fire starting, and of course the telling of tales beyond tall. Shopping is plentiful on Trader's Row, but you won't find

stuffed toys or Lake of the Ozarks shot glasses. You will find anything that might have been crafted more than 150 years ago. Handmade items, folk art, and widgets from the past are the stock in trade here. The founders of this event are sticklers for accuracy, and Trader's Row is monitored for authenticity. Additionally, you can stay at the rendezvous in a primitive campsite, but with the requirement of dressing in period attire and utilizing only those things available at the time. In short . . . be prepared to start your own fire, tote your own water, and live without air-conditioning and MTV. $5 adults; free for ages 15 and younger. In one of the few instances where the 21st century encroaches on the celebration, real money is preferred over beads, pelts, or wampum.

October **Eldon Turkey Festival** (573-392-3752; www.eldonchamber .com), Eldon, Mo. Miller County, Mo., is one of the country's top producers of domestic turkeys. During the last Saturday in October, the town of Eldon pays homage to this distinction with its annual Turkey Festival. This is one of those attractions that, for pure fun and quirkiness, should not be passed by. Activities include a turkey egg toss, turkey trot, and (my personal favorite) frozen turkey bowling. However, the games are just the beginning of the fowl goings-on. Vendors, music, a quilt show, live music, and an old-time steam-operated farm machinery exhibit all contribute to the carnival atmosphere. And as for food, you just haven't lived until you've had some turkey fingers or made like King Henry VIII and strolled around chomping on your giant smoked turkey leg.

Old Tyme Apple Festival (573-378-4401), Versailles, Mo. If an apple a day keeps the doctor away, then the physicians of Versailles must be hard up for work. The first Old Tyme Apple Festival took place in 1980, and today the event boasts more than 400 vendors, a parade, apple pie and fiddlers' contests, tractor show, car cruise, demolition derby, and gospel-singing extravaganza. Held the first Saturday in October—the car cruise is held Friday night—this local festival now draws more than 35,000 locals and visitors. Small wonder it is consistently voted one of the best festivals in the state by the readers of *Rural Missouri* magazine.

Mid-November–New Year's Day
Annual Lake Lights Festival. The lake is not shy about celebrating the holidays, and from just before Thanksgiving to the first of the year both land and water are alive with sights, sounds, and twinkling lights. The festival begins when businesses along the major thoroughfares (US 54, SR 42, SR KK, and SR HH) turn on all the bright yuletide displays.

Parades generally begin the next day, when Ameren UE (the company that bought out Union Electric, builders of the lake) flips the switch at Bagnell Dam.

As the season progresses visitors can enjoy the **Annual Enchanted Village of Lights** at Laurie. Held at the Laurie Fairgrounds, on SR O off SR 5, more than 27 acres feature nearly 200 lighted Christmas scenes, decorated trees, 4-by-8-foot "greeting cards," and other displays (admission is free). Sights of the season are also dramatic at Tan-Tar-A Resort in Osage Beach and St. Patrick's Church in Laurie. For those who enjoy the simpler times, a favorite is the annual Versailles **Old Fashioned Christmas** held in front of the Morgan County Historical Society Museum and the Versailles Area Chamber of Commerce office. Those in attendance can revel in caroling, watch the big bonfire, and sip free hot cider or hot chocolate. Horse-drawn buggies and wagons are available to view the various light displays around town.

THE OSAGE LAKES DISTRICT

Y ou might call the Osage Lakes District the "anti–Lake of the Ozarks." This is a quiet area, the lakes of relatively recent (less than 50-year-old) construction. In many ways the surrounding region consists of small towns that have changed little over the years, places that treasure traditional rural ways and are coincidentally located next to a lake. While many vacation homes overlook both Stockton and Pomme de Terre Lakes, they could in most instances be regarded as simple weekend vacation cabins. Both lakes are creations of the Army Corps of Engineers, and building down to the water's edge is prohibited. This has limited rampant development such as that found at the Lake of the Ozarks, and kept boating, fishing, and camping locales as pristine as possible.

This is not a part of the world where you will find five-star restaurants, glitzy nightclubs, go-cart tracks, luxurious resorts, cute boutiques, or antique-bedecked bed & breakfasts. It is a locale where you will find peace and quiet, family fun, and beautiful scenery. The pace is slow, a fact to which many travelers will attest if they've come up behind a tractor on the two-lane blacktops, following a farmer on the way to his fields. Urban magazines and newspapers often write of "the heartland," but quite frankly few have visited; fewer yet have any idea where it's truly located. It is here, one of countless rural regions dotted about the Midwest, villages where the Friday night football game draws packed bleachers and the Sonic Drive-In is still part of the strip cruised endlessly by local teens in pickup trucks.

This is not to say that the region is without amenities or history. In the latter case, it is reputed that the French explorer LaSalle gave the Pomme de Terre River its name ("apple of the earth," referring to the potato bean that grew wild and was an Indian staple) when he crossed the Ozarks in 1682. This was Osage Indian country, home to the proud and legendary tribe that inhabited the Ozarks for hundreds of years prior to the arrival of Europeans. To the west, in Lamar, you will find the birthplace of Harry Truman, Missouri's only president. Though small motels and numerous franchise food operations are prevalent on the main drags of the larger towns, equally as evident are family-owned restaurants, pretty parks, fairs, and festivals.

The Osage Lakes District is one of those increasingly rare parts of America where the words *neighborhood* and *community* still hold deep meaning. This is not a region that time forgot, but it is an oasis where the more objectionable,

The Osage Lakes District

Point of Interest

KANSAS
MISSOURI

Little Osage R.

N

Miles
0   5   10

SCHELL-OSAGE WILDLIFE AREA

Osage Village State Historical Site

Harry S Truman Reservoir

Osceola

Hermitage

Pomme de Terre State Park

Pomme de Terre Lake

Weaubleau

Humansville

Bolivar

Southwest Baptist University

Snow Bluff Ski & Fun Area

Cedar Springs

El Dorado Springs

Horse R.

Stockton

Stockton State Park

Stockton Lake

Greenfield

Golden City

Nevada

Harry S Truman Birthplace State Historical Site

Lamar

Prairie State Park

© The Countryman Press

frenetic facets of modern life have been relegated to the back burner. Luckily, visitors are welcome.

AREA CODES All of the towns and cities in the Osage Lakes District fall under the **417** area code.

GUIDANCE When traveling in the Osage Lakes District, several area chambers of commerce provide complete information on events, dining, lodging, lake activities, and area history. The **Pomme de Terre Lake Area Chamber of Commerce** (417-745-2299 or 1-800-235-9519; www.pommedeterrechamber .com) is located in Hermitage, Mo. To the southwest, everything you wish to learn about Stockton Lake can be acquired from the **Stockton Lake Association** (417-276-5161; www.stocktonlake.com). Many visitors choose to stay in Bolivar, Mo., the largest town in the area. The **Bolivar Area Chamber of Commerce** (417-326-4118; www.bolivarchamber.com or www.bolivarmo.com) offers a wealth of advice and history. If your goal is to visit the birthplace of Harry Truman, contact the **Barton County Chamber of Commerce** (417-682-3595; www.bartoncounty.com).

GETTING THERE *By car:* From the south, the area is easily accessible by several major highways that branch off I-44. From Springfield, both SR 13 and US 65 will put you, respectively, in the vicinity of Bolivar and Pomme de Terre Lake. Lamar, Mo., is on US 71, approximately 20 miles north of Carthage, Mo. To reach Stockton Lake and Greenfield, drive north on SR 39 off I-44. If arriving from Kansas City, take US 71 South to US 54 East. Then turn south onto SR 39.

By air: Less than an hour from most of the Osage Lakes District, **Springfield-Branson National Airport** (417-868-0500; www.sgf-branson-airport.com), 2300 N. Airport Blvd., Springfield, Mo., is the most convenient choice for air travelers. **Lambert–St. Louis International Airport** (314-426-8000; www.flystl .com), 10701 Lambert International Blvd., St. Louis, Mo., **and Kansas City International** (816-243-5237; www.flykci.com), One International Square, Kansas City, Mo., are located within a half day's drive.

MEDICAL EMERGENCIES Citizens Memorial Hospital (417-326-6000; www.citizensmemorial.com), 1500 N. Oakland Ave., Bolivar, Mo. Citizens Memorial is a 74-bed hospital with 23 physicians and dentists offering a range of services from outpatient to emergency care.

Barton County Memorial Hospital (417-681-5100; www.bcmh.net), 29 N.W. First Ln., Lamar, Mo. A 25-bed critical-access hospital with emergency services, Barton County has provided health care to area residents since 1949. This hospital is virtually new, having moved into new facilities at a new address in 2007. In addition to its full range of offerings, the hospital features a sports injury clinic.

✳ Wandering Around

EXPLORING BY FOOT For a look at some relatively unmolested remnants of the Osage Indians who first inhabited the area, take a walk on the 3-mile **Indian**

Point Trail at Pomme de Terre State Park. Located on the south (Pittsburg) side of the park, the trailhead for Indian Point is across from the campground entrance. Follow the signs for just shy of 1.5 miles and you will encounter the first of the Osage cairns, used as burial markers, monuments, and topographic signposts. Continue straight ahead and in just a few minutes (about 0.1 mile) you will reach Indian Point Overlook, which offers fantastic views of Pomme de Terre. After peeking out at the lake from the overlook, return to the trail and turn left. At roughly the 2.5-mile mark you will find a second cairn, an ideal spot to ponder the lives and times of those who built it. Continue to walk straight, and in 0.5 mile you will return to the trailhead and parking lot.

✳ Towns and Villages

Bolivar, Mo. In July 1948 President Harry Truman and Venezuelan president Romulo Gallegos came to town. In order to thank the residents of Bolivar, Mo., for celebrating the man who had liberated their country, Venezuela had donated a large statue of Simon Bolívar, leader of the 1817–1825 South American revolution. Truman and Gallegos performed the unveiling of the sculpture, and the locals applauded with gusto. The two dignitaries apparently never realized that Bolivar, Mo., was in fact named for a town in Hardeman County, Tennessee.

Founded in 1835, Bolivar (pronounced *BALL-uh-ver*) is now home to 11,169 residents, not to mention Southwest Baptist University. The North Ward School Museum and the Ella Carothers Dunnegan Gallery of Art are also found here, but the area holds true to its Ozark roots. The annual **Country Days Rodeo** is held the second weekend of every July, followed by the **Diamond S Bull Blast** the first weekend of August.

Greenfield, Mo. Established in 1842, the county seat of Dade County is called home by 1,220 citizens. In town you'll find an 1888 opera house (restored in 1986 and the site of local theater productions), but the real reason to visit Greenfield is the **Buffalo Days** festival. Held annually for more than 30 years, the fair features all the best of small-town festivals. There is a midway, quilt contests, townwide BBQ, cakes, pies, and food galore. The Buffalo Chip-Chucking Contest is a highlight: Those with a good throwing arm compete to see who can toss hunks of dried buffalo dung the farthest.

SIMON BOLÍVAR

Hermitage, Mo. Hickory County was named in honor of Andrew Jackson, nick-
named "Old Hickory." Thus it is fitting that the county seat, Hermitage, is
named for the plantation owned by the seventh president of the United States.
With a population of just 411 souls and located just north of Pomme de Terre
Lake, Hermitage boasts of several popular festivals. The annual **Ozark Market
Day,** held on the Saturday closest to July 4, finds the town square transformed
into an old-time marketplace. Literally hundreds of Ozark craftsmen show up to
both display and sell their creations. On the first Saturday after Labor Day, the
Pomme de Terre Fall Festival kicks into gear. Again, the regional artisans
descend with their unique, handmade products. Last but not least, the Pomme
de Terre Rendezvous is held just south of town each May. Also found in Hermitage is the Hickory County Historical Society Museum, housed in an 1855
antebellum home.

Lamar, Mo. Harry Truman only lived in Lamar for the first 11 months of his
life, but that's long enough to give the town bragging rights as his birthplace.
Lamar is an interesting little town of 4,418 residents, and the Truman birthplace
might be the least interesting stop. Held in late August, the Barton County Free
Fair is Missouri's largest free fair (there are no gate fees). The downtown square
is transformed into festival grounds, and the number of contests, events, activities, and displays held at the fairground proper is truly impressive. The square is
something to see in and of itself, being the second largest downtown square
shopping district in the state of
Missouri. There you will find the Barton County Historical Society and

LADY LIBERTY GUARDS THE LAMAR
SQUARE

Museum, the county courthouse, a
Civil War cannon, a 1913 bandstand,
a 16-foot-tall replica of the Statue of
Liberty, and a memorial to Harry Truman. Yet another unusual attribute of
Lamar is its Stilabower Public Observatory, designed to allow accessibility
to both the handicapped and small
children.

A little-reported historical tidbit
regarding Lamar is that, at age 22,
lawman Wyatt Earp was the town's
first constable (he departed after the
death of his wife, Urilla; the couple
had been married hardly a year).
Also, the town was literally ripped
apart by the Civil War, as the sympathies of the residents were equally
divided between North and South. It
was only in 1910 that veterans of the
opposing sides met on the courthouse
lawn, shaking hands over the barrel of
the cannon.

Stockton, Mo. With 2,007 residents, the county seat of Cedar County is the gateway to both Stockton Lake and Stockton State Park. The Corps of Engineers lake is well known for fishing and scuba, but surprisingly it is one of the most popular lakes for sailing in the state of Missouri. There is even a Stockton Yacht Club, which holds various races and regattas throughout the year. Though not many towns pride themselves on being nuts, Stockton has good reason to crow over such an attribute. It is the home of the Hammons Products Company, the world's premier processor and supplier of American eastern black walnuts for both food and industrial uses.

✳ To See

MUSEUMS 🐾 ✎ **Polk County Museum** (417-326-6850; www.rootsweb.ancestry .com/~mohspcm), 201 W. Locust, Bolivar, Mo. Open May 15–mid-Sept., Mon.–Sat. 1–4. $2 adults, $1 ages 6–12. Built in 1903, the former North Ward school features exhibits in 13 different rooms on three floors. Local Indian artifacts, farm implements, and toys from years past are featured. As proof of local pride, one room is dedicated to a teacher who instructed area children for nearly 50 years. On the museum grounds you can examine a two-story log cabin that dates from 1867.

🐾 ✎ ♿ **Hickory County Historical Society Museum** (417-722-4403), Museum St. on the town square, Hermitage, Mo. The threat of a stay in the primitive 1871 stone jail in Hermitage was no doubt an effective deterrent for more than a few 19th-century chicken thieves. Today both the jail and other historical build-

HERMITAGE'S 1871 STONE JAIL

ings can be found on the northeast corner of the town's courthouse square (the 1896 courthouse is still in use). The Hickory County museum, which resides inside an 1855 antebellum home, is a treasure trove for those who seek a trip to the past. To keep the theme complete, an antiques and gift shop is found in a building constructed the same year as the home.

🌸 ✎ ♿ **Barton County Historical Society and Museum** (417-682-4141; bartoncountyhistorical.org), basement level, Barton County Courthouse, Constitution Square, Lamar, Mo. Open Mon.–Fri. 12:30–4:30. As is true with the county seats of many Ozark towns, the Barton County Courthouse dates from the late 1800s. While the Barton County museum (lower level of the courthouse) is interesting in and of itself, the entire courthouse grounds offer a glimpse into the textured history of the area. A Civil War cannon, a bandstand built in 1913, and a 16-foot-high replica of the Statue of Liberty surround the edifice. Plus, the shopping and dining choices found around the well-designed square will give you plenty to do when it's time to return to the present.

CULTURAL SITES 🌸 ✎ ♿ **Simon Bolívar statue,** College St. and SR Bus. 13, Bolivar, Mo. Bolivar is allegedly the largest town in the U.S. named for the leader of the South American revolution. Thus it is fitting that the country of Venezuela presented local citizens with a statue of the heroic leader. Technically, Bolivar was named for the village of Bolivar, Tenn. However, since Bolivar, Tenn., was in fact named for the "Great Liberator," the gift was graciously accepted.

🌸 ✎ ♿ **Ella Carothers Dunnegan Gallery of Art** (417-326-3438; www .dunnegangallery.org), 511 N. Pike St., Bolivar, Mo. Open Mon., Wed., Fri. 1–4. Free admission. Right across the street from the Polk County Museum is this fine art gallery, a true prize for a town of this size. Displaying a wide range of styles and subjects, the gallery features the works of artists indigenous to Missouri as well as those known around the world. Special exhibits are held during the year (call for more information), and the gallery is the permanent home of both the Dunnegan and Wainscott art collections.

🌸 ✎ ♿ **Stilabower Public Observatory** (417-682-2745), Sixth and Maple Sts., Lamar, Mo. There are very few public observatories in the nation, but you'll find one in Lamar. The Stilabower Public Observatory features a 14-inch telescope, digital imaging, and computerized tracking. Better yet, it has been specially designed to accommodate both young children and handicapped individuals. Call ahead for viewing times; the observatory (located right across from Lamar High School, adjacent to the football field) is open by appointment.

HISTORIC SITE 🌸 ✎ ♿ **Harry S Truman State Birthplace Historic Site** (417-682-2279; www.mostateparks.com/park/harry-s-truman-birthplace-state -historic-site), 1009 Truman St., Lamar, Mo. Open Wed.–Sat. 10–4, Sun. noon–4. One of America's most famous presidents, and the only one born in Missouri, Harry Truman was born in the back bedroom of this tiny 1884 frame home. The 560-square-foot house, which young Harry's parents purchased for $685, has been re-created with period authenticity. Four downstairs and two

THE STILABOWER OBSERVATORY

upstairs rooms feature modest furnishings and lack both electricity and plumbing. Thus it was good that the grounds included a water well and outhouse. A little-known bit of historical trivia is that the Trumans sold this home to the Earp family. Relatives of the famous western marshal lived there until the late 1950s.

✳ Wild Places

🐾 🐻 ✍ ♿ **Prairie State Park** (417-843-6711; www.mostateparks.com/prairie .htm), 128 N.W. 150th Ln., Mindenmines, Mo. Open Apr.–Oct., Wed.–Sat. 10–4; Nov.–Mar., Thurs.–Sat. 10–4. Much of Missouri was once native prairie, but the changes that came with settlers, farming, and development reduced the tallgrass from 13 million acres to 65,000. Prairie State Park, at nearly 4,000 acres, is the largest remaining tallgrass prairie in the state. Full of wandering buffalo, prairie chickens, tallgrass (some of which can reach heights of 8 feet), and wildflowers, the park offers three hiking trails, picnicking, and an excellent visitors center. Camping is allowed with approval of the park naturalist. To reach this unique area from Lamar, drive 16 miles west on US 160. Turn right onto SR NN, drive 1 mile, then turn left onto the gravel Central Rd. for 3 miles. Turn right onto 150th Lane and head 1.3 miles to the park visitors center.

🐾 🐻 ✍ ♿ **Pomme de Terre State Park/Pomme de Terre Lake** (417-852-4291; www.mostateparks.com/pommedeterre/geninfo.htm), SR 64 B, Pittsburg, Mo. In the late 1950s the U.S. Army Corps of Engineers dammed the Pomme de Terre River as part of the flood-control plan for the Missouri River Basin. The result was the 7,800-acre Pomme de Terre Lake (113 miles of shoreline) and the accompanying 734-acre Pomme de Terre State Park. Much more quiet and peaceful than many of the more publicized parks in the Ozarks, Pomme de Terre is a near-perfect choice for a quiet weekend of camping and fishing. Split into two parcels (one on the Hermitage side of the lake, the other on the Pittsburg side), the park features more than 250 campsites, four paved boat launches, marinas, numerous picnic sites, a playground, several hiking trails, and two public beaches. But the best part of Pomme de Terre is the fishing; this is an angler's paradise. A very cool and clear lake, Pomme de Terre holds the usual Ozark species such as bass, catfish, bluegill, and carp. The addition of two other species, however, has made Pomme de Terre a favorite with the hook-and-line set. For starters, fine-tasting walleyes have been introduced into the lake, and they're thriving thanks to the coolness and clarity of the waters (the Pomme de Terre River—which forms the lake—is spring fed). The true prizes, though, are the lake's northern muskies. These are large, hard-fighting, hard-to-catch fish, and this is the only lake in Missouri that has them. Anyone who has ever hooked a muskie will attest that the wait is worth it; the fish is so aggressive that, when it does decide to take a lure, you'll think you have a Volkswagen on the end of the line.

🦐 🐾 ✂ ♿ **Stockton State Park/Stockton Lake** (417-276-4259; www.mostate parks.com/stockton.htm), 1900 S. SR 215, Stockton, Mo. You don't normally think of the Ozarks as a Mecca for sailboats, but the 25,000-acre Stockton Lake is that and more. The open topography and prevailing southwest winds of Stockton have made this body of water so popular with sailors that it not only has its own yacht club, but is the home of numerous regattas and contests as well. Formed when the U.S. Army Corps of Engineers dammed the Sac River in the early 1970s, Stockton Lake's 298 miles of shoreline and 12 parks (one state owned, the rest operated by the Corps of Engineers) provide ample opportunities for boating, fishing, scuba, camping, and sailing. The 2,175-acre Stockton State Park encompasses 29 basic and 45 electric campsites (there are many more spots in other areas around the lake as well), picnic areas, a full-service marina, a dining lodge, and a small motel. Just shy of an hour north of Springfield, Mo., this is another lake that has not suffered the pangs and perils of excess development. The pace of Stockton is slow and relaxing, stressing simple fun and a back-to-nature approach over five-star hotels, T-shirt shacks, and neon lights.

STOCKTON LAKE

✳ Lodging

RESORTS AND LODGES

✍ ᴦ ✳ **Eagle's Nest** (417-852-4301; www.eaglenests.com), HC 76, Box 2690, Pittsburg, Mo. Located 2 miles west of Pittsburg on SR J, Eagle's Nest offers five different rustic (but well-appointed) log cabins ranging from $79–95 per night. All come with full kitchens and bath and include a propane grill on the deck for evening BBQs. For those on a budget or who seek only a clean room and soft bed while on a blast-and-cast expedition, five "Fish and Hunt" cabins run $49–57 per night. All the cabins are nonsmoking, and pets are not accepted. The rates are based on a two-night stay with double occupancy, but the fee for additional guests is only $6 per person. Eagle's Nest offers a couple of options not found in many small resorts. Fishing and duck hunting guides are available, and—most unusual of all—the **Eagle's Nest Art Gallery** is on-site. In between catching muskies (or rather, trying to catch muskies) you can view the works of numerous local artists.

✍ ᴦ ✳ **Stillwater Resort** (417-282-6241; www.stillwaterresort.com), CR 544 and T4, Wheatland, Mo. With its blue and white housekeeping cabins, Stillwater is a bit reminiscent of an early-1960s resort. This is a good thing, as the atmosphere is relaxed and peaceful. The 10 cabins rent for $65–120 per night (three-night minimum between Memorial Day and Labor Day, double occupancy; four-night minimum on major holidays), with a $7 charge per night for each additional person. Pets are not accepted, and you must go out on the deck to smoke. All the cabins include color TV, bed linens and towels,

microwave, refrigerator, coffeemaker, dishes, utensils, and pots and pans; three have ovens. Also, all have decks with furniture and a BBQ grill, and a playground is located at the edge of the lake. Each cabin has its own covered boat slip (bring your own craft; the charge for the slip is $7 per day). Fishing guide services are available, and for the RV enthusiast there are numerous camping spots with full hook-ups.

✍ ᴦ ✳ **Sunflower Resort** (417-282-6235 or 1-800-258-5260; www.sunflowerresort.com), Lake Road 254-15, Wheatland, Mo. The Sunflower offers numerous kitchenette-equipped rooms running $55–99 per night. Very family-friendly, the facility includes a playground; boat, motor, and paddle-boat rentals; horseshoe pits; volleyball; tetherball; and indoor table tennis. The individual lodging units appear clean and modern, and again are priced for those on a budget.

✍ **The Old Country House** (417-276-5822; www.theoldcountryhouse.com), 14411 S. SR 32, Stockton, Mo. Within walking distance of Stockton Dam, this century-old home comes equipped with linens, dishes, silverware, and all the usual amenities (a BBQ grill and picnic table are in the backyard). Smoking and pets are not allowed, but the home is a very good choice for the large family. Prices per night begin at $75, depending upon the number of people staying, which makes it extremely affordable (compare this with the average economy room at a Holiday Inn). This is just a nice, much-loved home, and a few of the owners' commonsense restrictions accentuate the rural character of the area. For instance, they ask that you not clean fish in the house or throw a noisy shindig that might disturb the neighbors.

♨ ⊘ ⟐ ❄ ⚲ **Orleans Trail Resort and Marina** (417-276-3566, 417-276-5161, 1-800-826-0230, or 1-877-525-3886; www.orleanstrail.com), 15857 S. 1525 Rd., Stockton, Mo. Open year-round, the Orleans offers 81 rooms (smoking, nonsmoking, WiFi, kitchenettes, a laundry, regular guest rooms, and suites). Prices run $45–230 per night, and children under 8 stay free. Pets are accepted in the older part of the resort for a $10 flat fee. A full-service marina provides sailboat slips, covered slips, fuel dock with pump-out, boat rentals, and a bait-and-tackle shop. Also on-site is the Orleans Trail Restaurant and Bar (see *Eating Out*).

CAMPGROUNDS

🦞 ♨ ⊘ ⟐ ❄ **Pomme de Terre State Park** (417-852-4291 or 417-745-6909; http://mostateparks.com/park/pomme -de-terre-state-park) SR 64B Pittsburg, Mo. Camping is available at 250 spots located on both the Pittsburg and Hermitage sides of the park. Each camping area includes restrooms, showers, picnic areas, and laundry. Some sites are open year-round, while others are closed Nov.–Mar. During the summer season, prices are $13 for a basic campsite, $21 for an electric campsite, $23 for a campsite with electricity and water, and $26 for a site with electricity, water, and sewer. Pets are OK but must be kept on a leash.

🦞 ♨ ⊘ ⟐ ❄ **Stockton State Park** (417-276-4259 or 1-800-334-6946; http://mostateparks.com/park /stockton-state-park), 19100 S. SR 215, Stockton, Mo. Stockton has fewer campsites than its sister lake, Pomme de Terre, but prices and services are virtually the same. The best campsites at Stockton are available through the park areas operated by the Army Corps of Engineers.

🦞 ♨ ⊘ ⟐ ❄ **Pomme de Terre/Army Corps of Engineers** (417-745-6411;

ORLEANS TRAIL RESORT IS HOME TO A MARINA AND RESTAURANT

www.nwk.usace.army.mil/pt/Camping .cfm), 2160 SR 254, Hermitage, Mo. The Army Corps has six campgrounds located around Pomme de Terre: Nemo Landing, Damsite, Outlet, Wheatland, Lightfoot Landing, and Pittsburg Landing. All are affordable and feature level sites, posts for lanterns, picnic areas, and fire rings. A number also include electricity, showers, dump stations, and play-grounds. Although prices vary per campground, the average is $12–14 for a nonelectric site, $16–30 for one with plug-ins. A single, day-use fee of $3 is charged for launching boats, and there is a $1 charge (for those over 12) for swimming at corps beaches.

🐾 🐕 🛶 ♿ ❄ **Stockton Lake/Army Corps of Engineers** (1-877-444-6777; www.nwk.usace.army.mil/st /Camping.cfm), Stockton Project Office, 16435 E. Stockton Lake Dr., Stockton, Mo. Eight of Stockton's 11 campgrounds (Cedar Ridge, Crabtree Cove, Hawker Point, Masters, Orleans Trail North, Orleans Trail South, Ruark Bluff East, and Ruark Bluff West) are managed by the corps. Consisting of nearly 4,000 total acres and nearly 600 total sites (400 nonelectric, 181 electric, and some group areas), amenities here include showers, dump stations, picnic areas, shelters, boat launches, and swim-ming beaches. Regular-season camp-ing fees are $12 for nonelectric basic sites and $14 for nonelectric prime sites (better lake views and access). The electric basic sites are $16, and the electric primes are $18. As is also true at the corps facilities at Pomme de Terre, the day-use fee for boat launching is $3, and the beach fee is $1 for those older than 12 (up to a maximum of $4 per car).

✳ Where to Eat

EATING OUT Orleans Trail Restaurant (417-276-3566 or 1-877-525-3886; www.orleanstrail.com), 15857 S. 1525 Rd., Stockton, Mo. Open for lunch and dinner Wed.– Sun. Breakfast served Sat., Sun., and on major holidays. A simple but nice restaurant located at the Orleans Trail Resort and Marina, the Orleans Trail offers some choices that differ from what you'll find at the local diners and franchise options more common to the area. You can order a black tuna sandwich for $8, or a bacon cheese-burger and chips for $7.50. For din-ner, a 12-ounce T-bone runs $14, and a number of fish and pasta dishes are available as well. Try the chicken-fried chicken for $8.

Tea Garden Cafe (417-326-3568), 113 N. Main Ave., Bolivar, Mo. When driving around Bolivar you will see every fast-food franchise known to humankind, as well as the obligatory local diners and family restaurants. Therefore, it is something of a shock to trip across the Tea Garden Cafe. Open Mon.–Sat. 11–3, this little oasis on the west side of the town square sits on the upper floor of the **Country Hearth Gift Shop.** A nonsmok-ing establishment, its bill of fare lists numerous specialty teas, chai, cappuc-cino, espresso, and flavored coffees. A menu of lighter foods is a far cry from the typical Ozark catfish and BBQ stop. The longtime favorite of the Tea Garden is the Sweet William sand-wich, which features bacon, turkey, ham, and Swiss cheese on a croissant. Tea time is 3–4 PM (good to know if you've traded the London fog for the Ozark hills) and features scones, crumpets, and desserts.

The Blue Top Cafe (417-682-5080), 57 S.E. First Ln., Lamar, Mo. The Blue Top has been in Lamar since 1941 (I first ate here when I was a kid more than four decades back) and is the quintessential small-town gathering spot. It's where the farmers and local working folks come to drink coffee, swap stories, and load up on biscuits and gravy in the morning. It's a tradition, and that alone is reason enough to stop. Breakfast is good and lunches are hearty, with your usual menu of pancakes, omelets, and sandwiches. At night you can order a 12-ounce T-bone for $8.95, a 16-ounce hamburger steak for $6.95, or chicken-fried steak for $5.95. The Blue Top prides itself on its fried chicken (three pieces for $6.25), which comes with a salad, choice of potato, homemade rolls, and honey. Longevity is worthy of respect, and the traveler should always take a chance on the Blue Top. You'll see the old weathered sign (reading FOOD) from US 71. Where else could you get a big pile of fried chicken livers for $2.85?

The Wild Plum Café (417-682-3225; www.wildplumcafe.com), 206 W. 10th St., Lamar, Mo. I'm not quite sure how the Wild Plum managed to pull this off, but it has made a name for itself via the slogan, "No fried foods . . . ever!" Non-Ozarkers might find that normal, but we hillbilly folk normally regard fried food as an essential building block of life. It's a little more important than oxygen, and just a little less critical than home-made hooch. Nonetheless, The Wild Plum, located inside The Gallery in Lamar, boasts of farm-fresh eggs and breads made with chemical-free flour. This place even composts and recycles, for cryin' out loud. You can try meatless chicken for $3.49, or grab the soup of the day (with house-baked herb bread) for just $2.95. The Wild Plum calls itself Lamar's "Healthy Gourmet Lunch Alternative," and there's a very good chance you'll catch

THE LEGENDARY BLUE TOP CAFÉ

a poetry reading while you're on the premises (no foolin').

✴ Entertainment

Barco Drive-In Theatre (417-682-2434), 57 S.E. 25th Ln., Lamar, Mo. Open Apr.–Oct. With space for 400 cars, the Barco Drive-In has brought the outdoor silver screen to Lamar area residents for 60 years. A living rendition of a simpler time, the Barco is one of the best, offering stereo sound and first-run movies. It's located 1.5 miles east of the Lamar town square. Prices are $6 for adults, $3 for kids ages 3–11. Monday nights offer admission of $9 for as many people as you can cram in a car.

✴ Special Events

Also see Towns and Villages.
May **Pomme de Terre Rendezvous** (www.pommedeterrerendezvous.com), Below Lake Dam, SR 254, Hermitage, Mo. The 1840s come alive over the first weekend in May as latter-day mountain men demonstrate their skills in such events as black powder shooting and knife and tom-

ahawk throwing. There are craft and food booths galore, as well as live music and old-time machinery exhibits. In the past, even a French colonial artillery brigade has shown up for the fun. Best of all, admission is only $2 for those 12 and older.

Truman Day Celebration (417-682-5554), 11th St., Lamar, Mo. The Truman Day Celebration was for years held in June on the Lamar town square. Recently the event has been moved to early May and takes place on Lamar's 11th Street near the president's birthplace (we're guessing Harry wouldn't mind). The staff of the historic site offers refreshments and informative programs, and booths stretching both east and west of the Truman home are full of food and drink, as well as historical and hand-made crafts.

July **Ozark Market Day** (1-800-235-9519), Hermitage, Mo. A free event held on the Saturday closest to Independence Day, Ozark Market Day finds the town square of Hermitage filled with literally hundreds of local artisans. Craftspeople from all over the Ozarks show up at this festival to

Black Walnut Festival (417-276-5161; www.stocktonlake.com), Stockton, Mo. The largest processor of black walnuts in the world, the Hammons Products Company is locally owned in Stockton, Mo. Such being the case, the biggest festival of the year celebrates this profitable nut. Held near the end of September (usually the third weekend of the month), it's a 51-year-old, four-day event in which the entire town participates. You'll find a parade, hordes of artisans and food booths, a horseshoe-pitching contest, live music, and carriage rides. Contests can include anything from the typical beautiful baby competition to talent contests, turtle racing, and pedal tractor pulls. Although the Hammons company doesn't usually give tours, it does offer guided explorations of all things walnut during the festival days, starting at 2 PM Wed.–Fri. and after the parade on Sat.

show off (and hopefully sell) their creations.

August **Barton County Free Fair** (417-682-3687), downtown square, Lamar, Mo. A fair in the old-time tradition, the Free Fair lives up to its name. In fact, it's the largest free fair (there is no gate admission) in the state. Visit this event and you can enjoy parades, a carnival midway, live music, an antique car show, livestock exhibits, and 4-H displays. Contests are prevalent, as they are at all the best fairs, in the vein of fair queen, prettiest baby, and ugliest truck. If you want a taste of what the rural Ozark fairs used to be (and sometimes still are), this is your prime choice.

September **Pomme de Terre Fall Festival** (417-399-5596), Hermitage, Mo. Taking place the first Saturday after Labor Day on the courthouse lawn in Hermitage, the Fall Festival features a plethora of craftsman booths, art, food, and music.

The Southwest Missouri Ozarks

3

THE OZARK MINING REGION

SPRINGFIELD, MISSOURI

THE OZARK MINING REGION

Despite their beauty, the Ozarks have always been a hard land. For early settlers particularly, the rugged and rarely forgiving country demanded fortitude, independence, and pioneer spirit. Perhaps nowhere in the Ozarks were these qualities more required and more apparent than in the southwest section of Missouri. This was and is a territory shaped by extremes. In terms of topography you need but look to see the contrast. The rolling Springfield Plateau, as found in the Joplin, Neosho, and Carthage areas, is far different from the bluffs, ravines, and wild scenery you experience as you drop down into the White River Valley near Cassville, Noel, and Roaring River State Park. In terms of wealth, the history of the region is a contest between flat broke and fabulously wealthy, a gulf between eking sparse stocks of corn from thin, rocky soil and the fortunes that emerged from lead, zinc, and limestone mines.

During the Civil War (and both before and after . . . it is often said that the War Between the States lasted 10 years in Missouri, and four years everywhere else), the southwestern Missouri Ozarks experienced nonstop battles and skirmishes. Missouri is actually third behind Virginia and Tennessee in the number of battles fought, and many of them took place on the Kansas-Missouri border. Residents of that time leaned toward the Southern cause, more out of a sense of independence and pride (the hill residents hated any government telling them what to do) than out of sympathies with slaveholders. Frankly, most people here didn't have the money to own slaves.

Though the Civil War officially began on April 12, 1861, and ended April 9, 1865, the unofficial fights between pro-slavery Missourians and free-state Kansans had long before exceeded the boiling point. The elected government of Missouri voted to secede from the Union, but federal troops had other ideas. They wished not only to hold control of the Missouri and Mississippi Rivers, but also to possess the valuable lead reserves that had been discovered in the southwest Missouri Ozarks. Ousted governor Clairborne Fox and members of the Missouri General Assembly (11 senators and 44 representatives), on the run from Union forces, met in Cassville and declared it the Confederate capital of Missouri. Soon thereafter, they went to Neosho and ratified the Articles of Secession.

Left to their own devices, it could strongly be argued that residents of this region would have largely ignored the war and continued to live as they always had, keeping to themselves and remaining more concerned with family and community than with political turf wars. Their stance, as was true with all Ozarkers (and to a degree, still is), was initially one of opinionated neutrality. They had their views and were quick to air them, but the daily tasks of growing a crop and putting food on the table superseded fighting and dying over the squabbles of politicians.

A strategic mistake by the Union generals changed all that. Border Missourians, and especially Ozarkers in the precious mining region, were indiscriminately viewed by federal forces as traitors and Rebels. Virtually all were treated with utter contempt. With the implicit blessings of the North, renegade Jayhawkers from Kansas (under the command of such men as Jim Lane and Jim Montgomery) rode through the borderlands, burning, pillaging, and plundering at will. The proud Ozarkers fought back with a vengeance, now supporting the

Rebel cause against those who would destroy their homes. They gladly harbored equally violent Missouri bushwhackers under the command of leaders such as William Quantrill and Bloody Bill Anderson (both the James and Younger boys perfected their future trade under the tutelage of these two men).

The ground ran red with blood, and before long, friend and foe were interchangeable. Justifiable paranoia and fear were rampant. The Union might show up at midnight to conscript troops, burn a barn, appropriate stock and valuables, or shoot suspected Rebels. The bushwhackers might do much the same, simply to prevent their blue-coated opponents from acquiring provisions. A sizable number of deserters from both sides, harboring a criminal mentality, saw the potential for a fat harvest. They tore through the land like a whirlwind, stealing what they could and murdering without hesitation.

Until the end of the war, the fighting and carnage were unprecedented. In addition to the atrocities of bushwhackers and partisans, the armies of North and South engaged in a deadly game of tug-of-war over mining region towns and settlements. Cassville was attacked time after time, sometimes held by the Gray and sometimes by the Blue. The Battle of Carthage saw that town burned to the ground, and by 1866 its population was nearly nonexistent. Two battles were fought at Newtonia. The village of Jollification, between Monett and Granby, was twice set to the torch. Oddly, or perhaps not, the Jolly Mill was spared on both occasions. This could be attributed to either luck or the fact that the Jolly

THE JASPER COUNTY COURTHOUSE IN CARTHAGE

Mill served as a whiskey distillery (it continued producing whiskey, illegally, until just before World War I).

The war eventually ended, as most wars do, and the rebuilding process began. Mining had taken place in the district since the early 1800s (Ozark explorer Henry Schoolcraft wrote in 1819 of how he had dug lead from a streambed, scratched out a shallow pit to melt it, and molded bullets on the spot). Concerted mining efforts had begun in earnest around 1850, and though the mining camps were deserted during the war years, by the 1870s the mines were in full production. Joplin transformed into a town of thousands literally overnight, with nearly 80 saloons and bawdy houses for the footloose miners.

Lead became a bonanza for mine owners, though not for the workers. The men who dug the ore were paid a pittance; they suffered from cave-ins, black lung, and temporary blindness from acidic waters deep in the earth. When the miners discovered that the "black stuff" clinging to the lead was in fact zinc (at first they'd tossed the unknown substance into piles that sometimes reached hundreds of feet in height), the boom increased proportionately. By 1880, the mining region shipped out more zinc than lead. The mines were money pits in the truest sense of the term.

Carthage, which seemed doomed to die by the ravages of the war, experienced a resurgence in the late 1800s due to the discovery of Burlington limestone, also known as Carthage white marble. The population swelled to nearly 10,000, and in the 1900 census it was the wealthiest town per capita in America. The gracious mansions and homes of Carthage, not to mention the magnificent Jasper County Courthouse, still stand today. They reflect the town's sincere reverence for, and devotion to, its past.

And what became of native Ozarkers after the war? Used to hardship and sacrifice, they simply returned to their farms and started over. New settlers seeking elbow room moved in from Tennessee and Kentucky, but also from Europe. Holding similar values to the Ozarkers, desirous of cheap land, and hearing that the streets of America were paved with gold, these latter immigrants moved to the Ozarks and were assimilated into the isolated communities.

For good or ill, civilization and progress came to the mining region in the 20th century. As always, the new and the old still bubble in a single Ozark pot, and this unique section of southwest Missouri remains a study in contrasts. When the mines petered out, agriculture took over. As agriculture suffered, the local economy received yet another blow. As recently as the 1980s, those driving into downtown Joplin would find a town in the grip of an ongoing recession.

However, with the rapid growth of the region—and the popularity and acclaim of nearby cities such as Branson and Springfield—the mining region has received yet another lease on life. Soft-manufacturing firms provide jobs to thousands without destroying the environment. The transportation industry—freight and trucking firms—is huge in the towns that border I-44. An influx of investment has allowed community pride to emerge anew, and those once wealthy towns that had fallen on hard times are quickly returning to their earlier grandeur. Just a quick trip through Carthage, with its stately mansions, manicured lawns, numerous parks, and unique shops will prove that time is a healer. A drive though Joplin, seeing the hustle and bustle, sampling the artistic venues, and walking the miles of greenway, will serve as testament to that town's endurance. A day at Roaring River State Park, experiencing the quaint and friendly hamlets of Cassville and Noel, will teach the lesson that old and new can live in harmony.

The Ozark Mining Region was a hard land of extremes and contrasts; you'll get no argument there. But more than that, it is a living example of the power of resiliency.

AREA CODES All of the cities and towns found in the Ozark Mining Region fall under the **417** area code.

GUIDANCE Numerous chambers of commerce and visitors centers serve the busy and growing Ozark Mining Region of southwest Missouri. For information on events, dining, lodging, and individual town services, the following are the most helpful.

Joplin Convention and Visitors Bureau (417-625-4789 or 1-800-657-2534; www.joplincvb.com), 602 S. Main St., Joplin, Mo.

Carthage Convention & Visitors Bureau (417-359-8181; www.visit-carthage .com), 402 S. Garrison St., Carthage, Mo.

Cassville Area Chamber of Commerce (417-847-2814; www.cassville.com), 504 Main St., Cassville, Mo.

Monett Chamber of Commerce (417-235-7919; www.monett-mo.com), 200 E. Broadway, Monett, Mo.

Neosho Area Chamber of Commerce (417-451-1925; www.neoshocc.com), P.O. Box 605, Neosho, MO 64850.

GETTING THERE *By car:* From either the east or west, I-44 is the main route to the Ozark Mining Region. It passes directly through Joplin, with Carthage approximately 28 miles to the north on US 71. Following US 71 South, you will arrive at both Neosho, the "Flower Box City," and Noel, the "Christmas City." To experience the beginning of the White River Valley and Roaring River State Park at Cassville, take US 60 from Neosho to the town of Monett. From there, turn south onto SR 37. At Cassville, continue south on SR 112.

By air: Travel by air becomes simpler for Ozark visitors as they move toward this growing region. Just 42 miles south of Joplin on US 71 is **Northwest Arkansas Regional Airport** (479-205-1000; www.nwara.com), 1 Airport Blvd., Bentonville, Ark. This airport is serviced by Allegiant, American Eagle, Continental Express, Delta, US Airways Express, and United. The **Springfield-Branson National Airport** (417-868-0500; www.sgf-branson-airport.com), 2300 N. Airport Blvd., Springfield, Mo., with all the conveniences and amenities of the greater Springfield area, is located less than 60 miles east of Joplin up I-44. It is served by American Airlines, Allegiant, United, and Delta. The airport offers facilities for buses, vans, rental cars, and hotel and hospitality limousines for groups. The **Branson Airport** (1-888-359-2541; http://flybranson.com), 4000 Branson Airport Blvd., Hollister, Mo., opened in May 2009; it holds the distinction of being the only privately owned, privately operated, commercial service airport in the United States. The airport offers direct, nonstop flights to a number of cities, and is serviced by AirTran, Frontier, and Branson Air Express. **Joplin Regional Airport** (417-623-0262; www.jlnairport.com), 7331 N. SR 43, offers service via American Airlines and American Eagle. There is no fee for parking at Joplin Regional.

MEDICAL EMERGENCIES Feeling a tad under the weather is no problem in the Ozark Mining Region. The following six hospitals, all full service with 24-hour emergency rooms, are but a short hop from any location in the area.

Freeman Neosho Hospital (417-451-1234; www.freemanhealth.com/neosho), 113 W. Hickory, Neosho, Mo.

Freeman Ozark Center (417-347-7600; www.freemanhealth.com/ozarkcenter), 3606 McClelland Blvd., Joplin, Mo.

Cox Monett Hospital (417-235-3144; www.coxhealth.com/body.cfm?id=1341), 801 Lincoln Ave., Monett, Mo.

McCune Brooks Regional Hospital (417-358-8121; www.mccune-brooks.org), 3125 Russell Smith Way, Carthage, Mo. This hospital is worthy of additional note, as it was just completed in 2008. McCune Brooks is a 145,000-square-foot facility featuring an outpatient clinic, 41 private patient rooms, an expanded women's program and ER services, and an all-new digital radiology department. McCune-Brooks's obstetrics program includes whirlpool baths, family rooms, and individualized care.

St. John's Hospital–Cassville (417-847-6000; www.stjohns.com/cassville), 94 Main St., Cassville, Mo.

✳ Wandering Around

EXPLORING BY CAR In the early part of the last century, the locals of southwest Missouri made a habit of tapping the sugar maple trees for their sweet syrup. Though you'll no longer see too many Ozark maple trees with spigots in their sides, you can still explore the beauty of the region via the 30-mile **Sugar Camp Scenic Byway.** Begin your trip on SR 112, just south of Cassville, Mo., and drive through **Roaring River** State Park. You'll be driving "down" into Roaring River, with the last mile falling away at a rapid 400-foot pace (in other words, go slowly and shift down). There is plenty to do in Roaring River—you might want to visit the fish hatchery, hike one of the numerous trails, tour the Chinquapin Nature Center, or take a stroll back to Roaring River Spring itself. As you prepare to leave the park, watch the road signs and turn onto Forest Road (FR) 197. Though this is a gravel road, it is in very good shape (surprisingly, most U.S. Forest Service roads are well maintained). This route travels 8 miles, and eventually hooks up with SR 86. In between—and this especially applies if you're traveling in fall—be prepared for some jaw-dropping colors and breathtaking ridgetop vistas. For a brief stop, pull into the **Onyx Cave Picnic Area.** The adventurous (or those who don't mind getting a bit dirty) can crawl nearly 100 feet into this little hole in the wall. Continuing ahead a few miles, you will

ROARING RIVER SPRING

turn left onto FR 2275 and enter the community of Eagle Rock. Just ahead is the road's intersection with SR 86. Drive back north on SR 86 to its junction with SR 76, and return to Cassville. If driven straight through, the whole loop requires a little more than an hour. Nobody does it that quickly. You'll want to stop, see the sights, and click off lots of photos.

EXPLORING BY FOOT 🏛 ⌀ ♿ **Carver Trail** (417-325-4151; www.nps.gov /gwca/index.htm), 5646 Carver Rd., Diamond, Mo. Because most visitors travel in summer, and because after April even the smallest Ozark weed patch transforms into a tick factory, it is wise to either (a) tuck your pant legs into your shoes and spray them heavily with DEET; or (b) take short hikes on trails that are well maintained and well beaten down. Thus, for both enjoyment and a lack of bloodsucking parasites, I recommend the 1-mile Carver Trail at the George Washington Carver National Monument in Diamond, Mo. The trail begins at Carver's bust just outside the visitors center (you can press a button and hear Carver's own voice reciting a poem). Walk ahead until you come across the tiny cabin where the brilliant man was born a slave. The trail follows the same paths George played upon and explored as a boy. You will pass his statue, cross a small, arched bridge, and walk around a pretty little spring-fed pond. Soon you will approach a second home, built by George's kindly "owner," Moses Carver, in 1881. The house is open to visitors and contains bits and bobs of interpretive information. Moving forward, you'll cross a couple of tiny creeks, a prairie area, and the cemetery where both Moses Carver and his wife, Susan, are buried. The trail ends back at the visitors center. The park is open daily 9–5 except on major holidays. Admission is free.

EXPLORING BY RIVER Starting just north of Noel in Pineville, Mo., the **Elk River** forms at the intersection of the Big and Little Sugar Creeks. Roughly 55 miles in length, the Elk is clear, pretty, and generally fairly slow. That said, the current can jump up to the Class II range after a heavy rain. The flow of the river is more or less north by northwest, and it eventually dumps into the Grand Lake of the Cherokees in Oklahoma. Until relatively recent times, you could count on an unspoiled and quiet trip down the Elk. These days, as more and more visitors continue to discover southwest Missouri, things can get a bit busy on good-weather weekends. There's a reason for that: The Elk is a gorgeous float with good fishing. Numerous access points, campgrounds, and outfitters make for an easy and relaxing day (or days) on the river.

Big Sugar Creek, one of the tributaries of the Elk, encompasses about 25 miles that are easily navigable by kayak or canoe. Just behind the Elk in terms of popularity with floaters, it has a good current but no whitewater that might surpass the abilities of the beginner. The creek is locally famous for its clear water and fine fishing. The Big Sugar can be floated almost any time of year, except of course for those spells when the occasional Missouri drought pays a long visit.

If the Elk and Big Sugar are too busy for your tastes, you might want to sample the nearly 8 miles of **Little Sugar Creek** that are consistently floatable. There aren't a lot of folks who opt for the Little Sugar, but that's only because most people prefer a longer float. For a day trip, this creek is perfect. It's pretty and clear; birds, trees, and wildlife are plentiful. Little Sugar would actually be my first choice if my goal were a lazy day of floating, assuming the cooler is full and there are plenty of eats.

The best time to hit **Indian Creek** is in the months of early spring; the water isn't deep enough to float during the rest of the year. When the rains of March and April come down, you can almost always count on a fairly swift current. Almost 27 miles in length, the Indian flows southwest until it dumps into the Elk. It's a fairly remote river (this is a relative statement—the rivers of southwest Missouri are all close to numerous towns) and shutterbugs will find ample scenery to record for posterity. There are a couple of low-water bridges and drops on the Indian, so the inexperienced floater should watch carefully. Don't be ashamed to pull to the bank and portage around such obstacles if you believe they're beyond your skill level. It's downright humiliating to get stuck under a bridge. The locals might not laugh in your face—that would be impolite—but they'll talk about the event for months.

✳ Towns and Villages

Carthage, Mo. Still full of grand Victorian homes, Carthage was considered the wealthiest town per capita in America at the turn of the 20th century. Mining barons made a killing with their lead and zinc operations, and Carthage white marble was renowned throughout the country. For examples, just look at the Field Museum in Chicago or the Macy's building in New York City. Founded in 1841, Carthage was burned to the ground during the Civil War. The July 5–6, 1861, Battle of Carthage and Battle of Wilson's Creek at Springfield were two of the first major conflicts in the War Between the States. Today, this town of

CARTHAGE IS FULL OF VICTORIAN HOMES

14,055 is one of the prettiest stops in the Ozarks. At no time is the beauty more evident than in early October, when "the Maple Leaf City" holds its annual Maple Leaf Festival. In Carthage you can take a tour of Victorian homes, sample numerous restaurants and specialty shops, or visit Civil War battle sites and museums. The town is perhaps best known as the home of the famous Precious Moments Inspiration Park, but it should be equally well regarded as the birthplace of zoologist Marlin Perkins and outlaw queen Belle Starr.

Cassville, Mo. For about five minutes in 1861 (actually, it was Oct. 31–Nov. 7), Cassville served as the Confederate capital of Missouri. Obviously, the designation was short-lived, as the Show-Me State ended up remaining in the Union. Things are mellower these days, and Cassville is a popular stop for trout fishermen on their way to Roaring River State Park, which is only 7 miles away. The town of 3,255 residents is surrounded on two sides by the Mark Twain National Forest. It's also the hub of the 30-mile driving loop known as the Sugar Camp Scenic Byway. Don't miss that drive if you want to see nature at its very best.

Diamond, Mo. The little town of Diamond made a major contribution to the world when it produced the genius of George Washington Carver. Born a slave, the humble Carver went on to become a scientist, teacher, philosopher, and inventor of all things peanut. The George Washington Carver National Monument in Diamond is a tribute to the great man. While there, be sure to check out the informative visitors center, walk the 1-mile Carver Trail, and view the bronze statue of Carver as a boy.

Granby, Mo. Just south of Diamond lies Granby, the original lead and zinc town of the Ozarks. Around the year 1850, the Jolly Mill was established. The name apparently arose from the fact that the mill was used as a whiskey distillery until World War I. The mill has been restored by the Jolly Mill Park Foundation, and the grounds now include a peaceful park and good fishing in Capps Creek.

Joplin, Mo. Though settlements were formed in the Joplin area in the mid-1800s, it wasn't until after the Civil War that times became interesting. Lead was discovered in huge quantities in 1870, and the town was the center of an unprecedented mining boom. "Wild and woolly" is an understatement, as the population grew to the thousands; more than 80 saloons, gambling houses, and pleasure parlors kept the rough miners entertained. Production of lead and zinc continued unabated for years (close to a billion dollars' worth was shipped from the region between 1900 and 1940), and the mines only shut down in 1970. Economic depression followed, and by the 1980s many of the buildings in downtown Joplin had locked doors and plywood-covered windows. I happened to work on a paper in Joplin during that period, and on any given day I could be greeted by a collection of panhandlers, hobos, or one unfortunate fellow who liked to wear a Santa Claus suit year-round.

That's the past. Now Joplin is a culturally diverse city of more than 50,208 that has pulled itself up by its bootstraps and created its own renaissance. It's clean, up-to-date, and growing at a remarkable pace. Theater, art, shopping, and restaurants have replaced the old saloons and inns of ill repute, and a downtown revitalization is in full swing. Local retail and national/regional firms employ more than 35,000 residents. Joplin boasts of beautiful parks, two regional health centers, an airport, colleges, and 40 separate trucking companies. Though it would come as a surprise to those who saw the town just a couple of decades ago, Joplin is now consistently listed as one of the most livable small cities in American. The Dorothea B. Hoover Historical Museum and the Everett J. Ritchie Tri-State Mineral Museum celebrate the past, and the Joplin Municipal Building features a mural by renowned artist Thomas Hart Benton. Just outside town, on Riverside Drive, you can view Grand Falls, the largest continuously running waterfall in Missouri. Of course, any discussion of Joplin would be incomplete without mention of the Hornet Spook Lights, an unexplained dancing orange ball that appears almost any night (in the same spot) on an isolated road near the town.

Monett, Mo. Originally known as both Plymouth and Billings, Monett received its permanent name in 1887. The town of more than 8,829 residents now features a 75-acre city park and nearly 10 miles of greenway trails. The town's proximity to Springfield, Joplin, and Branson—it's less than an hour from each—has made it popular as a bedroom community for those who wish to enjoy a more rural lifestyle combined with city amenities.

Mount Vernon, Mo. The seat of Lawrence County, Mount Vernon and its 4,580-plus residents are most proud of their nationally known festival, Apple Butter Makin' Days. A three-day extravaganza that has been held annually for nearly 40 years, the event consistently draws nearly 50,000 visitors. Music, food, contests, parades, and pageants all center on the preparation of apple butter, which is cooked in huge copper kettles over open fires. More than 100 different regiments camped in and around Mount Vernon during the Civil War. The town

flew either the Stars and Bars or the Stars and Stripes, depending on which uni-
form was in residence.

Neosho, Mo. When rated on a basis of sheer pretty, there are few small towns
that can compare with Neosho. Nationally known as the Flower Box City, in the
mid-1950s the town received a grant to experiment in city beautification. As a
result, planters were placed in every location imaginable. Flower boxes are still
found in front of virtually every business, church, school, and home in town. As
if that weren't enough, Neosho's Morse Park holds the world's largest flower box
(formerly a 66-foot-long, 8-foot-wide railroad gondola car) filled with flowers,
shrubs, and trees. Also in town is Big Spring Park (a popular site for weddings,
set around the spring itself, which pumps out nearly 900,000 gallons daily) and
the oldest national fish hatchery in the U.S. Festivals are popular in Neosho;
October brings Barnyard Days, which draws artisans and craftsmen from around
the nation.

Noel, Mo. The Christmas City of the Ozarks, Noel is a pleasant little town of
1,615 situated on the Elk River. Canoeing is popular here, down the Elk, Big
Sugar Creek, and Indian Creek. The Elk River bluffs literally reach out to create
a ceiling above SR 59 between Noel and the small town of Lanagan. Just 2 miles
south of Noel is the commercial Bluff Dweller's Cave and Browning Museum.
As caves go this is a good one, featuring the 10-ton Balanced Rock, which can be
moved by the pressure of a finger, and the Musical Chime formation, which pro-
duces a tone when thunked. As mentioned, however, Noel's big claim to fame is
its designation as the Christmas City of the Ozarks. Since the 1930s, the town
has invited people from around the world to send their stamped, personal
Christmas cards to the local post office. In return they receive the red and green
NOEL postmark. More than 100,000 cards a year are still received (town volunteers help out and affix the special mark). There is no charge for the service. Just
package up your Christmas cards, make sure they are stamped, and send them
to: Postmaster, Noel, MO 64854.

THE WORLD'S LARGEST FLOWER BOX

✳ To See

✐ ઠ ✳ **Neosho National Fish Hatchery** (417-451-0554; www.fws.gov/midwest/neosho), 520 E. Park St., Neosho, Mo. Free. Established in 1888, this is the oldest operating federal fish hatchery in the U.S. The city of Neosho eventually grew around the hatchery, and today the facility attracts more than 100,000 visitors each year. Due to high public interest, the hatchery constructed a 9,200-square-foot visitors center in 2009. Tours are offered Mon.–Fri. 8–4:30 by appointment. In addition, a 3-mile paved walking trail (very popular with joggers) meanders around and through the hatchery.

MUSEUMS ✐ ઠ ✳ **Newton County Historical Society Museum** (417-451-4940; www.neoshocc.com/interest7.html), 121 N. Washington St., Neosho, Mo. Open Wed.–Sun. 12:30–4:30. Free. Originally the county jail and home of the sheriff, the Newton County Historical Society Museum holds, among other things, frontier-era farming equipment, tools, and household items. Also on the grounds are the restored **Newton County School 111**—an 1896 structure built by the county's Anti-Horse Thief Society—and an 1850s log cabin built by the great-grandfather of a Neosho businessman.

✐ ઠ ✳ **Longwell Museum** (417-451-2332; www.newtoncountyhistoricalsociety .org/longwell_museum_crowder_college.htm), 601 Laclede St., Neosho, Mo. Call for hours. Free. Located in the Elsie Plaster Community Center at Neosho's Crowder College, the Longwell Museum possesses many artifacts regarding

GRANBY MINERS MUSEUM

Thomas Hart Benton and the Daisy Cook Collection. In addition, the museum displays 5,000 photos, manuscripts, and records from the days when Crowder College was Fort Crowder. At that time the facility served as a World War II Army Signal Corps training facility and a POW camp for German and Japanese soldiers.

Granby Miners Museum (417-472-3014; www.facebook.com/pages/Granby -Miners-Museum/137781292960202), 218 N. Main St., Granby, Mo. Thurs.–Fri. 1–4, Sat. 11–4. Admission is free, but donations are accepted. The redbrick building on Granby's Main Street could easily be an old five-and-dime. If you spot the MINERS MUSEUM sign and take a step through the doors, though, you'll soon find yourself journeying into the past. The little village of Granby is the oldest mining town in southwest Missouri, the locale where the bonanza of lead and zinc was first discovered. The photos, tools, and history found in the museum will leave no doubts that the pioneer miners were a tough and inventive lot.

✔ ♿ ❀ **Joplin Museum Complex** (417-623-1180; www.joplinmuseum.org /about.htm), Seventh St. and Schifferdecker Ave., Joplin, Mo. Tues. 10–7, Wed.–Sat. 10–5, Sun. 2–5. $2 adults; children under 5 admitted free; family passes available for $5. Located in Schifferdecker Park, the Joplin Museum Complex holds several different museums that thoroughly detail the history of Joplin and the mining operations that built the town. The **Everett J. Ritchie Tri-State Mineral Museum,** founded in 1931, displays an impressive collection of lead and zinc ore. Also on hand are numerous mining tools, equipment, and histories exemplifying the rugged work and lives of the miners. **The Dorothea B. Hoover Historical Museum** puts its focus more on the town of Joplin itself. Geared heavily toward Victorian days, the collections include dolls, a circus room, a children's playhouse, and an ancient American LaFrance fire engine. Various submuseums (larger displays) are located within the complex, such as the Empire District Electric Company Museum, the Joplin Sports Authority Sports Hall of Fame, and the National Historical Cookie Cutter Museum.

♟ ✔ **Civil War Museum** (417-237-7060; www.carthage-mo.gov), 205 E. Grant St., Carthage, Mo. Mon.–Sat. 8:30–5, Sun. 1–5. Free. This museum chronicles the Civil War in the Ozarks, and one of its bragging points is a 7-by-15-foot mural detailing the Battle of Carthage. The museum also contains many artifacts of the War Between the States. Visitors can purchase souvenirs and signed, numbered prints of the mural.

♟ ✔ ♿ **Powers Museum** (417-237-0456; www.powersmuseum.com), 1617 W. Oak St., Carthage, Mo. Open June–Nov., Tues.–Sat. 10:30–4:30, Sun. 1–4:30. Closed Mon. and Dec. 18–Mar. 9. Free. Yet another jewel hidden away in a small town, the Powers Museum highlights a nearly complete history of Carthage during the 19th and 20th centuries. Opening in 1988, the museum resulted from a bequest left by lifelong Carthage resident Marian Powers Winchester. Housing an artifact collection of more than 10,000 items, Powers has more than four dozen main gallery exhibits and has hosted nearly 40 traveling exhibits and displays. It also features a gift shop, research library, and media presentations. The museum was seriously damaged by a blizzard in 2011 (apparently the roof leaked and water damage was severe). It also turned out that

POWERS MUSEUM

history-loving squirrels had taken up residence in the storage area. Since the Carthage city budget is tight, you best call ahead to make sure the museum is open.

🎗 ✐ **Lawrence County Historical Society Museum** (417-466-2185; www .mtvernonchamber.com), 11110 Lawrence (Farm Road 1137), Mount Vernon, Mo. Open Memorial Day–Oct., 1–4. Free. Located inside the lovely **Jones Memorial and Chapel,** this museum offers far more than you might expect. Inside are an 1865 hearse and a statue of Lady Justice, removed from the top of the Lawrence County Courthouse. One area of the museum celebrates the involvement of locals in conflicts ranging from the Civil War to Desert Storm; another focuses on the Depression era. The Hall of Time is a fine vignette of life during the 1950s, '60s, and '70s (polish up those disco boots). There is a gift shop within the museum, and adjacent is the historic, fully restored **1845 Adamson Cabin.**

The Country Caboose (417-624-3861 or 1-800-371-3861; www.countrycaboose .com), 1100 N. Prosperity Rd., Joplin, Mo. Mon.–Fri. 8–5 by appointment or "by chance." The owners used to call this shop "southwest Missouri's premier gourmet kitchen and gift shop," selling their wares from cabooses and passenger cars resurrected from the Santa Fe, New Jersey Central, and Frisco railroad lines. But a funny thing happened. The kitchen items weren't all that popular, but the railroadiana was. Such being the case, The Country Caboose is now southwest Missouri's only railroad museum . . . or at least the only such museum housed in railroad cars.

CULTURAL SITES 🍴 𝒮 ♿ **Neosho downtown square/murals.** Many of the buildings in downtown Neosho are listed on the National Register of Historic Places. Murals celebrating the town's heritage add to the charm of the Flower Box City. A five-panel mural chronologically depicting the history of Newton County is located on the main floor of the Newton County Courthouse, the *Centennial Mural* is found in the Municipal Auditorium, and the *Skaggs Tile Mural* is on the Mills Park Centre Building in Big Spring Park.

🍴 𝒮 ♿ **Webb City Praying Hands** (417-673-6297; www.webbcitychamber .com), 555 S. Main St., King Jack Park, Webb City, Mo. Free. More than 32 feet high and weighing 100 tons, *Praying Hands* was created in 1972 by local artist Jack Dawson. It serves as a symbol of spiritual growth for local residents and draws visitors from a four-state area.

🍴 𝒮 ♿ **The Kneeling Miner** (417-673-1154), 555 S, Main St., King Jack Park, Webb City, Mo. Free. Another creation of Webb City artist Jack Dawson, the 10-foot-tall *Kneeling Miner* commemorates Webb City's legacy as a lead-mining town.

🍴 𝒮 **Red Oak II** (417-237-0808; http://redoakiimissouri.com), 3 miles north of Carthage on SR 96, then 1 mile on SR 12. Open Mar.–Dec. This little-known spot north of Carthage continues to grow both because of its unique sights and cheap ($1) admission. The abandoned town of Red Oak was moved 25 miles by Lowell Davis and preserved as a reasonable facsimile of a 1929 Ozarks town. There are Burma Shave signs, a Phillips 66 station, an operating general store, and a blacksmith's shop with penny arcade games. Also on the site is a café and a little museum detailing the life of Belle Starr (the Ozarks are proud of their outlaws).

🍴 𝒮 ♿ **George A. Spiva Center for the Arts** (417-623-0183; www.spiva arts.org), 222 W. Third St., Joplin, Mo. Tues.–Sat. 10–5, Sun. 1–5; admission varies depending on exhibits and educational programs. With its two galleries, numerous classes, and extensive library, the Spiva Center offers regularly changing exhibits by local, regional, and national artists. The gift shop allows visitors the opportunity to purchase an infinite number of original works of art.

PRAYING HANDS

HISTORIC SITES ✐ 占 ✳ **George Washington Carver National Monument** (417-325-4151; www.nps.gov/gwca), 5646 Carver Rd., Diamond, Mo. Born a slave, kidnapped, orphaned, and nearly killed by whooping cough, George Washington Carver overcame all odds and mastered chemistry, botany, music, herbalism, art, cooking, and massage, eventually heading the Department of Agriculture at the Tuskegee Institute. His groundbreaking work with the peanut began in 1903, and he discovered more than 500 uses for the legume. Rather than seek profit, Carver spread his information for free with the aim of helping African American farmers escape poverty. His monument in Diamond, Mo., the home of his birth, was the first such park to honor an African American scientist and educator. The visitors center features a film and exhibits and is open daily. The **Carver Discovery Center** offers interactive displays for both adults and children, and the 1-mile **Carver Trail** wanders the woods Carver explored as a child and passes by his statue.

✐ 占 ✳ **Newtonia Civil War Battle Site** (417-592-0531), 520 Mill St., Newtonia, Mo. Free. Two major Civil War battles were fought in Newtonia, one on Sept. 30, 1862, and the other on Oct. 28, 1864. Approximately 20 acres of the battlefield and the 1852 **Ritchey Mansion** and cemetery (built by early settler Colonel Matthew Ritchey and his wife, Polly) are now preserved by the Newtonia Battlefields Protection Association. The site is open to the public on a daily basis, and tours are by appointment. Legend has it that the ghost of Polly still roams the mansion on cold nights, covering guests with blankets. This a handy thing to know if you're prone to chills. Newtonia is approximately 25 miles east of Neosho on SR 86.

✐ 占 **Battle of Carthage State Historic Site** (417-682-2279; www.mo stateparks.com/carthage.htm), E. Chestnut Rd., Carthage, Mo. Missouri originally seceded from the U.S. On July 5, 1861, Missouri governor Clairborne Fox led 6,000 Confederate troops against a 1,000-member Union force commanded by Colonel Franz Seigel. The Rebels won the day in a 12-hour running battle that began 9 miles north of Carthage and was fought throughout the streets of the town. This 7.4-acre plot in Carthage is where Fox's troops camped after their victory. An interpretive shelter explains the history of the battle, and

GEORGE WASHINGTON CARVER NATIONAL MONUMENT

HISTORIC PHELPS HOUSE

the area has changed little in nearly 150 years. As a side note, it is said that, after the battle, casualties were cared for in the Jasper County Courthouse. According to local lore, one of the nurses was Carthage resident Myra Belle Shirley, who later went on to be known as the infamous Belle Starr.

Phelps House (417-358-1776; www.phelpshouse.org), 1146 Grand Ave., Carthage, Mo. Open for individual, family, and group tours Apr.–Nov., Wed. 10–4. Call for rates. All that marble money pouring into Carthage led to some pretty nice shanties. Of those that remain, one of the best is Phelps House. A three-story Victorian constructed in 1895 of Carthage limestone, the home contains rare woodwork, original light fixtures, hand-painted wallpaper and mosaic tiles, a Shakespearean library, and 10 fireplaces.

✍ & **Kendrick Place** (417-358-0636; www.visit-carthage.com/phpyellow/full page.php?ckey=40), 131 Northwoods Rd., Carthage, Mo. Open Apr.–Dec., Wed.–Sat. 10–4. Donations accepted. Sold to the Kendrick family in 1860, this historic home was built by slaves in 1849. An old-style mansion in the true sense of the word, it was regarded at one time as one of the most opulent residences in Missouri. Apparently the Kendrick clan was of a diplomatic bent, as they managed to convince both Union and Confederate troops of their neutrality during the Civil War. The home was occupied by troops of both sides at one time or another (though one wonders what might have happened if they arrived at the same time) and survived the conflict unscathed. This was no small feat, as most of the homes in the Carthage area were plundered, ravaged, and burned. It's a true museum of living history. Guided tours are available, and the home can be rented for weddings or other special occasions.

ZOOS ✍ **Reptile World Zoo** (417-206-4443; www.reptileworldzoo.com), 1733 Kodiak Rd., Joplin, Mo. Open Mon.–Fri. 10–5:30; Sat. 11–4. $8 adults, $4.50 for children under 12. No vacation is complete (assuming you have a 12-year-old boy and a sister he wants to scare) without a visit to a reptile farm. Joplin has a good one in the Reptile World Zoo. From Ugandan black forest cobras to yellow anacondas to American alligators and Nile crocodiles, all things slimy and slithering are here under one roof.

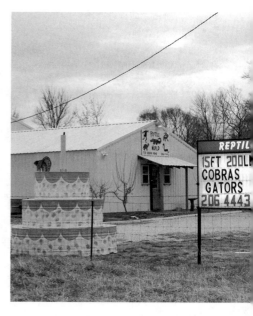

REPTILE WORLD ZOO IN JOPLIN

✍ �& 米 **Promised Land Zoo** (417-271-3324; www.plzoo.com), 32297 SR 86, Eagle Rock, Mo. Located south of Cassville on SR 86, near the town of Eagle Rock and Table Rock Lake. Open daily 10–7. Admission is $12.95 for adults, $8.95 for kids and seniors. Not your typical zoo, the drive-through Promised Land was created for the breeding of rare and endangered species. You'll see everything from camels and zebras to monkeys and llamas. A petting zoo is provided so that both kids and adults may touch and feed the animals. Feed is available for an additional charge.

URBAN OASES ✍ �& 米 **Big Spring Park** (417-451-1925; www.neoshocc.com), W. Spring St., Neosho, Mo. Just three blocks off the Neosho town square (across the street from the chamber of commerce), the 7-acre Big Spring Park offers lush gardens, a kids' wading pool, a gigantic floral clock, and numerous picnic areas. Of course the park's namesake is in residence at all times, gushing out nearly 900,000 gallons of frigid water each day. Big Spring is a must for the photographer, and weddings are a regular occurrence here.

✍ �& 米 **World's Largest Flower Box** (417-451-1925; www.neoshocc.com), North and College Sts., Neosho, Mo. I'm not sure if there is a Guinness record for flower boxes, but if there were, the box in Neosho's Morse Park would certainly be in the running. Residents took a former railroad gondola car (66 feet long, 8 feet wide, and 44 inches deep) and transformed it into a wonderland of flowers, trees, shrubs, and plants. These folks take the Flower Box City moniker very seriously, a lucky turn for those smart enough to stop and smell the flowers.

🐾 ✍ �& **Schifferdecker Park** (417-624-3533; www.joplinparks.org), 506 S. Schifferdecker Ave., Joplin, Mo. There are 23 different parks in the city of Joplin, comprising a total area of nearly 1,000 acres. One of the finest is the 160-acre Schifferdecker, home of the Joplin Museum Complex. The park also features a swimming pool, 12 tennis courts, a picnic pavilion, a baseball diamond, and an 18-hole golf course.

✹ To Do

FOR FAMILIES Also see *Zoos*, above.

✄ ♿ **Route 66 Carousel Park** (417-626-7710; www.route66carouselpark.com), 3834 W. Seventh St., Joplin, Mo. Featuring go-carts, amusement rides, arcades and games, 36 holes of miniature golf, batting cages, picnic areas, and all sorts of food and refreshments, Route 66 is open Mar.–Oct. Admission itself is free, but you'll have to cough up a bit of cash for the individual rides and activities.

UNEXPLAINED MYSTERIES
The Hornet Spook Light, Joplin, Mo. If you're up for a scary tale, wait until the night is dark and meander south of Joplin toward a little-used road called the Devil's Promenade on the Oklahoma border. If you're lucky, and literally thousands of people have been, you will catch a firsthand glimpse of the legendary Hornet Spook Light. Located near the ghost town of Hornet, the light is most often described as a yellow or orange ball that travels east at a high rate of speed. It dips, dives, throws off sparks, and may even land on your car hood. Approach it, however, and the Spook Light will disappear. It is alleged that in 1946 the Army Corps of Engineers attempted to study the flaming ball, finally giving up and labeling it a "mysterious light of unknown origin."

Theories abound as to the source of this friendly spook. Some say it is the ghost of a Quapaw Indian couple; others say that it's either a miner or an Osage Indian chief who is searching for his missing head. More scientific theories include marsh gas, minerals and gases arising from the earth, refracted headlights from I-44 (doubtful, as the light was first seen in the 1800s), subatomic disturbances from the New Madrid fault, and the ingestion of way too much beer. The most popular local explanation claims that the Devil's Promenade was at one time the site of an old wooden bridge. Those who walked across the bridge at midnight could summon up the devil, who would either ask three questions, grant three wishes, or kill you on the spot. Personally, I tend to believe the "too much beer" hypothesis.

To get to the Devil's Promenade and the Hornet Spook Light, head west on I-44 out of Joplin. Take the next-to-last exit before Oklahoma and drive south on SR 43. In approximately 4 miles a potholed, paved road crosses SR 43. This is Spooklight Road. Turn right and keep driving a mile or three until you find a convenient place to park. Or just look for the other cars. At times the road can get a tad crowded with Spook Light hunters.

🐾 ✒ ♿ **Precious Moments Inspira-tion Park** (1-800-543-7975; www .preciousmoments.com/content.cfm /park_chapel), 4321 Chapel Rd., Carthage, Mo. The brainchild of Samuel Butcher, creator of those cute little figurines and dolls treasured by collectors, Precious Moments is an entertainment monument to ceramic angels. You can visit the Precious Moments Chapel (featuring 52 bibli-cal murals), view the Fountain of Angels, or stroll the heavily mani-cured grounds. The visitors center doubles as the world's largest Precious Moments gift shop (gee . . . what a surprise). From Mar.–Dec. you can tour the chapel from 9–5 daily (excluding major holidays).

THE ENTRANCE TO PRECIOUS MOMENTS INSPIRATION PARK

✒ ♿ **Crystal Springs Trout Farm** (417-847-2174; http://crystalspringstrout farm.com), 16595 Farm Road 1120, Cassville, Mo. If either you or the kids want a stringer loaded with rainbow trout, do not miss a stop at Crystal Springs. Developed in the 1950s, the farm hatches trout for stocking operations. How-ever, a sizable area is also reserved for private fishing. Simply put, you will catch fish. There's no fishing license required, no limit, and you only pay for what you catch. This is where potential anglers should take note. While free bait and tack-le are gladly provided, and while the friendly Crystal Springs staff will clean and ice your catch, you are charged in the range of $4 per pound. The fish bite so quickly and easily here that if you don't watch it, you could easily end up with 20 pounds of trout in your cooler. Don't let that fact put you off. This is a fun spot, and kids love it. The farm is located on Partridge Lane off SR Y, and visitors would be well advised to call ahead for specific directions. The season for fishing here runs Feb. 15–Nov. 15.

GOLF Carthage Golf Course (417-237-7030; www.carthage-mo.gov), 2000 Richard Webster Dr., Carthage, Mo. A small-town course with a big reputation, this 18-hole facility was labeled one of the Top 10 Hidden Gems in Missouri by *The Kansas City Star.* The Carthage links feature two ponds, one with a foun-tain, more than 30 bunkers, and narrow fairways. Greens fees for 18 holes are $29 (cart included) Mon.–Thurs., $17 if you walk. Rates Fri.–Sun. are $31 with cart and $19 without.

Cassville Golf Club (417-847-2399; www.cassvillegolfclub.com), SR 112 South, Cassville, Mo. Just a short distance from Roaring River State Park, the Cassville Golf Club was listed among the Top 10 Public Courses in Missouri by *The Kansas City Star.* Its 18 holes will provide a challenge, but perhaps the true joy of this course is the surrounding beauty of the deep-woods Ozarks. It's very affordable as well: Weekday greens fees average $23 for 18 holes ($14 for nine holes), and weekend fees are $26 for 18 holes ($16 for nine holes). Cart rental is $9 for nine holes and $14 for 18.

Schifferdecker Memorial Golf Course (417-624-3533; www.joplinparks.org), Seventh St. and Schifferdecker Ave., Joplin, Mo. An 18-hole, par-71 course, Schifferdecker's greens fees are $11.50 on weekdays, $14.50 on weekends. Cart rentals are $5.25 and $10.50 (per person) for nine and 18 holes, respectively. The course is open year-round, sunrise to sunset.

✳ Wild Places

Grand Falls. The Ozarks are not known for waterfalls, but the largest continuously flowing one is located just south of Joplin. Though it only drops about 25 feet (and that's during the spring runoff), this spot is so pretty that it's more than worth a look. Just head south on SR 86 from I-44. Drive 1 mile, cross the Shoal Creek bridge, and immediately turn right. Go straight ahead for approximately 3 miles and you'll see the falls on your right. It's just a short hike down to the water and a great photo opportunity.

PARKS ☗ ♂ ♿ **Roaring River State Park** (417-847-2539; www.mostateparks .com/park/roaring-river-state-park), 12716 Farm Road 2239, Cassville, Mo. One of the oldest state parks in Missouri is located 7 miles south of Cassville on SR 112. Donated to the state in 1928, Roaring River is extremely picturesque, and the spring that emerges from the base of the limestone bluff churns out 20 mil-

GRAND FALLS

lion gallons of water per day. Roaring River is basically cut out of a mountain valley—part of the rugged, White River section of the Ozarks—and trout fishermen flock here by the thousands. The 2.5-mile spring branch, fed by the creek, is divided into three separate fishing zones (the one that allows wading is catch-and-release only). Approaching nearly 3,400 acres in size and adjacent to one of the southwest sections of Mark Twain National Forest, the park features a trout hatchery, a beautiful blue-green spring pool, a swimming pool, picnic areas, and a store. Seven trails totaling more than 10 miles in length are prized by both hikers and bicyclists, and the **Chinquapin Nature Center** offers interpretative displays and programs by park naturalists. Accommodations are abundant here. There are 187 campsites ranging from primitive to electric, and the **Roaring River Inn** is equipped with 26 guest rooms and a restaurant. In addition, 26 rustic cabins with full kitchens are available for rental (make your reservations early if visiting in summer).

🐾 ✂ ♿ ❄ **Mark Twain National Forest** (Cassville Ranger District: 573-364-4621; www.fs.fed.us/r9/forests/marktwain), SR 248 East, Cassville, Mo. One of the nine districts of the 1.5-million-acre Mark Twain National Forest can be

THE JOPLIN TORNADO OF 2011

During the late afternoon of May 22, 2011, a disaster of unimaginable consequences forever altered the landscape of Joplin. The skies had possessed an eerie quality for the entire day, and even 90 miles distant, I wondered at the incredible amount of lightning that filled the sky. The flashes lit the clouds virtually every second, so far away that no thunder was heard.

The 50,000 residents of Joplin had no idea that an EF5 tornado, the strongest such storm possible, was bearing down on the town. The storm sirens worked, people did have opportunity to seek shelter, but the power of the storm was so horrific that normal safety precautions were almost moot. The multi-vortex twister was more than a mile wide, with top wind speeds in excess of 250 mph. The storm ripped through the center of Joplin, traversing the entire town. In total, this most destructive single tornado in American history left a path of destruction more than 22 miles long.

All told, 160 Joplin residents lost their lives. Though people find this hard to believe, more than 30 percent of Missouri's fourth largest city was basically wiped off the map, completely obliterated. It's generally considered something of a miracle that the death toll wasn't higher, as graduation ceremonies had been held at many area high schools and colleges earlier in the day. Insurance payments are expected to exceed $2 billion.

The killer storm destroyed St. John's Regional Medical Center, Joplin High School, the Franklin Technology Center, Home Depot, Walmart, and countless found adjacent to Roaring River State Park. More than 70,000 acres of the forest are found in Barry and Stone Counties, with endless hiking, fishing, horseback riding, camping, and goofing-around possibilities. Some of the developed areas include **Big Bay Campground, Big Bay Picnic Ground and Boat Ramp,** and **Shell Knob Recreation Area.** If you're seeking to tour by car (particularly in fall, when the colors are beyond outrageous), do not miss the Sugar Camp Scenic Drive (FR 197), Onyx Picnic Area, and **Piney Creek Wilderness.** The last is of particular interest for hikers. Found 20 miles east of Cassville, Piney Creek encompasses 8,100 acres crisscrossed by 13 miles of trail. The north trailhead has a parking area, bathroom facilities (as in "modern outhouse"—there isn't running water here), camping areas with fire rings, quite a few hitching posts for horses, and the Piney Lookout Tower.

Big Sugar Creek State Park (417-847-2539; http://mostateparks.com/park/big -sugar-creek-state-park), Big Sugar Creek Road, Cassville, Mo. Take US 71 south from Joplin to Pineville; get off at the SR W exit, and follow Eighth St. east for 5 miles along Big Sugar Creek. The mission of 2,082-acre Big Sugar Creek State Park, which is still in the developmental stages, is to preserve in its pristine state

homes and businesses. It's another figure that's hard to imagine, but in the space of a few minutes more than 7,000 Joplin houses were simply . . . gone. The landscape of the town became something of a set from a horror movie. Rubble, twisted metal, foundations of what had once been homes, and a debris field that stretched for miles (X-rays blown from the hospital were found 70 miles to the east) were all that remained. Trees, those few left standing, were mere skeletons, stripped of bark and leaves. The residents walked the streets in a state of shock.

National, state, local, and regional resources descended on the area. Volunteers, firemen, and emergency medical personnel poured in from around Missouri and from Arkansas, Kansas, and Oklahoma. There is not a town within Missouri that, at the time of this writing in August 2011, is not still collecting donations for Joplin residents.

The recovery is proceeding at a rapid pace. Roughly 400 of the 500-plus businesses that were destroyed have either reopened or are in the process of rebuilding. St. John's is erecting a new hospital approximately a mile from its former location. Walgreens, two Commerce Banks, Home Depot, and Walmart all plan on remaining in the town. Travelers are advised to call ahead before visiting Joplin, at least up until the summer of 2012. Specific businesses, locations, and hours may well be different than prior to the storm.

Joplin should be well on its way to recovery by the time this book sees print; however, the scars left by the May 22 twister—physical, emotional, and mental—will no doubt remain forever.

a portion of the Elk River section of the Ozarks. Close to the Arkansas border as it is (you can hit Arkansas if you spit real hard), some of the park's flora and fauna take on a distinct southern bent. For instance, don't be surprised by the number of flattened armadillos (or "sail-cats," as we call them) that you might see on area roads. Hikers will want to try out Big Sugar Creek's **Chinquapin Trail,** a 3-mile loop that follows a stream through deep valleys. Walking this trail, you'll understand the too-often repeated Missouri Ozarks adage that "our mountains ain't much for height . . . but our valleys are mighty deep."

CAVES ✎ **Bluff Dweller's Cavern and Browning Museum** (417-475-3666; www.bluffdwellerscavern.com), 2 miles south of Noel, Mo., on 954 SR 59 South. Open daily year-round: Mar.–Oct. 9–5; winter hours vary. Discovered in 1925, this commercial cave is lighted and features a 45-minute guided tour. A tad more natural than some show caves, it takes its name from the discovery of the bones, tools, and relics of a flat-headed man who once inhabited the 56-degree hole (Fred Flintstone should be so lucky). Among the highlights of the tour are the **Musical Chimes,** a rock formation with a heavy iron content that elicits different tones when tapped by the guide. The cost to tour Bluff Dwellers Cave and the adjacent Browning Museum (full of rocks, mineral, antiques, spear points, and arrowheads) is $12 for ages 12 and up, and $6 for ages 4–11. Those under 4 are admitted free.

✳ Lodging

BED & BREAKFASTS

Joplin, Mo.
🐾 ✳ **Prosperity School Bed and Breakfast** (417-673-0833; www.prosperitybandb.com), 4788 CR 200. During the height of the mining boom, the little town of Prosperity boasted 5,000 residents. In 1907 the imposing two-story, redbrick schoolhouse was constructed. Alas, booms have a tendency to go bust. The school held on for a number of years, but the final bell rang in 1962. Now revitalized, this B&B features four lovely rooms ranging from $125–140 per night. This establishment is rumored to be haunted, and was featured nationally in an April 2011 edition of the A&E Network's *My Ghost Story.* The owners are happy to recommend the rooms reputed to have the most spook activity, but are also quick to point out that the resident spirits are friendly and hospitable. Antiques are everywhere, and the feel of being in an old schoolhouse is both pleasant and comforting. A full breakfast is served Saturday and Sunday, with continental breakfast on weekdays. Neither dogs, smoking, children under 14, nor childish, smoking dogs under 14 are permitted.

Lakeside Cottages of Joplin (417-781-9230; www.lakesidecottagesof joplin.com). Lakeside Cottages prides itself on being so luxurious and secluded that the proprietors won't give out the physical address until you make a reservation (something Brad Pitt and Angie might appreciate after they tire of cruising the strip in his hometown of Springfield). These romantic-getaway cabins (which start at $150 per night) include feather bed, fireplace, overstuffed leather love seat, Jacuzzi tub, and thick, king-sized towels. The kitchens are modern and well stocked, so you can prepare your own meals whenever you wish. The cottage porches hold a slide-swing chair that faces out over a 6.5-acre lake. Smoking is not permitted inside the cabins (it's OK on the porch; you're even provided with an ashtray), and neither children nor pets are permitted.

Carthage, Mo.

🍴 ✿ ❋ **The White Rose Bed & Breakfast** (417-359-9253; www.white rosebed-breakfast.com), 13001 Journey Rd. When Jim and Jan O'Haro claim that their inn is an Irish estate, there's not a bit of blarney involved. This stately 1900 home, constructed of Carthage marble, resides on a lush 10 acres of maples, oaks, magnolias, and tulips. Lovingly decorated with antiques from the 18th through 20th centuries, the B&B's Italian marble fireplace, high ceilings, chandeliers, and stone portico will make you wish you could move in permanently. And that's before you even get a taste of either the food or the Irish hospitality. Full Irish breakfasts are served, made

GRAND AVENUE BED & BREAKFAST

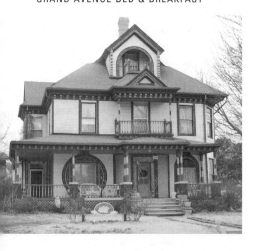

with ingredients both imported and grown in the O'Haros' garden. Luxurious gourmet dinners are available in the White Rose's restaurant, a nice touch all too infrequent in the B&B world. The menu features such delights as salmon pâté and fresh vegetables, French onion soup, Ballycanally chicken in Guinness and honey, home-baked bread, fresh-roasted asparagus, and an exceptional crème brûlée draped in sumptuous strawberries. Though specials are frequently offered, the normal lodging rates at the White Rose are $89–105. As expected, there are no facilities for pets, and smoking is not permitted indoors.

🍴 ✿ **Grand Avenue Bed and Breakfast** (417-358-7265 or 1-888-380-6786; www.grand-avenue.com), 1615 Grand Ave. Built in 1893, this graceful Victorian mansion is unmistakable due to its huge, wraparound front porch. The interior is an aesthetic masterpiece, with curved plaster walls, antique wainscoting, gas lamps, a large stained-glass window in the sitting room, a library, a miniature upright piano, and period furniture. Four tastefully appointed rooms run from $99–119 per night, and a variety of corporate and weekend specials are offered. Several times a year the Grand features a **Murder Mystery Weekend;** call ahead for dates and reservations. While the rooms may appear to be turn of the 20th century, they are fully equipped with private bathroom, high-speed Internet connection, a business center, cable TV, VCR, phone, coffee service, and deadbolt lock. Breakfasts are an important part of the Grand; no cold doughnuts or soggy cereal here. The morning meal includes fruit, yogurt, coffee, orange juice, a main entrée, sausage, and bacon. According to local legend, a mine owner named Albert Carmean bought the mansion in 1933 and died of illness just a few months later. It is said that certain guests have noticed a whiff of his trademark cigar smoke from time to time. This is a dubious assertion, as smoking is not permitted inside the home.

Noel, Mo.

Ginger Blue Inn (417-436-2273; www.gingerblueinn.com), 88187 N. Old Ozark Trail. The original Ginger Blue was constructed by a railroad tycoon in 1915. The establishment, named after a 1700s-era Indian chief from the area, operated success-fully under various owners until it burned to the foundation in the 1990s. Today, Ginger Blue owners Lynn and William Mosby have re-created the old lodge. Visitors are greeted by a 9-foot fireplace, 20-foot ceilings, and a grand piano. Five themed rooms and a carriage house are available at rates that range from $110–250 per night. Contact the owners for details on stay-ing with kids and pets.

RESORT 🐾 🐾 🦮 ♿ ❄ **River Ranch Resort** (1-800-951-6121; www.river ranchresort.com), 101 River Dr., Noel, Mo. A large, family-style resort with more than a mile of riverfront camping, River Ranch offers tent camping, floating, cabins, RV spots, a store, and a café with an $8.77 Sunday breakfast buffet. Cabins sleep from 6 to 10 people, and start at $175 per night. Tent camping sites start at $9 per night, but you'll need to cough up another $12 per night if you have a dog. RV spots are $15 per night, with a four-person minimum. Numerous

float trips are available beginning at $22.50 per adult per day. The resort also specializes in church retreats and on-site catering.

CANOE OUTFITTERS, CAMPING, AND RVS 🐾 🦮 **Eagles Nest Campground and Canoe Rentals** (417-475-3326 or 1-800-843-7080; www .4noel.com/eaglesnest), 53 Eagles Nest Ln., Noel, Mo. Situated on 40 acres, Eagles Nest offers campsites ranging from primitive tent areas to full RV slots with power and water. Camping rates run $7–25 per night. The facility features two beaches on the Elk River, fishing, swimming, a volleyball court, and a store. Tubes, kayaks, and canoes are available for rent, with the latter starting at $34. Dogs are permitted on a leash, but the management frowns on aggressive breeds.

🐾 🦮 ♿ **Shady Beach Campground** (1-800-745-6481; www.shadybeach .com), P.O. Box 473, Noel, MO 64854. Catering heavily to the floater, Shady Beach provides canoe, kayak, and six-person rafts. Prices for a two-person float start at $35; primitive tent sites run $7 and up (note that these sites are not marked; this is first come, first served); and any of the 23 RV slots go for $28 and up. Though pets are not allowed in Shady Beach's cabins (they are allowed at camp-sites), these rustic structures are a good choice, sleeping six people. While the cabins do have electricity, they do not have private baths or showers. Cabin prices are $70 per night double occupancy, with a $7 charge for each additional person. This campground is geared toward families, and such noisemakers as boom boxes, ATVs, motor scooters, fireworks, and your Dirty Harry .44

Magnum are not permitted. Neither are foul language or loud drunks.

❦ ✍ Elk River Floats and Wayside Campground (417-475-3561 or 417-475-3230; www.elkriverfloats.com), P.O. Box 546, Noel, MO 64854. With floats on both the Elk River and Big Sugar Creek, Elk River rents canoes, kayaks, and rafts (six- and eight-person). Canoe prices range from $40 (a 6-mile float with plastic canoe) and up. For those who would prefer to play along the shoreline, paddleboats and tubes are also available. This is another good family spot, and the shallow, slow waters on the banks of the Elk make for an excellent kids' swimming hole. Tent camping (first-come, first-served) sites start at $8, and 98 RV sites (32 of these have sewer service) begin at $35. Aside from its two separate campgrounds (RV and tent), the campground features hot showers, a snack bar and gift shop, firewood, swing sets, and a pleasant gravel beach. Your dog is welcome if he isn't too big and snarly, but he must be kept on a leash.

✍ ❦ ❋ Big Elk Camp and Canoe (417-223-4635 or 1-800-813-0907; www.bigelkcampcanoe.com), 402 S. US 71, Pineville, Mo. Located on the south side of the Elk River bridge. Aside from being a pretty camp-ground, Big Elk is known for being an alcohol-free facility. This makes it an excellent choice for both families and teetotalers. Canoe floats begin at $18 for a 4-mile float, making it probably the best floating value in the Ozarks. Rafts and kayaks are also for rent. Tent camping is $7 per person (leave Fido at home; he's not particularly welcome here), and an electric RV site for two people starts at $25. This operation also features miniature golf,

free WiFi, a game room, volleyball, and a tackle and gift shop. Big Elk Camp is open year-round.

❦ ✍ Camp Tilden (417-223-7568 or 1-877-646-1418; www.camptilden .com), 8739 Big Sugar Creek Rd., Pineville, Mo. Situated right on Big Sugar Creek, Camp Tilden offers floats on the Big Sugar, Elk River, and Indian Creek. The cabins were built in 2001 and feature a screened porch, tiny cooking area, a regular bed and sofa sleeper, and a loft bedroom for the sleeping-bag set. The draw here is location, set in a lovely spot shaded by the trees overlooking the water. Prices for cabin rental begin at $75 per night; tent camping for two people is $15 per night. As with most camp-grounds, linens and towels are not provided, so you'd best remember to bring your own. Pets are OK if kept leashed. Six- and 8-mile canoe trips are available, with prices provided upon reservation. Don't bring fire-works or pistols.

❦ ✍ ❋ Big Red Barn RV Park (417-358-2432 or 1-888-BIG-BARN; www.bigredbarnrvpark.com), 5089 SR 138, Carthage, Mo. One of those mega RV sites (with the advantage of very little highway noise), the Big Red Barn provides 70 level sites, 62 of which feature full hook-ups. You can rent by the night, week, or month (for $30 your space will include 50-amp electric, water, sewer, and 40 cable TV channels), and will find plenty of supplies and ice on-site. There is an adult game room with pool table, cen-tral BBQ area, air-conditioned laun-dry, free WiFi, and Jacuzzi hot tub. Pets are OK as long as both pet and owner behave responsibly. For off-season travelers, the park is open all year long.

🐾 ✍ ♿ ❋ **Joplin KOA Campground** (417-623-2246 or 1-800-562-5675; www.koakampgrounds.com/where /mo/25106), 4359 SR 43, Joplin, Mo. This RV site offers eighteen 50-amp sites and can accept vehicles up to 70 feet in length. Tent camping begins at $25 per night, RVs at $38, and cabins at $48 with a two-night minimum. The facility features a store and gift shop, laundry, WiFi access, and a catch-and-release fishing pond.

🐾 ✍ ♿ ❋ **Roaring River State Park** (417-847-2539; www.mostateparks .com/roaringriver.htm), 12716 Farm Road 2239, Cassville, Mo. Of the three camping areas at Roaring River, one is open the entire year. The remaining two are open Apr. 1–Feb. 25. Fees are $13 for a basic campsite, $21 for an electric campsite, $23 for a site with electricity and water, and $26 for electricity, water, and sewer. Pets are OK in Missouri state parks, but they must be kept on a leash or tie-out no longer than 10 feet. The Missouri state parks reservations number is 1-877-422-6766.

🐾 ✍ ♿ ❋ **Big Sugar Creek State Park** (417-847-2539; www.mostate parks.com/bigsugar.htm), CR SE W-24, Cassville, Mo. The same rates apply for Big Sugar Creek as they do for Roaring River State Park. The Missouri state parks reservations number is 1-877-422-6766.

🐾 ✍ ♿ ❋ **Mark Twain National Forest** (573-364-4621; www.fs.fed .us/r9/marktwain). Consisting of more than 1.5 million acres, the Mark Twain is a superb wilderness dotted by rivers, streams, and some of the largest natural springs in America. Broken into nine different ranger districts, the forest includes hundreds of miles of hiking trails, numerous scenic drives, seven congressionally designated wilderness areas, 40 camp-grounds, and thousands of acres of primitive and semi-primitive areas. The Mark Twain is a true playground for hunters, fishermen, hikers, equestrians, and campers.

❋ **Where to Eat**

EATING OUT ✍ ♿ ❋ ♈ **The Kitchen Pass** (417-451-6500; www.kitchen pass.net/neosho/neoshohotel.html), junction of US 60 and US Bus. 71, Neosho, Mo. Open daily 11–10. Located at the Neosho Inn adjacent to Neosho's 27-hole golf course, the Kitchen Pass offers a wide and varied menu for breakfast, lunch, and dinner. A blue cheese burger with grilled onions goes for $6.45, while a southern-fried steak sandwich is $6.75. Dinner is a bit of an odd mix here, ranging from stock Chinese dishes to Mexican to Ozark. The cashew chicken is $9.25, the quesadillas are $9.25, and the 8-ounce catfish fillet is $10.25. The lounge features a full bar and occasional live entertainment.

✍ ♿ **Stone's Throw Dinner Theatre** (417-358-9665; www.stonesthrow dinnertheatre.webs.com), 796 S. Stone Ln., Carthage, Mo. For an evening of dinner and a show, check out this relaxed venue in Carthage. Most productions are of the comedy genre, although occasionally a dramatic or children's performance will be offered as well. Admission to most productions is $22 for adults, $19 for kids and seniors. The actors for the shows come from the talented Community Theatre of Southwest Missouri.

🍦 ✍ ♿ **Carthage Deli & Ice Cream** (417-358-8820; www.carthagedeli .com), 301 S. Main St., Carthage, Mo.

Mon.–Fri. 7–5, Sat. 7–4. Sometimes you just have to have ice cream. When the urge strikes in Carthage, locals head for this 1950s-style hangout that has been serving the community for more than 30 years. Aside from old-fashioned malts, shakes, sundaes, sodas, and cones, you can also order smoothies, brownies, and cappuccino. If you're still feeling a might peckish, the Reuben sandwiches, double-deckers, and subs are delicious. Best of all, you'll be hard-pressed to find anything here that costs more than $6. The sandwich menu is extensive; try the steak sub or the Big Bear.

🦌 ✪ ♿ **Lucky J Steakhouse and Arena** (417-358-2370; www.luckyj arena.com), 11664 Fir Rd., Carthage, Mo. Mon.–Fri. 5–10; weekend hours vary but often include lunch Sat.–Sun. There's just something nice about watching a cowboy break a bronc while you dive into a steak or burger. In the Lucky J you can do just that, viewing rodeo activities in the adjoining arena through large glass windows. The menu here is traditional and leans heavily toward meat. The smoked brisket entrée in $10.99, and a 14-ounce rib eye is $20.99. Chicken-fried steak and catfish dinners are both $11.59. You could get a salad, if you really feel you must, but at $6.99 the gigantic, battered, fried pork tenderloin sandwich is a much better deal.

✪ ♿ **The Red Onion** (417-623-1004), 203 E. Fourth St., Joplin, Mo. Located downtown at Fourth and Virginia Streets. Mon.–Thurs. 11–8, Fri.–Sat. 11–9. The one piece of advice you might take to heart if eating here is to bring some spare change. This is a very popular lunch place, and parking can sometimes be a problem

around noon. Just drive into the adjacent lot and stick a few quarters in the meter. The Onion has an extensive lunch and dinner menu featuring appetizers, entrée salads, unique sandwiches, and specialty dinner items. If you're hungry, go for the Blue Moo Sandwich, a thin-sliced rib-eye steak with Monterey Jack, lettuce, tomato, and red onion served on focaccia bread and topped with blue cheese dressing. For dinner, a much-requested item is the lemon-grilled tilapia. This white fish is char-grilled with lemon, and then accented with a lemon and caper mayonnaise sauce. It's served with wild rice and a butter-fondue broccoli.

🦌 ✪ ♿ **Granny Shaffer's Restaurant** (417-624-3700 or 417-659-9393; www.grannyshaffers.com), 2207 W. Seventh St. and 2728 N. Rangeline, Joplin, Mo. Open Mon.–Sat. 6 AM–8:30 PM, Sun. 7 AM–3 PM. Neither over the river nor through the woods, Granny's is popular enough to warrant two locations in Joplin. Granny's has won local Best Breakfast awards every year since 2001, and has also taken the prize for Joplin's Best Spaghetti Dinner. All this aside, the real reason to hit Granny Shaffer's is the freshly made pies and baked goodies. A long list of standard pies (chocolate cream, coconut cream, apple, rhubarb, and many more) go for $10 each. Premium pies, such as pecan, blueberry, and black walnut fudge, are $12. For those on special diets there are many sugar-free pies (also $12), and a large blackberry or cherry cobbler is $19.50. The breads and rolls are very tasty as well, with a loaf of banana nut bread costing only $3. Any place that makes and sells gooseberry pie is the real deal.

DINING OUT ✒ ❄ ⟡ **Wilder's Steakhouse** (417-623-7230; www .wilderssteakhouse.com), 1216 S. Main St., Joplin, Mo. Open Mon.– Thurs. 5–9:30, Sat. 5–10. Wilder's has operated as a restaurant in Joplin since the 1930s (it started off as the local drugstore). The current owners, who also own the popular Kitchen Pass restaurant, have restored Wilder's to its original glory. You'll find a 40-foot mahogany bar, 16-foot-high ornamental tin ceilings, and what are arguably some of the best steaks, chops, ribs, and seafood in the region. The wine list is long at Wilder's, but far better than the fruit of the vine is the establishment's menu of fine, single-malt scotches. A restaurant that serves a 16-year-old Lagavulin is a rarity in this part of the country, and it's one of those touches that transform your basic eatery into something a cut above. A 24-ounce T-bone goes for $39, and fresh Chilean sea bass is $29. While you're there, do not miss the bourbon-pecan pie. Reservations are needed at Wilder's; eat there and you'll see why.

✸ Entertainment

🍴 ✒ ♿ **Joplin Memorial Hall** (417-623-3254; www.joplinmemorialhall .com), Eighth and Joplin Streets, Joplin, Mo. With seating for more than 3,000, Joplin's 80-plus-year-old Memorial Hall was created as a tribute to the local men and women who had served in the military. The events held in this venue are legion, not to mention constant. Concerts by nationally known performers, circuses and carnivals, basketball tournaments, boxing and wrestling matches, trade shows, conventions, and opera are just a few of the many possibilities. The venue has hosted acts ranging from Garth Brooks and Larry the Cable Guy to The Moscow Ballet and the Shrine Circus.

LIVE MUSIC ✒ **The Woodshed** (417-358-1800 or 417-359-7426; www .morninmail.com/woodshed.htm), 311 S. Main, Carthage, Mo. Located in back of the Main Street Mercantile on the town square. Live bluegrass and gospel can be heard every first and third Friday of the month starting at 7:30 PM. Admission is free, but donations are accepted.

✒ **Mudflats** (417-358-6808), 2048 Suburban St., Carthage, Mo. On the Fridays when live music isn't offered at the Woodshed, you can head to Mudflats. Beginning at 6:30 PM every second and fourth Friday of the month, local and regional players line up to take the stage with country, bluegrass, and gospel music. If you wish to perform, you can sign in at 5:30 PM and will be allowed 20 minutes (groups) or 10 minutes (individuals) to serenade the crowd. Admission is free, and this is a smoke- and alcohol-free environment.

THEATER ✒ ♿ **Joplin Little Theater** (417-623-3638; www.joplinlittle theatre.org/wordpress), 3008 W. First St., Joplin, Mo. Presenting between four and six shows per year, the Joplin Little Theater is one of the (if not the) oldest operating community theaters in the Midwest. Productions involve local and regional actors and behind-the-scenes crews. Call ahead for show dates, times, and prices.

✒ ♿ **Stained Glass Theatre West** (417-624-1982; www.sgtjoplin.org), 1318 W. 26th St., Joplin, Mo. The Stained Glass Theatre generally puts on half a dozen productions each year, most centering on a family or Christian theme. Call ahead for show dates, times, and prices.

Also see Stone's Throw Dinner Theatre under *Eating Out*.

DRIVE-IN THEATER 🐾 ♿ **66 Drive-In Theatre** (417-359-5959; www.comevisit.com/66drivein), 17231 Old 66 Blvd., Carthage, Mo. A dying breed, the 66 Drive-In is allegedly the last outdoor theater in the U.S. named for the "Mother Road." It operates Apr.–Sept., Fri.–Sun. nights. $7 adults; $3 children 12 and under; young children (of car-seat age) admitted free. Make sure to bring cash, as credit cards are not accepted. Shows start at dusk, and the drive-in features the required playground and concession stand.

✳ Selective Shopping

Richardson's Candy House (1-800-624-1615; www.candyhouse.net), 454 Redings Mill Rd., Joplin, Mo. Mon.–

Sat. 9:30–5:30, Sun. 12:30–5:30. Those with a sweet tooth will find pure Nirvana at Richardson's. In operation since 1970, the candy house is located in an old rock tavern. The establishment has expanded since this guide was first written, and expanded in a fashion that proves Ozarkers *really* like their candy. There are now two locations in Joplin, and two more in Springfield. All Richardson's delights come from family recipes and are made from fresh, natural ingredients. The chocolates are hand-dipped, rich beyond belief. This shop is the ultimate stop when you are ready to break your diet. Just walk in the door and you'll gain 5 pounds (and be happy about it). If you have a craving for the sweet stuff right now, Richardson's offers an online store.

Vintage Stock (417-782-2778; www.vintagestock.com/joplin), 3120 S. Main St., Joplin, Mo. When you seek some new tunes, games or movies, Vintage Stock in Joplin offers a huge selection. You'll also find new and preowned sports collectibles, trading

THE LANDMARK 66 DRIVE-IN

cards, games, comics, magazines, books, and toys. This growing chain that now consists of 21 stores started in 1980 as Joplin's Book Barn. Hours are Mon.–Sat. 9–9, Sun. 11–7.

Courtney's Candles and Creations (417-624-1838 or 1-866-723-6873; www.courtneyscandles.com), 2029 Willard, Joplin, Mo. Sure, it's got a huge selection of candles, but what's really nice about this spot (if you're into things that tick and tock) is the large selection of rhythmic, musical clocks. Should you tire of listening to the tunes and telling time, take a deep breath and enjoy the many scented jar candles and fragrance lamps. Ceramics, ornaments, wicker animals, and much more fill the shelves in this fun and attractive store. The store has expanded online and has diversified to include everything from bird feeders to ventless fireplaces.

The Old Cabin Shop (417-358-6720; www.oldcabinshop.net), 155 N. Black Powder Ln., Carthage, Mo. Tues.–Fri. 10–5, Sat. 9–5, Sun. 1–5. If you like history and if you like things that go bang, this is your type of place. The shop is the site of the 1830s cabin where the Jasper County government was formed in 1841. In 1980 the cabin became a retail gun operation, and additions were completed over recent years to better house the business, indoor archery lanes, and a museum featuring Indian artifacts and a fantastic gun collection. Anything involving guns, archery, knives, optics, or virtually any type of outdoor item can likely be found under this roof. Take a class on hunter education, qualify for a concealed carry license (you can do that in Missouri), purchase traps, or just browse to your heart's content.

Unique Turnings (417-847-2742; www.uniqueturnings.com), RR 2, Box 2722, Cassville, Mo. Artist Jerry Crowe takes wood burls (those giant, bulbous growths that pop up on the sides of trees) and—with chain saw, tools, and wood lathe—transforms stones such as turquoise and lapis. Small wonder Jerry's work is becoming ever more popular in galleries from coast to coast.

✳ Special Events

April **Missouri's Largest Garage Sale,** Neosho, Mo. For those seeking bargains galore, widgets beyond counting, and perhaps even a treasure trove of eight-track tapes, Missouri's Largest Garage Sale should prove satisfying. It happens in Neosho on the first Saturday of every April, and has been taking place every year since 1988. More than 400 individual garage sales are put on by local residents, schools, churches, and civic organizations; bargain hunters arrive by the thousands. If you can't find it here, it probably doesn't exist.

Spring Dogwood Tour (417-451-8050), Neosho, Mo. Neosho is loaded with literally thousands of dogwood (the state tree of Missouri) and redbud trees. In early spring the Neosho Chamber of Commerce provides maps to a local driving tour that highlights these gorgeous pink, purple, and white trees, as well as the infinite flowers that bloom all over town. The tour is a bit dependent on weather conditions, but in a normal year prime viewing time will be in early April.

June **Carthage Acoustic Music Festival** (417-359-8181; www.visit-carthage.com), Carthage, Mo. Held on the Carthage courthouse square, this one-day festival in June brings out some of the greatest performers you will never hear (unless you're in Carthage). It's free to the public, and the music plays 10–10. Should you wish to join in, just bring your instrument and take part in the open-mike sessions from 10–1. Groups are allowed 20 minutes on stage, individuals 10 minutes. The popularity of this event has led to major growth, and you can stroll through various exhibits and look for bargains at the bazaar.

Boomtown Days (417-624-4150; www. boomtowndays.com), Landreth Park, Joplin, Mo. Celebrating the heartland of America, Boomtown Days was originally known as the Festival of the Four States. What was a regional festival has grown into a three-day festival featuring top-notch live entertainment (Blues Traveler headlined in 2011), a chili cook-off, a half marathon, a dog show, and copious amounts of food. Tickets generally run $5 per day, or $10 for a three-day pass.

Hillbilly Boogie Skydiving Festival (1-800-598-5867), Mount Vernon Airport, Mount Vernon, Mo. Personally, I can think of no quicker way to experience coronary vapor lock than by jumping out of a perfectly good airplane. Still, watching others take the leap is fairly interesting. You can do just that (or if you're nuts, you can also jump) at the Hillbilly Boogie Skydiving Festival. Hundreds of jumpers show up for this annual event in mid-June, falling from the sky both in single and tandem format. Admission is free if you're merely a spectator. Just remember, the fall isn't what kills you. It's the sudden stop.

July **Newton County Fair** (417-451-1925), Newton County Fairgrounds,

Neosho, Mo. Taking place each year in early to mid-July, the Newton County Fair draws nearly 20,000 visitors from a four-state area. This is a fair of the traditional variety, featuring a full carnival midway, rides, craft booths, livestock exhibits, agricultural displays, music, and (of course) tons of food. The fairgrounds are located just south of Neosho near Crowder College.

George Washington Carver Day Celebration (417-325-4151; www .nps.gov/gwca), 5646 Carver Rd., Diamond, Mo. Though the date varies by year (either late June or early July), the Carver Day Celebration commemorates the Carver National Monument with educational programs, live gospel music, storytelling, nature walks, and numerous exhibits. Admission is free.

All Summer **Gatherin' on the Square,** Neosho downtown square. At one time almost every small town in the Ozarks had a bandstand on the courthouse grounds, with local musicians and town bands performing for the pleasure of locals and visitors alike. The trend has long passed in most areas, but not in Neosho. During the summer months, bluegrass, country, and gospel musicians descend on the square every Thursday evening and fill the air with music. There is no charge for this weekly event. Just drop by, and feel free to bring your guitar or banjo.

October ♪ **Apple Butter Makin' Days** (417-466-7654; www.mtvernon chamber.com), Courthouse Square, Mount Vernon, Mo. They cook it in huge copper kettles over open fires, just the way it was done for hundreds of years. No, even though this is the Ozarks, we're not talking moonshine.

We're talking apple butter, and the residents of Mount Vernon are crazy about the stuff. This festival, now nearly 50 years old, draws nearly 50,000 people over a three-day weekend in October. As festivals go, it's not only one of the most unusual, but also one of the best. How often do you see a nail-driving competition or turtle race? How often can you take part in apple-biting or apple-pie-eating contests while listening to old-time fiddle music? The entertainment here is geared for kids of every age, from the bubble-gum bubble blow-off to the rope climb to the parade of pets. Nearly 400 craftsmen from around the country set up in booths to peddle their wares. There's a gunfight on the square, dramatic skits, and a never-ending procession of country, folk, bluegrass, and Christian musicians. Least you forget the food, be prepared to dive into apple dumplings, caramel apples, funnel cakes, turkey drumsticks, kettle corn, bratwurst, stuffed baked potatoes, and the ever-popular hamburgers and hot dogs.

Barnyard Days (417-862-3838; www .circle-r-festivals.com/barnyard_days .html), 10970 Old Scenic Dr. at the Circle R Ranch, Neosho, Mo. For pure authenticity, Barnyard Days is one of the best local festivals you will find. It's a three-day affair that places craftsmen from around the country in a natural barnyard setting. The fall colors are spectacular, the crafts (with more than 150 exhibitors) unique. Entertainment is plentiful, with continuous music every day. Also on the agenda are a scarecrow-building contest, a petting zoo, and an antique

tractor display. Hours are Fri.–Sat. 8:30–6, Sun. 8:30–4. Circle R Ranch can be found 4 miles north of Neosho off US 71. Just turn west onto Iris Rd. and drive 3.2 miles.

Maple Leaf Festival (417-358-2373; www.carthagechamber.com/mapleleaf homepage.html), Carthage, Mo. The big shindig of the year. For a full week each October the town of Carthage celebrates full tilt with its Maple Leaf Festival. Held both on the historic square and at venues all over town, events include beauty pageants (to crown the Maple Leaf Queen), an old-time bazaar, and a wine and beer tasting. The list of activities is a mile long, with a quilt show, lip-sync competition, beautiful baby contest, bratwurst cook-off, auto show, marching band extravaganza, bull-riding rodeo, dog show, petting zoo, and a huge parade being just a sample of myriad options. Many of the events are free, but some of the individual sponsors charge admission fees.

December **Dickens Christmas Faire and Parade** (417-451-1925), downtown square, Neosho, Mo. Christmas begins in Neosho during the first weekend in December, when the lights come on both at Big Spring Park and throughout the historic downtown area. The latter is of particular interest, as this little Ozark town begins to take on the presence of Tiny Tim (the Dickens character, not the ukulele-playing tulip man) and Ebenezer Scrooge. Downtown features characters, carolers, horse-drawn carriage rides, food, and craft exhibits.

SPRINGFIELD, MISSOURI

The third largest city in Missouri, with 157,630 residents (more than 400,000 counting the suburbs and greater metropolitan area), Springfield has long been known as the "Queen City of the Ozarks." At least that's how it's inevitably labeled by historians and travel writers. For the locals, it's where you're headed if you're going to town, those times when you find yourself in desperate need of a Sam's Club, sporting events and concerts, great dining and shopping, health care, or even an education. Though the city's population continues to expand at a highly accelerated rate, thanks in part to its beauty and atmosphere but mostly due to the continued explosion of nearby Branson, Springfield has somehow never forgotten its roots. It's the major city of the Ozarks, yet it still manages to feel like a small town.

This aspect of the place can be attributed to the people, who seem to view themselves more as country folk than city folk. You will find Springfieldians a friendly and helpful bunch, proud of their Midwest values, their Ozark heritage, and the fact that their town is utterly up-to-date with the 21st century. Just about the only time you will find a hint of the pretentious is if you watch local news broadcasts, listen too long to the party line from the chamber of commerce, or happen to stumble across one of the myriad eponymous restaurants in town. The more upscale business element of Springfield sometimes tries a bit too hard to distance itself from the stereotype of the hillbilly. Still, this attempt to appear "cutting edge" should not in any way be construed as disingenuous or even obnoxious. If anything, you'll think that perhaps those creating the public relations image don't realize that the inherent gifts of Springfield are far more attractive and valuable than the urban/media ideals they would emulate. Either way, it's not a big deal. This is a city that, for the most part, truly likes what it is. That's good, for there's plenty to like.

You will find hundreds of restaurants covering virtually all styles and ethnicities. Entertainment runs the gamut from small rock or jazz clubs to major concerts by nationally known entertainers (Jerry Seinfeld and Elton John appeared in 2011) to a plethora of collegiate and semipro sporting events. There are a number of major hospitals in Springfield, all state of the art. For families, the vast number of parks, greenways, historic sites, and festivals (not to mention a great zoo) make the city seem almost idyllic.

Springfield

© The Countryman Press

Shopping is also big in Springfield, as evidenced by Bass Pro Shop's Outdoor World. This massive store (it's the firm's international headquarters) is a marvel to behold and succeeds beyond description in promoting (and selling) the romance with the outdoors that is the hallmark of the Ozarks. It's nice, it's classy without hype, and it's also the largest single tourist attraction in the state of Missouri (more than 4 million visitors annually).

All in all, this is just a great town, a community that draws new citizens like a spinster draws cats. Employment is good; housing is reasonably priced. Springfield has an excellent educational system and has birthed more than a few famous native sons. Brad Pitt went to Kickapoo High School, and former attorney general John Ashcroft attended Hillcrest High. Just to prove that the price was right, game-show icon Bob Barker learned his early lessons at Central High. Neither is higher education forgotten. Missouri State University boasts more than 17,000 students, while Ozarks Technical Community College, Drury University, and Evangel College teach 9,256, 1,631, and 1,657 students, respectively. Then there are Baptist Bible College, Central Bible College, Forest Institute of Professional Psychology, Vatterott College, and Bryan College. Those who believe the Ozarks to be a wholly uneducated locale will quickly have their preconceptions shattered in Springfield.

Founded in 1829 by John Polk Campbell, Springfield was a hotbed of action during the Civil War. Major bloodshed occurred between 1861 and 1863. The largest majority of residents were Southern sympathizers, and during the war itself Republicans were known to keep silent about their pro-Union leanings. After the war the town was the epitome of untamed frontier, with Wild Bill Hickok shooting Dave Tutt in 1865 in what is commonly acknowledged as the first "real" shootout of the Old West. Today it is one of those midsized cities that remain something of a secret to the vast majority of Americans.

Perhaps the best description of Springfield is this: It's a nice place to visit . . . but you'll probably want to live here.

AREA CODES Springfield, Mo., and the surrounding area are all covered by the **417** area code.

GUIDANCE The main source of information for Springfield and the surrounding communities is the **Springfield Missouri Convention and Visitors Bureau** (417-881-5300 or 1-800-678-8767; www.springfieldmo.org), 3315 E. Battlefield or 815 E. St. Louis, Suite 100, Springfield, Mo. Both locations offer a visitors center, plenty of pamphlets, and helpful information. Additional area facts and assistance can be gathered at the **Nixa Area Chamber of Commerce** (417-725-1545; www.nixachamber.com), 105 Sherman Way, Suite 108, Nixa, Mo., and the **Aurora Chamber of Commerce** (417-678-4150; www.auroramo chamber.com), 121 E. Olive, Aurora, Mo.

GETTING THERE *By car:* Springfield can be reached either from the east or the west via I-44, which passes right through the northern section of the city. From north and south, US 65 is the most favored route. Other, somewhat more scenic approaches include SR 13 to the north (a great alternative route that it is now four-laned) and US 160 to the south.

By air: **Springfield-Branson National Airport** (417-868-0500; www.sgf -branson-airport.com), 2300 N. Airport Blvd., Springfield, Mo., is served by American Airlines, Allegiant, United, and Delta. The airport offers facilities for buses, vans, rental cars, and hotel and hospitality limousines for groups en route to Branson or other Ozark locations. The airport underwent a multimillion-dollar expansion between 2006 and 2009, resulting in a new midfield terminal and expanded services.

MEDICAL EMERGENCIES Cox Medical Center North (417-269-3000; www.coxhealth.com), 1423 N. Jefferson Ave., Springfield, Mo., and **Cox Medical Center South** (417-269-6000; www.coxhealth.com), 3801 S. National Ave., Springfield, Mo., are part of the massive Cox network and include 770 beds.

Mercy St. John's (417-820-2000; www.stjohns.net), 1235 E. Cherokee St., Springfield, Mo., is an 866-bed center. All of these hospitals operate satellite clinics in surrounding counties. **Ozarks Community Hospital** (417-837-4000; www.ochonline.com), 2828 N. National, Springfield, Mo., formerly known as Doctor's Hospital, consists of two hospitals, 14 clinics, and more than 800 employees. **Lakeland Regional Hospital** (417-865-5581 or 1-800-432-1210; www.lakeland-hospital.com), 440 S. Market St., Springfield, Mo., has served Springfield for more than 100 years. It now provides psychiatric services for children, adolescents, and their families.

✳ Wandering Around

EXPLORING BY CAR Battle of Springfield Driving Tour (417-881-5300 or 1-800-678-8767; www.springfieldmo.org), Tourist Information Center, 3315 E. Battlefield Rd., Springfield, Mo. For Springfield, one of the major battles of the Civil War took place in January 1863. At that time, Union troops defended the town when Confederate forces swarmed in to obtain supplies and secure the Queen City for the Stars and Bars. To memorialize this bloody event, 12 markers chronicling the battle have been placed in strategic, historically accurate locations. For a map detailing this interesting driving tour, contact the Springfield Missouri Convention and Visitors Bureau at the number above.

EXPLORING BY FOOT 🌿 ✿ ✦ ♿ **Galloway Creek Greenway** (417-864-2015; www.ozarkgreenways.org). The trailhead is located at Seminole and Pine Streets at the Pershing Middle School in Springfield. Admission is free. Greenways are defined as long stretches of undeveloped areas of natural habitat that generally pass through urban areas. Often following streams or old railroad tracks, they are often hard-surfaced paths accessible to walkers, runners, bicyclists, in-line skaters, wheelchairs, baby strollers, and old folks on Rascal scooters. The Ozarks Greenways organization has been instrumental in creating eight such trails in the Springfield area, with one of the favorites being the Galloway Creek Greenway. The Galloway, designated a National Recreation Trail by the National Park Service, stretches 8 miles from Pershing Middle School to Sequiota Park to its ending at the Springfield Conservation Nature Center. Wandering this way and that under US 60 and US 65, the trail also crosses over the scenic James River Bridge. At the end of this bridge, you will come across a well-tended pet cemetery where many locals have laid their beloved critters to rest. The trail passes through and by a number of Springfield neighborhoods and along Springfield Lake. Best of all, if you get hungry or tired along the way, you can always take a break at the **Galloway Station Restaurant.**

✳ Towns and Villages

Aurora, Mo. Located 33 miles southwest of Springfield, Aurora was one of the original mining centers of the Ozarks. In 1885 some fellows digging a well set off a powder keg and exposed huge chunks of galena ore. After that, the lead boom was on, with rich veins being found one after another. Today Aurora is home to

MARIONVILLE TAKES PRIDE IN ITS ALBINO SQUIRREL POPULATION

more than 7,440 residents. More importantly for those who can't resist the combination of smoke, spice, and pork, it is also the home of the most excellent Richard's Hawgwild BBQ.

Marionville, Mo. The billboard at the edge of town reads MARIONVILLE WELCOMES YOU. While there's nothing unusual in that, the accompanying photo of a giant white squirrel raises a few eyebrows. You see, Marionville is the White Squirrel Capital of the United States. Nobody knows how they got there, but a colony of more than 100 pure white squirrels resides in this town of 2,167 located 28 miles southwest of Springfield. The locals feed and protect them, and hunters should beware: Injuring one of the town's beloved albinos results in a $500 fine (and you'd likely get a whuppin' from the locals if you were stupid enough to brag about it).

Nixa, Mo. Since its founding in the mid-1800s, Nixa has always served as a crossroads of sorts, first for farmers and later for teamsters traveling north from Arkansas. Today the town of 19,458, situated in the prosperous corridor between Branson and Springfield, serves the same purpose. A very pretty place in spring and fall, with its flowering dogwood and vibrant autumn colors, Nixa is also home to the legendary Sucker Day festival, held in early May for 50 years. Even the schools officially close on Sucker Day. Residents and thousands of visitors chow down on these nasty-looking, deep-fried bottom feeders (which taste great, by the way) while enjoying live music, a parade, and carnival rides.

Ozark, Mo. The seat of Christian County, Ozark was founded around pioneer John Hoover's gristmill in the 1830s. The town of 18,458 continues to prosper due to its proximity to both Springfield and Branson; it's grown a whopping 91 percent since the year 2000. The popular Lambert's Cafe (home of the "throwed roll") is found in Ozark and is regionally famous for the staff's propensity to toss fresh-baked biscuits at dining patrons.

Republic, Mo. Another early crossroads town just 14 miles west of Springfield, Republic's 14,300 residents are justifiably proud of their pumpkins. On the first Saturday of October, growers from across the region show up for **Pumpkin Daze** to have their giant pumpkins (plus squash and watermelons) weighed and recorded. This effort is part of the Great Pumpkin Commonwealth, an international competition that awards more than $25,000 in prize money. In 2004 the prize-winning pumpkin from Republic weighed in at 770 pounds, a new Missouri record. We have big pumpkins in these parts (and we're also easily amused).

✳ To See

MUSEUMS ✿ ♂ ♿ Springfield Art Museum (417-837-5700; www.springfield mo.gov/art), 1111 E. Brookside Dr., Springfield, Mo. Open Tues., Wed., Fri., and Sat. 9–5; Thurs. 9–8; Sun. 1–5. Admission is free. Founded in 1928, the Springfield Art Museum houses more than 8,895 artistic objects covering literally thousands of years of culture. Painting, watercolor, sculpture, and prints are just a start of the collection, and a 329-seat auditorium offers a variety of programs. Past presentations have included a collaboration with the Springfield Opera, with special recitals performed once each week. The museum expanded in 2008, adding a new wing with an entry hall, galleries, gift shop, and library.

♂ ♿ Wilson's Creek Civil War Museum (417-732-2662; www.civilwarmuseum .com), 5228 S. SR ZZ, Republic, Mo. Closed Dec.–Mar.; open daily 8–5 the rest of the year. Admission is free with a $5 adult admission to the Wilson's Creek National Battlefield. Up until around 2009 this museum was named after General Thomas "Fightin' Tom" Sweeny. Why the Wilson's Creek honchos decided to lop his name from edifice remains both a mystery and a local irritation. Political correctness is suspected, because the story of "Fightin' Tom" is not exactly all bunnies and rainbows. Born in 1820 in Ireland, Sweeny immigrated to the U.S. at the age of 12. He lost his right arm to a musket ball at the storming of Churubusco, and in the 1850s was an Indian fighter in the West. During the Civil War he fought in the Battle of Wilson's Creek near Springfield and took another musket ball in the thigh. With the 52nd Illinois at Shiloh, he suffered numerous bullet wounds and only left the field when forced to by loss of blood. "Fightin' Tom" survived, however, and lived to the age of 72. A linguist of sorts, Fightin' Tom could reportedly curse fluently and with gusto in three languages. The museum that used to bear his name contains Civil War artifacts and takes visitors through the highlights of the War Between the States. Sadly, this museum is not nearly as cool as it once was; I'm told many of the original items are now in storage. Still, it's worth a stop.

♂ ♿ Air and Military Museum of the Ozarks (417-864-7997; www.ammo museum.com), 2305 E. Kearney St., Springfield, Mo. Open year-round, Tues.–Sat. noon–4. $5 adults, $3 ages 6–11. Established in 1989, this museum is dedicated to all those who gave their lives in the defense of American freedoms and liberties. It specializes in the restoration, preservation, and display of military history, and more than 5,000 pieces of memorabilia are exhibited. I'm not just talking bayonets and medals. You can take a simulated flight (while sitting in the cockpit, no less) of a restored Cobra AH-1S military helicopter. This is a great experience for both kids and adults, as you start the engine, take off at 100 knots, and blast away at enemy tanks with a laser-sighted, six-barreled machine gun.

Historical Museum for Springfield/Greene County (417-864-1976; www .springfieldhistorymuseum.org), 830 Boonville Ave., Springfield, Mo. Open Tues.–Fri. and the second Sat. of each month 10:30–4:30. Admission is free, but a small donation of $1–3 is appreciated. Located on the third floor of city hall, the museum contains more than 3,000 square feet of exhibit space and features both permanent and rotating exhibits. Historical eras on display range from prehistoric times, through early settlement, through the Civil War, and up to the

1950s. Two interpretative videos can be viewed, and a hands-on area for kids offers an Indian grinding stone, Civil War tent, and household items from the pioneer days. Rotating exhibits have included such presentations as the 140-year history of Springfield baseball.

✐ ♿ **Missouri Sports Hall of Fame** (417-889-3100 or 1-800-498-5678; www .mosportshalloffame.com), 3861 Stan Musial Dr., Springfield, Mo. Open year-round, Mon.–Sat. 10–4, Sun. noon–4. $5 adults, $4 seniors, $3 children 6–15. A 22,000-square-foot celebration of Missouri sports and the athletes who played them, the museum is loaded with a wide array of sports memorabilia and inter-active displays. More than just football, basketball, baseball, and golf, virtually every sport imaginable is represented, including fishing.

✐ ♿ **The Softball Museum** (417-887-5817; www.springfieldsoftball.com/Pages /softball_museum.html), 2141 E. Pythian St., Springfield, Mo. Open year-round, Mon.–Fri. 11–5. Admission is free, but donations are welcome. Springfielders love their baseball and softball, and this museum offers a Hall of Fame com-memorating players from both the Springfield and Missouri Amateur Softball Associations. Displays trace local accomplishment back to the 1920s. There is even a display featuring softball achievement from Isesaki, Japan, Springfield's sister city.

❦ ✐ ♿ **Aurora Historical Society Museum** (417-678-4150), 121 E. Olive St., Aurora, Mo. Open year-round, Mon.–Fri. 9–4. Admission is free. A small museum filled with a trove of items from the past, most of which were donated by members of the community, the Aurora museum is located in a 1906 Mis-souri Pacific Railroad depot.

CULTURAL SITES ❦ ✐ ♿ **Wommack Mill** (fghps.org/mill.html), Main St. and SR 125, Fair Grove, Mo. Open year-round. Tours by appointment. Admission is free. Located roughly 10 miles north of Springfield on US 165, the town of Fair Grove is home to the historic Wommack Mill. Built in 1883 and in operation until 1969, the mill was rescued and restored by the Fair Grove Historical and Preservation Society. Today it holds its original burr stones and a nice collection of early 20th-century farm tools and horse-drawn machinery. If you visit the mill on the second Saturday in July, you will find yourself smack in the middle of the annual ice-cream social.

❦ ✐ ♿ **Springfield Conservation Nature Center** (417-888-4237; www.mdc .mo.gov/regions/southwest/springfield-conservation-nature-center), 4601 S. Nature Center Way, Springfield, Mo. Open year-round, Tues.–Sat. 8–5; also open Sun. noon–5 Mar.–Oct. Admission is free. Owned and operated by the Missouri Department of Conservation, this establishment's motto is "A place to enjoy nature's gifts and to learn about taking care of them." Located within the city limits of Springfield, the center consists of 80 acres of forests, fields, and creeks, with frontage on Lake Springfield. Six hikes are possible on 3 miles of trail, wildlife is prevalent, and a very cool boardwalk crosses the marshy shallows of the lake. However, the inside of the center is just as entertaining and informa-tive as a walk on the grounds. There are classrooms, exhibits, an information desk, a bookshop, and a 150-seat auditorium. Planned events might include a

ASSEMBLIES OF GOD HEADQUARTERS

presentation on bears and cougars, a day spent learning primitive living skills, tips on nature photography, classes on wood carving and tree identification, or perhaps even a Halloween party. Missouri has one of the best-funded conservation departments in the nation (for decades, a ⅛-cent sales tax has been earmarked for conservation), and the Conservation Nature Center is a prime example of those funds being put to good use.

🐾 ✐ ♿ **Assemblies of God Headquarters** (417-862-2781; www.ag.org/top), 1445 Boonville Ave., Springfield, Mo. Tours are held year-round, Mon.–Fri. at 1:30 and 2:30 PM. Admission is free. A note on local custom here: If you're taking the guided tour of the international headquarters of the Assemblies of God Church, it is considered in bad taste to ask questions about defrocked AG ministers such as Jimmy Swaggart or Jim Bakker. Even a joke about that duo will be met with roughly the same enthusiasm as screaming "bomb" in a crowded airport. Now that that's out of the way, this is an interesting tour of a religious group boasting 2.9 million members in the U.S. The headquarters is a massive complex consisting of 18 buildings spread over 10 city blocks. Part of the facility is the **Gospel Publishing House.** The church paper printed there—*The Pentecostal Evangel*—sizes out at 268,000 copies per week, utilizing enough newsprint to cover 214 miles.

HISTORIC SITES ✐ ♿ **Wilson's Creek National Battlefield** (417-732-2662; www.nps.gov/wicr), 6424 W. FR 182, Republic, Mo. Open year-round, daily 8–5. $3 per person or $5 per vehicle. Kids under 16 are admitted free. You can nearly hear the guns and smell the smoke at Wilson's Creek, a 1,750-acre battlefield that is little changed since the bloody fight of August 10, 1861. On that day, 12,000 Confederates and 5,400 Yankees engaged in fierce combat, resulting in 2,300 deaths in just five hours of engagement. The Rebels won the day but lost the war. Today this National Park Service facility features a visitors center, a 13-

minute film, a museum, rotating exhibits, and a 5-mile, self-guided auto tour. Easy foot trails lead to the various battle sites.

 Gray/Campbell Farmstead (417-725-4921; www.graycampbellfarmstead .org), 2400 S. Scenic Ave. in Nathaniel Greene Park, Springfield, Mo. Open May–Sept., weekends 1:30–4:30; Sun. only in Apr. and Oct. Admission is free. The original home of John Polk Campbell, the nephew and namesake of the fellow who founded Springfield, this historic 1856 residence offers visitors a chance to see the detached log kitchen, corncribs, and family cemetery. In-season, tours are given by costumed guides (historical costumes—not Spider-Man or anything like that).

Wild Bill Hickok Shootout. Markers are located downtown in Park Central Square at Boonville St. and Park Central. The very first gunfight of the Wild West took place in downtown Springfield in July 1865. Wild Bill Hickok (who had unsuccessfully run for sheriff of Springfield and was a gambler of inveterate proportions) had lost a poker game to his onetime friend, Dave Tutt. Short on funds, Hickok gave Tutt his pocket watch as collateral, telling him not to show it off in public or brag about it. Tutt, of course, embarrassed Hickok by displaying the timepiece all over town. Animosities grew, and eventually Tutt fired a shot at Hickok, barely missing his head. With lightning speed and from 75 yards away, Wild Bill pulled his pistol and plugged Tutt directly through the heart (it can be assumed he retrieved his watch). If you stand by the plaque on the southwest corner of Park Central Square, you will be walking in Wild Bill's footsteps. If you want to visit Dave Tutt, go to the **Maple Cemetery.**

ZOOS **Dickerson Park Zoo** (417-864-1800; www.dickersonparkzoo.org), 3043 N. Fort Ave., Springfield, Mo. Open Apr.–Sept., daily 9–5; Oct.–Mar., daily 10–4. $8 adults, $5 seniors, and $5 ages 3–12. For a relatively small city, Springfield's Dickerson Park Zoo is a shining jewel. Exhibits include a South American

THE GRAY/CAMPBELL FARMSTEAD

area, with Chilean flamingos, squirrel monkeys, toucans, and maned wolves. The Australian area holds red kangaroos, wallabies, and black swans, while the "Missouri Habitats" display features a boardwalk overlooking black bears, coyotes, bobcats, raccoons, river otters, deer, and turkeys. The popular Africa area includes cheetahs, kudus, cranes and storks, ostriches, giraffes, lions, and Asian elephants. The list goes on and on; you can easily spend a full day or more at Dickerson, viewing more than 500 animals representing 170 species, and never become bored.

✴ To Do

FOR FAMILIES Also see *Zoos,* above.

🦆 ✎ ♿ **Archery Quest** (417-863-8060; www.archeryquestinc.com), 2900 E. Pythian St., Springfield, Mo. Open Mon.–Thurs. noon–9, Fri.–Sat., noon–6. Fees vary per hour and number of shots fired. If you're looking for something different, or if you suddenly become delusional and believe yourself to be William Tell, a trip to Archery Quest is in order. With indoor archery ranges and a "3-D techno hunt" (sort of like virtual-reality-meets-Robin-Hood), you can twang the string and fire the shaft to your heart's content. If the bug really hits you, Archery Quest sells top-name bows and supplies.

🦆 ✎ ♿ **Andy Dalton Shooting Range & Outdoor Education Center** (417-742-4361; www.mdc.mo.gov/regions/southwest/andy-dalton-shooting-range), 4897 N. Farm Road 61, Ash Grove, Mo. Open Sept. 14–Apr. 14, Mon.–Thurs. 9–4:30, Fri.–Sun. noon–4:30; Apr. 15–Sept. 13, Mon. 9–4:30, Thurs. 9–7:30, Fri.–Sun. noon–4:30. Prices on the rifle/pistol range are $3 per hour per booth. Prices on the skeet range are $3 per person per round of 25 clay birds. Prices for static and 3-D archery ranges are $3 per hour. Featuring a 100-yard baffled rifle/pistol range with 20 covered booths (two of which are handicapped accessible), four trap and skeet fields, and archery facilities, this center is a favorite among local hunters and shooters. A great trip for the entire family, it's the perfect spot when either adults or kids want to practice their shooting skills. The shooting range also offers a training center with indoor classrooms and outdoor pavilion, and it is a leader in providing both gun and hunter safety courses. It is a bit hard to find: Take SR 160 west from Springfield (past the town of Willard but before Ash Grove) and watch for Greene County FR 61. The center will be near a white, stone barn.

🦆 ✎ **Fun Acre** (417-889-1872), 2500 S. Campbell Ave., Springfield, Mo. Open Feb.–Nov. For miniature golf (an 18-hole course) and batting cages, you can't beat the price at Fun Acre. At last check, golf was $2 for adults and $1 for children. If you want to make like Babe Ruth, the batting cage price is a mere 25 cents for seven pitches.

✎ ♿ **Mediacom Ice Park** (417-866-7444; www.icepark.org), 635 E. Trafficway, Springfield, Mo. Hours vary, but public skating is available for several hours seven days a week. $5.50 adults, $4 kids and seniors. Skate rental is $2.50 per person. Open since 2001, the Ice Park offers public skating and skating lessons for all ages; it's home field for the Missouri State University Hockey Bears, The

Springfield Youth Hockey Association, and the Jordan Valley Figure Skating Club, too. Formerly the Jordan Valley Ice Park, the complex also may be rented for birthday parties and special events.

GOLF Oscar Blom Golf Course (417-833-9962; www.parkboard.org/info/golf /info/oscarBlom.htm), 1825 E. Norton Rd., Springfield, Mo. For just plain fun, spend an afternoon playing this public, nine-hole, par-27 course. Open year-round (weather permitting), the course is lighted on evenings between May and November. Greens fees are $10 for adults for a nine-hole round, $14 for 18 holes. Those 17 and younger can play Mon.–Fri. for just $5.

Bill & Payne Stewart Golf Course (417-833-9962; www.parkboard.org/info /golf/stewart/index.html), 1825 E. Norton Rd., Springfield, Mo. Situated on a luscious 129 acres, this par-70, 6,162-yard public course is open year-round, every day, sunrise to sunset. That said, sunrise and sunset varies with the season, so plan accordingly. On this course you will find a driving range, practice greens, and snack bar. Greens fees for 18 holes are $18 on weekdays and $23 on weekends. Cart rental for 18 holes runs $12 per player.

Y **Deer Lake Golf Course** (417-865-8888; www.deerlakegolf.com), 5544 W. SR 266, Springfield, Mo. Deer Lake is a par-71, 18-hole public course with driving range, practice green lessons, and a bar and lounge. The 6,899-yard course is open year-round, 6–6 during the warmer months and 7–5 in winter. Greens fees begin at $22 for a walking round of 18 holes. Add a cart and the fees rise to $37. The course is under new management, and now features a full-service fitness club.

Horton Smith Golf Course (417-891-1639; www.parkboard.org/info/golf /horton/index.html), 2409 S. Scenic, Springfield, Mo. Open sunrise to sunset every day except Christmas, Horton Smith is a par-70, 6,312-yard, 18-hole public course. Greens fees are $18 weekdays and $23 weekends for 18 holes. Carts run $12 for 18 holes. Lessons, a driving range, and a snack bar are also found at this nice little course.

Rivercut Golf Course (417-891-1645; www.parkboard.org/info/golf/rivercut /index.html), 2850 W. Farm Road 190, Springfield, Mo. Without doubt the best public course in Springfield, Rivercut was named one of the top five public courses in Missouri by *Golf Digest*. A par-72, 7,066-yard course, its prime links offer 18 holes of championship-level golf, a driving range, lessons, club rental, and a snack bar. Open every day except Christmas; greens fees for 18 holes are $39 on weekdays and $48 on weekends.

✳ Wild Places

✿ ☕ ✎ **Busiek State Forest and Wildlife Area** (417-895-6880), 18 miles south of Springfield off US 65. Open year-round. Admission is free. A 2,505-acre wildlife area managed by the Missouri Department of Conservation, Busiek is loaded with trails for hikers, bikers, and the horseback crowd. Mostly forested, with several seasonal and one permanent stream, the area also allows camping, hunting, fishing, and target shooting.

URBAN OASES

With more than 50 public parks within the city limits, Springfield offers ample opportunity to enjoy the great outdoors or take part in sporting activities. For complete information on all parks, sports fields, and golf courses, visit the city's park website at **www.parkboard .org.** The following is a collection of some of the best Springfield has to offer.

MIZUMOTO JAPANESE STROLL GARDEN

The 6.5-acre **Loren Street Park** (2155 W. Catalpa St.) will appeal to the model-airplane buff, as it includes a model plane pad/landing strip. Loren Street is also Springfield's first off-leash dog park. The **Chesterfield Family Center and Park** (417-891-1616; 2511 W. Republic Rd.) is more than just a 40-acre expanse of green. This facility holds a family center, fitness center, gym, physical fitness course, playground equipment, and a 2-mile walking trail. Sports fans will love the 127-acre **Cooper Park** (417-837-5817; 2300 E. Pythian) with its five lighted baseball diamonds, 14 outdoor soccer fields, 1.5-mile fitness trail, and concession stands. **Dickerson Park** (417-864-1800; 1400 W. Norton Rd.) is more than just the home of a first-rate zoo; it's also a gorgeous and relaxing public park full of picnic tables, grills, shelters, playground equipment, and a lake. Have your burger while listening to the trumpeting of Asian elephants. At the **Doling Park and Family Center** (417-837-5900; 2600 N. Campbell), a swimming and wading pool shares 40 acres with horseshoe pits, two lighted tennis courts, bocce courts, picnic tables and grills, and a gym. For handball players, **Fassnight Park** (S. Campbell and Meadowmere) is the place to be. In addition to its two lighted handball courts, the park includes both swimming and wading pools, a lighted softball field, an outdoor basketball court, and plenty of picnic tables and grills. If you or the kids want to take a spin on your bike, one of the hallmarks of the 41-acre **James Ewing Sports Complex** (Scenic and Bennet Streets) is an unlighted BMX track. If Frisbee golf is more to your liking, drop by the **Oak Grove Park and Center** (417-891-1635; 1538 S. Oak Grove), where you will find a nine-hole course.

Jordan Valley Park (417-866-7444; 635 E. Trafficway) is known for its huge fountain, paved walking trails, and amphitheater featuring concerts and public events. Jordan Valley also encompasses the Mediacom Ice Park (see *To Do*). If you seek history, the **Nathaniel Greene Park** (417-897-1653; 2400 S. Scenic) is an ever-expanding botanical center with more than 20 varieties of plants and the city nursery. Also on this site are the Gray/Campbell Homestead and the Mizumoto Japanese Stroll Garden. Not to be forgotten is **Phelps Grove Park** (950 E. Bennett) with its lovely rose and xeriscape gardens, or the 246-acre **Ritter Springs Park** (3683 W. Farm Road 92). The latter is home to the Sac River bike trail, an archery range, horseshoe pits, picnic tables, play-ground equipment, grills and tables, and a scenic lake.

🐾 ♿ **Mizumoto Japanese Stroll Garden** (417-864-1049; www.parkboard .org), Nathaniel Greene Park, 2400 S. Scenic Ave., Springfield, Mo. Open May–Oct. $3 adults, free for kids. You don't expect to find lovingly tended Japanese gardens in the Ozarks, but that's exactly what you'll discover at this elegant, 7.5-acre site located within Nathaniel Greene Park. The garden features lakes, a teahouse, winding paths, a moon bridge, and much more. The care and expertise that have gone into fashioning this pristine environ-ment are astounding.

🐾 ♿ **Jefferson Avenue Footbridge** (417-864-7015; www.springfield mo.org/things-to-do/cat/Attrac/menu/121/client/65905), 201 E. Commercial St., Springfield, Mo. Open year-round. Admission is free. This century-old, 562-foot bridge crosses 13 sets of railroad tracks; it is often referred to as Springfield's largest piece of public art. The bridge, fully restored for pedes-trian traffic, is a great place to watch the trains that cruise by literally inches below your feet. This is a particularly cool spot at night, as the area is well lighted and the train-watching takes on an entirely different tone than dur-ing the daylight hours.

THE JEFFERSON AVENUE FOOTBRIDGE

🐾 ☃ ✿ **Compton Hollow** (417-895-6880), 20 miles east of Springfield. Take the SR B exit south for 5 miles, then travel 1 mile east on Compton Hollow Rd. Open year-round. Admission is free. For fishing, hunting, target shooting, camping, bird-watching, or even some frog-gigging, this 840-acre Missouri Department of Conservation area makes for a relaxing and tranquil day trip. There are several small ponds within the area (you'll see plenty of wildlife), and a rather tough 5.5-mile trail is available for hiking, biking, and horseback riding.

CAVES ✿ ♿ **Fantastic Caverns** (417-833-2010; www.fantasticcaverns.com), 4872 N. FR 125, Springfield, Mo. Open year-round except for major holidays. Hours are 8–8 in summer; closing time is one to four hours earlier in other seasons. $22.50 adults, $14.50 ages 6–12. Kids under 5 are admitted free. If you're going to tour a cave, this is the way to do it. Fantastic Caverns is the only ride-through cave in America, with passengers on the 50-minute excursion comfortably seated in Jeep-drawn tram cars. This makes the attraction very popular among those who suffer limited mobility, have small children, or just don't like the idea of huffing and puffing around in a cave. Discovered in 1862 (a farmer's dog reputedly found it), Fantastic Caverns is still a family-owned business. Deep underground, the tour follows a submerged riverbed and passes by massive formations. Almost everyone visits a cave or two when visiting the Cave State, and given its ease and comfort, this subterranean sojourn is highly recommended.

✳ Lodging
BED & BREAKFASTS

Springfield, Mo.

✿ ♿ **Virginia Rose Bed & Breakfast** (417-883-0693 or 1-800-345-1412; www.bbonline.com/mo/virginiarose/index.html), 317 E. Glenwood St. A 1906 country Victorian home, this green-roofed inn is notable for its wooded acre located in the heart of Springfield. The "rose" aspect of this establishment is not to be ignored—nor could you. Rose wallpaper is prevalent in many rooms, and the breakfast table is set with collectible Virginia Rose pattern dishes. This is a very well-kept inn that prides itself on hospitality, and one of its drawing points is its location, just a few minutes from the Bass Pro Shops complex. Another is the food. Breakfasts are plentiful, often featuring quiche, fruit, and homemade muffins or biscuits. Rates for any of the four guest rooms (all of which have private bath) start at $65, though a suite of two rooms is available in the $100 range. The parlor includes a TV, DVD, books, and games. Guests are invited to play a tune on the piano, assuming they can play. Kids are permitted, though smoking and pets are not.

✿ ♿ **The Mansion at Elfindale** (1-800-443-0237; www.mansionatelfindale.com), 1701 S. Fort St. Situated on 13 tree-covered acres down a lovely lane, the inn is the epitome of Victorian luxury.

Missouri's largest bed & breakfast, the castlelike Elfindale mansion has a long and varied history. It's too bad these walls can't talk. Built between 1890 and 1893 by John O'Day, attorney for the St. Louis–San Francisco Railroad, the original home was constructed by 50 German stonemasons with raw materials quarried on the property itself. At 27,000 square feet, Elfindale had 35 rooms and seven baths. Alas, soon after the mansion was completed, O'Day and his wife, Clymena Alice O'Day, were divorced. She received the property as a divorce settlement, a highly unusual event in that time, perhaps indicating John was a very bad boy. Clymena built an island in the property's stream, complete with iron and stone pagoda; constructed a lake, boathouse, summerhouse, and greenhouse; and imported trees from all over America and Europe. Within six years she blew through all her money. Though she was offered nearly $300,000 for the property, she sold it to a Catholic order of nuns for $30,000. From 1906 to 1964, Elfindale was the St. d'Chantel Academy for girls. The nuns built a chapel (now used for weddings) and a three-story classroom building. The property was again sold in 1977 to a group of Iranian businessmen for $1.54 million (it was to be a safe house for the shah of Iran). Springfield's Cornerstone Church acquired the property in 1979 (the shah didn't need it anymore, as he was deposed in that year and died the next) and completed a full restoration in 1990.

Today Elfindale's 13 guest rooms (check out the Art Deco Suite) feature private bath, phone, period antiques, stained glass, and hardwood floors. Some rooms have a fireplace. Rates range from $129–179, and a full breakfast is served in an elegant dining room. Corporate rates are available, and the facility is suitable for banquets, meetings, reunions, and retreats. Also, thanks to the on-site chapel, weddings are a regular occurrence at Elfindale. Event planners are available by calling the main mansion number. Children are welcome, but smoking is not permitted. Alcohol of any kind is neither served nor allowed on the Elfindale grounds.

THE MANSION AT ELFINDALE

🌊 ♿ **Walnut Street Inn** (417-864-6346 or 1-800-593-6346; www.walnutstreetinn.com), 900 E. Walnut St. This Queen Anne Victorian, with its hand-painted Corinthian columns, is charm personified. Though it may not have quite the unusual history of Elfindale, the Walnut Street Inn equals (and perhaps surpasses) its competitor in terms of pure class and elegance. Best of all, it accomplishes this task with relaxed and friendly grace. The main house of this 12-room establishment was built in 1894 in the heart of Springfield's Walnut Street Local Historic District, which is included in the National Register of Historic Places. Each room at the inn, which was voted Best Bed and Breakfast in the Ozarks by readers of the *Springfield News-Leader* four years in a row, was decorated by a different designer. All include private bath, king or queen bed, two-line phone, and cable TV. Most have WiFi access, private balcony, and stocked beverage bar. The inn also boasts of two parlors with fireplaces, comfortable chairs and chaise lounges, and a large front porch and veranda.

WALNUT STREET INN

Rooms run $99–179 and are found in the main house, the **1894 Carriage House,** or the **1904 Cottage Inn.** Walnut Street Inn is within walking distance of great restaurants, shops, a health club, theaters, and Hammons Field. Business rates are available, and the inn does rent for special occasions—it's a popular venue for wedding and family reunions. (The inn's wedding planner, Kristi Ball, can be reached at 417-880-6689.) Last but not least, ask about weekend packages for honeymoons, birthdays, and anniversaries. As expected, smoking and pets are not permitted, though kids are OK as long as they're well behaved.

✳ Where to Eat

Springfield is food crazy. There are restaurants on every corner, sometimes two or three on every corner, and they cover the cuisine spectrum. Literally hundreds of options exist, and it seems new establishments open on a weekly basis. As would be expected in the Ozarks, diners, BBQ, burger, buffet, and catfish joints are prevalent. Happily, the overall quality is exceedingly high and the ambience honest and authentic. Then there are the more upscale choices.

Moving beyond frying and smoking, you'll find Mediterranean, French, Italian, Vietnamese, and Thai restaurants. There are Caribbean, Cajun, German, Indian, Japanese, and Korean eateries. There are tearooms and bistros. Also, you'll find a number of high-end places that fly in their fish (flying fish?) three to five times per week. Strangest of all, this town seems to hold more Chinese restaurants per capita than any other locale in America. In fact, there is a vast amount of evidence (from people who have way too much time on their hands and spend years researching Chinese food trivia) that Springfield is the home of cashew chicken. It was created, so the story goes, in the early 1960s by a restaurateur who thought mixing Chinese style with fried chicken would improve his business with grease-addicted Ozarkians.

That's the good news. The other side of the coin is that quite a few Springfield restaurants strive to emulate their big-city cousins, hoping to display the epitome of faddish style. The slightly embarrassing thing is that often what the owners perceive as the cutting edge is 5 or 10 years behind the times. It's a little like thinking tanning beds, leisure suits, Rubik's Cubes, and the DeLorean are the next big things. Eponymous restaurants are the current rage, which is OK for a run-down diner with an EAT sign but sort of silly and pretentious otherwise. Chrome, stainless steel, and odd decor crop up way too frequently in Springfield. You get the impression that some of the local restaurateurs hope to distance themselves from the hillbilly image of this part of the world, when in fact they should celebrate their local strengths and specialize in subtle class (for an example of folks who do this right, see the listing for Bijan's). Springfield should strive to be uniquely Springfield, not a poor copy of San Francisco or Manhattan.

The town even passed one of those politically correct, highly obnoxious, and downright silly smoking bans in April 2011. This means you can't smoke in Springfield bars or restaurants. Some folks like that, mostly the kind of folks who Ozarkers don't really cotton to. The rest of us take it as a personal affront to individual rights (even if we don't smoke).

While space limitations prevent a comprehensive critique of Springfield's huge array of fantastic eats (that would require an entire book), the following are a sample of some of the best. Heck, there's even an eponymous joint or two included. A misdirected attempt at image creation doesn't mean the food isn't swell.

EATING OUT

Springfield, Mo.

⬥ ♂ ♿ **Ziggie's Café** (417-833-0900), 2222 S. Campbell St. Open 24 hours a day. Possessing what seems to be the lengthiest menu in the Western world, Ziggie's now has four locations in and around Springfield. The original Ziggie's, on South Campbell, is the only one open 24 hours a day. Breakfast is the specialty here, available anytime. These folks have any style of omelet you could name, and quite a few you couldn't. Sure, you can have your Denver ($5.99), plain ($4.29), or veggie omelet ($5.49). But for a change, go for the Greek omelet (at $7.19 it boasts gyro meat, green peppers, onions, mushrooms, tomatoes, and feta cheese). You won't go away hungry here, as all house omelets come with your choice of toast, muffins, biscuits, biscuits and gravy, or pancakes. Traditionalists might want to opt for the chicken-fried steak with eggs ($7.99). The lunch and dinner menu at Ziggie's is equally extensive; they should call this place "sandwich world." Choose from burgers, melts, dips, gyros, or croissants. If you're really hungry, go for the half-pound "Monster Burger" ($5.99). Dinner includes steaks, chicken, seafood, BBQ, Greek, Italian, and Chinese dishes. The most expensive item on the menu is the house rib eye for $15.99. Most entrées run in the $8–13 range.

🍴 ♿ **1955 Maple Cafe** (417-865-5656), 2253 N. Glenstone. Hours are Mon.–Sat. 5 AM–9 PM. This is an alcohol-free restaurant. Appropriate to the name, it was established in 1955 on historic Route 66. The meals have that homemade taste, and you can still get a traditional and simple breakfast for $2.99. Biscuits and gravy are big here.

🍴 ♿ 🍷 **Nonna's Italian American Cafe** (417-831-1222; www.nonnas cafe.com), 306 South Ave. Open Mon.–Sat. 11–10, Sun., noon–9. Nonna's offers a full bar and wine list. This is a friendly restaurant, well lit and happy. I have to admit that the chefs seem to go a bit garlic crazy here—which is great, since I can't get enough of the stuff, but diners without the same tastes might want to request that the kitchen tone it down a bit. The price for entrées is well within budget. Fettuccine Alfredo is only $6.99, but for an even better deal order the seafood lasagna. At $9.99, this is a fantastic entrée that should fetch a far higher price.

🍷 🍴 ♿ **Carlos O'Kelly's Mexican Cafe** (417-890-0220), 4100 S. Campbell St. Opens daily at 11 AM. Carlos O'Kelly's is part of a growing chain that has sprung up around the Midwest. The huge menu runs the gamut from nachos and quesadillas to fiesta platters, steaks, and chicken. A full bar is offered, and as you might expect, a wide variety of margaritas are available.

♿ 🍷 **W. F. Cody's** (417-887-8083), 3138 E. Sunshine St. Open Mon.–Sat. 11 AM–midnight, Sun. 11–10. A second location can be found at 1440 E. Republic Rd. Depending on your take on such things, you may or may not want to bring the kids with you for lunch or dinner. The environment is early American bar (which is not a bad thing—and in this case it's a very good thing), featuring a full liquor selection. This place is an institution in Springfield (the original location has been in operation for more than three decades), and the reason you come is for the burgers. Yes, there is also plenty of bar food (the wings are good; in the old days they were complimentary, but such is a thing of the past), but the burger is the stuff of myth, the Excalibur of chopped meat. For $6.95 you can get a 1-pound cheeseburger on a giant bun sized to fit. The fixin's come on the side, allowing you to pile on as much lettuce, tomato, and onion as you see fit. I'm not sure why the burgers here are so good, but it seems the meat is all very fresh. More than that, I suspect they're cooked the old-fashioned way: slapped onto a very hot, oiled griddle and then weighed down with the equivalent of a small anvil. Last, it tastes as if the buns are warmed on the same griddle, soaking up just enough burger juice to flavor the bread. Then again, none of this matters. Nobody cares what makes the rainbow; they just enjoy looking at it. At W. F. Cody's, simply order a beer (always cold) and a 1-pounder, and prepare to experience cheeseburger Nirvana.

🎈 🍴 ♿ **Incredible Pizza Company** (417-887-3030; www.incrediblepizza .com/springfield), 2850 S. Campbell

Ave. Buffet hours Sun.–Thurs. 11–8, Fri.–Sat. 11–9. The game room is open until 9 Sun.–Thurs., and until 10 Fri.–Sat. Though this is not the typical restaurant listed in this guide, it makes the cut because of its price, quality, and innumerable opportunities to entertain youngsters who might well be tired of viewing Civil War battlefields. The original location of franchises that are popping up around the country, Incredible Pizza's fare is much better than you might expect from a buffet pizza establishment. All items are made from scratch, including sauces, and more than 30 different types of pizza are made each day. At a price of just $7.99 for diners age 12 and older, $5.99 for seniors and kids 8–11, $4.59 for kids 4–7, and free for kids 3 and younger, you can try not only all the pizza you wish, but also a pasta bar, baked potato bar, and 100-item salad bar. There are soups galore, desserts aplenty, and fresh, hot cinnamon rolls.

But food is just one aspect of this restaurant; the interior (this is an estimate, but at a minimum it must be 70,000 square feet) includes a Route 66 miniature golf course, bumper cars, and a go-cart track. Last but not least, the Fairground area features more than 100 games of skill, from Skee-Ball to air hockey to all the video options imaginable. There's also a safe funland where the smallest kids can bounce, climb, and basically go wild. As you would assume in a family establishment, alcohol is not permitted.

🦪 🐟 **Crosstown Barbecue** (417-862-4646), 1331 E. Division St. Open Mon.–Sat. 11–9. For its size, Springfield possesses a huge array of restaurants. Moreover, I don't know that I've ever come across a single town with so many good BBQ joints. Standing head and shoulders above the crowd is a tough job, though it seems as if the Crosstown achieves such status without breaking a sweat. This is BBQ, pure and simple. A casual place

CROSSTOWN BARBECUE

(down to the paper plates), this little slice of smoked pleasure consistently churns out some of the best ribs, hot link sausage, sandwiches, and BBQ platters you'll ever find. A regular-sized smoked beef, pork, ham, or turkey sandwich plate is $6.49 for the small version and $8.25 for the large (you'd better be hungry—large means *large* at Crosstown). The hot link plate is $7.99, and a combo sandwich—your choice of any of the meats, but no side—goes for $4.99 or $5.99. If you want to splurge, and it's worth it, go for the $7.75 rib sandwich. A specialty sandwich named "The Bluto" consists of smoked brisket, sausage, and rib meat. It comes with a choice of the Crosstown's homemade coleslaw, potato salad, or baked beans (go for the pit-smoked baked beans, and don't forget to order some fries, too). A full slab of ribs is $18.95, and the $12.95 "Big Papa" dinner (brisket, sausage, and ribs) arrives with bread, a choice of two side orders, and sauce on the side. Finally, keep in mind that Crosstown has not forgotten the salad crowd. For $6.95 you can order a chef's salad, but it's hardly suited for vege-terrorists. This plate of greens features smoked ham, turkey, burned ends, and shredded cheese. You gotta love it. If you're in a hurry, Crosstown has a drive-through and sells both family packs and BBQ by the pound.

Pappy's Place (417-866-8744), 943 N. Main Ave. Hours are Mon.–Sat. 11–8:30. Pappy's is not for the claustrophobic. It's a crowded little place that would be just as at home (if not more so) in the 1940s and '50s than the 21st century. The staff is not huge (usually one person) and the surroundings aren't fancy. Why go to Pappy's? A couple of reasons. For starters, a 14-ounce beer is only $2. And to go with that beer, order the smoked pork sandwich at $6.95 (often one of the daily specials). This sucker is big, smoked just right, and tender as a toddler's dreams. Sauce is served on the side (if a place doesn't serve it on the side, it's likely covering something up), and the atmosphere will take you back to a simpler time. This establishment is not really set up for the handicapped. Remember to bring cash or a check, as Pappy's doesn't take credit cards.

&. ¥ **Springfield Brewing Company** (417-832-8277; www.springfield brewingco.com), 301 S. Market Ave. Open Mon.–Tues. 11–11; Wed.–Thurs. and Sun. 11–midnight; Fri.–Sat. 11–1 AM. While there is a large selection of appetizers, pizza, sandwiches, entrées, and desserts at the Springfield Brewing Company (appetizers start at $3.50, sandwiches and entrées at $6.95), the real reason to come is the beer. This two-story restaurant and pub—complete with a beer garden on the roof for warm weather—is actually owned by the Paul Mueller Company, a brewery equipment fabrication firm. From this facility, Mueller manufactures and markets its beers to domestic and international markets. Its unfiltered wheat, pale ale, Munich lager, and porter are all local favorites, and there's a constantly changing selection of ales and lagers from around the world. The Springfield Brewing Company also offers a full bar. Live music is featured Wed.–Sun. On Fri.–Sat., live jazz is played 6–9, followed by hot area bands 10–close. You can usually catch some fine acoustic tunes Sun. from 7–10. The music can be a little loud at times (not terrible, just a bit beyond the auditory pleasure level of old fogies like me)—but then again, such is to be expected in one of Springfield's top hangouts.

Aurora, Mo.

Richard's Hawgwild BBQ (417-678-4294), 22 E. Olive St. Hours are Mon.–Sat. 10:30–9. Nonsmoking and no alcohol. Those who seek the die-hard BBQ experience might be a little disappointed that Richard's doesn't serve beer. But don't let that keep you from dropping in. This is a large place, seating more than 150, and has the typical look of a rustic BBQ joint, complete with place mats shaped like a pig. The fare here is billed as Memphis-style BBQ (as if you couldn't guess that from the Elvis stuff on the walls), which generally is defined as slow-smoked over wood, then pulled apart or diced (sometimes the definition encompasses a semi-sweet sauce that inevitably includes molasses). Richard's lives up to the Memphis reputation at least in part. The meat has a nice, smoky taste, and the pulled pork is very good. Your best bet here is to order the pit plate ($15.99), which comes with ribs, pulled pork, beef, sausage, two side dishes, and bread. It might not be truly authentic Memphis (sorry, but you can only get that in Memphis), but this is some mighty tasty Q.

Hurley, Mo.

W & W Cafe (417-369-6255), 108 E. Main St. Mon.–Sat. 6:30 AM–8:30 PM. Aside from the pretty scenery, there is another reason to drive to the small town of Hurley, 28 miles southwest of Springfield. That would be the W & W Cafe. This is a true small-town diner, but the food is beyond excellent. Simplicity can be magnificent at times, as witnessed by the fact that W & W's menu offers a fried bologna sandwich and Frito pie. The folks here even cook their fried chicken in a cast-iron skillet. For urban types who have never tasted food from a country café, the W & W will quickly educate you as to what you've been missing. Best of all, try the pie—neglecting to do so would be a cardinal sin. These are home-baked standards in the vein of pecan, apple, and coconut cream, and just a couple of bucks a slice. The W & W does not serve alcohol, though it does have a smoking section.

W & W CAFÉ

Ozark, Mo.

🌸 ✎ ♿ **Century Buffet** (417-582-2188), 5493 N. 17th St. Open daily 11–9. You won't find smoking or alcohol at the Century Buffet, but you will find tons of food at a reasonable price. This family-friendly restaurant is right across the street from the semi-legendary Lambert's Cafe. If you're seeking passable Chinese food and want to stay within the vacation budget, the Century is unbeatable. The lunch and dinner buffets offer extensive selections, and it's tough to find an individual entrée costing more than $10. Toss in discounts for kids and seniors, and you'll agree that the Century is the deal of the century. That said, low prices mean nothing if the quality is subpar. Happily, this is one buffet that serves good food, not to mention keeping the buffet line free of spills and dried gravy splotches. The fruit and salad bar offers fresh selections (even strawberries at times), and the Chinese buffet line will leave you (a) confused and (b) stuffed. Spring rolls, tiny crab rangoon, cashew chicken, shrimp, and peanut chicken are really but a tiny sample of the choices. Of course (think about where you are) you'll find American dishes in the vein of catfish and macaroni and cheese. If you so choose—and this is an acquired taste that I never acquired—you can also chow down on fried okra.

DINING OUT

Springfield, Mo.

✎ ♿ 🍷 **Metropolitan Grill** (417-889-4951; metropolitan-grill.com), 2931 E. Battlefield Rd. Hours are Mon.–Fri. 11:30–2:30 for lunch and 4–10 for dinner. On weekends, the Metropolitan is open Fri.–Sat. 4–11, Sun. 5–10. Full bar and wine list. This is one of Springfield's top spots for lunch, particularly a midday meal of

🌸 ✎ ♿ **Lambert's Cafe** (417-581-7655; www.throwedrolls.com), 1800 W. SR J, Ozark, Mo. Open daily 10:30–9. No smoking and no alcohol. Credit cards are not accepted, but personal checks are (they're real proud of that . . . I'm not sure why). With three locations (the original is in Sikeston, Mo.; another is in Foley, Ala.), Lambert's is frequently featured on national travel shows as "the home of the throwed rolls." For those out of the loop, "throwed rolls" does not refer to a secret dough-making process. It refers to the fact that Lambert's waiters toss 5-inch fresh-baked rolls at you from across the room (it's more fun than it sounds, OK?). Other than that claim to fame, there are certain factors that should be taken into consideration before you eat here. First, the portions are huge, coming with side orders, rolls, and "pass arounds." This last item could be anything from fried potatoes to fried okra, macaroni and tomatoes to black-eyed peas, or sorghum and honey for your throwed roll. Servers patrol the floor with large pots full of these delicious goodies and will heap your plate with as much as you want, as many times as you want. Next, you should expect a wait. Despite the fact that the

the business variety. The menu has a tendency to change every six months or so, but there are some specialties that are area favorites. For a treat, order the $8.99 flash-fried spinach, and I guarantee you'll never look at Popeye's addiction in quite the same way again. For dinner, the apple-brined, bone-in Berkshire pork chop with bacon and maple onion rings is available for $19.89. For an outstanding meal, opt to spend the $36.89 and feast on the 8-ounce beef tenderloin with shrimp, scallops, squid, and crab.

♂ & ♈ **Bijan's Sea and Grill** (417-831-1480; www.bijans.com), 209 E. Walnut St. Hours are Mon.–Thurs. 5–10 PM, Fri.–Sat. 5–11 PM. The **Julieta Cigar and Martini Bar** is open Mon.–Sat. 5 PM–1 AM. Reservations are suggested. Here is the perfect example of a great restaurant that strives to establish its own identity— and succeeds. Others might try to imitate Bijan's, but they will never duplicate its particular style. That would be defined, quite simply, as pure class. From the long bar to the low lights to the comfort of dark wood and leather, Bijan's may well be the best restaurant in Springfield. Fresh seafood is flown in three times a week, and it's impossible to get a bad meal. The wine list is extensive (the restaurant is a four-time *Wine Spectator* magazine Award of Excellence winner), and choices run from $17 to $1,400 per bottle. For appetizers, the escargot ($10.75) includes a tasty combination of mushrooms and just the right amount of herbs and garlic, and the corn-dog lobster ($9.75) is not to be missed. The most renowned entrée at Bijan's is the Chilean sea bass ($26.75), which offers a hint of cedar and arrives with a crust of cashews, pecans, and caramelized onion. The lobster for two ($37) is deep fried and encrusted in a coconut and banana chip crème brûlée.

restaurant seats close to 350 people, it is not unusual to experience an hour's delay in getting a table. This is not because of poor service (in fact, the service is great, and entertaining to boot), but because so many folks like this place. You can kill time looking at the memorabilia or perusing the gift shop. Just keep in mind that the rule here is "first come, first served." And last, don't expect a calm and quiet dining experience. This is southern cooking on a mammoth scale, with servers who are just as likely to make jokes and sing songs as they are to deliver your meal. Speaking of which, hog jowls and turnip greens, fried chicken livers, and fried chicken gizzards are readily available. You can also order very good ribs or BBQ pork steak, a rib eye, catfish, roast beef, or chicken-fried steak. The menu here is large. Lambert's aims to please, and prices for adults vary from around $9–21. Kids under 10 can eat for $5–7. Don't leave without ordering a hubcap-sized cinnamon roll.

Did I say popular? Last year Lambert's baked 2,246,400 rolls and served 73,440 pounds of okra. It cooked 132,743 pounds of beef, more than 180,000 pounds of chicken, nearly 48,409 pounds of catfish, and 33 tons of french fries.

Wood-fired rib-eye steaks, pork chops, and filet mignon are available, but for a true surprise check out the slow-roasted Long Island duck ($21.50). If you just want to relax and listen to some soft music, you'll enjoy the gorgeous martini and cigar bar with its walk-in humidor.

🦞 🍴 ♿ ⅄ **Hemingway's Blue Water Cafe** (417-891-5100; www.hemingways bluewatercafe.com), 1935 S. Campbell (fourth floor of Bass Pro Shops). Open Mon.–Sat. 7 AM–10 PM, Sun. 9–7. Breakfast is served 7–10 Mon.–Sat.; brunch is available Sun. 9–3. You expect big things from any venture associated with Bass Pro Shops, and Hemingway's doesn't disappoint. It's a casual place that seats more than 350, set off by a 30,000-gallon saltwater fish tank. Many people come to Hemingway's for the buffets. The breakfast version ($6.25 adults, $3.50 ages 5–10) features the usual suspects of scrambled eggs, bacon, sausage, ham, pancakes, French toast, and biscuits and gravy. However (again, it's the Ozarks), you can also dig into deep-fried catfish, plenty of potatoes, and apple dumplings. The lunch buffet ($8.75 adults, $3.95 kids) offers carved roast beef, ham, or turkey; catfish (surprise, surprise); rice; vegetables; corn bread; soup of the day; a full salad bar; and several desserts. The spectacular dinner buffet ($18.96 adults, $6.95 kids) is loaded with snow crab legs, popcorn shrimp, ham, roast beef, BBQ ribs, clam chowder, vegetables, rice, dessert, and much more.

The restaurant has a full bar and an extensive wine list, and should you choose to forgo the buffet and order from the menu, you will find plenty of options. Nowhere else in Springfield

offers alligator tail ($7.95) as an appetizer. If you want something more traditional, go for the fried mozzarella ($5.95). The catfish sandwich ($8.95) is a safe bet for lunch, and the evening entrées make for a delicious cross section of American fare. The pan-fried Ozark trout is $12.95, and a tasty, blackened rib-eye steak will run you $16.95.

🍴 ♿ ⅄ **Haruno** and **Haruno Next Door** (417-887-0077; www.haruno sushi.com), 3044 S. Fremont Ave. Haruno is open for lunch Mon.–Fri. 11–2; Sat. 11:30–2:30. Dinner is served Mon.–Thurs. 4:30–10, Fri.–Sat. until 10:30. Haruno Next Door is open Mon.–Sat. 4:30–close. I'm not sure exactly what fuels the American sushi fixation, but I'm pretty sure it has more to do with social conformity than it does health. At any rate, the desire to eat hunks of raw fish shows no signs of stopping anytime soon. Such being the case, the wise owners of Haruno provide sushi in a big way. Luckily, for those who aren't raw-fish fans, Haruno also offers an extensive and excellent menu of Japanese appetizers and entrées. The main restaurant (the original space, which opened in 1999) offers such lunch selections as donkatsu (a fried pork cutlet with soup and salad) for $8.50. Shrimp or vegetable tempura is $7.50. Almost all lunch dishes are less than $12, including the sushi lunch, which consists of one tuna roll, one cucumber roll, and five nigiri. For dinner, a large number of appetizers are available, with good choices being the beef sashimi (rare, thin-sliced beef) at $8, and sumai (Japanese shrimp dumplings) at $4.50. Dinner includes such choices as chicken katsu (breaded chicken cutlet with special sauce) or donkatsu (deep-fried breaded pork with special sauce) for $13. You can also sit at the sushi bar (it holds half a dozen people) and watch the chefs chop up the fish (a hobby also enjoyed by those who frequent marinas and bait shops).

Haruno Next Door is the result of an expansion—very modernistic with lots of reflecting stainless steel, and very blue (that's blue as in the color, not blue as in melancholy). It offers a full menu and sushi menu, but also 30 different types of sake and a giant martini list. If your sushi desire hasn't been sated yet, Haruno Next Door features a midnight sushi bar, not to mention live jazz Wed.–Sat. It's something of an odd combination for an Ozark town, granted, but it's also something that seems to draw large numbers of customers night after night.

✍ ♿ ♈ **Avanzare** (417-567-3463; www.avanzareitaliandining.com), 1908 S. Glenstone Ave. Sun.–Thurs. 5–10, Fri.–Sat. 5–11. I like Avanzare for its sense of tradition. The tablecloths are white, the bar is black, the menus are bound in leather, and the wait staff is both friendly and knowledgeable. While you can order numerous entrées showcasing the lighter, seafood-oriented fare of northern Italy ("light" in comparison with southern Italy), Avanzare also shows a bit of inventive style. At $30, the filetto brandy features a pan-seared, center-cut fillet topped with a brandy and tomato cream sauce. The pollo balsamico is also a fine choice. At $17 it's a chicken breast sautéed in a balsamic vinegar reduction topped with melted fontina cheese and diced tomatoes. Avanzare also offers a very good wine list (close to 200 selections).

✍ ♿ ♈ **Gem of India** (417-881-9558; www.gemofindia.net), 211 W. Battlefield. Open daily 11–3 and 5–9:30. Lunch buffet daily 11–2:30; dinner buffet Mon.–Tues. 5–9. With every other ethnicity found within the Springfield dining demographic, it was high time that the curry crowd received its due. The Gem of India fills that requirement quite handily. One great thing about this place is the massive offerings of freshly baked Indian breads. At $35.95, the Gem's dinner for two includes mulligatawny soup, meat samosa, shrimp curry, tandoori chicken, and a number of other items you are advised not to even attempt to pronounce. If you're not truly acquainted with Indian food (and I count myself among that caste, believing that mulligatawny is that town in Pennsylvania where the groundhog sees his shadow), just ask; the folks at Gem of India will be happy to assist. There are many veal, chicken, and vegetarian entrées in the $9–15 range, and in the seafood arena you should try the shrimp biryani. This entrée features jumbo shrimp cooked with basmati white rice, fresh onions, green peppers, nuts and coriander; it will set you back only $12.95. Tandoori specialties (cooked in a tandoor, or clay oven) are numerous and have the benefit of being nonfat. Combination meals and dinners are available, as is a full bar and wonderful desserts. To end your meal, do not pass up the kheer ($2.95). This rice pudding, cooked in sweet milk with raisins and nuts, will make your tongue very happy.

✍ ♿ ♈ **Tong's Thai Restaurant** (417-889-5280), 3454 S. Campbell Ave. Open Mon.–Sat. 11–2:30 for lunch, 5–10 for dinner. I have a theory that most people who claim they don't like Thai food have never tasted Thai food (or at least not the real deal). I'll freely admit to have been among that group until I stumbled upon an incredible little Thai place in Naples, Florida, during the late 1980s. After that, I was hooked. Those who have yet to be initiated into Thai cuisine would likely have a similar experience if they wandered into Tong's. For an appetizer (you can't go wrong here) order the satay. This is chicken marinated in Thai spices and coconut milk, then fried and served on skewers. A traditional favorite here is the panang shrimp, steamed in panang curry sauce and served with pasta. A great meal is the siam beef , a sliced rib-eye steak marinated in garlic, ginger, pepper, soy sauce, and wine before being stir-fried with onion, green onion, red and green peppers, and carrots. Tong's has a nice wine list and a full bar. As usual with a Thai place (this is true of Indian joints as well), you would be wise to ask your server about the heat quotient of some of these meals. If such is your wish, the chefs will gladly tone down the spice to suit your palate. Diners are encouraged to try different sauces on different dishes. Tong's is well on its way to becoming one of the most popular (and certainly consistent) restaurants in town. Prices vary, but a safe bet is to budget around $15 per person for dinner.

✳ Entertainment

✐ ♿ **Juanita K. Hammons Hall for the Performing Arts** (417-836-7678; www.hammonshall.com), 525 S. John Q. Hammons Pkwy., Springfield, Mo. A 2,264-seat multipurpose perform-

ance venue, Hammons Hall is located on the Missouri State University campus near Springfield's historic Walnut Street district. Named in honor of the wife of famed hotel magnate John Q. Hammons, who spearheaded the private funding campaign to build the hall, this facility's events and performances run the gamut of entertainment. Regular tenants include the **Springfield Symphony,** but you will find anything from Broadway shows to jazz jams, kids' shows to chamber groups here. The spot offers only the best; recent performers have included The Blue Man Group and Bela Fleck and the Flecktones. Check the Hammons website for current and upcoming shows.

✐ ♿ **Springfield Ballet** (417-862-1343; www.springfieldballet.org), 411 N. Sherman Pkwy., Springfield, Mo. Founded nearly 40 years ago, the Springfield Ballet presents four major dance productions throughout its Sept.–May season. Having recently established its own professional company, which visits schools and public events, the community-supported endeavor continues to expand awareness of the arts through dance. All performances take place at the Landers Theatre, and tickets are available for individual shows. A season subscription is available at the ballet's website.

THEATER ✐ ♿ **Springfield Little Theatre** (417-869-1334; www.landers theatre.org), 311 E. Walnut, Springfield, Mo. On average there are nine performances per year (six main-stage performances and three children's shows) at the Landers Theatre. Admission price varies but is roughly $20 for adults and $12 for kids. The oldest (1909) and largest civic theater in Missouri, the Landers is on the National Register of Historic Places; John Philip Sousa and Fanny Brice performed on this stage. The season's plays and musicals are attended by more than 50,000 people.

✑ ♿ **Springfield Contemporary Theatre** (417-831-8001; www.vc theatre.com), 305 E. Walnut St., Springfield, Mo. The Vandivort Center hosts 12 main productions per year. Ticket prices vary, but they average $22 for adults and $18 for kids and seniors. Visitors can expect to see well-done and professional productions in the historic 1907 Vandivort Theatre. Past shows have included *Evita, Dirty Rotten Scoundrels,* and *Glenngarry Glenn Ross.* Given its great value, flexible seating, and impressive talent, the Vandivort has long been a Springfield favorite.

DRIVE-IN THEATER ✑ ♿ **Sunset Drive-In Theater** (417-678-6609; www.sunsetdriveinaurora.com), 1601 E. US Bus. 60, Aurora, Mo. Open Apr.–Sept. and Nov. $6.50 per ticket. Kids under 5 are admitted free of charge. This is one place of which it can truly be said "They don't make 'em like this anymore." In business since 1951, the Sunset holds 325 cars and, due to a lightning storm in 2001, utilizes digital FM for sound (sadly, no more poles with speakers). The concession stand is great, offering entrées such as a Sunset chili burger, ice-cold dill pickles, chili cheese fries, and Sunset nacho pie. Of course, there is plenty of popcorn, candy, and Coke as well. This is a trip to the 1950s in the sense that Sunset is not a re-creation. It's the real deal. For the kiddies, there is a playground up

front. Some compromise has been made with technology, as the theater now provides free WiFi (something about that just seems SO wrong), but this is still the coolest place in the Ozark Mining Region.

SPECTATOR SPORTS

⚾ ✑ ♿ **Springfield Cardinals (417-863-0395;** http://web.minorleague baseball.com/index.jsp?sid=t440), 955 E. Trafficway, Springfield, Mo. The season for this Double-A minor-league baseball team runs Apr.–Sept. Admission runs $6–47, depending upon seating choice. You will find few small cities that are as baseball crazy as Springfield, but for years the town had trouble attracting a team. Then hotel magnate and Springfield native John Q. Hammons stepped in. In 2004 Hammons not only built a $32 million, 10,000-seat stadium (Hammons Field), but he also convinced the legendary St. Louis Cardinals to buy the El Paso Diablos minor-league team and move it to Springfield. Cards games at Hammons are a great time in a spectacular setting, and for those on a budget, the price is right. General admission tickets start at $6, though if you're willing to splurge, for $24 per person you can have a seat in the **Redbird Roost,** located above the concourse on the third-base line—the view is perfect. Plus, all food and soft drinks are included in the price. This makes the seats worth it, as food at Hammons is excellent. Try the hot dogs, bratwurst, salad bar, chips, cookies, and a variety of Coca-Cola products. Redbird Roost members also have access to private restrooms (always a good thing at a ballpark). The brand new (as of 2011) **Champions Club** offers indoor seating (read: air-conditioned), a couple of 60-inch flat-screen TVs, and four 34-inch flat-screens. Tickets are $47 per person, but they include a great view of the ball field (along the first-base side). They also include all-you-can-eat hot dogs, bratwurst, popcorn, fresh-baked cookies, a nacho bar, salad bar, and specialty pasta dishes. Ticket holders get unlimited Coke, not to mention four, adult-drink tickets good for mixed drinks, wine, or Budweiser products. It's pricey, but look at it this way: Going to see the minor-league Cards and opting for the Champion's Room is cheaper than buying a seat in the nosebleed section at most major-league games.

🖉 ♿ **Drury University Panthers** (417-873-6389; www.drurypanthers .com), 900 N. Benton Ave., Spring-field, Mo. Indoor events (basketball and volleyball) are held in the brand new (as of 2010) O'Reilly Family Event Center (replacing the old Weiser Gym). The $13.5 million facility seats 3,100 people and was funded entirely through private donations. The O'Reilly family of Springfield—

owners of a large chain of auto parts stores—kicked in almost half that. The center also hosts major concerts and shows (Sheryl Crowe was there recently).

🖉 ♿ **Missouri State University Bears** (417-836-7678; http://missouri statebears.com), 685 S. John Q. Hammons Parkway, Springfield, Mo. A variety of collegiate events take place at the nearly 20,000-student Missouri State University. Basketball, volleyball, swimming, and diving can be viewed at the 8,900-seat **John Q. Hammons Student Center.** The season for both the MSU Bears and the Lady Bears runs Nov.–Mar., and single-game tickets range from $7–15 for adults. MSU football games take place at the 16,300-seat **Robert W. Plaster Sports Complex** (Sept.–Dec.), and admission begins at $10.

✳ Selective Shopping

Battlefield Mall (417-883-7777; www.simon.com), 2825 S. Glenstone Ave., Springfield, Mo. Open

HAMMONS FIELD

Mon.–Sat. 10–9, Sun. noon–6. The largest shopping center in southwest Missouri, Battlefield Mall offers more than 150 stores and restaurants. Name brands are prevalent here, in the genre of **Dillard's, Macy's, JCPenney,** and **Sears.**

Waverly House Gifts and Gallery (417-882-3445; www.waverlyhouse .com), 2031 S. Waverly Ave., Springfield, Mo. Hours are Tues.–Fri. 9:30–5:30; Sat. 10–4. Far more than your stereotypical gift store, Waverly House offers fine art, contemporary American crafts, and a year-round Christmas room. You will find ceramics, wearable art, kaleidoscopes, jewelry, sculpture, stoneware, and turned wood. In addition to a large supply of unique Santa figurines, the Christmas room contains holiday decor and ornaments from many different countries.

Half Price Books (417-889-9042), 1950 S. Glenstone Ave., Springfield, Mo. Open Mon.–Fri. 9–6, Sat. 9–5. With more than 4,000 square feet of space, Half Price Books has upward of 100,000 new and used books for sale. An independent bookseller, its stock includes everything from fiction and romance to westerns, mysteries, audio books, cookbooks, biographies, and much more.

✒ **Ted E. Bear's Toy Factory** (417-823-7883; www.tedebearstoyfactory .com), 2752 S. Campbell, Springfield, Mo. Open Mon.–Fri. 10–7; Sat., 10–8; Sun. 1–5. Admission is free, but the final cost of your custom-designed critter can run $9–20. A nice place to take your young kids, Ted E. Bear's lets you create your own teddy bear from scratch. Customers pick out the unstuffed body and then install eyes, stuff it until it feels just right, trim it, brush it, select one of myriad outfits, and then receive an official certificate of adoption. It's reminiscent of the Cabbage Patch doll factory, but without the vegetable motif.

Commercial Street Historic District (417-864-7015), on Commercial St. between Washington and Lyon. This six-block federal historic district has been refurbished to resemble a turn-of-the-20th-century railroad town. It's a great place to take a stroll, especially if you're looking for neat little shops offering antiques, art, and a wide range of clothing (some normal, some a bit odd). You can also have a drink or two in **Lindberg's,** Springfield's oldest tavern. The rehab of Commercial Street has been going on for quite a number of years—the area was pretty unsavory when the project began—and oftentimes it seemed as if progress was slow or nonexistent. However, as of 2011, Commercial Street seems to have hit its stride. Definitely check it out, especially on weekends when the weather is nice.

Grizzly Industrial (417-887-9191 or 1-800-523-4777; www.grizzly.com), 1815 W. Battlefield Rd., Springfield, Mo. Open Mon.–Sat. 8:30–6. This is the tool man's dream store. The second largest machinery showroom in the world (Grizzly also owns the largest, in Pennsylvania), the Springfield location features 150,000 square feet loaded with literally thousands of tools, accessories, and wood- and metalworking machines. From table saws to planers, from hand tools to power tools, from milling machines to welders, if you can't find it here, chances are it doesn't exist. The store also specializes in live demonstrations and has a first-rate cutlery area. I should probably mention that this place has me deep in the throes of addiction, and has somehow managed to take large sums of money from my wallet.

Bass Pro Shops Outdoor World (417-887-7334; www.basspro.com), 1935 S. Campbell St., Springfield, Mo. Open 364 days a year, Mon.–Sat. 7 AM–10 PM, Sun. 8–8. If asked to name the most popular tourist attraction in Missouri, most people would mention the Gateway Arch in St. Louis or Silver Dollar City in Branson. They would be wrong. Drawing more than 5 million visitors per year, Bass Pro Shops Outdoor World in Springfield wins the title. The original location and international headquarters of what is now the world's largest mail-order sporting goods store, Springfield's Bass Pro is one of 62 huge retail stores located around the country. The firm also owns and operates subsidiaries such as Tracker Boats and the Big Cedar Lodge. Not bad, considering that founder Johnny Morris opened his first small store in 1971. John's original location was a small corner in the back of his dad's liquor store, and his warehouse was a U-Haul trailer full of fishing supplies.

The 300,000-square-foot Bass Pro is something to behold. The store's main lobby boasts a four-story, natural stone waterfall that empties into a pond stocked with fish and ducks. That's just the beginning. Shopping areas cover hunting and archery (with indoor ranges so you can try before you buy), ladies' and men's apparel, wildlife jewelry, golf gear, every type of sporting equipment and athletic clothing imaginable, home decor and custom glassware, footwear, the **White River Fly Shop,** a gargantuan fishing and marine area, camping equipment, and a 40,000-square-foot Tracker Boat and RV showroom. In addi-

✳ Special Events

February **The Lawn and Garden Show** (417-833-2660; www.ozark empirefair.com/Events), 3001 N. Grant Ave., Springfield, Mo. Call ahead or check online for exact dates. The three-day Lawn and Garden Show at the Ozark Empire Fairgrounds takes place in mid-February. Hours are generally Fri.–Sat. 9–6, Sun. 11–5. Admission is $4, with kids under 12 admitted free. More than 100 exhibitors show up with services and shopping revolving around the latest in lawn and garden equipment and supplies. Pools, ponds, landscaping, grills . . . if you don't find it here, you won't find it.

March Horsefest (417-833-2660; www.horsefest.net), I-44 and SR 13, Springfield, Mo. Held Fri.–Sun. 8:30–5 on a weekend in mid- or late March; call ahead or check online for exact dates. This event, held at the Ozark Empire Fairgrounds, is a fun and interesting shindig for both the professional horseman and those who simply like looking at Trigger. Clinics are held to assist owners in training, and a huge trade show features the latest in equine products. You'll see some beautiful horses here, as top breeders arrive en masse to show off their prize animals. Admission for adults is $10 per day; kids are charged $5. Those under 12 are admitted free.

tion, the complex offers **Hemingway's Blue Water Cafe** (see *Dining Out*), a barbershop, an art gallery, a golf driving range, a taxidermy store, rod and reel repair, and a fine-gun room. Exhibits and seminars are a regular occurrence at Bass Pro, covering topics from hunting and fishing to fly tying and turkey frying.

BASS PRO SHOPS OUTDOOR WORLD IN SPRINGFIELD

May **Artsfest on Walnut Street** (417-831-6200; www.springfieldarts fest.org). At this open-air celebration on historic Walnut Street in downtown Springfield, hundreds of musicians, artists, artisans, and dancers gather to display both their talents and their wares. The event is always held on the first Saturday and Sunday in May, and information as to exact dates and times can be obtained by contacting the Springfield Regional Arts Council at the number above. Admission is $3, with kids 12 and younger admitted free.

Sucker Day (417-725-1545; www .nixasuckerday.org), downtown Nixa, Mo. You get the impression that Nixa's current city fathers don't really like publicizing Sucker Day all that much. Perhaps it strikes them as too "hillbilly" or something. That's a shame, because this is one of America's most all-time amusing festivals. Taking place in mid-May (even the public schools shut down on Friday for the parade), Sucker Day is a festival celebrating the catching and eating of bottom-dwelling fish with odd-shaped mouths. They taste good (really), and more than 15,000 people descend on this suburb of Springfield—just 5 miles south on US 160—to enjoy the giant fish fry, parade, live music, carnival rides, craft booths, and games. The parade starts at 6:30 on Friday night, and the festival kicks into high gear Saturday from 9 AM–8 PM. Admission is absolutely free, but a full sucker meal goes for about $7.50. If you might be wondering how to catch a sucker, it's done by snagging the little devils with a treble hook or jabbing them in the dead of night with a pointy stick. In the old days of this festival (which began more than 50 years ago; it was the brainchild of a Nixa barber named Finis Gold), local fishermen would start weeks in advance and sometimes nab as many as 500 suckers per day per person. Should you wish to help in this effort, the town is always on the lookout for volunteer sucker snaggers. Just call the chamber of commerce for further information.

June **Sheep & Wool Days** (417-581-7485), Gray/Campbell Farmstead, Nathaniel Greene Park, 2400 S. Scenic Ave., Springfield, Mo. Held on the second Sunday in June, this one-day, nearly 20-year-old event features a scene from sheep-shearing day on an 1860s farm. You'll see shearing, stock dogs in action, and demonstrations involving the carding and spinning of wool. Admission is free and there are plenty of games, door prizes, and music.

July–August **Ozark Empire Fair** (417-833-2660; www.ozarkempire fair.com/index.htm), 3001 N. Grant Ave., Springfield, Mo. Call ahead for exact dates. Hours are 11–11; carnival rides open at 1 PM daily and gates close at midnight. Running for 10 days beginning near the end of July, this huge regional fair features a full midway, countless livestock and craft halls, innumerable carnival rides, and major concerts. General admission is $6, with kids 6–12 admitted for $2.

Extra charges apply for rides, concerts, food, and drink. The grandstand holds several thousand people, and there are great concerts most every night (heck, I even got to see what was left of Foghat one time).

August **Ozark Booster Club Fall Bull Riding Spectacular** (417-485-2535), Finley River Park, Ozark, Mo. The two-day event generally occurs in late August. Admission is approximately $10 for adults, $5 for kids, and free for kids under 5. More than 50 professional bull riders travel from all around the country to compete in this $10,000 purse competition. Sanctioned by the North American Bullriding Association, this particular rodeo also features some of the toughest, meanest bulls in America.

September **Japanese Fall Festival** (417-864-1049; www.parkboard.org), Nathaniel Greene Park, 2400 S. Scenic Ave., Springfield, Mo. $5 adults, $3 for children 12 and younger, free for toddlers. Taking place at the Mizumoto Japanese Stroll Garden in early September, this three-day event includes performers from Japan, music, local artists, Japanese food, and tea ceremonies.

Greater Ozarks Blues Festival (417-864-6683; www.greaterozarks bluesfest.com), Springfield, Mo. More than 10,000 blues lovers flock to this two-day festival, held the weekend after Labor Day, to hear nationally known players as well as regional and local musicians (recent headliners have included the legendary Buddy Guy). The location of the main stage varies from year to year, but regular updates are provided on the website. Music runs 4:30–11 Fri. and 11:30–11 Sat. On Saturday night a blues pub crawl takes place all over downtown

Springfield, with more than 15 local bars presenting live blues acts. Ticket prices are a mere $25 if purchased in advance.

Cider Days on Walnut Street (417-831-6200), Walnut Street, Springfield, Mo. An end-of-summer celebration in mid-September. As with Artsfest, craftsmen and musicians descend upon historic Walnut Street to demonstrate their crafts. There are plenty of booths, not to mention lots of locally produced apple cider. For further info, contact the Springfield Regional Arts Council at the number above. Admission runs about $4, with kids 12 and younger admitted free.

Steam-O-Rama (417-833-2749; www.steamorama.com), 7175 W. Farm Road 170, east of Republic, Mo., on the south side of US 60. A four-day event held in mid-September (call for exact days, times, and admission), Steam-O-Rama is sponsored by the Ozark Steam Engine Association. The 35-acre show site (half of which is set aside for camping and parking) displays equipment from days gone by. The show—which celebrated its 50th year in 2011—typically averages 400 tractors, 20 steam-driven traction engines, hundreds of gasoline engines, and numerous crawlers, garden tractors, and classic and antique trucks. Both a full-sized working sawmill and a thresher are belted to steam-driven engines. Also on the site is a large flea market and vendor booths. An antique-tractor pull (tractors must be from 1938 or before) takes place Friday night.

October **Farmfest** (417-833-2660; www.ozarkempirefair.com/pdf/Ozark-Fall-Farmfest.pdf), 3001 N. Grant Ave., Springfield, Mo. Farmfest generally falls on the first weekend of October; call ahead for times, dates, and admission. This is the biggest agricultural event in the Ozarks, with more than 40,000 farmers and ranchers arriving from far and wide to view close to 1,000 farm-related exhibits and upward of 500 head of registered livestock. There is machinery both large and small (as well as old and new), products for the home, an incredible number of booths, and numerous breeds of purebred cattle, goats, sheep, pigs, and exotic critters.

The Ozark Heritage Region

4

THE ORIGINAL OZARKS

THE OZARK NATIONAL
SCENIC RIVERWAYS

THE ORIGINAL OZARKS

Most who venture into this unique section of southern Missouri, the western side of what is commonly referred to as the Heritage Region of the Ozarks, will eventually realize they are witnessing a number of sudden changes. The land alters. The hills become hillier and the curved, blacktop roads become curvier. The slight aroma of distant wood smoke seems to float on the breeze, a sultry counterpoint to the ghostly fogs that hang low and long in the valleys and hollows. The forests are thick, the rivers are cold, the wildlife is prevalent, and the sounds of chain saws, crows, coyotes, and wild turkeys can arise at any given moment.

And more is affected than the five senses. If you linger in this region, you will begin to feel an internal change as well. This is an ancient place, something you will know without being told, something that seeps into your bones. This is a part of the world that I always think of as the Original Ozarks, where geography and culture come together to paint a picture of magical authenticity. With just a little imagination, you can picture the first Scots-Irish settlers of this land as they struggled to make a living from hillside acres that grew little but rocks, moss, and copperhead snakes. You will notice that the accent is a bit more southern here, the attitudes of people more akin to traditional hill dwellers than the farmers or suburban residents who reside in the northern Ozarks. There's a sense of humor here, and, if you're not nosy or pushy or rude, a friendly welcome.

This is the part of the Ozarks where language becomes colorful, where a lazy neighbor is "slow as molasses in January," where a difficult decision leaves you "stuck between the devil and the deep blue sea." This is a spot where, on a hot day, you will "sweat like a stuck pig" and the completion of a big meal will leave you "fuller than a tick." Distances are referred to in terms of "as the crow flies," and there is a healthy disrespect for the clock. An appointment will not necessarily be set for a certain time; more likely it will be "oh . . . three o'clock or thereabouts." Those who function without thought or engage in patently stupid behavior will be labeled as "not having the brains God gave a goose." And strangers who do something silly will inevitably hear the query, "You're not from around here, are ya?"

And on and on and on. Asking directions of locals can (depending on their mood) result in either a monosyllabic grunt or a 20-minute dissertation involving stories of third cousins twice removed, busted-up marriages, natural disasters, and local lore. Finally, your question will be answered with a modest, "Just go a couple miles and turn left at the first crossroads."

This is a good part of the world, mostly honest, mostly fun, and mostly gorgeous. Contrary to ignorant representations provided by the media and entertainment elites of the East and West Coasts, it is not wholly populated with toothless inbreds the likes of which would walk out of *Deliverance* or *Ma and Pa Kettle Date Their Cousin*. In many ways it's just as up-to-date as anywhere else. The difference lies in attitude. The Original Ozarks are a slice of heaven on earth that stays just as it wants to stay, despite the best efforts of outside, urban civilization to bring about a politically correct homogenization of culture, belief, and speech.

Modern society has long sought to drag the residents of the Heritage Region of the Ozarks into the 21st century. But this is a headstrong crowd. For the most part this land is populated by rugged individualists who often possess more than their fair share of brains, common sense, well-developed funny bones, and a streak of stubborn independence a mile wide. They like who they are, they're proud of who they are, and "they ain't changin' for nobody."

Yes, modern society has tried to force residents of this area to join the 21st century. It is with happiness I can report that modern society has failed miserably.

AREA CODES With the exception of the towns of Licking and Mountain View (which fall in the 573 area code), the region covered in this chapter lies in the **417** area code.

GUIDANCE Information on area events, sights, and activities is readily available in this region of what is usually considered the traditional heartland of the Ozarks. The **Ava Chamber of Commerce** (417-683-4594; www.avachamber .org), 810 S.W. 13th Ave., Ava, Mo., offers a plethora of advice on such topics as the annual Foxtrotter horse shows and the beautiful Glade Top Trail. For ideas on things to do in the Houston area, home of famed clown Emmett Kelly, contact the **Houston Area Chamber of Commerce** (417-967-2220; www.houston mochamber.com), 501 East Walnut St., Houston, Mo. The **Mansfield Chamber of Commerce** (417-924-3525; www.mansfieldchamber.com), P.O. Box 322, Mansfield, MO 65704, will be happy to provide you with a wealth of details on its most famous resident, the late Laura Ingalls Wilder of *Little House on the Prairie* fame. For those who wish to enjoy the splendor of Bull Shoals Lake, get in touch with the **Theodosia Chamber of Commerce** (417-273-4245; www .theodosiaareachamber.com), P.O. Box 11, Theodosia, MO 65761. The largest town in the region, West Plains, offers both an up-to-date welcome center and two different websites. The **Ozark Heritage Welcome Center** (417-256-7176; www.westplains.net), 2999 Porter Wagoner Blvd., West Plains, Mo., will gladly supply you with all the information you could possibly want. Also, the **Greater West Plains Chamber of Commerce** (417-256-4433; www.wpchamber.com), 401 Jefferson, West Plains, Mo., includes further details on the growing town itself.

Last but not least, for numerous links to events and organizations, check out the **Willow Springs, Mo.,** website (417-469-5519; www.willowspringsmo.com /chamber.html).

GETTING THERE *By car:* This area, which becomes increasingly rugged as you travel east and south, is roughly bordered on the north by US 60 and on the east by US 63. For a scenic drive along the southern section, US 160 travels all the way from Branson, Mo., to West Plains, Mo.

By air: **Springfield-Branson National Airport** (417-868-0500; www.sgf-branson -airport.com), 2300 N. Airport Blvd., Springfield, Mo., located 40 miles north of Branson, is served by American Airlines, Allegiant, United, and Delta. The airport offers facilities for buses, vans, rental cars, and hotel and hospitality limousines for groups. The airport underwent a multimillion-dollar expansion between 2006 and 2009, resulting in a new, midfield terminal and expanded services. The **Branson Airport** (1-888-359-2541; http://flybranson.com), 4000 Branson Airport Blvd., Hollister, Mo., holds the distinction of being the only privately owned, privately operated, commercial service airport in the United States. The airport offers direct, nonstop flights to a number of cities, and is serviced by Air-Tran, Frontier, and Branson Air Express.

MEDICAL EMERGENCIES Texas County Memorial Hospital (417-967-3311; www.tcmh.org), 1333 S. Sam Houston Blvd., Houston, Mo. A not-for-profit, acute care facility with 66 beds, Texas County Memorial is located on the southern edge of Houston along US 63 and SR 17. It features full surgical and obstetrical services, as well as departments for emergency care, X-rays, physical and respiratory therapy, critical care, and cardiac rehabilitation. The hospital covers the health needs of those living in an approximate 40-mile radius of Houston and also provides for outpatient needs.

Ozarks Medical Center (417-256-9111; www.ozarksmedicalcenter.com), 1100 Kentucky Ave., West Plains, Mo. With a staff of more than 1,100, the 114-bed, not-for-profit OMC serves a population area of 11 counties and 150,000 residents. The medical staff consists of more than 100 physicians in virtually every specialty imaginable. The complex is certified as a Level III Trauma Center, and emergency services are provided 24/7. Four ambulance services are managed by OMC, and **Air Evac**—a local helicopter ambulance service—utilizes the hospital as its home base. The hospital complex encompasses a 20,000-square-foot surgical center, an urgent care clinic, and a state-of-the-art cancer treatment center; it offers a lengthy menu of rehabilitation services. In 2011, OMC Heart Care Services saw approximately 1,200 patients each month, including cardiac rehabilitation patients. In 2010, OMC opened a state-of-the-art, 16-bed emergency department. In-house are outpatient imaging services such as MRI, mammography, nuclear medicine, and more. In other words, if you have to get sick in the vicinity of West Plains, this is the place to do it.

✳ Wandering Around

EXPLORING BY CAR Glade Top Trail (417-683-4428; www.fs.fed.us /wildflowers/regions/eastern/GladeTopTrail/index.shtml), Ava/Cassville/Willow Springs Ranger District, 1103 S. Jefferson St., Ava, Mo. At a length of 23 miles, winding its way through the Mark Twain National Forest and bordering the Hercules Glade Wilderness Area, the Glade Top Trail is Missouri's only National Scenic Byway. Gorgeous any time of year, Glade Top takes on special majesty in fall. Visitors are inundated with shades of yellow, deep red, and orange. These colors are present not only on the common oak, walnut, elm, and hickory trees, but also on the brilliant "smoke tree" that's found in very few other Missouri locales. During the third week of October the town of Ava hosts its **Flaming Fall Festival** in honor of the explosion of color. Spring is almost as grand, as dogwood, redbud, rosebud, serviceberry, and wild fruit trees come to life in vibrant hues. This season is celebrated in Theodosia, Mo., with the **Spring Flowering Tour.**

To access the Glade Top from Ava, Mo., just head south from town on SR 5. Watch on the east side of the road for the **Ava/Cassville/Willow Springs**

Ranger District Office. Wheel in there and you can receive not only a map, but also suggestions and advice for places to stop and picnic, take pictures, hike, fish, camp, or hunt. If you miss the ranger station, keep going 8 miles to SR A. Head west for 3.5 miles, take a left onto a gravel road, and follow the signs reading GLADE TOP TRAIL. One of the first things you should come to is a picnic area with a sign offering a general overview of the trip.

During this drive you will often traverse Ozark ridges and view wildlife ranging from deer and turkeys to roadrunners and rattlesnakes. Popular stops along the route are the **Caney Lookout Tower** (a 1937 fire observation tower), the **Pinnacle** (where legend has it a somewhat addled old gal spent years digging—unsuccessfully—for gold), and the **Three Sisters** (a trio of bald limestone knobs). The entire trip does not take long—roughly an hour if you zip through end to end—but such is no fun at all. Just take your time, pack a picnic lunch, and remember to bring your camera.

EXPLORING BY FOOT Wildwood Trail (417-273-4245; www.theodosiaarea chamber.com/ThingsToDo.htm), Theodosia, Mo. If you want a pretty trail that is right in town but makes you feel as if you are in the depths of the wilderness, take a walk on Theodosia's Wildwood Trail. The 4-mile trek, built in large part by the Theodosia Chamber of Commerce and a local Cub Scout pack, will require about two hours. It should be noted that the trail, though fairly flat, can get pretty rough in places. If you're either very young or very old (or very clumsy, or out of shape at any age), you should take a bit more than average care. The trail winds through an oak, hickory, and dogwood forest, tops out on a cedar glade, and provides great views of Bull Shoals Lake; this is the sort of trek that requires a camera. The odds are good you will stumble across a bald eagle, white-tailed deer, turkey, or at least an armadillo or two. Also, you will cross a wet-weather stream, view interesting rock formations, and pass a sinkhole.

EXPLORING BY RIVER Bryant Creek is one of those stretches of water beloved by those who detest crowds and love the occasional spell of great fishing. The largely spring-fed Bryant starts in Douglas County. It wanders approximately 40 miles through the Mark Twain National Forest before dumping into Norfork Lake in Ozark County. Except during extensive dry spells, almost the entire length is floatable. That said, the most enjoyable and reliable float can be had by putting your canoe in the water at the low-water bridge on SR 95 south of the town of Vanzant. If it's been a wet year, you could encounter some light whitewater on the Bryant, but nothing too serious unless you're in the midst of a full-scale flood (in which case you shouldn't be floating anyway). I've known people who've caught massive fish out of the Bryant, most species being of the generalized carp variety, but it also has some great catfish holes. Floaters should note that this is the antithesis of a commercialized float stream; if you see one or two other folks on the water, you can pretty much bet they're locals. If you float far enough on the Bryant, you'll pass a couple of historic mill sites.

Another stream that isn't heavily traveled, **Beaver Creek** is one of the tributaries of the North Fork of the White River. Flowing alongside the Hercules

Glades Wilderness Area, it's known primarily for relaxed floating and smallmouth bass fishing. More fun to catch, however (and easier, as they'll strike almost anything), are goggle-eye, a smaller bass hybrid. Like the Bryant, Beaver Creek begins in Douglas County, running roughly 41 miles to Bull Shoals Lake in Taney County. This is a good float for families with kids, as there are plenty of gravel bars along the way that seem custom-made for a picnic lunch or wienie roast.

The **Osage Fork of the Gasconade** isn't as much of a drunken pretzel as its namesake, the Gasconade, but neither could it be considered straight as a string. This tributary begins in Webster County and travels roughly 60 miles northwest before merging with the Gasconade. A pretty and largely isolated river, the Osage Fork features only a few outfitters. On the other hand, the fishing is excellent (all sorts of bass, bluegill, and catfish). The generally slow flow of the river offers the chance to enjoy great scenery. Also, plenty of gravel bars allow for overnight camping if you seek a two- or three-day float. The water can get a little low in summer, so try to plan a float for the spring; the numerous redbud trees will make you ooh and ahh. The Osage Fork is largely uncrowded, even on holiday weekends, which makes it a diamond in the rough.

I would call the **James River** pretty much the ultimate beginner's float. Very slow and placid, with absolutely no surprises, it begins in Webster County and meanders to the southwest before emptying into Table Rock Lake. A little more than 60 miles long, the James is a good stream to wet a line. This is another good choice if you're traveling with younger kids, as you're not going to find obstructions or drop-offs that can lead to tipped canoes, wet younguns, and your cooler floating off downstream.

One of the best-loved rivers in the Ozarks, the **North Fork of the White River** (a tributary of the legendary White River in northwest Arkansas) is highly regarded for having Missouri's largest population of wild rainbow and trophy-sized brown trout. Thirteen miles of officially designated trout water stretch from Norfork Lake back upstream to Rainbow Spring. The spring churns out 137 million gallons of icy water every day, making the North Fork prime trout habitat. The river begins in Texas County and runs approximately 80 miles to the aforementioned Norfork Lake. You'll see plenty of traffic during the summer months, but don't let that dissuade you. Float on a weekday, rather than the weekend, if you seek a more placid experience. The North Fork is not a fast river, but it does have some low-water bridges and more than a few drops and small waterfalls. None of these is more than a couple of feet, but floaters should still take care and consider a portage, especially in times of higher water. As with everything else, simply exercise a bit of common sense based on conditions and individual ability. The worst time to admit that your skills are lacking is when your canoe ends up sideways against a boulder, you're freezing wet, and your camera is at the bottom of the river. Numerous outfitters handle the North Fork, and there are several Forest Service campgrounds along its route. Also check out the **River of Life Farm** (see *Resorts*) for great accommodations, river advice, and guided trips.

NORTH FORK OF THE WHITE

✳ Towns and Villages

Ava, Mo. The seat of Douglas County, Ava is strategically located for growth. Less than an hour from both Branson and Springfield, the town's 3,186 residents pride themselves on being the site of the world headquarters for the Missouri Foxtrotting Horse Breed Association. Two internationally regarded horse shows are held here each year, celebrating the officially designated state horse of Missouri. Also in or near Ava are the beginning of the stunning Glade Top Trail, the eminently fishable Bryant Creek, and the historic Douglas County Courthouse. One of the best times to visit Ava is in fall, when the trees change color and the town holds its annual Flaming Fall Festival.

Cabool, Mo. You could probably consider Cabool the geographic heart of the Ozarks, rising up from the middle of the Ozark Plateau to elevations in the 1,600-foot range. With 2,135 residents, it is primarily a farming and ranching community that prides itself on traditional values. Although mass communications have propelled all of the Ozarks into the 20th century (and some into the 21st, believe it or not) spending a bit of time in this town will leave you with the impression that its Ozark roots run deep.

Gainesville, Mo. Four of Gainesville's courthouses have burned down, but the seat of Ozark County, with its nearly 596 residents, just keeps plugging along. Close to Gainesville are six historic mills—Hodgson's, Dawt, Hammon, Zanoni, Topaz, and Rockbridge. Of these, the last is a must-stop. Now a 3,000-acre recreational complex known as the Rainbow Trout and Game Ranch, its owners have utilized several refurbished historical buildings, offer excellent trout fishing, and run a fine restaurant. Also, the third weekend in September brings Gainesville's annual Hootin an Hollarin festival.

Houston, Mo. Burned several times during the Civil War, Houston is the county seat of Texas County, not to mention the hometown of legendary clown Emmett

Kelly, who originated the "Weary Willie" character. The first weekend of each May, Houston hosts the Emmett Kelly Clown Festival, which gives everyone an excuse to don greasepaint and squeeze into little tiny cars. Houston is also the locale of the Texas County Memorial Hospital, which is no doubt helpful when once-a-year clowns trip on their giant shoes and require medical assistance.

Mansfield, Mo. Roughly 1,315 residents call this Wright County town home. You will rarely hear the name *Mansfield* without also hearing the name *Laura Ingalls Wilder*. The noted author of the Little House books fell in love with the Ozarks, and wrote all of her books from her cherished Rocky Ridge Farm. Laura's home and museum are visited by fans from all parts of the globe.

Marshfield, Mo. Supposedly possessing the highest elevation on I-44 east of the Rocky Mountains (1,494 feet), this town of nearly 7.250 is located roughly 20 miles east of Springfield. Marshfield is the birthplace of astronomer Edwin P. Hubble, for whom the Hubble Space Telescope was named. Also, fans of blues and folk music might know the old song "Marshfield Tornado" by John W. "Blind" Boone. The tune immortalized the April 18, 1880, tornado that barged through the heart of Marshfield, killing 65 residents and doing $1 million worth of damage.

Theodosia, Mo. In the 2004 movie *Million Dollar Baby* (starring Clint Eastwood and Hilary Swank), Theodosia was trashed as a redneck hole populated by fat folks who lived in trailers with tires on the roof. Theodosia's 250 residents were less than thrilled. The fact of the matter is that Theodosia is situated in an area of incredible beauty. Not only is it the gateway to Bull Shoals Lake (the record bass capital of Missouri), but it's also surrounded by rugged bluffs, creeks, rivers, and deep forests. The scenery witnessed during spring and fall—via redbud, dogwood, oak, and smoke trees—is beyond description. I suppose you could find some fat folks with tires on the roofs of their trailers if you looked hard enough, but you could find the same thing in L.A. or New York. Such spottings only prove you're looking for all the wrong things and are in desperate need of an attitude adjustment. The Theodosia area is an outdoor paradise.

West Plains, Mo. This town has experienced some phenomenal growth in recent years. The population of this seat of Howell County now stands at more than 12,003. The Mark Twain National Forest is but a stone's throw away, and within minutes of West Plains are more than 350 miles of floatable water, 63,000 acres of pure wilderness, and more than 100 miles of hiking, biking, and horseback trails. West Plains features the 30,000-square-foot West Plains Civic Center, the Ozarks Medical Center, the Harlin House Museum, and numerous motels, restaurants, and bed & breakfasts. Famous residents included the late icon Porter Wagoner (you know, the big-haired boy who introduced the world to the equally big-haired Dolly Parton) and the legendary left-handed Brooklyn Dodgers pitcher Preacher Roe. West Plains was utterly destroyed during the Civil War and didn't really begin to rebuild until the 1870s. In 1928 (and on a Friday the 13th, no less) 37 young adults were killed in West Plains when the Bond Dance Hall exploded. No cause of the explosion was ever determined. If you ask some of the very old locals (and they're in a talking mood) it's quite possible you'll hear a number of theories.

MUSEUMS ✤ ✐ **Douglas County Museum and Historical Society** (417-683-5799; www.facebook.com/pages/Douglas-County-Museum-and-Historical -Society/181238348565358?sk=info), 401 E. Washington Ave., Ava, Mo. Open year-round, Sat. 10–2. Admission is free, though donations are appreciated. This stately old white home was purchased and transformed into a local historical museum in 1988. Today, along with numerous antiques, the museum concentrates on the history of the Ozarks and the beginnings of Douglas County. Explore 12 rooms of displays and a research museum.

✤ ✐ **Harlin House Museum** (417-256-7801; www.harlinhousemuseum .homestead.com), 405 Worcester St., West Plains, Mo. Open Tues.–Sat. noon–4. Free admission with any donation. The Harlin House Museum is home to more than 200 original sketches and paintings created by the late Lennis Leonard Broadfoot. The artist, who was born in nearby Shannon County, chronicled the early Ozarks and its resilient, independent characters in his 1944 book, *Pioneers of the Ozarks.* In addition to the Broadfoot Collection, the two-floor museum is home to a wide variety of artifacts ranging from farm machinery and war memorabilia to an authentic Ozark moonshine still. Indian artifacts found in Harlin House date from 5000 B.C. The photos and historical minutiae devoted to country singer Porter Wagoner are not nearly that old.

✐ ♿ **Fire Museum of Missouri** (417-469-4589; www.usfirehouse.com), 908 E. US Bus. 60/63, Willow Springs, Mo. Open Apr.–Nov. $5 adults, $3 ages 10–17. If

DOUGLAS COUNTY MUSEUM

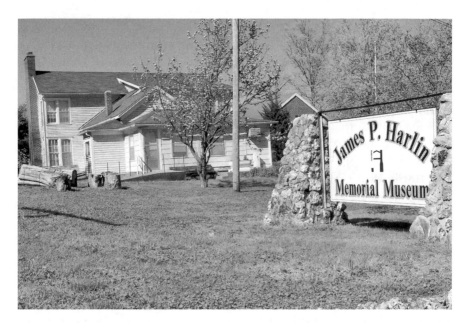

HARLIN HOUSE MUSEUM

you like to drink soda, you will like this place. It possesses what is arguably the largest collection of soda bottles in the world. If you get tired of gawking at the empty Mountain Dew receptacles, take a look at the museum's large collection of fire trucks. I've really no idea how these two topics were incorporated into one museum, and thus can only say "Welcome to the Ozarks." You'll also find some antique cars and antique soda-pop vending machines. It's probably a good idea to call before making the drive to Willow Springs. Hours seem to be a bit open to interpretation at this museum.

✐ ♿ **Laura Ingalls Wilder Museum and Home** (417-924-3626 or 1-877-924-7126; www.lauraingallswilderhome.com), 3068 SR A, Mansfield, Mo. Open Mar.–Nov., Mon.–Sat. 9–5, Sun. 12:30–5. Admission is $8 for adults, $4 ages 6–17, and free for children under 6. Those over age 65 are admitted for $6. Fans of Laura Ingalls Wilder's Little House books (or even those who liked the TV show of the same name) will love this historic spot in Mansfield, Mo. **Rocky Ridge Farm,** where Laura penned her famous tomes, has been restored with a dedication to authenticity, and in many ways the residence looks just as Laura left it. The talented woman did not even begin to chronicle her life on the prairies until age 65 (urged by her daughter, Rose Wilder Lane, a noted author, journalist, and world traveler). All her books were composed in this lovely and tranquil Ozarks home.

MONASTERY Assumption Abbey Monastery (417-683-5110; www.assumption abbey.org), SR 5, Ava, Mo. Located roughly 20 miles southwest of Ava off SR 00 (call for exact directions lest you get lost), Assumption Abbey has existed in the Ozarks since 1950. The residents are Trappists, more formally known as the

Cistercian Order of the Strict Observance. The atmosphere here, as you would expect, is very peaceful. Those who come from cities might at first feel a bit disconcerted by the silence, but it will grow on you if given the chance. Guests, both men and women, are welcomed to the abbey and are invited to stay in a simple guest house. Usually no more than six or eight guests are present at any one time, and the goal here is contemplation via an appreciation of the surrounding beauty and silence. If you wish to stay at the abbey, call the main number for a reservation. Also, the order is known around the country for its delicious fruitcakes. You can order one of these delights—which weigh 2 pounds and cost $29.50—by calling 1-888-738-0117.

✳ To Do

GOLF Oakwood Country Club (417-967-3968), Country Club Dr., Houston, Mo. A nine-hole course located 2 miles from Houston (off SR B in Oakwood Estates), this small facility offers a driving range, lessons, and cart rental. Greens fees run $8 for nine holes, $15 for 18.

🍸 **Theodosia Country Club** (417-273-4877; theodosiacc.50megs.com), Country Club Dr., Theodosia, Mo. A nine-hole, par-34 course, the Theodosia Country Club offers a pro shop, lounge, driving range, and cart rental. Open year-round, it's located 0.5 mile east of Theodosia off US 160. Greens fees are $20 for 18 holes. Cart rental is $13.

♿ **West Plains Country Club** (417-256-7197), 1402 Country Club Dr., West Plains, Mo. This semiprivate, 18-hole, par-70 course is one of the older links in the area (built in 1926). Open year-round, its fees are $42 for 18 holes on the

LAURA INGALLS WILDER MUSEUM AND HOME

HISTORIC SITES: MISSOURI GRISTMILLS

If you're into taking photos of old gristmills, you have just hit the mother lode. The original mills (built from the mid-1800s to about the turn of that century) served a dual purpose. Yes, they ground the grains to provide flour for area families, but they were also a general meeting spot for families and friends who rarely had the opportunity for neighborin' (that would be "socializing" for you non-Ozark types). Taking grain to the mill could sometimes be a several-day event, a time of excitement, music, tall tales, whoppers, lies, and fun. The Civil War (when many mills were burned), the advent of the railroad, and mass production of goods led to the death of the mill lifestyle, but a number of these structures remain in the Missouri Ozarks.

The **Rockbridge Mill,** built in 1868, was once the site of a small village, complete with bank and general store. This mill didn't actually close until the 1940s, and it's now restored in detail. Even better, it is the home of the Rainbow Trout and Game Ranch (see *Resorts*). You can get some great photos of this old red mill, catch rainbow trout near the waterfall, and have drinks and a meal. The old bank has been transformed into an antiques store, and the resort has a restaurant that offers excellent food. There are even rooms for rent should you wish to spend the night. To get to Rockbridge, head north of Gainesville on SR 5 until you reach the tiny town of Wasola (more of an eye-blink than a town), then go 4 miles farther until you hit SR N. Take this road 17 miles north and you will eventually come to Rockbridge.

The **Zanoni Mill,** located in Ozark County, was allegedly still grinding grain until 1951. Today the property serves as a B&B (see *Bed & Breakfasts*), and the mill is open for viewing. In front of the Zanoni Mill is a lake, fed by Zanoni Spring, which is a favorite of those staying at the inn's rental cabin. If you wish to see the Zanoni Mill, drive 3 miles west of Sycamore, Mo., on SR 181. Watch on the north side of the road for the sign.

The **Hodgson Mill** is not open to the public, but you can still see the building from a pull-off area along the road. Constructed around 1860 on Bryant Creek, this old red mill was in operation until at least the 1940s; it acquired quite a name for putting out stone-ground meal in the area. When the original mill was closed, a new one was built in Gainesville. That operation, which still sells products under the Hodgson Mill name, was then sold to the Siemer Milling Company. To find the original mill, take SR 181 north of

Gainesville for about 15 miles. Pass Zanoni; the mill will be on the north side of the road in roughly 4 miles.

The **Dawt Mill** was built in 1887 by Alva Hodgson, the same man who built Hodgson Mill. Though it burned in 1896, it was rebuilt almost immediately and is still open to the public as a first-rate resort (see *Resorts*). Inside the mill you can see much of the old equipment along with a gift shop selling everything from bread to T-shirts. This is a popular spot for those canoeing on the North Fork of the White River, and at the on-site store you can rent a campsite or a canoe. Also, a variety of lodging options is available here. Dawt is one of the best mill photo opportunities you will encounter in the Ozarks.

Located approximately 14 miles west of the town of Cabool, the **Topaz Mill** (built in 1895) was also once the center of a community, complete with store, blacksmith, cannery, and post office. Now privately owned and not open to the public, the Topaz Mill can be reached by taking SR 81 south of Cabool to SR 76. Turn right, then turn left onto SR E (a gravel road). Go straight for roughly 4 miles and you will come to the mill.

HODGSON MILL

weekend; a cart is included in the price. This is a nice course, with water hazards coming into play on eight different holes.

&. **West Plains Municipal Golf Course** (417-256-9824), 1724 N. Terra St., West Plains, Mo. This 18-hole, par-72, somewhat hilly public course has water hazards on five different holes. Weekend greens fees, with cart included, are $32.

&. **Willow Springs Municipal Golf Course** (417-469-1214), 123 E. Main St., Willow Springs, Mo. A nine-hole, par-35 course, Willow Springs Municipal charges $20 for 18 holes on weekends (cart included). There is a restaurant on-site, open weekends 11–4.

✳ Wild Places

Mark Twain National Forest (573-364-4621; www.fs.fed.us/r9/marktwain). Consisting of more than 1.5 million acres, the Mark Twain is a superb wilderness dotted by rivers, streams, and some of the largest natural springs in America. Broken into nine different ranger districts, the forest includes hundreds of miles of hiking trails, numerous scenic drives, seven congressionally designated wilderness areas, 40 campgrounds, and thousands of acres of primitive and semi-primitive areas. The Mark Twain is a true playground for hunters, fishermen, hikers, equestrians, and campers. In this region, two sections of the Mark Twain are under the management of the Ava/Willow Springs District. In the Willow Springs area, you'll find the Devil's Backbone Wilderness Area. The North Fork of the White River and its nine major springs also provide myriad recreational opportunities. Closer to Ava, the Mark Twain features such attractions as the Glade Top Trail, Hercules Glades Wilderness Area, and Caney Mountain Refuge.

Hercules Glades Wilderness (573-364-4621). Consisting of 12,413 acres, Hercules Glades is located in southwestern Taney County. A combination of steep, rocky hills, forests, and open meadows, it is a fairly isolated area that hosts a number of types of wildlife not really found in other parts of the Ozarks. In fact, much of Hercules Glades seems to be out of the Southwest; it's not uncommon to see rattlesnakes, roadrunners, lizards, or tarantulas. On the other hand, it can appear pure Ozarks, with redbud, dogwood, red cedar, oak, and smoke trees, along with plenty of raccoons and white-tailed deer.

Caney Mountain Conservation Area (417-256-7161; www.mdc.mo.gov), Wildlife District Supervisor, Ozark District Office, Box 138, West Plains, Mo. Located 5 miles north of Gainesville on SR 181, Caney Mountain is owned and managed by the Missouri Department of Conservation. A popular spot for squirrel, deer, and turkey hunting, it consists of 7,899 acres and features caves, a headwaters creek, old-growth forests, glades, and savannas. Should you plan on hiking, remember that this is a very steep part of the country (and full of ticks during the warm to hot months). A couple of interesting historic buildings are found here. One is a 1941 log cabin that belonged to Starker Leopold, son of the famous naturalist and writer Aldo Leopold. Starker was the resident biologist for Caney Mountain.

🦆 🐾 ♿ **Elephant Rocks State Park** (573-546-3454; www.mostateparks.com /elephantrock.htm), 7406 SR 21, Belleview, Mo. Sometimes a name can say it all, and such is the case with Elephant Rocks State Park. These hunks of igneous rock are to normal boulders what the Sears Tower is to an out-house. (The biggest rock in the park is 27 feet high and weighs 680 tons!) The geology behind the Elephant Rocks is one-of-a-kind. The massive stones were not left behind by glaciers, as glaciers never reached as far south as the St. Francois Mountains (the range that includes Taum Sauk, Johnson Shut-Ins, and Elephant Rocks). Rather, the Elephant Rocks were formed 1.5 billion years ago, granite hunks that sheared off as differing joints of volcanic magma cooled and split. The rocks hid beneath ancient seas, and only emerged after countless eons of erosion and uplift. To look at the Elephant Rocks is to look back at the beginnings of the Earth itself.

Though the park consists of only 132 acres, that's more than enough. Trails wind through this garden of stone, and you will find 30 picnic areas scattered about. Also, the park offers a Braille Trail featuring Braille signs, a paved and gently sloping surface, railings, and guide ropes. Neither camp-ing nor pets are permitted inside this park. Elephant Rocks is roughly 5 miles south of the town of Belleview on SR 21.

ELEPHANT ROCKS STATE PARK

Devil's Backbone Wilderness Area (417-683-4428), Willow Springs Office, Ava/Cassville/Willow Springs District Office, Old Springfield Rd., Willow Springs, Mo. Take SR CC about 15 miles west of its junction with US 63 in West Plains, Mo. This rugged 6,595-acre area, located within the Mark Twain National Forest, is noted for both its trails and its beauty. In spring you can revel in the blooms of oak, hickory, dogwood, and redbud. In fall the oaks, sweet gums, and sugar maples turn the forest all shades of red. The Devil's Backbone is loaded with all sorts of wildlife. Day hiking, backpacking, camping, and horseback riding are all much-loved activities here (take note, however, that both biking and motorized vehicles are prohibited). There are 13 miles of manicured trails, but you can hike anywhere you wish. At the north end of the Devil's Backbone is the **North Fork Recreation Area** (which locals may call Hammon Mill or Hammon Camp)—a great spot for camping or picnics on the North Fork River. You will find a boat launch there, and if you care to take a half-mile hike, have a look at **Blue Spring,** one of the main springs of the North Fork.

LAKES Norfork Lake (870-425-2700; www.swl.usace.army.mil/parks/norfork), Mountain Home Project Office, 324 W. Seventh St., Mountain Home, Ark. Only 10 percent of Norfork Lake is located in Missouri (at Gainesville and Tecumseh). The rest of its 30,000-plus acres stretch to the south into Arkansas. With 550 miles of shoreline, it is a favorite tourist spot, well known for all water sports, camping, and hiking. Fishermen love this lake for its rainbow trout and largemouth bass. Constructed in 1941 by the Army Corps of Engineers for flood control and hydroelectric power in the Upper White River Basin, Norfork boasts of having one of the largest federal trout hatcheries east of the Rockies. On the Missouri side it's fed by both Bryant Creek and the North Fork. This makes for some fantastic early-spring fishing. During the first part of March, walleye migrate to the north end of the lake. Later on, into April, various species of bass are easily caught here, particularly smallmouths, which migrate down the rivers. Norfork is surrounded by 32,000 acres of public land, with numerous resorts, services, restaurants, marinas, and U.S. Army Corps of Engineers–managed campsites. Scuba divers from all over the world visit Norfork because of the crystal clarity of the water.

Bull Shoals Lake (870-425-2700; www.swl.usace.army.mil/parks/bullshoals), Mountain Home Project Office, 324 W. Seventh St., Mountain Home, Ark. Another Army Corps project that came about to control flooding in the Upper White River Basin, the 45,000-acre Bull Shoals is nearly 100 miles long. With 1,050 miles of shoreline, Bull Shoals Dam was started in 1947 and completed in 1951. Located 7 miles north of Cotter, Ark., on the White River, it is a major source of hydroelectric power. Most of Bull Shoals Lake can be found in Arkansas, although its northern arms extend into Missouri from Cedar Creek (in the west, south of Branson), through the town of Protem in the middle range, and to Pontiac and Theodosia in the east. The entirety of the lake, on both the Missouri and Arkansas sides, has become increasingly popular with retirees. This migration can be attributed partially to the beauty of the area and the wealth of easily accessible recreation activities. Another factor is that, compared with other lake areas of the country, real estate taxes are low and housing prices are surprisingly affordable.

There are 19 developed parks around Bull Shoals, not to mention countless marinas, boat launches, restaurants, lodges, and resorts. This lake is known far and wide for its largemouth and striped bass fishing, but it is almost as popular with anglers in search of catfish, trout, crappie, and walleye. Divers also flock to Bull Shoals; in some spots it is nearly 200 feet deep. Visibility is in the 25- to 30-foot range.

✴ Lodging

BED & BREAKFASTS ✐ **Garden Gate Guest House** (417-256-1199), 119 S. College St., West Plains, Mo. This 1891 Victorian cottage offers a full kitchen, two baths, a fireplace, and laundry facilities. Kids are accepted, and rates run $125–185. Smoking is permitted in a designated area.

Zanoni Mill Inn (417-679-2181), HC 78, Box 1010, Zanoni, Mo. The grandfather of the owner of this bed & breakfast built the actual Zanoni Mill in 1905 (his great-grandparents had settled in the area more than three decades prior). In front of the old mill and beside the remnants of an Ozarks pioneer village now sits this huge Colonial-style home. Located in the midst of a 1,750-acre working ranch, Zanoni offers a cabin rental directly across from the mill. It includes a sofa and recliner, fireplace, and small kitchen with all appliances. There is a half-bath on the main floor along with a rustic shower. In addition, the cabin includes a loft with a queen-sized bed. If you're planning on some fishing and floating, this inn puts you close to Bryant Creek, the North Fork River, and Norfork and Bull Shoals Lakes. Call for pricing and reservations. Pets are usually negotiable.

✐ ♿ **Aunt Bess's Stoneridge Inn** (417-261-2177; www.stoneridgeinn bedandbreakfast.bravehost.com), HC

ZANONI MILL INN

79, Box 3000, Dora, Mo. As an item of musical trivia, the tiny town of Dora is best known as the birthplace of legendary R&B artist Steve Cropper, the guitar player in the Blues Brothers Band with Dan Aykroyd and John Belushi. Also worthy of note in town, however, is this fine stone-and-cedar B&B. With its bird and butterfly sanctuary, small spring-fed lake, and huge screened-in porch (all rooms open onto it), Stoneridge Inn is a prime spot for relaxation in the deep Ozarks. You are close to canoeing and fishing on Bryant Creek or the North Fork, and can tour several of the old mills that dot the region. The rates at Stonebridge, which include gourmet meals and tax, begin at $110 per night. That would be cash only; no checks or credit cards are accepted. The food is renowned here, and breakfasts can include such offerings as blackberry soufflé, pancakes, omelets, and sausage. Aunt Bess herself also creates fresh-baked goods, and even those who are not staying at the inn can call ahead and have a meal served by appointment. There are four guest rooms, all with ceiling fan, queen-sized bed, and private bath. Kids are accepted at Stoneridge, and smoking is permitted outside only. Call to inquire about pets.

Windstone House (417-967-2008; www.bedandbreakfast.com/missouri /windstone-house-bed-breakfast.html), 539 Cleveland Rd., Houston, Mo. A relatively new home, constructed in 1977 primarily of native stone, Windstone offers three guest rooms (two upstairs and one down). The two-story inn features covered, wrap-around porches and a huge balcony on the second floor that is perfect for relaxation, reading, or even breakfast.

The home is chock-full of antiques, and features three different common areas and a dining room with wood-burning fireplace. Double-occupancy rates are $65 per night (single occupancy is $55), and kids over 12 are allowed. A large apartment is available at $110 per night. Pets cannot stay at Windstone, but smoking is permitted in designated areas.

🦃 ♿ **The Dickey House** (417-468-3000; www.dickeyhouse.com), 331 S. Clay St., Marshfield, Mo. Built between 1910 and 1913, this impressive Greek Revival mansion has been featured in *Time* magazine and has played host to the likes of President George H. W. Bush and Barbara Bush. It's set on 2 acres, complete with an aviary full of white turtledoves. Guests can stay in one of the mansion's three guest rooms or in four additional suites located in cottages around the property. All the rooms and suites come equipped with cable TV and VCR, and the suites feature a fireplace, double Jacuzzi, refrigerator, and coffeemaker. Special touches in both the individual rooms and suites have come after much thought, and those staying at Dickey House can expect electric fireplaces in some rooms, four-poster or canopied beds, brass beds, and a plethora of period antiques. In the sunroom you'll find a therapeutic hot tub (57 jets) capable of comfortably holding eight adults. A full breakfast is served each morning (try the caramel French toast), and kids 12 and older are welcome. Smoking is absolutely not permitted within the rooms or suites; inquire in advance if you are traveling with a pet. Rates at the Dickey House range from $89 for a room to $169 for the largest suite.

FLOATING THE RIVER OF LIFE

🐟 ✐ ♿ **River of Life Farm** (417-261-7777; www.riveroflifefarm.com), RR 1, Box 4535, Dora, Mo. You don't have to believe me when I tell you River of Life Farm is one of the coolest resorts in the Ozarks; after all, I've known owner Myron McKee on and off for nearly 20 years and might be biased. But you should believe NBC's *Today* show, *The Wall Street Journal,* the *St. Louis Post-Dispatch, Missouri Life* magazine, and countless smaller publications. It seems everyone who visits this idyllic resort in the heart of Mark Twain National Forest has nothing but rave reviews. Consisting of 120 acres that have been in Myron's family for three generations and fronting on the Wild Trout Management Area of the North Fork of the White River, this gated getaway offers the ultimate in lodging, wade fishing, float fishing, canoeing, hunting, hiking, and camping. River of Life is peaceful—the number of guests on-site at any one time is limited—and the scenery is nothing short of spectacular.

Aside from the outdoor glory, one of the main draws of ROLF is the lodging. Myron is a craftsman in every sense of the word, and his "tree house" lodging options are works of art. Your choices, which rise high into the trees (hence the name), range from the 590-square-foot **Cedar Chest Cabin** and **Tree Top Hideaway Treehouse** to the 1,200-square-foot **Mountain Log Lookout.** While this is just a sample, all the choices come with private bath, fireplace, fully equipped kitchen, and queen-sized bed. The facility now also includes a restaurant—new since this book first came out in 2006—and is fully set up for meetings, banquets, and catering. Guided hunting trips or custom-designed trips are popular here; contact the resort to discuss pricing. Because of its location, ROLF offers endless hiking opportunities. Also, for those who would prefer to camp under the stars, a campground (the only one in the Ozarks found in the Wild Trout Management Area) features picnic tables, fire pits, hot showers, and bathrooms with running water. RV spots are also available. Those considering ROLF need to call ahead for reservations and should note that most lodging choices have minimum-stay requirements.

Weddings are a fairly frequent occurrence here; contact the owners as to prices and details.

RESORTS ✐ **Bucks and Spurs Guest Ranch** (417-683-2381; www .bucksandspurs.com), HC 71, P.O. Box 163, Ava, MO 65608. This dude ranch south of Ava, which has been featured on NBC's *Today* show, offers horseback riding, cattle drives, horse drives, and horse training on 1,000 acres along Beaver Creek. You can swim, fish, canoe, or even go on a turkey hunt. This, while enjoying the beauty of the Ozarks and digging into some hefty meals. Every guest receives personalized attention, and riders are provided with mounts based upon their experience and ability. Lodging at Bucks and Spurs includes several options, including beautiful and large lodges and cabins. A three-night stay (that's the minimum during spring, summer, and fall; there's a two-night minimum during the winter) costs $180 per night for adults, $146 per night for kids 8–16, and $108 per night for kids 4–7. Weekly rates are also available. All vacation packages include meals, lodging, horseback riding, fishing, canoe trips (on the ranch), and any special event. To reach the ranch, head 5 miles south of Ava on SR 5 to SR A. Continue south on SR A for another 5 miles, then turn north onto SR A-422 for 2 miles. Ask about the various discounts when you call for reservations.

✔ ♿ **Golden Hills Trail Rides** (417-457-6222 or 1-800-874-1157; www .goldenhills.com), 19546 Golden Dr., Raymondville, Mo. Open mid-Apr.–early Nov. With more than 250 miles of trails on 5,100 privately owned acres, Golden Hills offers far more than stunning scenery and trail riding galore. There are horse-and-rider clinics, fishing, hiking, and even a biannual re-enactment of a mountain man rendezvous. Capable of hosting 1,100 guests, the facility's lodging options run the gamut from campsites with electricity and water, to bunkhouses, to private rooms with two queen-sized beds. Entertainment can include cowboy bands, hayrides, marshmallow roasts around the campfire, line dancing, mountain biking, and much more. There is a weight room, swimming pool, creeks on the property, and a store. Three hot meals

are served daily, and prices start at a low of $40 per night for accommodations in the lodge. RV sites with full hook-ups are also available. Individual rates for horse rental start at $30 per day. There are too many riding options to list (they're all available on the website) and you are welcome to bring your own horse.

✔ ♿ **Turkey Creek Ranch** (417-273-4362; www.turkeycreekranch.com), HC 3, Box 3180, Theodosia, Mo. Owned by the same family for nearly 50 years, this 700-acre resort and working cattle ranch on Bull Shoals Lake was named one of the Top 25 Cottage Resorts by *Midwest Living* magazine. The ranch offers a string of well-trained saddle horses, and trails range all over the property. Open Mar.–Nov., with rates starting at $109 per night. Accommodations include deluxe cabins with two to five bedrooms, two baths, full kitchen with microwave and range, a master suite, and central air. The standard cottages are slightly smaller, with two to three bedrooms. Both options include a grill; picnic table; screened porch; all pots, pans, and linens; coffeemaker; and TV. Also available are studio-sized "casitas," which sleep two to four people and offer private bath, full kitchen, porch, and picnic area complete with grill and table. Aside from horseback riding, there are plenty of recreational amenities at Turkey Creek. A game room, gift shop, hot tub, indoor pool, tennis courts, basketball, volleyball, and shuffleboard are only the beginning of pastimes that will keep the kids from getting bored. Pets are not accepted.

✔ ♿ **Theodosia Marina-Resort** (417-273-4444; www.tmrbullshoals .net), Lake Rd. 160-25, P.O. Box 390,

Theodosia, MO 65761. In business since 1952, Theodosia Marina-Resort has grown from a dock, café, and motel to a full-service marina and resort with boat sales and service. On-site you'll find a motel, cottages, lodges, and an RV and camping park. Prices for the motel begin at $45 per night, and the two-bedroom cottages (with complete kitchen, private bath, and TV) begin at $125 per night (that's per person, with a four-person minimum). If you prefer to rent a lodge, they have a good one here. The 2,000-square-foot log structure includes four bedrooms, two baths with Jacuzzis, complete kitchen with dishwasher, three TVs, a fireplace, and a porch with lake view. Prices start at $200 per person per night with a six-night minimum. The season for both the cottages and lodges runs Mar.–late Nov. For those who arrive with an RV, sites at the **Fort Cook RV Park** (with water, electricity, restrooms, and hot showers) begin at $20 for two people. As Theodosia Marina

is right on Bull Shoals, boat rental is popular. Rental for a fishing boat (a 16-footer with a 60-horse outboard, trolling motor, and depth finder) is $75 for a half day and $125 for a full day. Skis, ski vests, life jackets, towropes, and safety gear are all included in the rental charge. Last but not least, the facility also features lighted tennis and basketball courts, an outdoor pool, and a family-style restaurant.

⚓ ♿ ⑂ **Dawt Mill** (417-284-3540 or 1-888-884-3540; www.dawtmill.com), HC 1, Box 1090, Tecumseh, Mo. The Dawt Mill, originally built in 1897, is the only remaining gristmill in Ozark County that is still operational. Much more than that, however, the facility for which the mill serves as centerpiece is a full-scale resort. Many folks choose Dawt Mill for canoe rental, as the three trips offered down the North Fork are all very pretty (easy to say, since there's not a single part of the North Fork that isn't gorgeous). With shuttle service included, the cost

DAWT MILL

of a nine-hour trip for two is $64.95. Shorter trips run $43.95 and $47.95. For those who wish to cast a line, fishing licenses can be purchased at the mill.

Lodging choices here are excellent. The Dinnel log cabin (which is three old cabins hooked together and renovated) has a full kitchen, bathroom, bedrooms, front deck, and air-conditioning. It rents for $159 per night during summer. Hodgson House, built in the late 1800s, is divided into four separate units, each of which can comfortably accommodate four people. Prices start at $86 for a standard suite in the summer months. A modernized cabin in the woods (creatively dubbed the Cabin in the Woods) also can sleep four and costs $86 per night. A recently constructed lodge, the Cotton Gin Inn, offers deluxe or standard suites (two rooms) beginning at $109. On the property are also 50 campsites for either RV or tent camping. RV spots with water, electricity, and sewer run $45, and tent sites begin at $10. Finally, the resort is the home of the popular Henegar's Grist Mill restaurant and Sawyer's Deli.

🐾 ✐ ⅄ **Rainbow Trout and Game Ranch** (417-679-3619; www.rock bridgemo.com), P.O. Box 100, Rockbridge, MO 65741. With more than 200,000 fish raised each year in this hatchery, the fishing is always good here at the site of the old Rockbridge Mill (the record is a 16-pound trout). In this idyllic setting in the deep Ozarks, sportsmen can also enjoy guided hunts for upland birds, turkeys, and white-tailed deer. Within the 3,000 acres of land that surround this facility, the possibilities are infinite. Also, a sporting clay area and hunter's archery range are of great

assistance in sharpening your marksmanship. For lodging, the game ranch features 29 motel rooms as well as five separate guest houses, each having a minimum of three bedrooms and two baths. Pets are not accepted in any of the homes; call ahead to inquire about keeping a pet in your hotel room. A fine restaurant (see Dining Out) is on the property, and open daily 8–8. In the old mill itself you'll find the **Grist Mill Club.** Open seasonally (closed in winter), this pub offers adult beverages, a relaxing setting, and a great view of the mill's waterfall.

Fishing permits are available not only to those staying at Rockbridge, but to anyone who might like to wet a line for an afternoon. Because this is a private enterprise, no other license or stamp is needed. You are required to keep any trout you catch (and you can catch a lot), and the cost averages around $4 per pound. For $250 (per eight hours) you can opt for a guided, catch-and-release fly-fishing trip. All equipment, plus lunch, is included in the price. Guided and nonguided hunt packages are offered for turkeys, deer, and upland birds. The packages vary greatly in price. Call the ranch for details.

CANOE OUTFITTERS AND CAMPING 🐾 ✐ Beaver Canoe Rental (417-796-2336; www.beaver canoerental.com), 159 SR W, Ava, Mo. This outfitter specializes in floating and fishing on Beaver Creek, a nice little stream featuring decent bass fishing and possessing lots of good gravel bars for picnics. Open Apr.–Oct., Beaver Canoe offers floats starting in the $40 per canoe range. Shuttle service is provided, and an on-

site store carries all the basic provisions. Beaver has four separate campgrounds, some of which feature full RV hook-ups and some of which are geared for tent camping. Amenities include toilets, hot showers, tent sites, fire pits, and picnic tables. Pets are allowed but must be leashed and attended at all times.

☠ ✆ ⚴ **Boiling Springs Resort and Canoe Rental** (573-674-3488 or 1-800-564-3285; www.boilingsprings resort.com), 15750 SR BB, Licking, Mo. The Big Piney River is a slow-moving body of water, and one that is far from overfished. Such being the case, you can expect to catch plenty of hard-fighting goggle-eye (a smallish bass derivative), smallmouths, and largemouths. Canoe rentals with shuttle begin at $45, and modern cabins (TV, air-conditioning, bathroom, linens, and full kitchen) begin at $70 per night. Pets are allowed, but they will cost you an extra $20 per night. Tent campsites begin at $7 per night, and RV sites begin at $10 per night plus a $6-per-person fee.

Twin Bridges Canoe and Campground (417-256-7507 or 417-256-2726; www.twinbridgescanoe.com), HC 64, Box 230, West Plains, Mo. Located on the North Fork River, Twin Bridges is a multipurpose outfitter offering canoes ($23 per person, two-person minimum), rafts ($25 per person with a four-person minimum), kayaks ($35 per person), tandem kayaks ($23 per person), and a variety of camping and lodging options. Both fishing and hunting are first-rate in this stretch of the Ozarks—what with the cold, clear North Fork and the Mark Twain National Forest—and over the years this operation has expanded to ensure that you can pur-

sue those pastimes in comfort. Either owning or leasing 1,200 acres with 5 miles of riverfront, Twin Bridges has built a number of log homes and cabins right on the river that sleep up to 16 people. Four separate camping areas are found both on Spring Creek and the North Fork, as well as another large, wooded site overlooking the river. These tent sites start at $8 per night per person and include picnic tables, grills, hot showers, and bathrooms with running water.

The log homes offered by Twin Bridges offer a good value for larger groups and those who seek more luxury than a tent. Situated on 250 acres with a mile of riverfront, the homes begin at $145 per night for two people, with $28 for each additional adult, and sleep up to 16. Cabins begin at $65 per night for two, with $12 for each additional adult. Call for rates on the large trout lodge, as well as for information on minimum stays. Pets are not permitted in the cabins or lodge. The Twin Bridges facility also features RV hook-ups, a camp store, and guide services.

For **Bucks and Spurs Guest Ranch, River of Life Farm,** and **Dawt Mill,** see *Resorts.*

✳ Where to Eat

EATING OUT ☠ ✆ ⚴ **Ava Drug Soda Fountain** (www.avadrug.com; 417-683-4127), 112 W. Washington St., Ava, Mo. You're going to like this place, located in Ava's local drugstore. This is a true old-fashioned soda fountain. You'll find limeades made from real limes, 1950s prices, banana splits, ice cream, shakes, and all the traditional stools and stainless steel you either (a) remember, or (b) wish you could remember. The menu is simple, and everything tastes wonderful. What you'll find here is a great atmosphere, a happy time, and the sort of sugar buzz that is mandatory from time to time. By the way, a cup of coffee is still 5 cents.

🐾 🍴 ♿ **Hillbilly Junction** (417-469-4296), 2364 SR 1270, Willow Springs, Mo. I would be utterly remiss were I not to include the landmark known as Hillbilly Junction, visible on the north side of US 60 as you approach Willow Springs. It's not that the food is that phenomenal (it's just OK . . . but you won't spend more than $5–10), and it's not like there's some sort of spectacular ambience. The reason you

THE AVA DRUG SODA FOUNTAIN

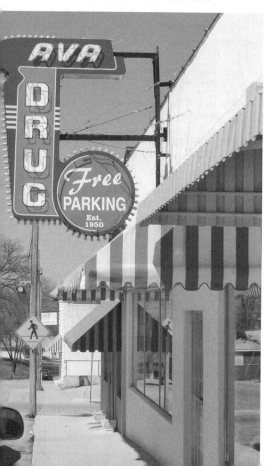

have to stop is that you will always regret it if you don't. You see, failing to visit Hillbilly Junction would be a bit like driving through South Dakota and failing to stop at Wall Drug. You do it so you can tell other people you did it, and also to pick up some tourist junk as evidence of your visit. Yes, this is the place to grab a meal (or sometimes hit the buffet) and then purchase stuff you don't need. It's the place for postcards featuring a giant bass in a tiny rowboat with a caption reading THE ONE THAT DIDN'T GET AWAY. It's the place to buy jam, honey, or pork rinds. It's the place where you get your silly-looking felt hillbilly hat or authentic corncob pipe. It's your prime source for the much-needed Ozark shot glass or the inevitable tiny spoon emblazoned with the Gateway Arch. Look, you have no choice. Just surrender gracefully to the inevitable, pull in, grab a burger, and stock up on bumper stickers. At the time of this writing in 2011, the entire Hillbilly Junction complex is on the market. It's still operating, no worries there, but the joint could be yours for around $700,000.

🍴 ♿ **Cookie's** (417-273-4444; www .tmrbullshoals.net/cookies.html), Lake Rd. 160-25, Theodosia, Mo. Located at the Theodosia Marina-Resort, Cookies is a family restaurant whose menu ranges from hot dogs to filet mignon. There's a full breakfast menu, lunch and dinner specials, Friday- and Saturday-night prime rib specials, and smorgasbords. Breakfast is in the $3–8 range, and a buffet is served Saturday, Sunday, and holidays during the summer season. The catfish lunch is $6.99. Also for lunch, a "steak-n-taters" salad (prime rib and sautéed potatoes with red onions all

HILLBILLY JUNCTION

served over a bed of greens) costs $8.95. A nice dinner appetizer is the breaded Cajun crawdad tails ($4.95), while a 16-ounce KC strip is $15.95. If you are by chance trying to sample every deep-fried catfish dinner in the Ozarks (which should make your cardiologist even wealthier), the version at Cookie's runs $9.95.

DINING OUT 🚲 ♿ ⅂ **Café 37** (417-256-3780; www.cafe37.food.officelive.com), 37 Court Square, West Plains, Mo. I never really expected to see a gourmet restaurant in West Plains. Then again, I never expected West Plains to have grown to the degree it has. This restaurant, located in the restored Opera House, involved more than a little thought. The inside is very well done, with a fine antique back bar and copper ceiling. It is in fact this combination of past meeting future that seems to be the hallmark of the contemporary Ozarks. Though the food is first-rate—as is true almost everywhere in this part of the world—the dress is casual. This isn't the most inexpensive place around (dinners are around $15–20 per person, on average) but you will not go away unhappy. You'll find both a number of standard entrées and also enough unique offerings to pique your curiosity. Particularly good is the Portobello Mushroom Two-Way. At $14.95, this is a portobello mushroom cap smothered with roasted garlic, chicken filling, and sautéed spinach with tomatoes. The dressed-up mushroom is broiled, then nestled in a bed of gorgonzola grits. If you're seeking a good lunch, you just won't beat the Mediterranean meat lover's pizza at $7.99.

Rainbow Trout and Game Ranch (417-679-3619; www.rockbridgemo.com), SR N, Rd. 142, Rockbridge, Mo. Located at the old Rockbridge

Mill, the restaurant of the Rainbow Trout Ranch is open to the public seven days a week from 8–8 (except for Christmas week). It's a great place to get a fine and relaxing meal after a day of fishing, hunting, or simply exploring the ranch's grounds and the old mill. Breakfast, lunch, and dinner are served. The morning meal options run the gamut from biscuits and gravy to a massive country-fried steak and eggs (be hungry if you order this). A variety of sandwiches, entrées, appetizers, and salads are offered for lunch. As for dinner, start with some frog legs for an appetizer, then move on to anything from fried chicken to a hefty selection of trout. That's the specialty here, and you can order it amandine, stuffed, broiled, batter fried, or baked. There's also Monterey trout, blackened trout, and lemon-pepper trout. Prices for any of these are in the $15–20 range.

✱ Entertainment

✎ ♿ **Avenue Theatre** (417-256-4420; www.theavenuetheatre.com), 307 Washington Ave., West Plains, Mo. Built in 1950 as an art deco movie house, the fully renovated Avenue now plays host to community plays and other local entertainment events. Prices and admission vary depending upon the event.

♨ ✎ ♿ **West Plains Civic Center** (417-256-8123; www.civiccenter.net), 110 St. Louis Ave., West Plains, Mo. From banquets to basketball games, from pro wrestling to ballet, from gymnasts to Ted Nugent, from gun shows to live theater, you never quite know what you'll find at the West Plains Civic Center. The main exhibit hall/arena here can hold more than 3,500 people,

and the smaller theater room seats 450. As expected, admission prices vary with the individual shows.

✎ **West Plains Opera House** (417-256-3780; www.westplains.net/tourism /historic.php), 37 Court Square, West Plains, Mo. Completely refurbished, this 1886 opera house now plays host to concerts, dancing, and performing arts of all types. Call for information on upcoming events and admission prices. This is also the home of Café 37.

✎ **Yellow House Community Arts Center** (417-372-3113; www.yellow housearts.org), 209 W. Cleveland St., West Plains, Mo. The center is open year-round, but call ahead for performance times and admission prices (generally in the $3–10 range). This 1903 house is now home to a variety of musical performances, speakers, and artistic presentations open to the public. The music is particularly good—everything from bluegrass to Celtic, country, and classical.

SPECTATOR SPORTS West Plains Motor Speedway (417-257-2112; www.westplains-speedway.com), 10603 US 63, West Plains, Mo. Generally considered one of the top three dirt tracks in America, this ⅜-mile oval is open Mar.–Aug. and offers seating for 17,000. Set on 100 acres with a large campground on-site, the facility includes hot showers, bathrooms, and full concessions. Races include IMCA modifieds, superstocks, hobby stock cars and trucks, and much more. The West Plains Motor Speedway is also home of the **Firecracker Classic.** Admission prices for the Saturday races are $5 for adults, free for kids 6 and younger.

WEST PLAINS OPERA HOUSE & CAFÉ 37

✳ Selective Shopping

Memory Lane Antiques (417-683-1063; www.mlava.com), 120 E. Public Square, Ava, Mo. Located on the town square at Memory Lane, you'll find just a bit of everything here. There's lots of glassware (carnival glass, Depression glass), old books and signs, jewelry, utensils, and even antique fishing plugs and gear. That's not all; there's also usually a wide range of collectible and antique furniture, not to mention dolls, old tools, and pottery.

✳ Special Events

May **Emmett Kelly Clown Festival** (417-967-2220), Houston Area Chamber of Commerce, Houston, Mo. If you suffer from coulrophobia (an intense fear of clowns), then you'd best avoid Houston during the first weekend in May. That would be the time of the annual Emmett Kelly

Clown Festival, when clowns of all shapes, sizes, colors, and descriptions descend upon this small town to make weird noises and flop around in greasepaint and such. Dedicated to Houston's favorite son, Emmett Kelly (his Weary Willie character is arguably the world's best-known clown), you'll experience not just clowns and the obligatory clown antics, but also a midway, circus acts, myriad booths stocked with crafts and food, face painting, music, balloons, and magicians. You have to wonder, considering the terrifying manner in which he portrays clowns in his books, if Stephen King ever attended this shindig.

June and September **Missouri Fox-trotting Horse Breed Association Show** (417-683-2468; www.mfthba.com), P.O. Box 1027, Ava, MO 65608. Riders from around the world love the equine breed known as the Missouri Foxtrotter. Whether used as merely a family horse, for ranch work, or for competition, the Foxtrotter is known for its smooth gait, rhythm, and friendly personality. Located in Ava, the headquarters of the Missouri Foxtrotting Horse Breed Association holds two international shows per year. The **Fall Show and Celebration** (held for a week in early September) and the **Spring Show and Three Year Old Futurity** (held for four days in early June) feature performance horses, trail rides, competition in a long list of different classes, food, drink, and fun.

July **Douglas County Fair** (417-683-4594; www.avachamber.org), 810 S.W. 13th Ave., Ava, Mo. Held for three days in mid-July, this county fair is of the traditional style, with games, music, food, and livestock. The Douglas County fair has been held annually for more than 75 years.

September **Hootin an Hollerin** (1-800-447-1290), held on the town square, Gainesville, Mo. Now more than 50 years old, the annual Hootin' and Hollerin' festival takes place the third weekend in September. It's dedicated to preserving the traditions, crafts, skills, and music of the Ozarks, and you'll hear everything from

gospel to bluegrass. If your feet are itchy, join in for some line dancing, clog dancing, or square dancing. Wandering around, you'll see folks demonstrating the arts of carving and whittling, blacksmithing, spinning, and much more. There are contests galore. Though they have yet to be sanctioned by the International Olympic Committee, sports such as outhouse racing, hog and husband calling, frog jumping, and turtle racing are old standards. Of course there will be tons of food and craft booths, as well as a parade, queen pageant, chili cook-off, and quilt show.

October **Glade Top Trail Flaming Fall Festival** (417-683-4594; www.avachamber.org/events.htm), 810 S.W. 13th Ave., Ava, Mo. Held the third weekend of every October, when fall colors on the famous Glade Top Trail are at their height, this festival includes live music, square dancing, and an arts and crafts show. On Sunday morning you can enjoy a sausage-and-pancake breakfast. Also on Sunday, a BBQ chicken dinner is held on a peak halfway down the trail at the Caney Tower Forest Service fire lookout.

THE OZARK NATIONAL
SCENIC RIVERWAYS

Even a novice to floating the rivers of the Missouri Ozarks knows the names of the Current and Jacks Fork. These two legendary waterways, along with 80,000 acres of land that surround their span, make up the Ozark National Scenic Riverways. More than 134 miles in length combined, the two rivers were federally protected by an act of Congress in 1964. Today they are a beautiful, albeit busy, favorite of canoeists, kayakers, campers, hikers, and fishermen.

The battle to save the Current and Jacks Fork from overdevelopment actually began at the dawn of the 20th century. As was true in most of the Ozarks, hillsides bordering these rivers had been logged nearly to the ground, resulting in a heavy degree of erosion and destruction. Though floaters love to picnic on the many gravel bars they encounter, the truth is that these respites are far from natural. In fact, they were created when gravel and rocks washed down denuded hills into the crystal-clear waters. Tourists began visiting the rivers with enthusiasm, and for many years there was more than a little debate over whether the lands now known as the ONSR should be preserved in a natural state, commercially developed, or (as almost happened) dammed by the Army Corps of Engineers for yet another Ozark hydroelectric facility and lake.

In the 1920s the state of Missouri purchased Big Spring, Montauk, Alley Spring, and Round Spring, designating them as fledgling state parks. In the 1930s the U.S. Forest Service (then less than three decades old) began buying up land bordering the rivers and, under the auspices of the Civilian Conservation Corps, planting pine trees and building trails. Also in the 1930s, the Army Corps of Engineers, which both then and now seems to erupt in fits of glee at the idea of damming anything larger than a kitchen sink, announced its intent to dam the Current and construct a massive lake. Many Ozarkers, used to a hardscrabble life, weren't terribly opposed to the thought. Jobs were jobs, after all, especially in a rugged land where keeping food on the table was a daily struggle. For other residents, though, the thought of destroying the Current was simply unacceptable. This contingent included Missouri's newspapers and politicians, who took the side of the preservationists.

The Ozark National Scenic Riverways

The battle for the Current was heated to say the least. Most locals, distrustful of the callous attitude of government as shown toward other Ozark communities, did not want the area under federal control as a national park. Still, the press and the pols won the day, and in 1964 President Lyndon Johnson signed legislation creating the ONSR. In 1972, Tricia Nixon Cox pitched a bouquet of flowers into Big Spring and officially christened the waters. Her father, President Richard Nixon, was apparently too busy to attend. Dick was in the process of tending to a water problem of his own, the Watergate scandal that would bring down his administration.

Today the Current and Jacks Fork are a haven for visitors from around the world. The area is home to more than 300 caves, and more than 60 percent of the rivers' flow arrives from uncountable springs (7 huge ones, 51 smaller springs, and infinite tiny jets of subterranean water). Big Spring alone pumps out an astonishing 276 million gallons per day. This is great news for floaters, as the Jacks Fork and Current are floatable year-round. The bad news for floaters is that the popularity of these rivers makes them heavily traveled. More than 60 percent of floaters arrive in summer, and about half that number paddle downstream in fall and spring. If you want a quiet and peaceful float, bundle up, bring a thermos of hot coffee, and launch your canoe during winter. You'll probably not see another living soul. (No firm figures exist on the numbers of disembodied souls you might encounter.)

If you do show up in summer, and wish a more tranquil day, you might opt to canoe the Eleven Point River. While designated a Wild and Scenic River, it is not part of the ONSR and thus receives less traffic. There's a trade-off with the Current and Jacks Fork that can be found in many federally protected areas. While a Park Service stewardship preserves and protects the land, the very act of designating a place wilderness or national park draws so many people that the wild aspect becomes something of a memory.

Be that as it may, the streams of the ONSR are still some of the most beautiful in the world. The springs boil without rest, and the caves, bluffs, and wooded glades are reminiscent of the forest primeval. Fishing is good, and wildlife is prevalent—112 species of fish, 196 species of birds, 58 species of mammals, and 25 species of snakes (4 of which have a poisonous disposition) are found in and along the lands of the ONSR. Visitors will also discover quaint and amusing little river towns such as Eminence, Doniphan, and Van Buren. There's plenty of bluegrass, plenty of BBQ, catfish, and trout. For those who choose to look, there are also plenty of hidden respites both on the river and in the woods that will make an incursion into the Ozark National Scenic Riverways a trip to remember.

AREA CODES With a few exceptions on the western border, which remain under the **417** area code, the Ozark National Scenic Riverways region falls under the **573** area code.

GUIDANCE As you could assume from the title of this chapter, most of the recreational opportunities in this region revolve around the outdoors. Rarely, if ever, will you find more scenic and enjoyable rivers than when exploring the Ozark National Scenic Riverways. Luckily, there is plenty of information in regard to floating, fishing, and having the time of your life.

For starters, the **National Park Service** website (www.nps.gov/ozar/index.htm) offers a great overview of these beautiful waters. Even better, for suggestions, recommendations, and advice beyond what you might anticipate, contact the **Salem Chamber of Commerce** (573-729-6900; www.salemmo.com), 200 S. Main, Salem, Mo. Its tourism packages are both lengthy and informative. For a good look at some of the sites along the Current River, or for a visit to Big Spring, either the **Ripley County Chamber of Commerce** (573-996-2212; www.ripleycountymissouri.org), 209 W. Highway St., Doniphan, Mo., or the **Van Buren Area Chamber of Commerce** (573-996-2212; www.vanburen.org), P.O. Box 1518, Van Buren, MO 63965, will happily send you a list of area sites and services.

One town you don't want to miss in this region is Eminence. It's a beautiful place, not to mention ground zero for those wanting to canoe the Jacks Fork River. Any insight you need into lodging, dining, camping, or canoeing can be gathered for you by the **Eminence Chamber of Commerce** (573-226-3318; www.eminencemo.com), P.O. Box 415, Eminence, MO 65466. And then there is Oregon County, which is blessed with such natural wonders as the Irish Wilderness, the Eleven Point River, Grand Gulf State Park, and Greer Spring. The **Thayer Chamber of Commerce** (417-264-7324; www.thayerchamber.com), 200 E. Walnut. St., Thayer, Mo., and the **Alton Chamber of Commerce** (417-778-6321; www.altonadvertiser.com/visit_altonmo.html), 101 Pine St., Alton, Mo., are your best bets when planning a trek to some of these Ozark treasures. Lastly, if you find yourself in the far southeast corner of this region, check out the **Greater Poplar Bluff Area Chamber of Commerce** (573-785-7761; www.poplarbluffchamber.org), 1111 W. Pine St., Poplar Bluff, Mo.

GETTING THERE *By car:* As you have no doubt noticed, there are only a few main thoroughfares traversing the Ozarks. In the Ozark National Scenic Riverways region, both US 60 and US 160 stretch the entire distance from east to west. From north to south your best bets are US 63 south from Rolla and US 67 from just south of St. Louis. Now, if you want a pretty drive (not necessarily the fastest, just the nicest), take SR 19 from Salem, through Eminence, and all the way south to the Arkansas border at Thayer.

By air: **Springfield-Branson National Airport** (417-868-0500; www.sgf -branson-airport.com), 2300 N. Airport Blvd., Springfield, Mo., is served by American Airlines, Allegiant, United, and Delta. The airport offers facilities for buses, vans, rental cars, and hotel and hospitality limousines. The airport underwent a multimillion-dollar expansion between 2006 and 2009, resulting in a new, midfield terminal and expanded services. The **Branson Airport** (1-888-359-2541; http://flybranson.com), 4000 Branson Airport Blvd., Hollister, Mo., opened in May 2009; it holds the distinction of being the only privately owned, privately operated, commercial service airport in the United States. The airport offers direct, nonstop flights to a number of cities, and is serviced by AirTran, Frontier, and Branson Air Express. Also, **Lambert–St. Louis International Airport** (314-426-8000; www.lambert-stlouis.com), 10701 Lambert International Blvd., St. Louis, Mo., serves a variety of major air carriers with nonstop service to and from many locations. Try to avoid taking I-270 South between 4–6 PM (weekdays), or you may find yourself in a traffic jam.

MEDICAL EMERGENCIES The hospital I'd choose if I became ill in the western part of this region would be the **Ozarks Medical Center** (417-256-9111;

www.ozarksmedicalcenter.com), 1100 N. Kentucky St., West Plains, Mo. See "The Original Ozarks" for a full description.

Salem Memorial District Hospital (573-729-6626; www.smdh.net), SR 72 North, Salem, Mo. Should you feel aches and pains in the vicinity of Salem, drop by this 25-bed critical access hospital. Services offered include cardiopulmonary, emergency, kidney dialysis, radiology, surgical, and more. A nonprofit, district-owned hospital, Salem Memorial provides care for the residents of Dent, Shannon, Crawford, and Iron Counties.

Ripley County Memorial Hospital (573-996-2141; www.rcmhospital.net), 109 Plum St., Doniphan, Mo. This facility has 30 beds and offers general medical and surgical care as well as an emergency department.

Poplar Bluff Regional Medical Center (573-785-7721; www.poplarbluff regional.com), 2620 N. Westwood Blvd., Poplar Bluff, Mo. (north campus), or (573-686-4111), 621 W. Pine St. (south campus). This 423-bed facility is the premier regional hospital in the southeastern section of the Ozark National Scenic Riverways region. It employs more than 100 physicians. Services include emergency, cancer treatment, pulmonary, X-ray and imaging, women's health, mental health, and much more.

John J. Pershing Veterans Administration Medical Center (573-686-4151 or 1-888-557-8262; www.poplarbluff.va.gov), 1500 N. Westwood, Poplar Bluff, Mo. This center holds 18 general medicine beds and 40 extended-care beds. It serves 24 counties in southeast Missouri as well as 6 counties in Northeast Arkansas.

✳ Wandering Around

EXPLORING BY CAR For pure scenery, you really can't go wrong traveling south on SR 19 from Salem to Eminence. SR 19 was designated a Scenic Highway by the Missouri legislature, and it's so curvy that you can't drive very fast. That's a good thing, because the route is so pretty that you'll want to dawdle, gawk, and occasionally take a short side trip to view various springs and mills, and of course the legendary waterways known as the Current and Jacks Fork Rivers. From Salem, head south on SR 19 for approximately 10 miles. The first stopping place for a photo opportunity will be **Standing Rock Bridge,** so named because the rocks look like they are standing on their ends (whether top end or bottom end is yet to be determined). Continue south on SR 19 for another 15 miles and take a right onto SR EE. Follow this road for 4 miles and you'll arrive at **Pulltite Spring,** home of the old **Pulltite Cabin.** After walking around for a time, seeing the spring, and dunking your feet in the Current River, return to SR 19 and head south. In 3 miles you'll cross Sinking Creek Bridge, the point at which Sinking Creek flows into the Current River. Roughly 2 miles farther is the entrance to Round Spring Campground, where (at least between Memorial Day and Labor Day) you can take a tour of **Round Spring Cave.** If you're not into spelunking, enjoy the ride for 20 miles to the south (still on SR 19) and arrive in **Eminence.** This is one of the coolest little towns in the Ozarks, with plenty of things to do and plenty of sites to see. You also may want to turn onto

SR 106 and drive east for 6 miles to the mill at **Alley Spring,** probably the most photographed structure in this part of (if not the entire) Ozarks.

EXPLORING BY FOOT Pine Ridge Trail/Montauk State Park (573-548-2201 or 573-548-2434; http://mostateparks.com/park/montauk-state-park), 345 CR 6670, Salem, Mo. What with all the caves, creeks, and springs found within the Ozark National Scenic Riverways, just about any given spot is good for a hike. You'll find one that's a bit more defined, however, at Montauk. The Pine Ridge Trail is not the easiest of treks, and can in fact get a bit slick if it's muddy (in other words, wear hiking boots). Remember to take note (as I didn't) that this 1.5-mile trail does not make a full loop, as most trails do. Due to the way the trail winds, you'll have another 0.5 mile (more or less) to walk after completing the trail (assuming you parked at the trailhead by the picnic shelter). The first part of the trail is steep, and begins by taking you through the Montauk Upland Forest Natural Area. This is a pretty 40 acres of oak and pine. After that you'll cross a highway and enter a grove of pines that, at least in spring, is loaded with songbirds. You may spy a deer or two, and chances are you'll hear woodpeckers as they jackhammer away at dead trees for insects. Continuing on, you'll come across the highlight of this walk, which is a great view (bring the camera) of Bluff Spring and Montauk Lake. If you're visiting in winter, watch the skies for bald eagles.

EXPLORING BY RIVER The **Current River** is the centerpiece of the Ozark National Scenic Riverways. While not a fast river by any stretch of the imagination, the Current is fed by innumerable springs. This is good for the floaters, and you can be nearly assured of an enjoyable canoe trip year-round. The river has its headwaters in Montauk State Park and travels more than 100 miles southeast into Arkansas. Most floaters, however, prefer the stretches between Montauk and Big Spring, near Van Buren. This is a beautiful river, clean and clear. Thanks to its federal designation, it has been largely protected from commercial disruption. For those seeking caves, deep forests, gushing springs, and a feast of color in both spring and fall, the Current is the preferred choice. That said, the federal designation is a double-edged sword. This is one stretch of water that can become exceptionally busy during the warmer months, with weekends witnessing literal flotillas of canoes. Still, the Current has been and remains the most well-known and popular float stream in the Missouri Ozarks.

A tributary of the Current and also part of the Ozark National Scenic Riverways, the **Jacks Fork River** has its headwaters in southeast Texas County and flows toward its confluence with the Current near Eminence. The lower sections of the Jacks Fork (below Alley Spring) offer a faster ride than many Ozark streams, with a fair amount of mild whitewater and small waterfalls. This is not the type of whitewater you'd find on a wild and woolly Rocky Mountain raft trip, and experienced floaters consider it very tame. In other words, while there is no outrageous danger here, you can receive a happy thrill in spots. This is particularly true in spring, when rains keep the water level high and eliminate the need for long portages around dry spots. Almost everyone loves the Jacks Fork, and almost everyone also manages to take at least half a dozen pictures of Alley Spring.

HEADWATERS OF THE CURRENT RIVER

Designated a Wild and Scenic River, the **Eleven Point** begins near the town of Willow Springs and heads to the southeast in Arkansas. Another river that is fed by innumerable springs, the Eleven Point is floatable year-round (more or less; I'm not saying you might not have to pull your canoe over a gravel bar from time to time). I would rate this river as having a bit more "wild and scenic" quality than either the Current or the Jacks Fork, what with the trees, wildlife, pastures, and tranquil farms that line its banks. As with the Jacks Fork, you will find some mild whitewater on the Eleven Point, which is always nice to break up the day. A slow and tranquil pace is fine and dandy, but there are times where it's nice to feel a few splashes and bump against a few boulders.

✳ Towns and Villages

Doniphan, Mo. Like many towns in the Ozarks, this seat of Ripley County was burned to the ground by Yankees during the Civil War. This is not to imply that said Yankees didn't have reason to be miffed. Doniphan was a hotbed of Southern guerrilla activity, and General Sterling Price and his Rebel troops were moving into the area from Arkansas. It does seem to hint, however, that the "civilized" Union often demonstrated a severe penchant for pyromania and probably just needed to work out deep-seated issues in a safe and nurturing therapeutic environment that would enable closure and healing. (In case you missed it, that was merely a sarcastic example of the sort of thing that would *never* cross the lips of any Ozarker worth his salt.) Today, located as always on the Current River, Doniphan is a pretty town that serves as home to the Current River Heritage Museum. Close by is a unique geological formation known as the Narrows—a high, thin ridge that separates the Eleven Point River from Fredrick Creek.

Eminence, Mo. This is another town that rates as one of my top five spots in the Ozarks. Eminence, population 548, was once named both Missouri's Top Outdoor Outpost and one of the 50 Top Outdoor Sports Towns in America by *Sports Afield* magazine. I was a hair away from buying a gorgeous bed & breakfast here in 1999, and have never stopped kicking myself for failing to do so. Surrounded by innumerable springs and caves of jaw-dropping beauty, bisected by the Jack's Fork, and surrounded by high, forested ridges, Eminence is a center for horseback riding, fishing, floating (the Current River is close by as well), and great fun. You'll be surprised at the shopping available in this seat of Shannon County, and you'll love the B&Bs.

Poplar Bluff, Mo. With 17,045 people, Poplar Bluff is on the southeastern edge of the cultural region that defines the Ozarks. Virtually deserted during the Civil War, it is now home to the Poplar Bluff Regional Medical Center, hosts major entertainment events at the Black River Coliseum, and boasts of the excellent Poplar Bluff Speedway. You'll also find many restaurants, museums, and even a kids' water park in the ever-growing seat of Butler County.

Salem, Mo. There is no false advertising in Salem's claim to being the Gateway to the Ozark Riverways. The town of 4,936, the seat of Dent County, is on the doorstep of Montauk State Park, the Ozark National Scenic Riverways, Indian Trail Conservation Area, and the Mark Twain National Forest. The residents of this Salem have never burned any witches; they just float the rivers, catch fish, breathe in the amazing scenery, and thank their lucky stars for being able to live in such a picturesque and charming town. While visiting Salem, make sure to drop by both the Dent County Museum and the Bonebrake Center of Nature and History.

Van Buren, Mo. With roughly 809 residents, Van Buren is well known to those who float the Current River. This is known as Big Spring Country, and the natu-

BIG SPRING IN VAN BUREN

ral feature that makes that name possible (pumping out 276 million gallons of water per day) is located just south of town. To see Big Spring is to know that residents of this area have an amazing talent for understatement. Like so many spots in the Ozarks, this small town is ecstatic in the knowledge that it remains a small town. For example, stop in Van Buren between May and October, and there's a good chance you'll enjoy one of the monthly street dances (complete with live music) held on the pavilion behind the stately, old, county courthouse. As we would say in these parts, "You can't beat that with a stick."

✳ To See

MUSEUMS ✐ & **Epps-Houts Museum** (573-785-2734; www.poplarbluff chamber.org/areaattractions.asp), 1540 SR 451, Poplar Bluff, Mo. Open year-round; donations are gratefully accepted. This interesting little museum holds paintings, cultural artifacts, and carvings from South Korea, southern Africa, Saudi Arabia, and 10 other countries. A huge number of rare cookbooks also are found in this historic homestead.

🍴 ✐ & **Moark Regional Railroad Museum** (573-785-4539; http://moark rail.org), 303 Moran St., Poplar Bluff, Mo. Open year-round, Sat.–Sun. 1–4. Admission is free. If you're into things involving steel rails and iron horses, you'll enjoy this tribute to the choo-choo. Inside are a very well-done model-train display and a large number of old photos covering almost every element of railroad life. You'll also find tools, lanterns, and even Morse code memorabilia. The Moark, a National Historic Site, is housed in a 1928 Frisco railroad depot.

🍴 ✐ **Poplar Bluff Historical Museum** (573-785-2220; www.poplarbluff chamber.org/areaattractions.asp), 1010 N. Main St., Poplar Bluff, Mo. Open year-round, Sun. 2–4. Admission is free. This museum not only centers on the history of Poplar Bluff and Butler County, but also takes things a couple of steps further. There are displays devoted to the Boy and Girl Scouts, veterans, and the U.S. Forest Service. There's even a Poplar Bluff Sports Hall of Fame, a nice touch of community pride.

🍴 ✐ & **Bonebrake Center of Nature and History** (573-729-3400; www .bonebrake.org), 601 N. Hickory, Salem, Mo. Situated on 12 acres, this property holds a spring-fed pond, stream, natural wetland area, and numerous walking paths. The centerpiece of this living-history museum is a restored, circa 1880 home. Visitors are free to stroll the nature paths at any time, and the home is open for viewing during planned activities. There are minimal charges for various programs held on the property.

🍴 ✐ **Dent County Museum** (573-729-6331; www.salemmo.com), 400 N. Pershing Ave., Salem, Mo. Open Memorial Day–Oct., Sun. 1–4. Admission is free, but donations are accepted. This 1895 Victorian home features three floors of goodies chronicling the history of the Ozarks. Inside you will find not only period furniture and decor, but also vintage clothing, antiques, glassware, and a huge loom. And if you don't see a trip to Philadelphia in your future, a reproduction of the Liberty Bell sits on the back porch of the home.

DENT COUNTY MUSEUM

🐾 ✎ ♿ **Current River Heritage Museum** (573-996-5298; http://doniphan missouri.org/the_current_river_heritage_museum_and_gift_shop), 101 Washington St., Doniphan, Mo. Open weekdays 9–4, Sat. 9–noon. Free admission. This museum is all about life on the river, both the way it was and the way it is. You'll soon learn the important role played by timber and logging operations along the banks of the Current and see how a life could be built via trapping, hunting, and fishing. Just a block from the museum is a restored 1880s pioneer homestead with log cabin, barn, and blacksmith shop.

🐾 ✎ ♿ **Margaret Harwell Art Museum** (573-686-8002; www.mham.org), 421 N. Main St., Poplar Bluff, Mo. Open Tues.–Fri. noon–4, Sat.–Sun. 1–4. Admission is free. Housed in a great old Victorian home, the Harwell Art Museum offers rotating exhibits for a wide array of local, regional, and national artists. There is a museum gift store on the premises, and you can arrange a tour by reservation.

HISTORIC SITES ✎ ♿ **Dillard Mill State Historic Site** (573-244-3120; http://mostateparks.com/park/dillard-mill-state-historic-site), 142 Dillard Mill Rd., Davisville, Mo. Open Mar.–Nov., Mon.–Sat. 10–4, Sun. noon–5; Dec.–Feb., Mon.–Sat 10–4, Sun. noon–4. Hard though it may be to believe, this old flour mill is still in working order. Many folks enjoy coming here for a picnic, and tours are readily available. The Dillard Mill is open year-round; admission is $4 for adults, $2.50 for ages 6–12. To find the mill, travel on SR 19 to the town of Cherryville. Turn left onto SR 49, and in 5 miles turn right to stay on SR 49. After 5 more miles, turn onto Dillard Mill Rd. and travel 1 mile.

🦐 🐾 ✎ ♿ **Fort Davidson State Historic Site** (573-546-3454; www.mostate parks.com/ftdavidson.htm), 118 E. Maple St., Pilot Knob, Mo. The Battle of Pilot Knob was one of the bloodiest Civil War battles of the Ozarks. On September 27, 1864, the South's General Sterling Price, with 12,000 men, attacked the 1,450 men holding Fort Davidson. More than 1,000 Confederate troops died in the assault (Fort Davidson had 9-foot earthen walls and a moat), and the Union forces escaped via a brilliant strategy. Muffling the wheels of their wagons and artillery, the troops snuck out on a stormy night. They also set a time-delay fuse and blew their powder reserves, thus keeping them from Rebel hands. Today this 77-acre site preserves the memory of both the battle and those who gave their lives. Also on-site is a visitors center with exhibits, a diorama of the battle, and an audiovisual presentation. Contrasting the violence of the past with the peace of the present, the grounds now hold a playground and picnic area.

✳ To Do

FOR FAMILIES ✎ ♿ **Bo's Hollow** (573-548-2429 or 1-877-313-8744; www .bohollow.com), 22516 Bo's Hollow Ln., Salem, Mo. Any place whose claim to fame is built upon beef jerky, Model A rides, and donkey petting is worth a look. Family created, owned, and operated, Bo's offers a re-created 1930s Ozark village complete with log cabin, outhouse, jail, and the obligatory "lost mine." You'll see Model A Fords in all stages of restoration, and when you tire of that you can pet the donkeys or feed the chickens. The gift shop is loaded with the aforementioned jerky (seven varieties at last count, including one specifically for

BONEBRAKE CENTER OF NATURE AND HISTORY IN SALEM

FORT DAVIDSON STATE HISTORIC SITE

dogs); I highly recommend the six-pepper version. However, the big draw here is a tour in one of the restored Model A's and a lunch of Ozark BBQ. Hours are Fri.–Sat. 10–4. The price for a 15-minute spin for $5. A brown-bag BBQ lunch is available for an additional $5. You might want to call ahead and make a reservation if you're traveling with a group. Tours of the Model A restoration barn are $30 for two people. Only one tour is offered per day

✒ �& **Bluff Falls Water Park & Entertainment Center** (573-776-7622; www .blufffalls.com), 2801 Cheshire Blvd., Poplar Bluff, Mo. While the water park section of this facility is only open while weather permits, the dry sections are open year-round (call ahead for exact days and hours). Built on 12 acres, Bluff Falls includes wave pools, water slides, go-carts, batting cages, miniature golf, an indoor arcade, a gift shop, and all the mandatory food concessions. Bluff Falls was in the process of changing their prices at the time of this writing, so call ahead if you want an exact quote.

GOLF ✒ �& ⅂ **Spring Creek Golf Club** (573-729-3080), Rolla Rd. off SR J, Salem, Mo. A semiprivate course located at the intersection of SR J and SR 322, Spring Creek is a par-36, nine-hole course open year-round. It's very affordable: Weekday prices begin at $10, and weekends start at $13. Cart rental runs $10–16. A clubhouse with TV, pool tables, shuffleboard, sandwiches, and a full bar is on-site.

Ozark Ridge Golf Course (573-686-8634; www.poplarbluff-mo.gov), 3045 Cravens Rd., Poplar Bluff, Mo. This 18-hole championship course features large greens, tree-lined fairways, and a number of tricky bunkers. On-site is a driving range and well-stocked pro shops. Fees with a cart are $18 and $28 weekdays (9 and 18 holes, respectively) and $20 and $31 on weekends and holidays. Walking fees are $11 and $14 during the week, and $13 and $17 on weekends and holidays.

HORSEBACK RIDING 🐾 🐎 **Coldwater Ranch** (573-226-3723; www.coldwater ranch.com), HCR 1, Eminence, Mo. Located just north of Eminence; turn east on SR 208 (off SR 19) and travel 1.2 miles. For those who wish to experience the Ozark hills and rivers via the back of a horse, Coldwater Ranch offers a variety of camping, lodging, and riding packages. A fully equipped lakeside cabin with two queen-sized beds begins at $89 for two people. For those with larger families, a line shack runs $178 for four people. RV and trailer sites (with electricity and water) are $17 per night, and if you bring your own horse, stalls are also $17 per night. Dogs and cats are welcome with prior approval and a $25 nonrefundable deposit. Hourly trail rides start at $42, including horse.

🐎 **Cross Country Trail Ride** (573-226-3492; www.crosscountrytrailride.com), P.O. Box 15, Eminence, MO 65466. If you never travel anywhere without your horse, and if you're a fan of bluegrass, Cross Country Trail Ride offers the best facility in an area known as the Trail Riding Capital of the United States. On SR 19 just 1 mile north of Eminence, on the banks of the Jacks Fork River, the facility offers camping on a 75-acre site, three meals a day, horse shows, major bluegrass and holiday festivals, and all the trail riding you could ever want. While you need to bring your own horse if you want to ride, many people from across America visit this establishment simply to enjoy the Ozarks, the Jacks Fork, and the food. The stunning facilities include a 63,000-square-foot indoor riding arena that's open 24 hours a day. Inside the arena you will find a western store, tack store, and restaurant. Nearly 3,000 horse stalls are available for rent at $15 per night, and plenty of hay and oats are available should you forget to bring your own. Those who wish to visit CCTR should call ahead for rules and regulations, specifically for state-required vaccination policies (for the horses, not the people).

HUNTING SayersBrook Bison Ranch and Lodge (1-888-854-4449; www .sayersbrook.com), 11820 Sayersbrook Rd., Potosi, Mo. For the price of $2,500 (two-person minimum) you can stalk the wily buffalo with your weapons of choice, whack it, and haul the big guy home. You will receive guidance from the ranch manager, and—just like the mountain men of old—you bring your own tent and sleep under the stars. Meat processing and taxidermy are not included in the price. However, if you'd like to go whole hog (or whole bull, as the case may be), you might opt for SayersBrook's Five-Star Trophy Hunt. This package (and though we can't get an exact price it appears to be upward of $10,000) includes three nights in the main lodge, meals prepared by a five-star chef, use of the sporting clay course and machine-gun range, personal guiding by the ranch's owner, the whacking of a buffalo, head mounting and hide tanning by a taxidermist, and all meat processing. If you've got the dough and always wanted a buff head on your wall, this is the trip for you. Those not into the whacking aspect can take a basic tour of the ranch if you've got a group of 20 or more ($12 adults, $6 ages 12 and younger), or enjoy a tour and delicious buffalo meal (these folks do great stuff with buffalo). Prices start at around $22 for students and $33 for adults.

✳ Wild Places

The Irish Wilderness (573-364-4621; www.fs.fed.us), Doniphan/Eleven Point Ranger District, 4 Confederate Ridge Rd., Doniphan, Mo. Just before the Civil War, Father John Hogan of St. Louis established a settlement for impoverished Irish immigrants deep in the Ozarks. Unfortunately for Father John and the Irish, the conflict between North and South got in the way. The Irish Wilderness became a haven for thieves and bushwhackers, both Blue and Gray, and the idea of utopia fell away. To this day it is not known what happened to the immigrants, and more than a few visitors to today's Irish Wilderness will attest that this section of the Mark Twain National Forest holds an eerie quality. Others will tell you it's chock-full of irritated ghosts with an Emerald Isle brogue and perhaps even an unnatural desire for a box of Lucky Charms. Such is the stuff of myth, but what is known for certain is that this 16,500-acre stretch of forest primeval is loaded with sinkholes, streams, caves, and an abundance of wildlife. It's located in Oregon County on the Eleven Point River. You can reach the Irish Wilderness from Doniphan by traveling 18 miles west on US 160. Turn north onto SR J and drive 7 miles to the Camp Five Pond Trailhead. This is the locale of one of three trailheads for the White Creek Trail.

Mark Twain National Forest (573-364-4621; www.fs.fed.us/r9/marktwain). Consisting of more than 1.5 million acres, the Mark Twain is a superb wilderness dotted with rivers, streams, and some of the largest natural springs in America. Broken into nine different ranger districts, the forest includes hundreds of miles of hiking trails, numerous scenic drives, seven congressionally designated wilderness areas, 40 campgrounds, and thousands of acres of primitive and semi-primitive areas. Literally hundreds of thousands of acres of the Mark Twain are located in close proximity to the Ozark National Scenic Riverways. For information or maps, contact the following district offices:

Salem District (573-729-6656), 1301 S. Main, Salem, Mo.

Doniphan/Eleven Point District (573-996-2153), 4 Confederate Ridge Rd., Doniphan, Mo.

Poplar Bluff District (573-785-1475), 1420 Maud St., Poplar Bluff, Mo.

Potosi/Fredericktown District (573-438-5427), SR 8 West, Potosi, Mo.

♣ ✐ **Indian Trail Conservation Area** (573-729-3182; http://mdc4.mdc.mo.gov /Applications/MOATLAS/AreaSummaryPage.aspx?txtAreaID=6201), Department of Conservation, P.O. Box 1128, Rolla, MO 65401. This 13,503-acre preserve is located off SR 19 between Salem and Steelville. While primarily forested, it is also the home of a 350-acre warm-water fish hatchery. Hunting can be fairly good here, but there are really no great fishing spots. Primitive camping is permitted, and an area has been set aside for campers and RVs.

✆ 🐾 **White River Trace Conservation Area** (573-368-2225; http://mdc4.mdc
.mo.gov/applications/moatlas/AreaSummaryPage.aspx?txtAreaID=8917). Located
8 miles west of Salem on SR H, this 2,044-acre site permits hunting, fishing,
camping (in designated areas), and hiking. Open fires are not allowed. This area
was purchased only about 30 years ago and used for an experimental planting of
endangered running buffalo clover. White River Trace is a getaway that is not
terribly rugged (about 80 percent of the land is open), making it perfect for
relaxed camping or picnics.

Roger Pryor Pioneer Backcountry (314-621-0239; www.pioneerforest.org
/pforest.php), P.O. Box 497, Salem, MO 65560. Part of the privately owned Pioneer Forest, this remote 61,000-acre area borders the Current River for 15 miles
to the southwest and is located in Shannon and Reynolds Counties off SR 19
north of Eminence, Mo. Pioneer Forest was established in 1951 to prove that
sustainable and commonsense forest management was possible in the Ozarks,
and today the Roger Pryor Backcountry is protected in part via a joint arrangement between the L-A-D Foundation and the Missouri Department of Natural
Resources. Fishing and hunting is permitted by anyone holding a Missouri
Department of Conservation license, 27 miles of fine trails are groomed for hiking, and the camping possibilities are endless.

🐟 🐾 ✆ ♿ **Peck Ranch Conservation Area** (417-256-7161; www.visitmo.com
/listing/contentguid/92c1deed-6f81-40d2-ae9a-ad197d286e16.aspx), SR H,
Winona, Mo. Located 8.5 miles west of Winona on SR H, the 23,048-acre Peck
Ranch is home to every kind of critter, from pileated woodpeckers to bobcats to
black bears, and full of caves, springs, creeks, and sinkholes. There's a great little
picnic spot known as Rocky Falls on the back side of Stegall Mountain. While it's
not on the ranch proper, it is still on the public lands of the Ozark Trail. The
hike is worth it for the chance to watch the waters of Rocky Creek drop 40 feet.
Hunting and hiking are very popular here, and there is a special zone set aside
specifically for disabled hunters. Primitive camping is permitted in certain areas,
but contact the District Ranger's office at the number above before dropping in
with your tent.

🐾 ✆ ♿ **Big Spring Conservation Area** (573-323-4236; www.nps.gov/ozar/plan
yourvisit/big-spring.htm), SR 103, Van Buren, Mo. The first white man to trip
across Big Spring was an obscure explorer with the unfortunate name of Pocahontas Randolph. That was in 1803, and because of the lack of roads and incredibly rough terrain, few other folks saw this spring until more than 100 years later.
Missouri made Big Spring a state park in 1925, and the National Park Service has
owned the site since 1971. Located 4 miles south of Van Buren, this is in fact one
of the largest springs in the world, pumping out more than 276 million gallons of
water each day. The area is open year-round, but campers should know that the
water (that would be drinking water, not the spring) is turned off Oct. 30–Apr. 15.
Viewing the spring is free, and 123 campsites are suitable for tents. The cost is
$17 per night for a regular spot, or $20 per night for one with electricity.

Red Maple Pond Natural Area (573-996-2153; http://mdc.mo.gov/discover
-nature/places-go/natural-areas/red-maple-pond), Doniphan/Eleven Point Ranger

District, 1104 Walnut, Doniphan, Mo. This is one of those off-the-beaten-path sights that is worth seeing simply because it's pretty. Consisting of nearly 100 acres located in a portion of the Mark Twain National Forest, this pond/swamp is in fact a strange sort of sinkhole surrounded by red maple trees and boasting of thick and unusual foliage. To find Red Maple Pond, take US 160 west from Doniphan to SR C. Head north on SR C for a little more than 10 miles and turn right onto FR 4912. When you reach the top of the hill you'll see a sign.

Greer Spring and Trail (573-996-2153; www.fs.fed.us/wildflowers/regions /eastern/GreerSpring/index.shtml), Doniphan/Eleven Point Ranger District, 1104 Walnut, Doniphan, Mo. Just a tad smaller than Big Spring (located on the Current River), Greer Spring shoots more than 220 million gallons of water per day into the Eleven Point River. This spring is so large that it actually doubles the flow of the Eleven Point. It's located off SR 19, roughly 20 miles north of Thayer. It's a bit of a walk to get back to the spring itself, but it's worth it.

🐾 ⚲ ♿ **Pulltite Spring** (573-323-4236; www.nps.gov/ozar/historyculture/pulltite .htm). Located on the Current River, 14 miles north of Eminence off SR EE, the 29-million-gallon-per-day Pulltite Spring got its name from the horse-drawn teams that had to "pull tight" on the reins while traversing a steep hill to the gristmill. Nearby is **Pulltite Campground,** which is open year-round (though the drinking water is turned off Oct. 1–Apr. 15). There are 55 campsites at Pulltite, but none with electrical or water hook-ups. The camping fee for a family site is $14–17 per night.

🎣 🐾 ⚲ ♿ **Alley Spring** (314-323-4236; www.nps.gov/ozar/historyculture/alley -mill.htm), Ozark Riverways, Van Buren, Mo. Possibly the most photographed spot in the Missouri Ozarks, Alley Spring can be found 5 miles west of Eminence on SR 106. The old red mill still stands proud, and the 81 million gallons of water that flow from the spring each day are typically of a gorgeous turquoise color. You can tour the gristmill Memorial Day–Labor Day, daily 9–4 (there is no charge), and a gift shop offers numerous books and postcards. The **Alley Spring Campground** is open year-round and offers 162 campsites at a price of $17 per night for non-electric and $20 for electric. There is no drinking water Oct. 1–Apr. 15. Also at Alley is the restored **Story's Creek Schoolhouse,** which is open May–Sept., Fri.–Sat. 1:30–4:30.

Devil's Well. If you travel south on SR 19 from Salem and then head 6 miles west on SR KK, you will see a sign for Devil's Well. Make sure you turn left onto this gravel road. What you'll discover is a sinkhole that opens into an underground lake the size of a football field. There's a viewing platform, and when you peer through the natural openings in the rocks you will see this subterranean swimming pool in all its glory.

Cave Spring. Really, the only way to see Cave Spring is when you're floating down the Current River. It is located on the river just about halfway between Akers Ferry and the Pulltite Campground, and you can paddle your canoe into it to the very spot where the spring rises. People have long liked to beach their canoes and picnic in this area. Also, if you remembered to bring your tackle, throwing in a line while floating directly over the spring may land you a fish or two.

ALLEY SPRING MILL

Akers Ferry. There are only a couple of old-time ferry operations still in existence in the U.S., and there's only one on the Ozark National Scenic Riverways. To reach it, travel 23 miles south of Salem on SR 19 and head south on SR K (when you're on SR K, make sure you're headed toward the town of Darien—otherwise you'll end up in Montauk State Park). Akers Ferry has been taking cars across the Current River for more than 50 years, and it was the way folks got from here to there when the Ozarks lacked bridges. The ferry is almost always open during daylight hours, and the cost is $4. Add a buck if you're pulling a trailer.

🐾 🎯 ✍ ♿ **Round Spring** (314-323-4236; www.nps.gov/ozar/planyourvisit/round
-spring-and-round-spring-cave.htm), Ozark Riverways, Van Buren, Mo. One of
the first state parks in Missouri (established in 1932, then integrated into the
Ozark National Scenic Riverways in 1972), Round Spring is located 13 miles
north of Eminence on SR 19. The spring rises up in a basin that was created by
the collapse of a cavern roof. Part of this cavern (see *Caves*) is open to the public
via National Park Service tours. Pumping 26 million gallons of water per day,
Round Spring also offers a campground with 60 sites. As with the other NPS
campgrounds on the Current River, the cost is $17–20 per night. Again, there is
no water Oct. 1–Apr. 15.

🐾 🎯 ✍ ♿ **Blue Spring** (314-323-4236; www.nps.gov/ozar/blue-spring.htm),
Ozark Riverways, Van Buren, Mo. If you travel 12 miles west of Eminence on
SR 106, you will trip across the prettiest spring in the Ozarks. It may not be the
biggest (69 million gallons per day), but it is for sure the bluest (hence the

name). Arising out of a very deep cave, this spring offers a color that has to be seen to be believed. For those who wish to sit a spell, Blue Spring offers a picnic area.

✎ **Rocky Falls Shut-In.** This seems to be a place most of the tourists miss. That's a shame, as it's quite an impressive little waterfall. I'm not talking Niagara Falls here. Instead, at Rocky, whitewater comes tumbling down, over, and around ancient stones into one of the best swimming holes you will find. If it's a hot day, this is the place to take the kids. There are picnic areas adjacent to the water, and aside from locals you will normally find Rocky to be relatively uncrowded. You'll find it approximately 9 miles southeast of Eminence on SR NN.

🐾 ⛺ ✎ ♿ **Two Rivers** (314-323-4236; www.nps.gov/ozar), Ozark National Scenic Riverways, Van Buren, Mo. As you could likely guess by its imaginative name, Two Rivers is the spot where two rivers come together. In this case the bodies of water in question are the Jacks Fork and the Current River. You can reach the spot—the site of an old ferry crossing—by traveling 8 miles east of Eminence on SR 106, turning left onto SR V, and then heading 3 miles farther. The pavement will end, and just a short hike downstream is where the ferry master used to ply his trade. Also at Two Rivers is a 19-site campground with basic spaces renting for $14 per night. Spaces with electricity go for $17 per night. You can camp free from Oct. 15–Apr. 15. There's no water or electric, but one of the restrooms usually works.

PARKS 🐾 ⛺ ✎ ♿ **Montauk State Park** (573-548-2201 or 573-548-2434; www.mostateparks.com/montauk.htm), R345 CR 6670, Salem, Mo. Sitting on the headwaters of the Current River (about 20 miles southwest of Salem), Montauk Park is noted for its exceptional trout fishing. On the opening day of trout season (Mar. 1–Oct. 31) anglers come from miles around, lining the banks in

MONTAUK FISH HATCHERY

anticipation of tight lines and ripped lips. The park, acquired in 1926, encompasses 1,353 acres and includes a gristmill, campground, motel, cabins, restaurant, store, and picnic areas. A fish hatchery (tours are available) managed by the Missouri Department of Conservation is on-site. The springs at Montauk pump more than 43 million gallons of water into the Current River every day, making it prime habitat for rainbow trout.

As at all state campgrounds, a basic campsite costs $13 per night. A campsite with electricity and water is $21 per night. When available, sites with water, sewer, and electricity are $26 per night. Camping is permitted year-round. The **Dorman L. Steelman Lodge** features a store, tackle, restaurant, ice cream, and campsite reservations and registration. The restaurant serves breakfast, lunch, and dinner; there are both motel rooms ($70–80) and cabins ($122–175).

🍴 🏠 ♂ ♿ **Taum Sauk Mountain State Park** (573-546-2450; www.mostateparks .com/taumsauk/trails.htm), 148 Taum Sauk Trail, Middlebrook, Mo. At 1,772 feet, Taum Sauk Mountain is the highest point in the state of Missouri. It's one of the oldest points as well, with rocks 1.5 billion years young. This is a stunning park, nearly 7,500 acres in size, and you cannot view sites such as Mina Sauk Falls without a sense of awe. Basic campsites are available for $13 per night, electric for $21, and whole-hog sites with water, sewer, and electricity for $26. You might want to remember that only tents are allowed here. Pop-ups and RVs are forbidden.

Many visitors choose Taum Sauk for its scenic hiking. A 33-mile stretch of the **Ozark Trail** (which, when completed, will stretch from near St. Louis all the way down to the Ozark Highlands Trail in Arkansas) runs through Taum Sauk, crossing numerous mountains, creeks, and even the east fork of the Black River. Eventually the trail leads into Johnson's Shut-Ins State Park, nearly 13 miles to the west. To reach Taum Sauk, at the town of Arcadia turn onto SR CC. In 5 miles you will reach the park entrance.

🍴 ♂ ♿ **Johnson's Shut-Ins State Park** (573-546-2450; http://mostateparks.com /park/johnsons-shut-ins-state-park), 148 Taum Sauk Trail, Middlebrook, Mo. Johnson's Shut-Ins is arguably the most popular state park in the Ozarks, due to its unique scenery, the incredible photo opportunities, and how much fun it is to slip around on smooth boulders coated with a spray of whitewater. The rocks are beyond old, the igneous remainders of ancient lava flows. As the waters of the east fork of the Black River enter this area, they meet the impenetrable rocks and become a maze. The waters twist and turn, leading to chutes and pools. The water knows not where to go, at times seeming to be trapped—hence the name Shut-Ins. At 8,549 acres, Shut-Ins also hosts a natural water slide.

If you're going to visit, I advise you get here early. The park is located approximately 13 miles west of the town of Graniteville on SR N. The day-use area holds only 100 cars—and this is a place nearly everyone seeks to visit. Camping, hiking, and swimming are allowed. The last is permitted only in the Shut-Ins area on the east fork of the Black River, and this is the place that can get crowded. To reach it, just take the 0.25-mile paved path that begins at the park office complex. Unlike most state parks in Missouri, pets are not permitted. The park suffered a major disaster in 2006, when a failure of the Taum Sauk reservoir resulted in a billion gallons of water hitting the Shut-Ins, but the state did a fantastic job of cleaning the place up and getting it reopened. Johnson's Shut-Ins has returned to its former glory, and you'll be doing yourself a disservice if you miss dropping by.

🐾 ✂ ♿ 🐾 **Grand Gulf State Park** (417-264-7600; http://mostateparks.com/park /grand-gulf-state-park), SR W, Thayer, Mo. This is the Missouri Ozarks' version of the Grand Canyon. The gulf is what remains of a cave system that collapsed 10,000 years ago (give or take a year). The "gulf" itself stretches for more than a mile between walls that are 130 feet high. It is spanned by a 250-foot natural bridge featuring a 75-foot-high opening. A creek drains into Grand Gulf, disappears, and then emerges to the surface 9 miles to the south at Mammoth Springs, Ark. (which spews out 8 or 9 million gallons of water per hour). Consisting of 322 acres, Grand Gulf is laced with trails and wheelchair-accessible overlooks that allow visitors to peer into the depths without taking a swan dive. To reach the park, head to the northwest on SR 19 at the town of Thayer. Turn right onto SR W, and you will head right into Grand Gulf.

LAKES Clearwater Lake (573-223-7777; www.swl.usace.army.mil/parks /clearwater), Army Corps of Engineers, Clearwater Project Office, RR 3, P.O. Box 3559-D, Piedmont, MO 63957. An Army Corps of Engineers project, Clearwater is a 16,000-acre lake that has retained much of its charm due to its lack of private boat docks. Five campgrounds can be found around the lake (two of those are on the banks of the Black River) and offer nine boat launch ramps, three swimming beaches, and seven playgrounds. In addition, the campsites feature grills, fire pits, tables, showers, and water. The fishing is often very good at Clearwater, particularly if you're after bass and catfish, but boating, skiing, hiking, and hunting on the surrounding corps-managed lands are equally popular. If you're looking for a lake that has avoided rampant overdevelopment, this would be it.

🐾 ✂ ♿ **Shawnee Mac Lakes** (573-739-3182; http://mdc4.mdc.mo.gov/Applications /MOATLAS/AreaSummaryPage.aspx?txtAreaID=7820), SR 411, Salem, Mo. Located 2 miles east of Salem on CR 41110, Shawnee Mac consists of two lakes (Turner Lake is 17 acres, Ziske Lake is 30 acres) sitting amid a total of 256 acres. This state conservation area is a popular spot for fishing (the bass bite particularly well here, though you can get some fair-sized catfish if you fish on the bottom and are patient), boating, camping, and hiking. There aren't any specific hiking trails at Shawnee Mac, but you can wander where you like. Also, the price is right (i.e., free), making the area a nice spot for a relaxed family picnic. Bring along your bow and arrow and make like Robin Hood on the free archery range.

🐾 ✂ ♿ **Fourche Lake** (573-364-4621; www.fs.fed.us/r9/forests/marktwain /ranger_districts/doniphan), Doniphan/Eleven Point Ranger District, 4 Confederate Ridge Rd., Doniphan, Mo. Located 15 miles west of Doniphan on US 160, then 2 miles farther on SR V, Fourche is a 49-acre lake perfect for a day of relaxed fishing. Full of bass and catfish, the lake also offers a boat ramp (though only electric motors are allowed). You'll also find picnic sites and restrooms.

☞ ఉ ❦ **Ripley Lake** (573-364-4621; www.fs.fed.us/r9/forests/marktwain/ranger
_districts/doniphan), Doniphan/Eleven Point Ranger District, 4 Confederate
Ridge Rd., Doniphan, Mo. Another good bass and catfish hole, the 29-acre Ripley Lake offers a boat ramp and 12 different picnic sites. To reach the lake, head
8 miles west of Doniphan on US 160. Turn north onto SR C and drive 1 mile,
eventually turning right onto FR 3240. Ripley Lake is about 1 mile ahead.

CAVES ☞ **Round Spring Cave** (573-858-3297; www.nps.gov/ozar/planyourvisit
/round-spring-and-round-spring-cave.htm), Ozark National Scenic Riverways,
National Park Service, P.O. Box 490, Van Buren, MO 63965. $5 adults, $2 kids.
Located on the Current River (roughly 18 miles north of Eminence on SR 19),
this cave is operated by the National Park Service. Lantern-light tours are
offered Memorial Day–Labor Day, Fri.–Sun. at 10 AM and 2 PM. Round Spring is
well worth the trip, in that this is a cave that remains largely in its natural state.
Keep in mind that this is a first-come, first-served affair, and each tour is limited
to 15 people. Arrive early, because no reservations are taken. Round Spring does
have 63 campsites, but the campground area closed in September 2011 for
repaving. Call ahead on this one. Fees are normally $14–17 for a standard tent
site, and $20 for a site with electricity.

✳ Lodging

BED & BREAKFASTS ☞ **Hawkins
House** (573-226-5944; http://hawkins
housebb.com), 210 Main St., Eminence, Mo. Built in 1913, this pretty
old home with its covered wraparound porch personifies the laid-
back atmosphere that is Eminence.
Four guest rooms are offered—
beginning at the $100-per-night
range—and a dessert is served every
afternoon. Kids are accepted, but pets
are not. There is, however, a nearby
kennel that can help accommodate
the needs of Fido and Spot.

☞ **Cottage Overnight Lodging**
(417-778-6497; www.cottageovernight
lodging.com), US 160 and SR 19,
Alton, Mo. If you happen to be floating the Eleven Point River or exploring the natural wonders in and around
Oregon County, these three cottages
in Alton have all the comforts of
home (two of them even include a
washer and dryer). They're clean,
quaint, and comfortable. The rental

price is just $65 per night for two peo-
ple, with $10 for each additional
guest, Apr.–Oct. Rates for two people
drop to $55 Nov.–Mar. Eleven Point
River Canoe Rental took over this
operation a few years back, so canoe
rental is on-site.

☞ ❦ ☞ ఉ **Big Spring Lodge and
Cabins** (573-323-4423; www.big
springlodgeandcabins.com), HCR 1,
P.O. Box 169, Van Buren, MO 63965.
You'll find more than just a huge vol-
ume of water in Big Spring Park.
You'll also discover trails, a restaurant,
and 14 rustic stone cabins dating from
the 1930s. Luckily for the traveler,
these great little getaways, built by the
Civilian Conservation Corps and on
the National Register of Historic
Places, are available for rent. Available
in a variety of sizes and prices
($80–120 per night), most include a
bathroom, shower, bed linens, two-
burner electric stove, sink, small
fridge, microwave, and coffeemaker.

Best of all, your dog is welcome for only $10 extra per night. The **Big Spring Dining Lodge** is also a must-see. It overlooks the spring itself and is open for business May–Oct.

✦ ♿ **River Birch Lane** (573-729-6965; www.riverbirchlane.us), RR 5, P.O. Box 454, Salem, MO 65560. If you want to stay in a hand-hewn stone home, then you'll like River Birch. Situated on 40 acres just outside Salem on SR 616 (call for directions), the home has been divided into an upper and lower suite with queen-sized bed, kitchen, bath, and porch. Breakfast is served in the owner's home, just a short walk away, where there is also a sitting room with comfortable chairs, a fire, and a piano. Kids under 12 stay free at River Birch, and there are several different pricings. A room alone is $70 per night; a room and full breakfast is $85. Additional guests are $15 and $20, respectively. This B&B is unique in that it offers reflexology classes and "Sherry's Herb Shack."

Plain and Fancy Bed and Breakfast (573-546-1182; www.plainfancy bb.com/index.html), 11178 SR 72, Ironton, Mo. A 1908 post-Victorian home, the Plain and Fancy is close to such sites as Elephant Rocks, Taum Sauk, and Johnson's Shut-Ins State Parks and the Black River. There are nice touches in this home, not the least of which are refurbished original pine and oak floors and a first-floor ceiling of patterned tin. You'll find a hot tub, wedding gazebo, creek, and patio with fire pit. Four suites are offered at Plain and Fancy. The Red Hat Suite ($140 per night) offers a sitting room, bedroom, private porch, cable TV with DVD, high-speed Internet, king-sized bed, and queen-sized sofa sleeper. Renting the Amish Room ($140) does not mean you are forced to wear black and rise at 4 AM to feed the chickens. Instead, you'll find a wealth of fine furniture handmade by the Amish, in addition to the same amenities found in the Red Hat Suite. Plus, I don't think the Amish provide the plush lounging robes offered by the innkeepers of this establishment (if they do, it's a well-kept secret). The Butterfly Room also rents for $140, and Scarlett's Hideaway (with its own fireplace) goes for $199. Smoking is permitted outside only, and you should call to inquire about children and pets. This establishment offers a huge variety of special packages.

RESORTS ✦ ♿ ☕ ☀ **Aguila Lodge** (573-226-5665; www.eminencelodge .com), HC 1, Box 17, Eminence, Mo. Right on the banks of the Jacks Fork, on Tom Akers Rd. near Eminence, the Aguila Lodge offers both a motel, cabins, and one particularly nice place on a high river bluff. The motel offers rooms from $65–104 per night. Cabins are very near the river and run from $94–109. The special "Bluff Side" cabin hangs above the Jacks Fork and includes a queen-sized bed, tables and chairs, cable TV, air-conditioning, shower and Jacuzzi, double sink, full kitchen, and much more. Pets are usually OK, but there's a nonrefundable charge of $60. Also at Aguila is the RS Steakhouse (see *Eating Out*) and a popular lounge with full bar.

✦ ♿ **River's Edge** (573-226-3233; www.rivers-edge.com), HCR 1, Box 11, Eminence, Mo. As mentioned earlier, around a decade back I came within a hair of purchasing an Eminence bed & breakfast just downriver from the River's Edge (instead I bought a beer and BBQ joint in the utterly heinous little village of Elk City, Idaho, thus losing much of both my shirt and my sanity, but luckily escaping with my life). River's Edge always struck me as having one of the nicest locations in the Ozarks, and many travelers like to come back year after year. A number of lodging options are possible. A large river cabin (sleeping up to 12) runs from a minimum of $99 per night in the off-season to a minimum of $389 Memorial Day–Labor Day. These cabins are completely equipped and access a private deck looking over the river. Motel rooms overlooking the river begin at $69 per night; suites start at $149. Smaller cabins, which include stone fireplaces, a great view, and all the electronic video goodies,

range from $69–149. Those with kids will appreciate River's Edge, as the folks here neither encourage nor permit crazy or alcoholic behavior. You can drink on the premises if you wish, just don't be stupid about it. Pets are not allowed, and smoking is permitted outside only. This is an establishment strongly dedicated to safe family fun.

Shady Lane Cabins (573-226-3893; www.shadylanecabins.com), P.O. Box 94, Eminence, MO 65466. Located right off SR 19 in Eminence, Shady Lane is but 150 yards or so from the banks of the Jacks Fork River. Nine RV sites with sewer, water, and electricity run $17 per night. Motel rooms, ranging from one to six beds, cost $35–160 per night. Small cabins begin at $39, and large cabins (with full kitchen and four queen-sized beds) are $99–199. If you have a large family or group and want some privacy,

RIVER'S EDGE RESORT

a modern home with barn and horse stalls can be rented (depending on the time of year) for $99–219. Kids are OK, but pets are not permitted in the private home, cabins, or motel rooms, and there's a $150 penalty if you try to sneak one in.

🐾 🦮 ♿ **Reed's Cabins** (573-548-2222; www.reedscabins.com), 9300 SR 19, Salem, Mo. A private enterprise located next door to Montauk State Park, Reed's offers 18 cabins with full kitchens. Prices begin at $72–87 per night, and pets are allowed with a $20-per-night surcharge (no pit bulls). An in-ground swimming pool and store are on-site. This latter offers not only a wide supply of grocery items, but also a deli, breakfast menu, and all sorts of fishing supplies from the likes of Bass Pro and White River Fly Tackle.

CANOE OUTFITTERS, CAMPING, AND RVS 🐾 🦮 ♿ Akers Ferry Canoe Rental and Campground

(1-800-333-5628 for Akers Ferry or 1-800-522-5736 for Jacks Fork; www.currentrivercanoe.com). More than 60 years old, this outfitter's operations include not only **Akers Ferry** and **Jason Place Campground** (23 miles south of Salem), but also **Jacks Fork Canoe Rental and Campground** in Eminence. The firm also rents canoes along the Current via **Round Springs Canoe Rental** and **Wild River Canoe Rental.** In other words, this outfitter covers the Current River nearly from start to finish. Canoe rentals begin at $22 per person per canoe per day. Camping rates start at $8 per night per person. Full RV hook-ups begin at $14 per hook-up per night. Cabin rentals range $90–110 per night. Jason Place fea-

tures a store, swimming pool, restaurant, and volleyball courts.

🦮 **Jadwin Canoe Rental** (1-800-937-4837; www.jadwincanoe.com), RR 1, Jadwin, Mo. Featuring canoes, kayaks, gas, groceries, and a campground, Jadwin (in business since 1966) offers trips ranging from several hours to several days. Rates for a one-day float begin at $44. Primitive camping rates are $3.80 per person per night, plus tax. Sites with electric hook-ups are $4.74 per night per person plus tax. Children 12 and younger may stay in the campground free.

For the **Pulltite, Alley Spring, Round Spring,** and **Two Rivers Campgrounds,** see *Wild Places.*

Harvey's Alley Spring Canoe Rental (573-226-3386; www.harveys alleyspring.com), HCR 3, Box 18, Eminence, Mo. Harvey's is located 6 miles west of Eminence on SR 106 (which is less than 0.5 mile from the Alley Spring Campground). With floats on both the Current and Jacks Fork, Harvey's has a fully equipped general store and a number of different rental options. Memorial Day–Labor Day, canoes begin at $45 per day, which includes hauling you and yours both to and from your campsite.

Windy's Canoe and Tube Rental (1-866-889-8177; www.windyscanoe.com), P.O. Box 151, Eminence, MO 65466. Just across the street from the River's Edge Resort, Windy's is perhaps the best-known float outfitter in Eminence. This place has been in business for about 50 years, always family owned and operated. The staff here knows the rivers, knows the best floats, has all the gear you could ever need, and offers floats ranging from three hours to seven days. Canoe and kayak rentals begin at $45 per day. If you'd prefer to go floating down the river on a big rubber inner tube, the cost is only $10. Of course, if you've got the financial wherewithal of Bill Gates, you could go whole hog and rent a canvas-covered tube for $15.

🛶 ♿ **Eminence Canoes, Cottages and Camp** (1-800-723-1387; www .eminencecanoescottagescamp.com), P.O. Box 548, Eminence, MO 65466. Located less than a mile north of Eminence on SR 19, this facility's name succinctly describes its offerings. Canoe and kayak rentals begin at $40 and $35 per day, while tube rentals are $15. A campsite without extras runs $7–9 per person per night, while one with water and electricity (for a tent) is $6. RV spaces with water, electricity, and A/C begin at $22. The campground does include hot showers, restrooms, a fire ring, and picnic table. A number of nice cottages can be rented in the $68–180 range (based on cottage type and number of guests). Amenities include air-conditioning/gas or electric heating, cable TV, VCR and free movies, bed and bath linens, dinnerware, cookware, coffeemaker and filters, toaster, refrigerator, stove with oven, microwave, and gas barbecue. Neither pets nor smoking are permitted.

🛶 ♿ **Silver Arrow Canoe Rental** (1-800-333-6040; www.silverarrowcanoe .com), 17685 S. SR 19, Salem, Mo. With headquarters roughly 17 miles south of Salem on SR 19, Silver Arrow offers float trips on the Current ranging 8–42 miles. Rates for a single canoe begin at $48 (there's a discount if you rent more than one), and kayaks begin at $25 per day. Campground rates begin at $5 per

person per night for a basic site. Add a buck for sites providing electricity. A large country cottage, capable of sleeping 10, is also available for rent. The charge for two people begins at $100 per night. The campground's amenities include tables, grills, electric hook-ups, and hot, pay showers. Best of all, this facility enforces "quiet hours" beginning at 11 PM.

Eleven Point River Canoe Rental (417-778-6497; www.11pointcanoe .com), RR 2, Box 2522, Alton, Mo. The Eleven Point River is usually less crowded than either the Jacks Fork or Current. It's also a bit deeper and offers some great fishing for wild rainbow trout, bass, and a variety of panfish. Eleven Point River Canoe Rental offers canoes starting at $38 per day and kayaks at $28 per day. If you wish (call for a quote on prices), you can also book for a guided fishing trip with experienced river pilots. This outfitter allows camping on its land, but you can also camp on gravel bars and riverbanks all along the Eleven Point.

🛶 **Running River Canoe Rental** (573-858-3371 or 1-800-226-6394; www.runningrivercanoe.com), Salem, Mo. Located on SR 19 about 25 miles south of Salem, Running River specializes in float trips down the Current. Prices begin at $46 a day, and trips can range from four hours to two or even three days. Should you wish to camp, the establishment has a small, private campground with store, restrooms, and showers. A basic campsite runs $5 per adult per night ($2 for kids). An electric site requires an additional $3, and a full RV spot (water, electricity, and sewer) is $25 per night for four people.

✳ Where to Eat

EATING OUT 🍴 ♿ 🍷 **Big Rock Candy Mountain** (417-932-4440 or 1-877-932-4440; www.bigrockcandy mtn.com), HC1, Box 570, Jadwin, Mo. Only 8 miles from Montauk State Park and half a mile from the Current River, Big Rock Candy Mountain offers a bar with occasional live entertainment (and this could be anything from a band to local folks pickin' and grinnin'), a simple menu, camping, cabins, and RV hook-ups. Another very local spot where nobody is a stranger, this is a nice little place to hang out and have a beer after a long day of floating. To reach Big Rock from Salem, go to Jadwin, turn right onto SR ZZ, and drive the 6.5 miles to Cedar Grove. Cross the bridges and turn right onto SR B. Drive half a mile to the top of the hill and you're there. Keep in mind that the grill is open to the public only from Memorial Day–Labor Day. The bar is open Mar.–Nov., Fri.–Sat. 6:30 PM–1:30 AM.

🍴 ♿ 🍷 **RS Steakhouse** (573-226-5665; www.eminencelodge.com), HC 1, Box 17, Eminence, Mo. Open Wed.–Sun. 5–9. Located at the Aguila Lodge in Eminence, the RS specializes in meat, particularly steaks and filet mignon. However, you can also choose plenty of burgers, sandwiches, and Ozark favorites. The 10-ounce filet and the 16-ounce T-bone are favorites, but grilled trout and the all-you-can-eat salad bar also bring in the crowds. The lounge can be a fairly hopping place in summer, with three pool tables, plenty of music, and a full bar. This place is sorta cool in that it promotes itself as a "smoking facility." RS claims it doesn't even have non-smoking areas. That's a refreshing change in this age of hypersensitivity and political correctness. I'd recommend them for that reason alone—just for having a well-formed Ozark stubborn streak—but the joint really does serves up a dandy plate of meat.

🍴 ♿ **Colton's Steak House & Grill** (573-686-3880; www.coltonssteak house.com), 2114 N. Westwood, Poplar Bluff, Mo. Colton's is part of a chain, but it's a small regional chain that offers some good value if you're traveling with the family. For lunch, you can try a fried catfish plate for $7.99, country-fried steak for $6.99, or a bacon cheeseburger for $6.99. For dinner, a variety of steaks range from $10.99–23.99, and a pretty standard seafood menu (more catfish, shrimp, salmon, and such) is all in the $12–15 realm. Actually, one of the tastiest things you can order from Colton's menu is the "tumbleweed" appetizer. That's a giant deep-fried blossomed onion served with dipping sauce. It's pretty good (especially for a chain outfit), and the price is $6.29.

✳ Entertainment

🍴 ♿ **Black River Coliseum** (573-686-8001; www.blackrivercoliseum .com), 301 S. Fifth St., Poplar Bluff, Mo. A 115,000-square-foot facility, the Black River Coliseum plays host to major concerts, rodeos, and other sporting events; family and trade shows; and conventions. Encompassing 5,000 concert seats, the building also houses an excellent fitness center. Call ahead or check the website for information on upcoming events and prices.

LIVE MUSIC 🍸 🍴 **Doniphan's Ozark Jamboree** (573-593-4348), downtown on Washington St., Doniphan, Mo. This is the sort of event that you're always wishing you could find, but never do. Every Friday and Saturday night the Doniphan locals meet up in a downtown location that formerly held a Ben Franklin store and make music. Groups are welcomed, or you can pick up the mike yourself and cut loose. You'll hear anything from bluegrass to gospel to classic country. There's no admission fee, though donations are accepted if you feel so inclined. All you have to do is be ready to have a good time.

❧ ✍ **Ozark Country Music** (573-729-4811), 202 N. Washington, Salem, Mo. Another authentic venue with tunes by the locals. Live music is performed every Fri. 7–10 in the Salem City Hall auditorium. Everyone is welcome to listen or dance, and again, the performers are paid by any donations you might wish to offer.

SPECTATOR SPORTS ✍ ♿ **Poplar Bluff Speedway** (573-785-8989; www.poplarbluffspeedway.com), 1989 Speedway Ln., Poplar Bluff, Mo. $8 adults, $5 ages 6–12. Races are held at this ⅜-mile, high-banked oval Mar.–Nov. Racing time is generally at 7:30 PM, with gates opening at 4:30. You'll find all the various classes here, everything from late model to super-street, from cruisers and hobby to open-wheel modified.

✳ Special Events

March 1 **Opening day of trout season** (573-548-2201 or 573-548-2434; www.mostateparks.com/montauk.htm), Montauk State Park, RR 5, Box 279, Salem, Mo. March 1 is the day when trout fishermen from all over the state (and parts unknown) descend on Montauk, wait for the bell to ring, and

flail the water to a creamy froth as they angle to hook that first trout of the year. It may be more fun to actually watch this event than to take part, as the word *crowded* becomes a vast understatement. Just sit back, take photos, and shake your head in wonder. You've never seen so many people trying so hard to catch the big one.

May **Upper Current River Pow Wow** (573-7274-3918; www.ucrpow wow.info), SR 72 and CR 2300, Salem, Mo. $3 adults, free for those 6 and younger. Taking place on Memorial Day weekend at the old Salem Middle School, the powwow features American Indian arts and crafts, jewelry, food, music, and much more. Of course there will be lots of drumming and dancing, and the event is open to the general public.

June–July **Cross Country Trail Rides Fourth of July** (573-226-3492; www.crosscountrytrailride.com), P.O. Box 15, Eminence, MO 65466. Drawing thousands of people and featuring big-name pickers, this annual bluegrass festival is an area favorite. Prices vary for the three-day event (including festival admission, camping, food, and a horse stall), but they basically run $210 for adults, $160 for kids 6–11, $80 for kids 3–5, and $15 for kids under 2. Located 1 mile north of Eminence, off SR 19.

July **Fourche Creek Bluegrass Festival** (1-800-457-3025), Fourche Creek Ranch west of Doniphan, Mo. in mid-July, This local bluegrass festival features a weekend of the best of local and regional players. Call ahead for information on camping and admission.

September **Labor Day Homecoming** (573-996-7980; www.ripleycounty

missouri.org), Doniphan, Mo. Held each Labor Day weekend, the affair includes a parade, antique-car show, games, and all types of vendor booths stocked full of arts, crafts, and calories of both the empty and nutritious kind.

October **Current River Days** (573-996-2212; www.ripleycountymissouri .org), Van Buren, Mo. Held on the first weekend of every October, Current River Days offers arts and crafts, artists, a beauty pageant, music and dancing, exhibits, a street dance, clogging, square dancing, food, and much more.

Naylor Pioneer Heritage Day (573-996-2212; www.ripleycountymissouri .org), downtown Naylor, Mo. Held the first Saturday of each October, this local festival features a themed parade, music, crafts, games, and exhibitions in such pioneer arts as soap making and blacksmithing. You might particularly enjoy the old-time dress contest and the decorated bicycle contest. You'd think there would also be an "old-time decorated bicycle in a dress contest," but perhaps such an oversight merely stems from the fact that no one has suggested the idea.

The Arkansas Ozarks

EUREKA SPRINGS AND
NORTHWEST ARKANSAS

THE WHITE AND THE BUFFALO

EUREKA SPRINGS AND NORTHWEST ARKANSAS

The plans of humans often differ from those of fate, with the latter having a tendency to win the day. There are those who, with seemingly zero effort, are rewarded with luck, fame, and riches. On the other hand, there are those who work and struggle for years only to see their well-planned ventures end with a fizzle rather than a boom. The theory applies to lands and regions as well as to individuals. All of us have seen the "unlucky corner" in any given town or city, the spot where business after business is doomed to failure no matter the quality of its goods or services. Just is prevalent is that little hole-in-the-wall, located far from traveled thoroughfares, a ma-and-pa operation that had the dumb luck to open in a spot that magically draws patrons and visitors from miles around.

Northwest Arkansas enjoys the sort of blessed luck reflected in the latter category. A hard and rugged country, albeit beautiful beyond words, it defies the imagination to think that this isolated region has consistently attracted guests and travelers from around the world. Even before the sun rose on the 20th century, Northwest Arkansas was the playground of the rich and famous. The attraction and accolades continue, in varied forms, to this day.

The first inhabitants of this region were the Bluff Dwellers, prehistoric people who resided in the bluffs and caves prevalent along Northwest Arkansas's many rivers. Later came the Osage, a proud and handsome tribe that was an offshoot of the Sioux. It is said that in 1541 the explorer Hernando de Soto traversed this land. He was followed by the likes of Marquette and Joliet, and innumerable French fur traders who filled their bellies with the bounty of the White River.

Skipping ahead, by 1856 local residents began to have a sense that the waters boiling from the ground in the Eureka Springs area (long regarded as holy by the Indians) had certain marketing potential. Eureka Springs went from nothing to a boomtown in just a few decades. By the 1890s the "healthful" water of Basin Spring was being shipped all over America (eat your heart out, Perrier). Eureka Springs boasted of graded, gas-lit streets, a municipal water system, modern sewage, stone sidewalks, parks, and even telephone service. Fires devastated the

Eureka Springs & Northwest Arkansas

© The Countryman Press

town on several occasions, and by the turn of the century most buildings were being constructed of locally quarried stone. The elite of the world came to take the healing water, receive pampering in the spas, enjoy more than 50 hotels (many world-class), and engage in a social whirl that rivaled anything found in New York or Boston. There were resorts such as Monte Ne, created by the eccentric silver baron William "Coin" Harvey. Built on 320 acres, Monte Ne was serviced by a railroad Harvey constructed. Visitors were picked up by gondolas at the train depot, then ferried by water to their rooms in one of two, 320-foot-long log cabins. Though business boomed for some years at Monte Ne, the advent of World War I saw the guest list dwindle. Harvey, deciding civilization was doomed, began construction of a pyramid that would serve as a time capsule of sorts, storing items from the present for future generations to discover. Alas, he ran out of money. The pyramid was never finished, and when Beaver Lake was built, Monte Ne sank beneath the waves. The luxurious resort made brief appearances in 1977 and 2006, when drought lowered the level of Beaver Lake and the ruins of Monte Ne rose to the surface. Contrary to Harvey's prediction, civilization still exists (more or less), and hundreds of thousands of visitors have descended on Beaver Lake to view the remains of a latter-day Atlantis. In 2011, the area remains popular with scuba divers.

A similar fate befell Eureka Springs. Though it was the hot spot of America for roughly 20 years, the combination of World War I and the Great Depression threw the town into a tailspin. A long fallow period followed, but by the 1960s Eureka Springs was beginning a resurgence. Today it has regained much of its past glory, with hotels, restaurants, shows, shopping, and a plethora of social events fueling the town's continuing success.

Just to the west of Eureka Springs, the towns of Fayetteville, Bentonville, Springdale, and Rogers have grown to the point that they seem one vast metropolis. Again, success just seems to ride the coattails of Northwest Arkansas. Bentonville is the birthplace and corporate home of Walmart, the world's largest retailer. Fayetteville is an eclectic, fun, and highly literate town that hosts the University of Arkansas. The entire area is loaded with live music and theater, museums, dining, and shopping of the sort you would not normally expect if you took to heart the media depictions of the state.

The region shows no signs of slowing down. Northwest Arkansas is geared toward the future. This should come as no surprise, as it has always been ahead of its time.

AREA CODES The majority of this section of Northwest Arkansas is located in the **479** area code. The exception is to the eastern edge of the area, such as Harrison, which falls under **870**.

GUIDANCE Luckily for travelers, the state of Arkansas provides one of the most complete, competent, and helpful tourism departments in the nation. For information on sites and events, contact the **Arkansas Department of Parks and Tourism** (501-682-7777 or 1-800-NATURAL; www.arkansas.com), 1 Capitol Mall, Little Rock, Ark.

When you wish to spend time in one of America's most unique towns, a place named as one of its Dozen Distinctive Destinations by the National Trust for Historic Preservation, make sure to check in with the **Greater Eureka Springs Chamber of Commerce** (1-800-638-7352; www.eurekasprings.com), 516 Village Circle Dr., Eureka Springs, Ark. Also, for information on the town of Rogers (and who could pass up a trip to the Daisy Airgun Museum?), contact the **Rogers/Lowell Area Chamber of Commerce** (479-636-1240 or 1-800-364-1240; www.rogerslowell.com), 317 W. Walnut St., Rogers, Ark. Yet another Arkansas stop that is increasingly rising in the estimation of national travelers is Fayetteville—a pretty town that not only boasts of great dining, music, and nightlife, but is also home of the University of Arkansas. Details on things to do and places to see can be obtained from the **Fayetteville Chamber of Commerce** (479-521-1710; www.fayettevillear.com), 123 W. Mountain St., Fayetteville, Ark.

If you are thinking of Walmart, then you're thinking of Bentonville, the hometown and global headquarters of the world's largest retailer. At the **Bentonville/Bella Vista Chamber of Commerce** (479-273-2841; www.bentonvillebella vistachamber.com), 200 E. Central St., Bentonville, Ark., you'll find there's much more going on than low prices. Just down the road a piece is Springdale, defined quite admirably by the **Springdale Chamber of Commerce** (479-872-2222; www.springdale.com), 202 W. Emma Ave., Springdale, Ark. Last but not least, on the far eastern side of this district you will discover the quaint little town of Harrison. The **Harrison Convention and Visitors Bureau** (1-888-283-2163; www.harrisonarkansas.org), P.O. Box 940, Harrison, AR 72601, can tell you everything you want to know. Or, drop by the **Harrison Chamber of Commerce** at 621 E. Rush St. in Harrison.

GETTING THERE *By car:* From the north, US 71 enters Arkansas from Missouri, and at Bentonville transforms into I-540. This major thoroughfare continues to travel south through Washington County (Springdale and Fayetteville) until it joins I-40. US 62 will take you on a drive from the western part of this region to the southeast, passing through Eureka Springs and Berryville until joining with US 65, which traverses Harrison as it continues on its journey to the south.

By air: Travel by air becomes simpler for Ozark visitors as they travel into Arkansas. **Northwest Arkansas Regional Airport** (479-205-1000; www.nwara .com), 1 Airport Blvd., Bentonville, Ark., is serviced by Allegiant, American Eagle, Continental, Delta, US Airways Express, and United. For even more flight opportunities, albeit requiring a bit more travel by car, you can fly to or from **Branson Airport** (1-888-359-2541; http://flybranson.com), 4000 Branson Airport Blvd., Hollister, Mo. This facility, which opened in May 2009, holds the distinction of being the only privately owned, privately operated, commercial service airport in the United States. The airport offers direct, nonstop flights to a number of cities and is serviced by AirTran, Frontier, and Branson Air Express. **Little Rock National Airport** (501-372-3439; www.lrn-airport.com), 1 Airport

Dr., Little Rock, Ark., is serviced by Delta, Southwest, American, American Eagle, United, Vision, Continental, and US Airways. At the far southwest edge of this region, **Fort Smith Regional Airport** (479-452-7000; www.fortsmithairport .com), 6700 McKennon Blvd., Fort Smith, Ark., is serviced by American Airlines and Delta.

MEDICAL EMERGENCIES **Northwest Medical Center of Bentonville** (479-553-1000; www.northwesthealth.com), 3000 Medical Center Pkwy., Bentonville, Ark. Part of the **Northwest Health** group, this hospital is one of the most modern in the Ozarks. Services include emergency care, surgery, neurosurgery, cardiac care, senior services, imaging, women's care, and obstetrics. Just to the south in Springdale, Northwest Health also operates the **Northwest Medical Center of Springdale** (479-751-5711), 609 W. Maple Ave., Springdale, Ark. Serving Washington County for more than five decades, the facility offers cardiac care, emergency services, surgery, a neonatal ICU, cancer care, and senior health services.

Mercy Health Center/St. Mary's Hospital (479-338-8000; www.mercy4u .com), 2710 Rife Medical Ln., Rogers, Ark. This 165-bed, not-for-profit health center features emergency care and a full menu of services ranging from cancer treatment and diagnostic imaging to outpatient care and a sleep disorder center.

Siloam Springs Memorial Hospital (479-524-4141; www.siloamsprings memorial.com), 205 E. Jefferson St., Siloam Springs, Ark., is a 73-bed not-for-profit acute care facility known for its primary care, internal medicine, surgical and obstetrical services, emergency care, and both in and outpatient clinics.

Washington Regional Medical Center (479-463-1000; www.wregional.com /washington-regional-medical-center), 3215 N. North Hills Blvd., Fayetteville, Ark. Washington Regional, founded in 2002, recently underwent a $64 million expansion. The 366-bed, acute care facility is also home to the Johnelle Hunt Women's Center and the Walker Heart Institute.

The Regency Hospital group operates facilities in Springdale and Fayetteville. **Regency Hospital of Northwest Arkansas** (479-713-7000; www.regency hospital.com), 1125 N. College Ave., Fayetteville, Ark., is a 25-bed, long-term acute care hospital designed to provide services to those people who have experienced catastrophic trauma, injury, or illness. **Regency Hospital of Springdale** (479-750-5800; www.regencyhospital.com), 609 W. Maple Ave., Springdale, Ark., is another 25-bed acute care facility located within Northwest Medical Center–Springdale.

North Arkansas Regional Health Center (870-414-4000; www.narmc.com), 620 N. Main St., Harrison, Ark., is a 174-bed hospital that employs a staff of more than 600. In operation for more than 50 years, this hospital can handle just about any ailment you could imagine.

Other area hospitals include the **Carroll Regional Medical Center** in Berryville and the **Eureka Springs Hospital** in Eureka Springs.

EXPLORING BY CAR Boston Mountains Scenic Loop. For many years US 71 was the only route through the Boston Mountains. This hallowed road, which travels from Louisiana to Iowa, takes on the attributes of a pretzel when it reaches Northwest Arkansas. It travels between I-40 to the south and Fayetteville to the north, and travelers could at one time count on twists, turns, hills, valleys, and a disconcerting amount of traffic. Take it from one who had occasion to travel this road while pulling a very large U-Haul trailer behind a very small Toyota (over-heating and in first gear all the way): In its glory days, US 71 was not for the faint of heart.

Today, though, while the twists, turns, hills, and valleys remain, traffic on US 71 is light-years away from the white-knuckle journey of the past. The main route through the Bostons is now I-540, which speeds along just a short distance to the west. The construction of that superhighway makes US 71 the perfect leisurely drive through the highest and some of the most scenic stretches of the Arkansas Ozarks. This is 42 miles of sheer beauty, and you'll find plenty of places to pull off, gawk at the scenery, and shoot photos.

The Boston Mountain Loop shows just how rugged this section of the Ozarks really is. Here, the mountains feel like mountains. To the south, just off I-40, the trip begins in the town of Alma. Drive north and you'll pass through the hamlets of Winslow and Mountainburg, experiencing jaw-dropping vistas, numerous farms, and the obligatory tiny motels common to small-town America. In Moun-tainburg, make sure to stop at the **Ozark Mountain Smokehouse** (www.ozark family.com). For about 60 years this place has been offering cured and smoked meats, homemade jams, jellies, pickles, and relish; it even has a "make-your-own-sandwich" bar. Throughout the trip you should keep your eyes peeled for more than a few off-the-beaten-path cafés, diners, gift shops, and antiques stores. Or just take your time and enjoy the views, rivers, creeks, and forests. Either way, you'll win.

EXPLORING BY FOOT Devil's Den Self-Guided Trail (479-761-3325; www .arkansasstateparks.com/devilsden), 11333 W. SR 74, West Fork, Ark. Located in **Devil's Den State Park,** this 1.5-mile trail can be a little strenuous in spots, but it will also provide a bird's-eye view of two fracture caves (the Devil's Den and the Devil's Icebox). Along the walk, which requires a couple of hours minimum, you'll come across numerous springs, waterfalls (in spring, at any rate), and ani-mals and plants galore. Unfortunately, as of April 2010, both caves were closed to the public. This move was supposedly to protect the bats from something called White-Nose Syndrome, which has killed a lot of the flying rats up in New England. Personally, I think that bats with "White-nose Syndrome" should go to rehab and deal with their obvious cocaine addiction. At any rate, the trailheads for this hike are just behind the Devil's Den State Park Visitor Center and by the SR 170 bridge at Lee Creek.

EXPLORING BY TROLLEY ❦ ✧ ♿ Eureka Springs Transit System (479-253-9572; www.eurekatrolley.org), 137 W. Van Buren, Eureka Springs, Ark.

Eureka Springs is a pain to walk, as there probably isn't a single flat spot in town. Here you only have two choices: up or down. Driving isn't much better; the streets wind this way and that, and it's easy to get lost. Luckily, the local transit system can solve all your problems. No smoke-belching buses here. Instead, you can explore the town via trolley car. The cars run all over town, are wheelchair accessible, and have seat belts and shoulder straps. Schedules are Nov.–Apr., Tues.–Sat. 9–5; May–Oct., Sun.–Fri. 9–6, Sat. 9–8. Rates are just $5 for an adult's all-day pass. A kid's pass (ages 7–11) is $1. A two-day pass is $8, and a one-ride pass is $3. You can also take a narrated trolley tour through the Eureka Springs Historic District at a cost of $10 for adults and $4.50 for kids under 12. The tours take place daily from late Apr.–Oct. Tours last just shy of an hour, and leave at 1 and 3.

EXPLORING BY RIVER Although the best portions of the best Arkansas Ozark rivers are covered in the next chapter, Northwest Arkansas does offer some opportunities for floating and fishing. The **West Fork of the Upper White River** starts south of Fayetteville (near Winslow), runs north through Fayetteville to Beaver Lake, then heads into Missouri to Table Rock Lake. From there it drops into Bull Shoals Lake and finally emerges as the famous **White River,** renowned for monster trout and land scams masterminded by an impeached president. While the West Fork isn't really a great floating river, it is floatable year-round. It offers few services, however, and you're probably going to need to bring your own canoe and shuttle yourself back and forth. If that doesn't bother you, this could be a peaceful little float largely absent of canoe traffic.

A more popular floating creek (when it's floatable—and during many dry summers it's not) is **War Eagle Creek.** This is the stretch of water to take if you're visiting in winter. The scenery is gorgeous, and at times you'll even come across

WAR EAGLE CREEK

a few rapids. War Eagle's headwaters are in the Ozark National Forest, and it flows in a generally northwestern direction through Withrow Springs State Park and on to Beaver Lake. If you're planning to both canoe and camp, Withrow is a good place to stop. It offers a couple of dozen campsites, restrooms, water, showers, electric hook-ups, and canoe rental.

The most popular body of water for canoeists and fishermen in Northwest Arkansas is the **Kings River.** Formed in the Boston Mountains of Madison County, the river flows more or less north, eventually joining with the White River, crossing the Missouri border, and dumping into Table Rock Lake. Roughly 90 miles from start to finish, the Kings is superb for both floating and fishing. Canoeists will encounter the occasional rapid, and deep pools make for some excellent bass and catfishing. The cats can get large, but the smallmouth bass population is the real draw. Don't think you'll only catch dinky fish here; it's not that unusual to take a lunker from the Kings. The best time to float this river— depending on rainfall, of course—is spring. That's also the best time to view the scenery, as the deep forests and bluffs that line the Kings are a sight to behold. A number of outfitters offer trips on the Kings River; you'll likely find the best choices in the Eureka Springs and Berryville areas.

✴ Towns and Villages

Bentonville, Ark. On Bentonville's downtown square stands a large statue of a Confederate soldier. Perhaps, though, the statue should be of Sam Walton,

BENTONVILLE'S CONFEDERATE WAR MEMORIAL

A EUREKA SPRINGS STREET SCENE

founder of Walmart. This is the home of the world's largest retailer, and the Walmart Visitor Center draws people from around the world. The center has been greatly expanded recently, and it now encompasses not only Sam's original five-and-ten store, but also an exhibit gallery and the Spark Café. One of the fastest growing towns in Arkansas (increasing in population from nearly 20,000 in 2000 to nearly 37,000 in 2011), Bentonville boasts beautiful old mansions and is just southwest of the Pea Ridge National Military Park. In September you won't want to miss the annual Harvest Music Festival.

Eureka Springs, Ark. Sometimes known as Little Switzerland, from the mid-1800s on, Eureka Springs was renowned for its "healing" waters. It's also renowned for being quirky, fun, and one of the steepest, hilliest towns in existence; the place is loaded with fine Victorian architecture, hotels, spas, restaurants, antiques, and much more. Just a few of the attractions here are the Turpentine Creek Wildlife Refuge (home to lions, tigers, leopards, and cougars), Opera in the Ozarks, and the seven-story sculpture, *Christ of the Ozarks.* An open-air trolley will show you the entire town (this is either a walking or trolley town; driving is not suggested), and thousands of people from around the world show up to see the outdoor theater presentation of *The Great Passion Play.* Because the area is less than an hour south of Branson, Mo., many visitors make sure to spend time in both places.

Fayetteville, Ark. There's no reason to worry if, when in Fayetteville, you happen to see folks walking around wearing plastic hog snouts. It's likely just football season, and the crowds are preparing for yet another Arkansas Razorbacks game. Fayetteville, with 77,142 residents, is home to the University of Arkansas. It was also home to former president Bill Clinton and his wife (you can take a tour of the small home where they were married) and is the site of the very hip Dickson Street, loaded with shops, restaurants, and live music. Devil's Den State Park is near Fayetteville, and for good fishing or floating it's hard to beat the White River.

Harrison, Ark. Just over the Missouri border (in fact, less than 70 miles south of Springfield, Mo.), Harrison is the seat of Boone County. Home to 13,183 residents, the site now occupied by Harrison was once home to a large Osage Indian village. That is, it was home to the Osage until around 1816. In that year the Cherokee tried to move in, and the Ozarks witnessed a full-fledged Indian war that lasted until both tribes were shipped off to Oklahoma. Harrison is a growing town that offers a host of activities and events for both locals and visitors. Two worth checking out are the Crawdad Days Festival in May and the annual Northwest Arkansas Bluegrass Festival in August.

Rogers, Ark. It's probably fair to say that what Walmart is to Bentonville, the Daisy BB Gun Factory is to Rogers. This was not always the case. For about 10 years, only Daisy's corporate offices and BB gun museum remained in town. The factory was moved to an underground facility near Neosho, Mo. However, Daisy is once again assembling its guns in Rogers, and all is well with the world. Rogers, with nearly 60,000 residents, is just minutes from the 30,000-acre Beaver Lake. It also has one of the coolest main streets in the country (2004 winner of the Great American Main Street Award).

Siloam Springs, Ark. Founded as a health resort in the 1880s, Siloam Springs is now an ever-growing town of nearly 15,000. A truly great event in Siloam is the annual **Dogwood Festival,** held the last weekend of every April. The party attracts more than 30,000 people, and you will not only view dogwood trees in full bloom, but also enjoy mountains of food and a wide variety of music. For a drive on the wild side, take a tour through the Wild Wilderness Safari, or just hop the state line into West Siloam Springs, Oklahoma, and try your luck at the Cherokee Casino. Both the casino and its restaurant are open 24 hours a day and offer live blackjack and more than 500 electronic gaming machines.

Springdale, Ark. People in Springdale probably don't care if you label their town a "fowl place," seeing as how it's the home of Tyson Foods. OK, bad puns notwithstanding, this progressive, small city of about 69,000 is home to more than 75 manufacturers, top-notch health care, and award-winning schools. Springdale is very close to Beaver Lake, and while in town you can hop on the Arkansas & Missouri Railroad for an up-close and personal tour of the Ozark hills. Also, because this is a town that loves its poultry, you won't want to miss **FeatherFest,** held every spring. It could be safely argued that nobody knows how to have a wing cook-off as well as the natives of Springdale.

MUSEUMS 🖼 ✎ ♿ **1875 Peel Mansion Museum & Heritage Gardens** (479-273-9664; www.peelmansion.org), 400 S. Walton Blvd., Bentonville, Ark. Open Tues.–Sat. 10–3. $5 adults, $2 ages 6–12. The home of a number of Benton County historical societies, the Peel Mansion is an Italianate structure built in 1875 by Confederate colonel Samuel West Peel. Authentic from top to bottom and loaded with period antiques, this living museum is the site of many events, tours, and Civil War re-enactments. The elaborate gardens feature roses, perennials, and native plants in keeping with the original 19th-century design. The gift shop and gatehouse of the mansion are found in the **Andy Lynch Log Cabin,** moved from a location near the original Battle of Pea Ridge to the Peel grounds. The mansion and grounds can be rented for private events and weddings.

✎ 🖼 ♿ ✳ **Crystal Bridges Museum of American Art** (479-418-5700; http://crystalbridges.org), 600 Museum Way, Bentonville, Ar. Mon. Thurs. Sat., Sun 11–6; Wed. and Fri. 11–9; Closed Tues. Free admission. Crystal Bridges is the first major institution dedicated solely to American art created in the past half century. Founded by Alice Walton, daughter of late Walmart creator Sam Walton, the 201,000 square-foot museum sits amidst 120 acres of land formerly owned by the Walton family. The Walton Family Foundation contributed $800 million to the museum as an endowment, and the free admission has been made possible via sponsorship by the Walmart corporation.

🖼 ✎ ♿ **Carroll County Heritage Center** (870-423-6312; www.rootsweb .ancestry.com/~arcchs/Tour/index.html), 403 Public Square, Berryville, Ark. Open Mon.–Fri. 9–4. Admission is $2 for adults and $1 for students. I tend to believe that the moonshine still is an almost integral part of any Ozark museum worth its salt. The CCHC has one, thus proving without doubt that it's a fine place. Located on the west side of the Berryville public square in the former courthouse, the center contains a wealth of artifacts from the early days of the county. Aside from the aforementioned still, another interesting item is the old-time funeral parlor (probably handy for those who imbibed too heavily from the still).

SAUNDERS MUSEUM

✿ ✎ ♿ **Saunders Museum** (870-423-2563; www.berryville.com/museum.html), 115 E. Madison, Berryville, Ark. Open Apr. 15–Nov. 1, Mon.–Sat. 10:30–5. $4 adults, $2 ages 6–12. If you like old guns, you'll like the Saunders Museum. They've a bunch of them here, the collection of the late Colonel D. B. Saunders, not to mention knives, antiques, and a variety of Victorian artifacts. You'll discover that the firearms are definitely not of the generic style, as some in the collection belonged to the likes of Wild Bill Hickok, Pancho Villa, and the notorious Jesse James. Also, take a gander at Sitting Bull's actual war bonnet.

✎ ♿ **Frog Fantasies Museum and Gift Shop** (479-253-7227; www.mizfrogs pad.com/frog_fantasies.htm), 151 Spring St., Eureka Springs, Ark. It's a fact that you can draw more flies with honey than you can with vinegar. It's also a fact that you can draw more frogs with flies than you can with vinegar. This is why vinegar has low self-esteem; its uses are relegated to making pickle brine and cleaning glass. At any rate, you'll find here a 7,000-piece collection of amphibians created from every material under the sun. There is also a gift shop where you can pick up all things froggy. After a tour in this establishment, you may have the urge to hit the closest restaurant and order frog legs.

✎ ♿ **Aviation Cadet Museum** (479-253-5008; www.aviationcadet.com), 542 CR 2073, Eureka Springs, Ark. Open Wed.–Sat. 10–6. $12 adults, $7 ages 5–12. Located at Silver Wings Field, this museum honors the fliers and support staff who have protected America's skies. All branches of service, including the U.S. Army Air Corps, Air Force, Navy, Marines, and Coast Guard, are represented. The permanent displays include not only a wealth of historic information but also an F-105 and an F-100.

✎ **Eureka Springs Historical Museum** (479-253-9417; www.eurekasprings historicalmuseum.org), 95 S. Main St., Eureka Springs, Ark. Open Mon.–Sat. 9:30–4, Sun. 11–4. The architecture of the **Calif House,** site of the Eureka Springs Historical Museum, is a perfect example of the classic homes to be found in this amazing little town. The structure was built in 1889 as a private residence, and since 1971 it has played host to the museum that celebrates the town (which, with its 62 separate springs, was at one time America's premier Victorian health spa town). There are three floors of artifacts to be viewed, as well as hands-on exhibits and a historic log cabin. Admission and tours vary, but in a good way. A self-guided tour is $5 for adults, $2.50 for kids. A tour by a costumed guide is $7 per person with a minimum of eight people (reservations required).

✎ ♿ **Arkansas Air Museum** (479-521-4947; www.arkairmuseum.org), 4290 S. School Ave., Fayetteville, Ark. Open Mon.–Fri. and Sun., 11–4:30, Sat. 10–4:30. $8 adults, $4 ages 6–12; $4 per person for a guided tour. A recommended stop by The History Channel, this museum features racing planes from the 1920s and '30s, as well as an early airliner and everything from Vietnam-era helicopters to Navy fighters. The displays rotate on a regular basis, as almost all of these craft are fully restored and are flown to different parts of the country from time to time. The museum also features engines, engineering, and a history of Arkansas aviation.

✏ ✒ **Clinton House Museum** (1-877-245-6445; www.clintonhousemuseum.org), 930 California Dr., Fayetteville, Ark. Generally open Mon.–Sat. 8:30–4:30. Admission is $5. Not only was this the first home of former President Bill Clinton and Secretary of State Hillary Clinton, but the couple were also married right in the living room. Inside, you'll find memorabilia of Bill Clinton's campaigns, a replica of Hillary's wedding dress, items on loan from the Clinton Museum in Little Rock, and of course a gift shop. For those with a hankering for all things Clinton, this is a must-stop. That said, it should be noted that the gift shop does not include any photos of Monica Lewinsky, Gennifer Flowers, or any of Bill's other girlfriends.

✒ ♿ **Headquarters House Museum and Garden** (479-521-2970; www.washco historicalsociety.org), 118 E. Dickson St., Fayetteville, Ark. It's a mystery how this 1853 Greek Revival home survived the Civil War. The Battle of Fayetteville took place in its front yard, and both Union and Confederate troops used it at one time or another as a headquarters. Tours are by appointment only. Prices vary, as a variety of tours and events are available.

✏ ✒ **Arkansas Country Doctor Museum** (479-824-4307; www.drmuseum .net), 109 N. Starr Ave., Lincoln, Ark. Open Wed.–Sat. 1–4. Admission is free, but they'll happily accept a donation. There are allegedly but two country doctor museums in America; this is one of them. Opened in 1994, this museum served as both a home and clinic to three different Lincoln doctors from 1936–1973; it's now both a tribute to country doctors everywhere and a historical record of the times. You'll see medical instruments, an antique horse and buggy, a vintage car, and loads of Ozarkian medical paraphernalia.

✏ ✒ ♿ **Daisy Airgun Museum** (479-986-6873; www.daisymuseum.com), 202 W. Walnut St., Rogers, Ark. Open Mon.–Sat. 9–5. Admission is free, but a donation of a couple bucks is expected. What started out in Michigan as the Plymouth Iron Windmill Company would become the best-known BB gun manufacturer in the world. Daisy, founded in 1895, sells what is for countless Americans their very first shooting iron. It's perhaps most famous for the Red Ryder model. The company left Rogers in the 1990s (guns were assembled in

DAISY AIRGUN MUSEUM

an underground plant at Neosho, Mo.), but the firm's manufacturing plant has happily returned to Rogers. Now, the assembly lines are running and Rogers is once again the home of cool BB and pellet ordnance. In the museum you will not only find the long and interesting history of Daisy, but also a collection of air guns that, believe it or not, date from the late 1600s. Of course there is also a Daisy gift shop, where you can pick up a few memories of your journey into BB gun history (and you don't even have to worry about shooting your eye out).

🔫 ♂ ♿ **Rogers Historical Museum** (479-621-1154; www.rogersarkansas.com /museum), 322 S. Second St., Rogers, Ark. Open Mon.–Sat. 10–5. Admission is free. One of the most respected museums in the state of Arkansas, the Rogers Historical Museum offers a tour of the **1895 Hawkins House,** re-created with authenticity to demonstrate how the average family lived at the turn of the last century. The First Street exhibit is a true-to-life rendition of an 1880s bank, barbershop, and general store in downtown Rogers. The Attic, a favorite with kids, features a replica of a Victorian-era attic; non-adults are allowed to try on old clothes, play with books and toys, crank an old phone, and type on a manual typewriter. The museum is loaded with countless items and offers a rotating selection of new and interesting presentations and exhibits.

🔫 ♂ ♿ **Shiloh Museum of Ozark History** (479-750-8165; www.shilohmuseum .org), 118 W. Johnson Ave., Springdale, Ark. Open Mon.–Sat. 10–5. Admission is free. This 21,000-square-foot facility, with beautiful grounds and six historical buildings, holds more than 100,000 pieces and more than 400,000 photographs. You could wander for days in this place and still not see everything. There is a huge collection of Indian and prehistoric artifacts, and eight other collections include everything from World War I items to household objects, furniture, tools, and much more. This museum tells the entire story of the Arkansas Ozark region.

CULTURAL SITES 🔫 ♂ ♿ **Walmart Visitor Center** (479-273-4000; http: //walmartstores.com/aboutus/287.aspx), 105 N. Main St., Bentonville, Ark. Open Mon.–Sat. 6:30 AM–9 PM, Sun. noon–5. You probably shouldn't go through Bentonville without stopping at old Sam Walton's original five-and-dime. This humble building—it recently went through an extensive remodeling—serves as a museum for the world's largest retailer and offers a history of the firm. Not only will you see Sam's original shop, you'll find a huge number of exhibits and a dandy café. Admission is free.

♂ ♿ **Blue Spring Heritage Center** (479-253-9244; www.bluespringheritage .com), US 62 West, Eureka Springs, Ark. Open Mar. 15–Thanksgiving, daily 9–6. $9.75 for adults, $6.50 for ages 6–17. Focusing heavily on modern impressions of the Indian culture, this heritage center offers a historic film, interactive classes, trails, an old mill site, and the remnants of a Bluff Dweller's cave. Used by the Osage Indians as a trading post, Blue Spring was also a stop for Cherokee forced to march the Trail of Tears in 1839. The spring itself, with its deep-blue lagoon, pumps out 38 million gallons of water per day.

♂ ♿ **Arts Center of the Ozarks** (479-751-5441; www.artscenteroftheozarks .org), 214 S. Main St., Springdale, Ark. A complete center for both the perform-

THE ORIGINAL WALMART

ing and visual arts, this center features classes, plays, an art gallery, and numerous musical events. The hours of the gallery itself are Mon.–Fri. 9–5, Sat. 9–3. For prices and times of performances, contact the box office.

🍴 ✏ ♿ **Christ of the Ozarks** (1-800-882-7529; www.greatpassionplay.com), 935 Passion Play Rd., Eureka Springs, Ark. Located on the site of *The Great Passion Play* (the most attended outdoor drama in the country). Visitors who take their religion literally might well assume from this statue that Jesus was really tall and really white. The huge sculpture of Christ, standing atop Magnetic Mountain, is more than 250 feet tall, weighs more than 2 million pounds, and was constructed of 24 layers of white mortar applied on a steel frame. Remarkably, sculptor Emmet Sullivan, who assisted in the creation of Mount Rushmore, fashioned the statue completely by hand. *Christ of the Ozarks* is open for viewing 24 hours a day, and admission is free.

HISTORIC SITES ✏ ♿ **Queen Anne Mansion** (479-363-6291; www.thequeenannemansion.com), 115 W. Van Buren St., Eureka Springs, Ark. This huge home, originally located in Carthage, Mo., was built in 1891. Apparently needing a change of locale, it was moved to Eureka Springs, piece by piece, over

CHRIST OF THE OZARKS

a two-year period ending in 1985. Featured in *Southern Living* magazine, the mansion boasts nearly $500,000 worth of antiques and is listed on the National Register of Historic Places. It's more than just a tourist site; you can hold your meetings, throw a party, or have your wedding here. A self-guided tour is $15, available Thurs.–Tues. noon–5:45. A docent-guided tour, available by reservation, is $25 and begins at 5.

❦ ✿ **Quigley's Castle** (479-253-8311; www.quigleyscastle.com), SR 23 South, Eureka Springs, Ark. Open for tours Apr.–Oct., Mon.–Wed. and Fri.–Sat. 8:30–5. Admission is $7 for adults; ages 14 and younger are admitted free. When Ozarkers take a notion to involve themselves in a project, they at times get carried away. This is the case with the home of the late Elise Quigley, whose love of rocks and flowers became a lifelong passion that was integrated into her dream home. The home, built in 1943 and on the National Register of Historic Places, features a perennial garden with more than 400 varieties of flowers, garden paths, birdbaths, and tropical plants (the last being inside the home, with some species stretching to the second story). A native of Italy, Elise Fiovanti married Albert Quigley during the Depression. He promised her a dream home and, good to his word, built the 32-window home with timber cut from their own property. It's a great story, and a labor of love you won't want to miss.

❦ ✿ ♿ **Thorncrown Chapel** (479-253-7401; www.thorncrown.com), 12968 US 62 West, Eureka Springs, Ark. According to architect E. Fay Jones, the style of the Thorncrown Chapel is "Ozark Gothic." With more than 6,000 square feet of glass and 425 windows, the chapel was constructed from all-organic materials and rises 48 feet high. As inspiration, Jones chose La Sainte-Chappelle in Paris, and his design won the 1981 American Institute of Architecture National Honor Award. Thorncrown ranked fourth on the AIA's list of the Top 10 Buildings of the 20th Century. A nondenominational chapel, Thorncrown is the premier location for weddings in Eureka Springs, and in fact has attracted happy couples from around the world. Also on the site is the **Thorncrown Worship Center,** also designed by Jones, which seats 300 and features a 75-foot glass steeple and a 50-foot-tall window. Thorncrown Chapel is open Apr.–Nov., 9–5; Mar. and Dec., 11–4 (closed Jan.–Feb.). Sunday services are held Apr.–Oct. at 9 and 11 AM. From November through the third week in December, a single service is held at 11 AM. There is no charge to tour the chapel and grounds, though donations are accepted. For information on wedding packages, call the Thorncrown directly at the number above.

❦ ✿ **War Eagle Mill** (1-866-492-7324; www.wareaglemill.com), 11045 War Eagle Rd., Rogers, Ark. Open daily 8:30–5. Located on the War Eagle River, the reconstructed mill is actually the fourth such structure to be built on the same spot. The first mill, dating from the 1830s, was washed out in a flood. The second mill, which went up in 1848, was burned by a Confederate general to prevent the Yankees from taking it. The third mill came to be in 1873, but again burned to the ground in 1924. In 1973 it was completely rebuilt by new owners. Today the 18-foot undershot waterwheel is the only operating type of its kind in the U.S. The stone buhr grinders are still milling, and more than 25 varieties of organically grown grains, cornmeals, flours, and buckwheats are offered for sale.

WAR EAGLE MILL

The mill is also loaded with crafts, and the gift shop features such items as graniteware dishes, kitchen items, knives, jams and jellies, and literally hundreds of other items. This is also the site of the renowned War Eagle Mill Crafts Show in early May and the War Eagle Mill Arts & Crafts Fair held each October. Last but not least, the mill is also home to the **Bean Palace Restaurant,** open for breakfast, lunch, and teatime.

Beaver Bridge. Located north of Eureka Springs on SR 187 is a 1949 suspension bridge (still in use) that you won't believe. Crossing the White River, Beaver Bridge is 554 feet in total length, with a main span of 312 feet. The bridge is only open to one-way traffic and has a weight limit of 10 tons. Bring the camera.

ZOOS ✍ ♿ **Turpentine Creek Exotic Wildlife Refuge** (479-253-5841; www.turpentinecreek.org), 239 Turpentine Creek Ln., Eureka Springs, Ark. Open daily 9–6 in summer, 9–5 in winter (closed Christmas). $15 adults, $10 kids and seniors. This refuge, dedicated to saving neglected or mistreated big cats and other critters, contains more than 100 lions, tigers, and leopards, not to mention bears, monkeys, deer, and birds. At this facility you can not only view the cats, but also sleep with them. This is not meant to imply that the animals are of limited virtue, but rather to inform that the refuge offers a variety of suites, tree-house dwellings, and a safari lodge. The RV park averages $25 per night. Most rooms are in the $150 per night range.

✍ ♿ **Wild Wilderness Drive-Thru Safari** (479-736-8383), 20923 Safari Rd., Gentry, Ark. Hours are 9–dusk daily. $10 adults, $8 kids. During the nearly 4-mile drive through this park you will encounter rhinos, hippos, giraffes, alligators, bears, and leopards. Situated on more than 400 acres, approximately 100 species either roam about freely or are contained behind high fences. In addition there are foot trails (no worries, they don't go into big-carnivore country) and a petting zoo. Keep in mind that credit cards are not accepted.

✳ To Do

FOR FAMILIES Also see *Zoos,* above.

✍ ♿ **Belle of the Ozarks** (479-253-6200; www.estc.net/belle), 354 CR 146, Eureka Springs, Ark. Cruising May–Oct. at 11 AM, 1 PM, and 3 PM, the *Belle* sets sail every day but Thurs. $20 adults, $8 for kids under 12. Travelers are taken on a 1¼-hour tour of Beaver Lake covering 60 miles of shoreline. The captain of the *Belle* narrates the excursion, pointing out such sites as a Bluff Dweller burial ground, Whitney Mountain, Whitehouse Bluffs, and Beaver Dam. If you choose and have a willing partner, you can even hold your wedding on the *Belle*.

✒ ♿ **Arkansas & Missouri Railroad** (479-751-8600 or 1-800-687-8600; www.amrailroad.com), 306 E. Emma St., Springdale, Ark. If you'd like to see the Ozarks the way travelers viewed them 100 years ago, climb aboard for this railway excursion. You'll enjoy riding in fully restored passenger cars with inlaid mahogany interiors, and the crew of the train will offer tidbits of info and trivia on the region. The Arkansas & Missouri features a wide variety of different trips. Travel the 134 miles round-trip from Springdale to Van Buren at prices ranging from $49–$79; enjoy the round-trip ride from Van Buren to Winslow for $35–$65; or ride the Fort Smith-to-Winslow train (70-mile round-trip) with seats ranging from $40–$72. You can ride in coach, an upgrade, or first class; the two latter options provide either lunch or snack bar and a souvenir photo. Departure times vary, and there are a variety of special foliage and holiday rides on the schedule. Reduced prices are offered for children.

✒ ♿ **Eureka Springs & North Arkansas Railway** (479-253-9263; www.esnarailway.com), 299 Main St., Eureka Springs, Ark. Open for regular excursions Apr.–Oct., the ESNA takes you back in time as you explore the Ozark hills from a 1940s diesel choo-choo. Not only can you ride this locomotive and listen to a historical presentation by the conductor, but you can also view a wealth of railroad artifacts and memorabilia. Excellent dinner service is available on the

THE ESNA RAILROAD

Eurekan Dining Car (see *Eating Out*). The trains take a 4.5-mile trek through the hills surrounding Eureka Springs, departing Tues.–Sat. at 10:30, noon, 2:30, and 4. Rates are $13.50 for adults, $6.75 for ages 4–10.

🐾 ⚭ ♿ **World's Largest Wind Chime** (479-981-3288), 381 SR 23 South, Eureka Springs, Ark. Erected by artist Ranaga Farbiarz in the parking lot of the **Celestial Windz Harmonic Bizaar,** this chime is roughly 32 feet long. The deepest-toned tube is 20 feet long, and the shortest, highest-pitched tube is 14 feet. The giant chime (and without doubt your neighbors would love you if you placed it a few feet from their bedroom window) is free for public viewing, but it will cost you $5 if you want to ring the thing. Hours are Fri. and Sun. noon–6, Sat. 10–6. Inside the store itself you'll find a huge selection of tuned musical wind chimes, bells, gongs, singing bowls, art glass and home decor, wind dervishes, spinners, beads, and sky chairs.

GOLF Golfing in Bella Vista, Ark. If you're truly a golf nut and plan to retire in Arkansas, you would be wise to check out Bella Vista. This place might not be for everyone, in that it's a master-planned, unincorporated community of nearly 25,482, which means lots of owner association rules. However, the golf courses here are excellent. The community's 18-hole courses include the **Bella Vista Country Club, Kingswood, Berksdsale, Highlands, Scotsdale,** and **Dogwood Hills.** Nine-hole courses are the **Brittany** and the **Branchwood.** Now, this is all well and good if you're a member or resident, but it appears that visitors to the area need to be sanctioned guests to play. For further information, you'll need to call 479-855-5079 and discuss rates and times with the powers that be.

🐾 **Razorback Park Golf Course** (479-443-5862; http://razorbackpark.com), 2514 W. Lori Dr., Fayetteville, Ark. An excellent value, this 18-hole course in Fayetteville is open to the public year-round. Greens fees are $20 if you walk your 18 holes, and $30 if you drive a cart. A new, lighted driving range offers a giant bucket of balls for $12.

🐾 **Stonebridge Meadows Golf Club** (479-571-3673; www.stonebridgemeadows .com), 3495 E. Goff Farms Rd., Fayetteville, Ark. Rated as one of the top 10 golf courses in the state by *Golf Digest* magazine, Stonebridge Meadows is an 18-hole public course with a 13-acre practice area and a clubhouse with snack bar. The greens fees cover everything (including cart, tees, and range balls) and range from $30 on weekday afternoons to $55 on weekends. Be prepared to hit long, for there are two 520-yard holes on this course. Stonebridge Meadows is open daily year-round.

The Creeks Golf Course (479-248-1000; http://creeksgolf.com/golf/proto /creeksgolf), 1499 S. Main St., Cave Springs, Ark. An 18-hole course convenient to both Springdale and Bentonville, The Creeks offers a full round of Mon.–Fri. golf for $22 per round walking ($33 with cart). Play on the weekends and the price is $29 ($42 with cart).

Big Sugar Golf Club (479-451-9550; www.bigsugargolfclub.com), 1101 Sugar Creek Rd., Pea Ridge, Ark. Open every day except Mon., this 18-hole championship course is part of the Big Sugar residential community, but it's open to the public. Fees for 18 holes and a full cart are $38 on weekdays and $48 on weekends. Also located within this pretty 165 acres is a practice range, putting green, pro shop, and food and beverage area.

❦ **Prairie Creek Country Club** (479-925-2114; www.realark.com/pc), 1585 Roundtree Dr., Rogers, Ark. A bargain of a course, Prairie Creek was rated the fourth best public course in Arkansas in 1996 by *Golf Digest*. Over the years more accolades have followed from the likes of *USA Today* and the *Arkansas Democrat-Gazette*. An 18-hole course, the upper nine of this course traverse the top of a ridge, while the bottom nine wind through a valley. An all-day greens fee (as many holes as you'd like to play) is $16 on weekdays and $18 on weekends. Cart rates are $20 for 18 holes, but walking is also allowed. Prairie Creek is open all year.

✳ Wild Places

❦ ✎ ❧ ❦ **Ozark National Forest** (479-964-7200; www.fs.fed.us/oonf/ozark). With 1.2 million acres, the Ozark National Forest offers literally anything the outdoorsperson could desire. From hiking, biking, and horseback riding to floating, kayaking, picnicking, and camping, this sprawling and rugged forest is a cavalcade of bluffs, mountains, rivers, and trees. The sections that lie within the region covered in this chapter begin roughly 25 miles south of Fayetteville off I-540. You can camp basically anywhere in the ONF for free if you don't mind roughing it. If you choose one of the established campgrounds that has a day-use area (and they are prevalent), the fee is generally $4 per car. Some areas offer cabins (historic) that generally run in the $30–100 per night range. Note that, if you're visiting in summer, Arkansas is noted for its ticks, chiggers, and snakes. Also, for campers and hikers, the black bear population is on the increase. Occasionally a traveler will stumble across one of these critters in the woods (it's rare—bears are shy by nature—but it does happen from time to time), and the old maxim regarding "an ounce of prevention" is a dandy policy to keep in mind. It's not a bad idea to carry pepper spray. Also, the tactic sometimes applied to grizzly bears (falling down and playing dead) does not work on black bears. They'll just think you're supper. Make plenty of noise, wave your arms, and try not to lose control of bodily functions while you look for a tree to climb.

Baker Prairie (www.naturalheritage.com/!userfiles/baker_prairie.pdf). Found within the city limits of Harrison, Baker Prairie is a 71-acre area co-managed by The Nature Conservancy and the Arkansas Natural Heritage Commission. Integrated in the Arkansas System of Natural Areas in 1991, this open field is a wonder of wildflowers and native grasses. It is, in fact, all that's left of this region's much-vaunted tallgrass prairie. Bring your camera, particularly in spring and summer. Such beauties as Indian paintbrush, shooting star, and pale purple cornflower are just a sample of the flora that abounds on this natural palette.

Pivot Rock and **Natural Bridge** (1-800-638-7352), 1708 Pivot Rd., Eureka Springs, Ark. Found right in Eureka Springs, back in the trees via a three-block walking trail, is Pivot Rock. This is one of those odd, natural geological formations that become the hallmark of many a family photo or visitors center post-card. If you're into odd rocks, take the short stroll and snap a picture or two. Let's just say the rock is unusually top heavy.

PARKS ✿ ✵ ✎ ♿ **Withrow Springs State Park** (479-559-2593; www.arkansas stateparks.com/withrowsprings), 33424 SR 23, Huntsville, Ark. Located about 5 miles north of Huntsville, this 732-acre park is best known for the waters that spill out of a small cave at the base of a steep bluff. The spring, named for Richard Withrow, who established the area's first gristmill on the site in 1832, spills into a deep and pretty pond. This is a peaceful place, with War Eagle Creek flowing along, heavy forests, and the aforementioned protective bluffs. Many folks enjoy tossing a line for catfish, bluegill, and bass at Withrow, but you can also take a canoe float, swim, hike, play a game of tennis, enjoy baseball and softball fields, or make like Robin Hood on the crossbow range. Camping at Withrow is facilitated by 30 nearly new sites with water, 50-amp electric, and sewer hook-ups ($28 per night). There are four different tent sites ($13), 16 sites with electricity and water ($14 per night), and five sites with electricity and water for tents only ($14 per night). The campgrounds also offer a bathhouse that is handicapped accessible.

✿ ✎ ♿ **Pea Ridge National Military Park** (479-451-8122; www.nps.gov/peri /index.htm), 15930 E. US 62, Pea Ridge, Ark. Set on 4,300 acres, Pea Ridge pays tribute to the strategically critical 1862 Civil War battle that forced Missouri to remain in the Union. On March 7–8 of that year, 16,000 Confederates unsuc-cessfully battled 10,250 Union troops, and the course of the War Between the States was changed forever. A complete visitors center is located at the park entry and features both an interesting museum and a movie titled *Thunder in the Ozarks*. Later, you can embark on a 7-mile, 10-stop, self-guided driving tour that will show the progress of the battle and the various events that transpired during those two days of blood and bullets. Also in the park is a hiking trail and backcountry horse trail. Pea Ridge is open May–Oct., daily 6 AM–9 PM; Nov.– Apr., daily 6–6. Visitors center hours are daily 8–5. Entrance fees are $5 per person for those ages 17–61, or $10 maximum per vehicle.

✿ ✵ ✎ ♿ **Prairie Grove Battlefield State Park** (479-846-2990; www.arkansas stateparks.com/prairiegrovebattlefield), 506 E. Douglas, Prairie Grove, Ark. The year 1862 was a nasty one in Arkansas, and on December 7, 2,700 soldiers lost their lives at the Battle of Prairie Grove. Revered by Confederate veterans and their families for decades after the battle, the site became a state park in 1971. Today, thanks to additional purchases of land, more than 750 acres of the origi-nal battlefield have been preserved. This has led to Prairie Grove being recog-nized as one of the best preserved Civil War battlefields in America. Coming here, you walk the ridges and valleys that witnessed the worst of the carnage, stroll along the 1-mile **Battlefield Trail,** or take a 6.5-mile driving tour. If you show up in December of an even-numbered year, you will witness one of the best battle re-enactments known to humankind. Also on the site are a museum, a pre–Civil War Ozark village, and plenty of picnic tables. Admission to the park is free, but if you wish to explore the museum and take a self-guided tour of the buildings, the charge is $3 for adults, $2 for ages 6–12. Even better, opt for the museum and guided tour, which is only $5 for adults, $3 for kids.

🦫 🐾 ✈ ♿ **Devil's Den State Park** (479-761-3325; www.arkansasstateparks.com /devilsden), 11333 W. SR 74, West Fork, Ark. At 2,500 acres, Devil's Den is known for its scenery, rustic cabins, and 8-acre lake. You'll find plenty of campsites as well as hiking, biking, and horse trails, not to mention a park café, store, and swimming pool. The stone cabins, built in the 1930s by the Civilian Conservation Corps, have all been modernized and come with full kitchen, heating and air-conditioning, and stone fireplace. Options and rates range from a studio cabin at $105 per night to a three-bedroom, two-bath version for $180 per night. There are 97 campsites in the park, and they run the gamut from primitive tent sites ($10) to RV spots with electricity, sewer, and water ($28). If you brought along a horse, a campsite for you and Trigger is $14. If playing in the water is your specialty, you can rent canoes, kayaks, pedal boats, and water bikes. For fishing, just make sure you have an Arkansas license. Caving used to be popular at Devil's Den (hence the name), but **Devil's Den Cave** and **Icebox Cave** are closed to the public because the resident bats are afflicted with a condition known as White-Nose Syndrome, which researchers recently determined is caused by a fungus. It is safe to assume that the caves will be closed until the fungus is either controlled or eradicated. More than 20 miles of well-marked horse-riding trails traverse the Lee Creek Valley where Devil's Den is situated. If you're in good shape, the 15-mile **Butterfield Hiking Trail** should provide all the ambulatory amusement your legs can stand. Just remember that, just as in the Missouri Ozarks, the ticks and bugs can get pretty vicious in spring and summer.

🦫 🐾 ✈ ♿ **Hobbs State Park–Conservation Area** (479-789-5000; www .arkansasstateparks.com/hobbsstateparkconservationarea), 20201 E. SR 12, Rogers, Ark. Comprising 11,964 acres along the south shore of 28,370-acre Beaver Lake, Hobbs is located roughly 10 miles east of Rogers on SR 12 and is always undergoing further development. Visitors to this park will discover a number of hiking trails, a 17-mile multiuse trail, a public shooting range, and seasonal hunting. One of the best trails is the handicapped-accessible **Van Winkle,** a half-mile trek that passes under SR 12 via a large tunnel and leads hikers to the site of the historic Van Winkle lumber mill and home. The centerpiece of the park is a $4.5 million, 17,531-square-foot visitors center that was completed in 2009. A few primitive campsites are available. Interpretive boat tours run $10 per person for adults, $5 per child. An interpretive kayak or canoe tour is $12 for each adult, and $6 for each child.

LAKES ✈ 🦫 ♿ 🐾 **Beaver Lake** (479-636-1210; www.swl.usace.army.mil/parks /beaver), 2260 N. Second St., Rogers, Ark. With 28,370 acres and 487 acres of shoreline, Beaver Lake, the headwaters of the White River, is one of the most popular recreation areas in Northwest Arkansas. Spring and fall are particularly gorgeous, as the area is loaded with redbud and dogwood trees. Fall is equally colorful, offering a cornucopia of colors. Add in a plethora of limestone bluffs, caves, and opportunities for fun on the water, and you have the makings of a

BEAVER LAKE DAM

perfect getaway. Managed by the Army Corps of Engineers, Beaver was completed in 1966. The corps has provided 12 developed parks featuring 650 individual campsites available (with electricity) for $16–$17 per night. The campgrounds are modern, with paved roads, fresh water, showers, restrooms, dump stations, and fire rings. Within seven of the parks are full-service marinas with gas, groceries, guides, and boat rental. Numerous private outfitters surround Beaver Lake, and the body of water is known for some fine bass fishing. However, those who want a real thrill should try to hook some of the monster catfish and hideously ugly spoonbill that inhabit the depths.

🐾 🌿 🏕 **Lake Leatherwood** (479-253-2866; www.arkansas.com/lakes-rivers /lake/id/42), 532 Spring St., Eureka Springs, Ark. A spring-fed body of water, the 85-acre Lake Leatherwood lies within the midst of the 1,600-acre Lake Leatherwood Park. Trails for hiking and mountain biking abound, and the lake itself is popular with local fishermen. Keep your eyes open and you are likely to spy plenty of herons, wild turkeys, and bald eagles.

CAVES 🌿 **Cosmic Cavern** (870-749-2298; www.cosmiccavern.com), 6386 SR 21 North, Berryville, Ark. Contrary to popular belief, the blind trout found in the subterranean lakes at Cosmic Cavern do not wear dark glasses or require the assistance of Seeing Eye bass. Still, both the sight-impaired fish and the cave itself are worth a look. This is the site of Arkansas's largest underground lake (in fact, there are two lakes), and the 1¼-hour tour leads through a number of rooms and across a rock bridge. You can even pan for gems in an authentic sluice if you wish, and to keep everything requires only a $5.50 surcharge. As a rule the cave is open 9–5 during the spring, fall, and winter. Hours from Memorial Day–Labor

Day are 9–6. Tours begin every 25 minutes during the summer and every 45 minutes the rest of the year. Tour fees are $14 for adults, $7.50 for ages 5–12.

✍ ☀ **War Eagle Cavern on Beaver Lake** (479-789-2909; www.wareaglecavern .com), 21494 Cavern Rd., Rogers, Ark. General hours of operation are Mon.– Sat. 9:30–5, Sun. noon–5. When you see the entrance to this cave, located in a box canyon, you will feel you are about to descend to the farthest depths of the earth. Open since 1978, War Eagle Cavern remains a very natural cave, and a wide, smooth walkway follows a creek that runs inside this subterranean attraction. If you're wondering about the difficulty of the trek, a person of average condition will have no problems. Plus, you will encounter no stairs. The guided public tour takes about an hour (roughly a half mile). Tours leave on the hour and half hour, and if your dog is on a leash, he can come along, too. The cost is $12.95 for adults, $7.50 for ages 4–11. A more extensive journey, the Spelunker Tour, requires a couple of hours and heads much deeper into the cave. This excursion is by reservation only and has a few restrictions. First off, you must be at least 4 feet tall and have a minimum group of four people. You'll see all sorts of strange formations and literally thousands and thousands of bats. Oh, lest you think this is a clean tour, please be advised that you will get both wet and muddy. Spelunkers must sign a release, wear appropriate clothes (jeans, a jacket, gloves, knee pads, and hiking shoes), and carry a couple of flashlights. The Spelunker Tour runs $50 per person and is available by reservation only.

✍ **Old Spanish Treasure Cave** (479-787-6508; www.spanish-treasure-cave .com), 14290 N. SR 59, Sulphur Springs, Ark. As the story goes (and keep in mind that most Ozark stories should be taken with portions of salt ranging from a grain to a pound), about 300 years back Spanish conquistadores buried a $40 million treasure in this cave. Now, there have been a few helmets, coins, and pieces of armor found in this cavern, so who knows? The only certain fact is that more than a few people spent years looking for the booty, and it has yet to turn up. A one-hour guided tour takes you deep into the earth at a price of $12 for adults and $6 for kids. Mar.–mid-Sept., the cave opens daily at 9 and the last tour leaves at 6. Additional hours during the Halloween and holiday seasons.

✍ **Mystic Caverns** (1-888-743-1739; www.mysticcaverns.com), SR 7 South, Harrison, Ark. Open Mar.–Dec., Mon.–Sat. at 9 AM. Last tour leaves at 5 Mar.–May and Sept.–Oct.; 5:30 June–Aug.; and 4 Nov.–Dec. $14.99 for adults, $7.99 for kids 4–12. Although it's had many names over the years, Mystic Caverns was once part of the often maligned, now defunct amusement park known as Dogpatch USA. Now, I happened to like Dogpatch USA when I was a kid (good rides and amusing Lil' Abner characters running to and fro), and thus can only state that detractors of the site were seriously humor impaired. Sadly, Dogpatch overestimated the draw of a hillbilly-based funland, and is now grown up in weeds. On the bright side, Mystic Caverns is still going strong. In fact, a tour of the cavern actually takes you into two separate caves. Mystic Caverns itself has all the normal formations you expect in a show cave, but the large **Crystal Dome Caverns** (discovered 100 years after Mystic) really do live up to their billing. You'll see an eight-story dome and some great crystal formations. It's a pretty place, a tad better than your average hole in the ground.

✳ Lodging

BED & BREAKFASTS There are so many lodging options in Eureka Springs—hotels, motels, luxury log cabins, and B&Bs—that space limitations do not allow an adequate description of them all. For an excellent list, you should check out the **Alliance of Better Bed and Breakfasts** website (www.allianceofbetter bandbs.com). Also, for a complete list of accommodations, go to the state of Arkansas's Eureka Springs lodging site (www.eurekasprings.com/lodging /index.html). As you will see, the possibilities are nearly endless.

❧ **Beaver Town Inn and General Store** (479-253-4060; www.beaver towninn.com), 102 SR 187, Beaver, Ark. Located at the foot of the Beaver Bridge, the Beaver Town Inn offers five different rooms and suites located above the Beaver Town General Store. This is a beautiful place, a local hangout since the day it was built as a trading post in 1901. Now completely restored and refurbished, this native limestone inn's rooms run $85–120 per night. Just about 10 minutes from Eureka Springs, this is a nice choice for those who wish to tour Eureka during the day and escape to some peace and quiet in the evening. Nonsmoking rooms are available, and kids are OK.

❧ **11 Singleton House** (1-800-833-3394; www.singletonhouse.com), 11 Singleton St., Eureka Springs, Ark. There's just something about this place that reminds me of the Hansel and Gretel gingerbread house. With its beautiful gardens and a location tucked back into a hill just a block from the Eureka Springs Historic District, the 1890 Victorian is colorful, fun, and loaded with antiques and trails. Five guest rooms each feature a private bath, with one option further providing a Jacuzzi for two and a treetop balcony. Some rooms include two beds, and one will sleep up to five. Amenities include cable TV, air-conditioning, rockers on the porch, hot tea and cocoa, and a gourmet breakfast. Also on the property, if you want more privacy, is the **Gardener's Cottage,** with fireplace, whirlpool tub, and full kitchen. Rates for the guest rooms range $95–150; the Gardener's Cottage, $125–165. Pets and smoking indoors are not permitted, but kids are OK if they are housebroken and well behaved.

❧ ♿ **Turpentine Creek Safari Lodging** (formerly Call of the Wild Bed and Breakfast) (479-253-5841; www.turpentinecreek.org/b&b.htm), 239 Turpentine Creek Ln., Eureka Springs, Ark. The proprietors refer to this establishment on the Turpentine Creek Wildlife Refuge not as "bed and breakfast," but rather as "bed and big cats." There are several lodging options, all unique. The first is the Tree House, which sleeps two to four and is modeled after similar lodgings in Africa. Yes, you'll be able to see the big cats (as in lions and tigers) right from your window. The Tree House has a kitchen, bath with shower, refrigerator, microwave, double futon on the main floor, and loft with two double-futon pallets. You'll receive a continental breakfast and have unlimited admission to the refuge during daylight hours. The cost for two is $150 per night. Other accommodations include the Blue Room and Green Room at $150 per night. The Zulu Safari lodges are (yup . . . you guessed it) $150 per night. Last but not least, an RV park is located outside the main compound and offers 10 spaces with 20-amp service, water, sewage, a picnic table, and a grill. Rates are $25 per day.

The Benton Place (479-253-7602 or 1-866-253-7602; www.bentonplace .com), 32 Benton St., Eureka Springs, Ark. With three Victorian suites ranging $135–155 per night, the Benton Place is known for its beautiful rooms, rock formations, gazebo, and intimate atmosphere. Two of the suites include a full kitchen, and all three offer such amenities as microwave, cable TV, inhouse massage by appointment, private dining area, breakfast, and Jacuzzi for two. This establishment is geared to couples only, and a smoking area is provided. According to the *2004 Book of Lists* published by *Inn Traveler* magazine, Benton Place ranks as the sixth most intimate inn in America.

✔ ♿ **Johnson House** (479-756-1095; www.innsite.com/inns/A000413.html), 5371 S. 48th St., Johnson, Ark. This two-story home was built in 1882 by one Jacob Q. Johnson. Constructed of brick and featuring impressive 12-foot ceilings and 8-foot windows, not to mention an elaborate spiral staircase, the home is loaded with antiques. Quite a few of these are apparently heirlooms of the Johnson family. Check with the owner on rates, as they sometimes vary. In a general range, expect to pay at least $70 per night. The nearly 2-acre grounds offer games such as horseshoes and croquet, and a full breakfast will start your day off on the right note. The little town of Johnson is located about halfway between Springdale and Fayetteville, and is convenient to the nightlife and shopping of both. Pets are forbidden, but kids are OK with prior approval. A designated smoking area is provided, and the home is partially handicapped accessible.

♣ **Maguire House Bed and Breakfast** (501-442-2122; www.arkansas.com /attractions/attr_detail.aspx?id=90817 &r=Ozarks&city=Elkins), 19154 SR 74, Elkins, Ark. Loaded with history, Maguire House is an antebellum home located just a few miles west of Fayetteville on SR 74. Built by state representative Hosea Maguire in the late 1800s, this inn is what a B&B should be. It's comfortable in the sense that both the first glance—that of an old, white, family home—and the cozy interior seem livable. Too many B&Bs make the mistake of feeling like a museum or art gallery, as if you shouldn't sit on the priceless antiques. Not this one. Set on more than 4 acres, Maguire House offers four bedrooms and two bathrooms upstairs. Guests are free to wander the orchard, check out the vegetable garden, watch the chickens, or just kick back in the parlor or gazebo. One great draw of this establishment is the food: Eggs are fresh from the resident hens, and the bread is homemade. Fruits and vegetables come straight from the orchard or garden. If your idea of breakfast is ham, fried potatoes, a three-cheese omelet, and lots of toast and homemade jam, this is the spot for you. Call ahead for the latest rates. Small weddings are encouraged. Leave the pup at home, check on bringing kids, and don't smoke.

♿ **Apple Crest Inn Bed and Breakfast** (479-736-8201 or 1-888-APP-LEUS), 12758 S. SR 59, Gentry, Ark. With its brown roof, splashes of blue trim, huge chimney, turrets, and gables, the Apple Crest looks a bit like a gingerbread house that's been hitting the gym. Situated on 5 acres, this Victorian home and carriage house has its own claim to history, having first been deeded by President Rutherford B. Hayes. Call ahead for the most current rates, but keep in mind that Apple Crest was voted Best Bed and Breakfast in Northwest Arkansas by the readers of *CitiScapes* magazine. Six guest rooms are decorated with antiques and collectible items, and guests are met with chocolate truffles. There's a hot tub outdoors, a gourmet breakfast, and plenty of books, games, and a TV in the common room. One room is handicapped accessible. There is no smoking inside the home, and as usual, it is wise to check with the innkeepers before you show up with a minivan full of children.

RESORTS ✐ ⴠ **Hotel Seville** (870-741-2321; www.hotelseville.com), 302 N. Main St., Harrison, Ark. By the time the Hotel Seville opened in 1929, total construction costs had topped the $150,000 mark (that was a truckload of greenbacks during the Great Depression). Now on the National Register of Historic Places, this "Spanish Castle of the Ozarks" was once the site of some of the swankiest affairs imaginable. You can just imagine the pomp and pageantry when you view the grand staircase, no doubt the site of many an impressive entrance. With its traditional Spanish Revival architecture, the hotel now provides the European plan in bed & breakfast style. All 12 suites offer a private bath and cable TV, as well as coffeemaker, kitchenette, and refrigerator. Room rates generally include breakfast and range $75–319 per night (the latter is for the Presidential Suite; it includes a couple of massages). Within walking distance of the historic Harrison Square, the Seville permits neither pets nor smoking.

This is a popular spot for weddings, and you should contact the hotel directly for prices and packages.

🐟 ✐ ⴠ **Lost Spur Crooked Creek Cabins** (870-743-4655; www.rent-a-ranch.net), 8148 Lost Spur Rd. Harrison, Ark. If you've come to Arkansas for some smallmouth bass fishing, Lost Spur can offer you a fine creek, a great lodge, and the chance to do some hiking and riding. What is cool about this place is that you are renting the entire 116-acre ranch. That's fantastic for groups, as you are allowed to bring along your horses, dogs, four-wheelers, and kids. The price for one to four people is $1,750 a week. Fees for five to eight guests are $150 per person per night. Horses and dogs are $20 each per night. Call ahead and get the entire scoop; your stay for a full ranch rental does not include maids, cooks, or wranglers, and some cleaning fees do apply.

Palace Hotel and Bathhouse (479-253-7474 or 1-866-946-0572; www.palacehotelbathhouse.com), 135 Spring St., Eureka Springs, Ark. In operation since 1901 and on the National Register of Historic Places, the Palace was at one time considered one of the premier spots in Eureka Springs. At the turn of the 20th century this was the location where the rich and famous arrived to partake of the "healing" waters. Today the Palace still offers its famous spa to visitors, along with eight guest suites. Each one features a king-sized bed, double-sized tub, wet bar, refrigerator, cable TV, and WiFi access. Victorian antiques are everywhere, and a continental breakfast is delivered to your room each morning. Rates are $169–179 per night, and all suites are nonsmoking. If you're here for the spa treatment, you will be met by an attendant who will take you to your private bath. Or perhaps you would enjoy a eucalyptus steam in a traditional wooden-barrel steam cabinet? The services are many and include packages with massage, mineral baths, and facials ranging in price from $45–$260.

✄ ♿ **1905 Basin Park Hotel** (479-253-7837 or 1-877-643-4972; www.basinpark.com), 12 Spring St., Eureka Springs, Ark. Located in the heart of Eureka Springs, the Basin Park offers 61 rooms with a variety of different suites ranging from $99–259 per night. This is a very historic place, having at one time hosted the likes of Pretty Boy Floyd. *Ripley's Believe It or Not* has also profiled the Basin Park, as every room in the multistory building is at ground-floor level. This is because (a) the hotel was built into the side of a mountain, and (b) Eureka Springs lies more vertical than it does horizontal. While staying in the Basin Park, you can also enjoy the Balcony Restaurant (see *Eating Out*) and a variety of spa services. The Basin also offers the **Lucky 7 Rooftop Billiards** emporium on its sixth floor. Grab a drink, shoot some pool, or watch a football game on the big-screen TV.

✄ ♿ ♈ **Grand Central Hotel** (479-253-6756 or 1-800-344-6050; www.grandcentralresort.com), 37 N. Main St., Eureka Springs, Ark. Thirteen suites range from $135–229 per night. The Grand Central, which is on the National Register of Historic Places, has been totally renovated and now features very high ceilings, some great oak woodwork, and English antiques. Within the hotel is the **Grand Taverne,** noted for its excellent food,

PALACE HOTEL AND BATHHOUSE

THE HISTORIC CRESCENT HOTEL

complete lounge, and extensive wine list. A trip to Eureka Springs just wouldn't be complete without a trip to the spa, and the Grand Central can provide you with the full treatment. Massage, reflexology, paraffin dips, facial wraps, and a variety of other pampering services are available. Prices for individual services range from $40 for a half-hour massage to $125 for an essential-oil delight It's an à la carte menu, so hit the spa buffet and get pampered to the extent your heart desires and your wallet dictates.

✐ ♿ ⚲ **The Crescent Hotel and Spa** (479-253-9766 or 1-877-342-9766; www.crescent-hotel.com), 75 Prospect Ave., Eureka Springs, Ark. When constructed in the late 1800s at a price of nearly $300,000, the Crescent was regarded as one of the most luxurious hotels in the U.S. Today its 71 rooms are still something special. Spa packages (generally $115–520) are readily available at the **New Moon Day Spa and Salon,** though individual services start at a mere $25.

The Crystal Dining Room (see *Dining Out*) offers breakfast, lunch, dinner, and Sunday brunch. For pure relaxation, Dr. Baker's Lounge offers a full bar, big-screen TV, and live entertainment on weekends. Suites at the Crescent come in a variety of styles and with varying amenities: $119–419 per night.

🦴 🐾 ✐ ♿ **The Retreat at Skywinds** (formerly Fairwinds Mountain Cottages) (479-253-9465 or 1-800-242-3128; www.fairwindsmountain.com), 637 CR 111, Eureka Springs, Ark. With their stone fireplaces, vaulted ceilings, full kitchens, and antiques (not to mention being within 2 miles of both Beaver Dam and the White River), the cabins at Skywinds are probably the nicest you will find in this area. All seven themed cabins have TV and VCR, stereo, a covered porch with swing and rocking chairs, and a charcoal grill. One cabin—"The Barkley"—is designed for guests and their dog. The cabins are set on 135 acres; you can fish in the stocked pond (with a floating dock) or head on down to the river. Other activities include hiking, horseshoes, badminton, and volleyball. Prices range from $175–199 per night and pets are accepted.

✍ ♿ **Cabin Fever Resort** (1-877-993-3837; www.cabinfeverresort.net), 15695 SR 187, Eureka Springs, Ark. Situated in the solitude of the hills about 15 minutes from downtown Eureka Springs, Cabin Fever provides well-outfitted log cabins that are barely 10 years old. All of the cabins (five at present) feature full kitchen, microwave, coffeemaker, Jacuzzi for two, grill, TV and VCR, full bath, and beautiful deck. This is a peaceful resort, but that's what you'd expect from an operation that remembered to include a porch swing with each cabin. $159–239 per night; smoking is allowed outside only. Kids over 14 are OK, but pets are not permitted.

✍ 🐾 **Sugar Ridge Resort** (1-877-498-1648; http://sugarridgeresort.com), 1216 CR 113, Eureka Springs, Ark. Sugar Ridge, which lies on 75 acres overlooking Beaver Lake and the Damsite Park, has eight luxury log cabins geared for adults only and two reserved for families. And for the fisherman, the great trout angling available from the White River is only 1.5 miles away. All the cabins come with TV, VCR, fully equipped kitchen, native stone fireplace, and 16-jet Jacuzzi. Throw in a private deck looking out over the lake. Pets and kids are allowed, but call ahead to learn about restrictions and policies. $99–429.

CANOE OUTFITTERS, CAMPING, AND RVS ✍ 🐾 ♿ **Spider Creek Resort on the White River** (479-253-9241 or 1-800-272-6034; www

.spidercreek.com), 8179 SR 187, Eureka Springs, Ark. Spider Creek offers the great fishing of the White River, not to mention 17 furnished cabins and houses with cable TV, Jacuzzi, and kitchenettes. Three of the cabins are reserved for smokers. $85–275 per night; no charge for kids under 12. Float rental is also available. Canoes and kayaks start at $45, rafts at $70, flat-bottomed jon boats at $65, and 20-foot river cruisers at $95. RV spaces are $40 a night, but no tents or pop-ups are permitted.

✍ **Riverside Resort and Canoes** (1-800-528-4645; www.riversideresortandcanoes.com), 3031 US 62 West, Berryville, Ark. People rave (and justifiably so) about the trout fishing on the White River. Less often heard, however, is the fact that smallmouth bass fishing on the Kings River is also excellent. Riverside Resort, just 5 miles from Eureka Springs, offers seven cabins, some of which have a fireplace, Jacuzzi, or hot tub. In all you can count on cable TV, a kitchen, and a grill on the deck. Pets are not allowed, and you should call for current prices. The resort offers both canoe rental and shuttle service (fishing guides are available as well) for the entire Kings River.

For **Withrow Springs State Park, Devil's Den State Park, Beaver Lake,** and **Ozark National Forest,** see *Wild Places.*

🐾 ✍ **Kings River Outfitters** (479-253-8954; www.kingsriveroutfitters.com), Eureka Springs, Ark. In business for more than a decade, Kings River Outfitters was named the 2001 Conservation Outfitter of the Year by the Arkansas Stream Team (part of the Arkansas Fish and Game Commission). Located 8 miles southeast of

Eureka Springs off SR 221, the firm rents canoes and kayaks, provides shuttle service, and has guides available for hire. The majority of canoes and kayaks rent for $60 per day. Also on the property is a primitive campground (your dog is welcome as long as he doesn't act up, bite, or spend all night baying at the moon). Camping is $10 per person.

✳ Where to Eat

EATING OUT

Eureka Springs, Ark.

✒ ⟁ ⟟ **Balcony Bar and Restaurant** (479-253-7837 or 1-800-643-4972; www.basinpark.com/balconybar restaurant.shtml), 12 Spring St. Open Mon.–Thurs. 11–9, Fri.–Sat. 11–11, Sun. 11–9. Located in the historic 1905 Basin Park Hotel, the Balcony is a relaxed establishment offering a full bar, alfresco dining overlooking downtown Eureka Springs, and frequent live music. The restaurant offers a good list of appetizers, including mozzarella sticks for $5.95. Salads, soups, and a variety of burgers fill out much of the menu. For dinner, entrées include the Downtown Crown (glazed pork legs braised in a sweet chipotle sauce) and Mediterranean pasta.

☙ ✒ ⟁ ⟟ **Forest Hill Restaurant** (479-253-2422 or 1-888-253-1907; www.foresthillrestaurant.com), 3016 E. Van Buren. For those with a large appetite or who wish to feed the family without totally breaking the bank, Forest Hill is a good choice. The breakfast buffet runs $6.95, while the lunch version is $7.95. Of course you can also order off the menu, and lunch finds the Ozark standards of chicken-fried steak for $6.95, deep-fried catfish for $7.95, a wide variety

of sandwiches in the $7 range, and personal-sized pizzas cooked in a wood-burning oven for less than $7. A Sunday brunch buffet takes place every week at this restaurant, and the nightly dinner buffet costs $9.75. Evening menu favorites include a rib-eye steak for $19.95 or (once again) catfish and hush puppies for $9.95. Forest Hill also serves beer, wine, and mixed drinks.

✒ ⟟ **Rogue's Manor at Sweet Spring** (1-800-250-5827; www .roguesmanor.com), 124 Spring St. Located at the very cool Rogue's Manor bed & breakfast, the Rogue's Manor restaurant offers casual fare in a fun yet classy environment. While one of the most popular entrées has a very boring name, you'll want to give it a try. The seafood casserole ($29) is a mesh of scallops, shrimp, and salmon sautéed in white wine, sherry, and herbs, then baked in hollandaise sauce and topped with Swiss cheese. You may also partake of rack of lamb ($44) and a number of pasta, chicken, and vegetarian entrées. For relaxing either before or after dinner, the **Hideaway Lounge,** with its deep leather chairs, offers a fine spot for a drink or three. You can even order one of its special hand-rolled cigars.

✒ ⟁ ⟟ **Sparky's Roadhouse Café** (479-253-6001; www.sparkysroad house.com), 147 E. Van Buren. The food at Sparky's is simple and casual, but the real reason to come is the beer. You can choose from a selection of nearly 100 domestics, microbrews, and imports. If you prefer your alcohol from grapes, there is plenty of wine as well as a full bar. This is just a fun little place, with indoor seating and a huge outdoor deck (nice in summer months). There are plenty of appetizers on the menu. Among them is the Picasso Platter ($12.95), which consists of fresh goat cheese, tomatoes, cucumbers, red onions, olive tapenade, and pita bread. Or you can go for standards such as nachos ($8.95) or the excellent Vidalia onion rings ($5.95). You may choose from a host of burgers and sandwiches in the $6–11 range. One of the best is the bistro burger. At $10.95, this half-pound patty is topped with Brie, grilled ham, and sautéed mushrooms. For an extra $3.50 (and you can do this with any burger), Sparky's will double the meat. There's nothing like a 1-pound burger for a light midday snack. Entrées more in the dinner vein include a slow-roasted Cuban pork dinner for $11.95 and an 8-ounce sirloin for $15.95.

✍ ♿ ❖ **The Eurekan Dining Car** (479-253-9623; www.esnarailway .com), 299 N. Main St. A service provided by the Eureka Springs & North Arkansas Railway, the Eurekan Dining Car wanders the hills and serves scrumptious dinners May–Oct. The trip departs at 5 PM and takes roughly 1½ hours. The dinner menu consists of a baked chicken breast, prime rib, or rainbow trout amandine (all $39.50) and comes with soup, salad, rice pilaf, and flaming baked Alaska. Wine and champagne are available, and the price includes both your train

✍ ♿ **AQ Chicken House** (479-751-4633; www.aqchickenhouse.net), 1207 N. Thompson St., Springdale, Ark. Also, AQ Chicken House (479-443-7555), 1925 N. College Ave., Fayetteville, Ark. With its two locations, this 55-year-old chicken house serves almost a million customers per year. That's a lot of bird, even for the state that is home to Tyson chicken, and there's enough evidence to form a decent argument that AQ (which stands for "Arkansas Quality") is the most popular restaurant in Arkansas. At least in part (if not mostly), such a reputation stems from the fact that the fried chicken is prepared much the same as it was back in 1947: pan fried in a cast-iron skillet. Start your meal at AQ with an order of Pickle O's. In short, these are dill pickles that have been battered and dunked in a deep fryer. I'd seen these on a menu years ago at the Atomic Cafe in Atomic City, Idaho (out in the middle of the desert), but AQ fried dills are far better. The menu also includes a number of sandwiches, and while I'm sure they're all good, you really come here for the chicken. The original, pan-fried meal, which arrives with three pieces and two side orders, is $8.79. I'm talking chicken like you would have at Grandma's house on Sunday. If fried food doesn't set with you, you can order it charbroiled or barbecued. The best deal here is the all-you-can-eat chicken buffet. For $11.99 you can eat chicken until you grow feathers, along with two side orders and a plate of spaghetti besides. This is the epitome of the Ozarks meal.

But AQ has branched out to more than chicken. Catfish from the White fare and meal. All diners must be older than 5. May–Oct., a one-hour lunch trip departs at noon. The cost is $22 for adults, $11 for kids under 8, and the meal consists of either beef stroganoff, chicken salad with fresh fruit, or a hot deli sandwich. Beverages, dessert, and homemade bread accompany your lunch.

DINING OUT *𝒮 ⅄* **James at the Mill** (479-443-1400; www.jamesat themill.com), 3906 Great House Springs, Johnson, Ark. Open Mon.–Sat. 2–10. Located next door to the **Inn at the Mill** (a four-star Clarion Hotel), James at the Mill has pioneered a unique dining style known as

Ozark Plateau Cuisine via the creative mind of chef Miles James. In 2000 this restaurant was named one of the 10 Best Restaurants in the United States by the *Nation's Restaurant News.* Also, this eatery is inevitably voted Best Overall Restaurant in Arkansas by the *Arkansas Times.* It's the sort of establishment where the food is not only delicious, but also a work of art on a plate. For an appetizer, you might try a local, warm, goat-cheese-salad with Yukon Gold potatoes, Arkansas peppered bacon, and warm frisée ($12). Or, for a novel twist on an Ozark favorite, order the chicken-fried filet of beef "Lewis May Style" with garlicky spinach, steamed

River prepared southern-style (fried), grilled, with lemon-pepper, or charbroiled is available for less than $8.99. And don't forget the hickory-smoked BBQ ribs, lunch and blue plate specials, a kids' menu, and the specialty combo platters. Restaurants like the AQ just aren't that common anymore; if you're within 100 miles, it's worth the extra drive.

AQ CHICKEN HOUSE

asparagus, house hollandaise, and reduced red-wine-sauce ($24). A number of other great salads, sandwiches, soups, and daily specials are also available. In the evening order the appetizer known as the homemade andouille sausage corn dog, which arrives with Johnson Valley mustard, salsa fresca, and whipped potatoes ($9). There are no mistakes to be had with the dinner entrées, but perhaps the all-time favorite is the hickory-grilled, bone-in rib eye for $36. It comes with Southwestern black beans, crispy cumin onion rings, salsa fresca, and grilled corn on the cob. Desserts run $8, with options such as a milk-chocolate pyramid with frozen-caramel hazelnut mousse, espresso anglaise, and fresh fruit. While at James at the Mill you'll also encounter a number of specialty coffees, espressos, and teas. The restaurant offers a full bar, and the wine list here is phenomenal, garnering a 2004 Award of Excellence from *Wine Spectator* magazine.

✍ ♿ ♈ **Crystal Dining Room** (479-253-9766; www.restauranteur.com /crystal), 75 Prospect Ave. Eureka Springs, Ark. Open Mon.–Sat. 7–10 for the breakfast buffet, 11–2 for lunch, and 5–9 for dinner. Sundays offer a popular brunch from 9:30–2. As with most fine restaurants in the Ozarks, the surroundings can be elegant, but you need not feel compelled to dress the part. With its hardwood floors, white tablecloths, and chandeliers, the Crystal is located within the famous 1886 Crescent Hotel and Spa. The restaurant offers a full bar and extensive selection of wines, and **Dr. Baker's Lounge** provides a relaxed setting for those who wish to view the big screen, enjoy some appetizers,

and occasionally hear live music during the summer season. The breakfast buffet is $9.95 for adults, $5.95 for kids ages 5–12, and $2.95 for children 5 and younger. A delicious appetizer for lunch, at a cost of $6.95, is the portobello fries (the tasty mushrooms are cut into strips and deep fried). Or, go for the Ozark trout cakes, a nice Arkansas twist on Maryland crabcakes priced at $7.95. An array of sandwiches, salads, entrées, and pastas are also available for lunch. The dinner choices cover the spectrum of beef, pork, fowl, and seafood. A filet mignon with Stilton blue cheese is $32, while a grilled trout will set you back $18. Twin lobster tails with drawn butter are $45, and the provolone- and sage-stuffed chicken breast is $20. If you're in search of excellent service and fine (yet casual) dining in Eureka Springs, it's hard to go wrong with the Crystal.

✍ ♈ **Gaskins Cabin Steak House** (479-253-5466; www.gaskinscabin .com), 2883 SR 23 North, Eureka Springs, Ark. Open Wed.–Sat. 5–9, Sun. 5–8. This restaurant isn't huge, seating just over 75 people, which just goes to show that quantity is not nearly as important as quality. Gaskins resides in an interesting setting: a historic log cabin built in 1864 by an early settler (and bear hunter) named John Gaskins. It is in fact the oldest standing structure in Carroll County, Ark. A relaxing and homey place, with its big fireplace burning whenever the mercury drops, this establishment is well regarded for its steaks and prime rib. It also has an extensive wine list and serves a variety of domestic and imported beers. For $11.95 the escargot appetizer is a good buy, and the certified Angus beef is all grown in the U.S. by Creekstone Farms. A boneless rib eye goes for $28.95, and the 18-ounce prime rib is $35.95. The deep-fried shrimp costs $17.95. The prices may seem a bit high at times, but steak lovers who wish to splurge will be graciously thanked by their taste buds.

⚐ ♿ ⅋ **Autumn Breeze Restaurant** (479-253-7734; www.autumnbreeze restaurant.com), 190 Huntsville Rd., Eureka Springs, Ark. Open Mon.–Sat. 5–9. A nonsmoking establishment, Autumn Breeze has been hailed by *Wine Spectator* magazine as having "one of the most outstanding wine lists in the world." Chef and co-owner Richard Bloch is a graduate of the Culinary Institute of America, and his dishes have received rave reviews since the opening of this restaurant in 1993. This is a restaurant that believes in the importance of details, and such care is reflected not just in the food, but also in the knowledgeable staff and intimate surroundings. There are a number of appetizers, but the coconut beer-battered shrimp ($7.95) is a far cry from the coconut shrimp that's now a staple at any number of chain restaurants. The veal Olympic ($16.95) is something special, a combination of veal medallions and jumbo shrimp in a brandy lobster sauce. You'll also find a 12-ounce lobster tail for $36.95, and a pound of king crab legs for the same price. The list goes on and on, from rack of lamb for $26.95, to Chinese-style baby back ribs at $14.95, to a 22-ounce porterhouse for $33.95. For a finishing touch, don't forget the chef's specialty, a chocolate soufflé that, at $6.95, will send you into chocolate Nirvana.

⚐ ♿ ⅋ **DeVito's** (479-253-6807; www.eureka-springs-usa.com/devito),

5 Center St., Eureka Springs, Ark. Open 4–9 every night but Wed. Not only was DeVito's voted Best Italian Restaurant in Arkansas by readers of the *Arkansas Times,* but it also has been praised by the likes of *The New York Times.* In this very special eatery, in operation since 1956, all the sauces, meatballs, Italian sausage, and bread are made from scratch. The trout that are DeVito's claim to fame are raised on the nearby family trout farm. For appetizers, the traditional toasted ravioli ($7) or the trout fingers ($8) will provide a teaser for the meal to come. Many regulars come back time and again simply for the spaghetti and meatballs ($12), but equally popular are such time-tested entrées as ravioli ($19), chicken Parmesan ($18), eggplant Parmesan ($18), and chicken piccata ($19). There are a wide variety of trout offerings under $20, such as pesto trout Parmesan, lemon trout, and char-grilled trout. DeVito's also serves beer and wine.

⚐ ♿ ⅋ **Bavarian Inn** (479-253-8128; www.eureka-net.com/bavarian), 325 W. Van Buren, Eureka Springs, Ark. Open daily 9–5. The Bavarian Inn is something you wouldn't expect in the Ozarks: an authentic Czech-German establishment serving both European and American favorites. Apparently the style and quality of entrées has been a hit, as the Bavarian has been written up in publications ranging from *Southern Living* and the *Arkansas Democrat-Gazette* to *The New York Times.* Dinners arrive with soup, salad, and a basket of renowned homemade rye bread. Better-known dishes include the sauerbraten ($15.95), Wiener schnitzel ($14.95) and jaeger schnitzel ($16.95). Selections with a more American appeal

include steak Madagascar ($22.95) and a fillet of salmon ($17.95). A children's menu is available, and you do not want to skip dessert at the Bavarian. For a treat, order the praline cheesecake ($5.75).

♂ ও ♈ **Cottage Inn** (479-253-5282; www.cottageinneureakspgs.com), 450 W. Van Buren, Eureka Springs, Ark. Open Thurs.–Sun. 5–9. Cottage Inn offers yet another style of fare not common to the Ozarks. In this case, the taste is Mediterranean. Guests with a hankerin' for the culinary stylings of Greece, Spain, France, and Italy, not to mention a large selection of wines, will not be disappointed. The menu changes here from time to time, but particularly noteworthy entrées have been in the genre of the French country duck trio ($22), a combination of roast duck confit, duck breast, and duck sausage served with seared fresh apple slices. Straying a bit further afield, this establishment has also been known to offer such delights as spicy Thai shrimp ($19) and roast rack of lamb ($34).

✳ Entertainment

LIVE MUSIC ♂ ও **Opera in the Ozarks at Inspiration Point** (479-253-8595 or 1-800-595-4849; www .opera.org), 16311 US 62 West, Eureka Springs, Ark. For all those who suffer from geographic snobbery, yes, we do have opera in the Ozarks. And no, it's not necessarily of the Grand Ole variety. True, we generally prefer bluegrass, blues, and country, but we are equal-opportunity providers when it comes to music. Therefore, no matter if your taste is Rossini, Verdi, or Puccini, you can catch a performance at Opera in the Ozarks. For curtain times and prices, call the box office.

♂ ও **Symphony of Northwest Arkansas** (479-521-4166; www.sona music.org), 605 Dickson St., Fayetteville, Ark. Performing for more than 55 years, the extremely talented Symphony of Northwest Arkansas performs on average once per month at the Walton Arts Center. From music of the movies to the classics, you can't help but enjoy the selections provided by these fine instrumentalists. The shows generally start at 7:30 PM, and tickets run $28–36. Call the box office for exact dates and times.

♂ ও **Ozark Mountain Hoe-Down** (479-253-7725 or 1-800-468-2113; www.hoedown.net), 3140 E. Van Buren, Eureka Springs, Ark. Shows are presented Mar.–Dec. every night but Tues. Tickets are $24.95. Children under 12 are admitted free. If you just didn't get enough of Branson, you can see a Branson-style show in Eureka Springs. The Hoe-Down is your expected fare of country, western, pop, and corn-fed comedy (i.e., guys in overalls and gals with a couple of blacked-out teeth).

♠ **Little O' Opry** (479-839-2992; www.littleoprey.org), 271 S. Campbell Ave., West Fork, Ark. This is not a fancy little theater, but it's the real deal. There seems to be a house band, but regulars and locals take the stage as well and join in with the jam. These are people who can play, who probably grew up with one hand on a banjo, guitar, or walking bass. Best of all, during the intermission you can chow down on cake and cookies and see if you won a door prize. At last check admission was $9 for adults, $7 for those over 55, and $4 for kids 4–11. Shows begin every Saturday at 7.

Pickin' in the Park (479-936-5487) Frisco Park, 3011 Blue Hill Rd.,

OZARK MOUNTAIN HOE-DOWN

Rogers, Ark. Among the nice things about the Ozarks, and there are many, are the community get-togethers you'll find on the town squares. It's a part of American life absent from many locales, but to which we hold more tightly than a snapping turtle with a headache. In Rogers's Frisco Park, Apr.–Oct. every Saturday at 6, you can join the 500 or so folks who show up with lawn chairs, picnic dinners, and maybe even a banjo, mandolin, guitar, washboard, or harmonica. Anyone can play and anyone can attend. As you stroll around you'll see various groups and soloists picking out tunes, some jams growing ever larger as other musicians arrive and join in. It's a great time, the music is great, and it's free. This little shindig is better than anything that costs cash money. The only requirement is that you play acoustic music; no electrics or amps are permitted. Also, leave the booze at home; it's not permitted.

THEATER AND MORE 𝒮 ♿ **The Great Passion Play** (479-253-9200; www.greatpassionplay.com), 935 Passion Play Rd., Eureka Springs, Ark. One of the best-known spectacles in the region, *The Great Passion Play* has been viewed by more than 7 million people over nearly five decades. It is, in fact, the world's most attended outdoor dramatic presentation. Chronicling the last seven days of Jesus Christ, the epic is held in a 4,100-seat outdoor amphitheater, involves 200 actors and a plethora of exotic animals, and runs for two hours. Performances take place early May–Oct. There are numerous shows each week, but call ahead for specific dates. Showtimes vary, but as a general rule you can count on an 8:30 PM curtain May–Aug. In Sept.–Oct. the performance begins at 7:30 PM. $26.50 for adults, $13.50 for kids 6–15. Prices are an additional $15.50 (adults) and $10.25 (kids 6–15) if you want to see the **Bible Museum, Sacred Arts Center,** and **Living Bible Tour.** Package prices are available for various other sites and activities at the facility, not the least of which is the **Passion Play Dinner**

Theater. It's priced at $27 for adults, $13.50 for kids 6–15, and features live gospel music.

♂ �& **Rogers Little Theater** (479-631-8988; http://rogerslittletheater .org), 116 S. Second St., Rogers, Ark. With performances held in the lovely and historic Victory Theater, which offered 750 seats upon its grand opening in 1927, the Rogers Little Theater offers a wide variety of concerts, plays, dinner theater, and performances for kids. To learn about presentations, times, and admission fees, call the box office. The Rogers Little Theater marks its 26th year in the 2011–2012 season.

♂ �& **Sager Creek Arts Center** (479-524-4000; www.sagercreekartscenter .com), 301 E. Twin Springs Rd., Siloam Springs, Ark. Located just across from the pretty Twin Springs Park in Siloam Springs, the Sager Creek Arts Center was incorporated in 1984 and is housed in a former Methodist church sanctuary. A large variety of events are featured. Community theater, musicals, dinner theater, art workshops, exhibits and competitions, concerts of every type, and many workshops are all part of the yearly agenda. For information, dates, times, and ticket prices for performances, call the center directly.

♂ �& **Walton Arts Center** (479-443-5600; www.waltonartscenter.org), 495 Dickson St., Fayetteville, Ark. Featuring performances by major names, classes, plays, and visual presentations, the Walton Arts Center holds two theaters, a multipurpose room, an art gallery, and an amphitheater. Call ahead for tickets, times, and the various entertainment du jour, but you can expect anything from jazz and symphony concerts to opera, musicals, and touring Broadway shows.

Also see **Arts Center of the Ozarks** under *Cultural Sites.*

✳ Selective Shopping

Eureka Springs Downtown Historic District (www.eurekasprings .org), Spring St., Eureka Springs, Ark.

THE GREAT PASSION PLAY

The historic district is the shopping, dining, and lodging center of Eureka Springs, and its main landmark is the 1886 Crescent Hotel. Just hop the trolley to downtown and start wandering; you're bound to find something you like.

Kaleidokites (479-253-6596 or 1-888-836-6251; www.kaleidokites.com), 1C Spring St., Eureka Springs, Ark. This store is reputed to have the largest collection of handmade kaleidoscopes in a four-state region. One look at the place and you can assume the claim to fame is true. Better yet, it stocks an amazing selection of psychedelic kites available in all shapes, designs, and sizes. You'll also find wind socks, spinners, tops, and a variety of other unusual cards and gifts.

Sweet's Fudge Kitchen (479-253-5810; www.sweetsfudgekitchen.com), 36 Spring St., Eureka Springs, Ark. In business since 1959, Sweet's makes all its chocolates from scratch, hand dipping in small batches to ensure freshness. However, chocolate alone does not a candy store make. This one also carries an extensive variety of homemade fudge and many different flavors of saltwater taffy. Candies, imported licorice, turtles, nut clusters . . . the spectrum of sugar is covered at Sweet's. Even if you end up with a stomachache from overconsumption, you could well find yourself saying, "Thank you, sir, may I have another?"

White River Tobacco Company (479-253-5350), 99 Spring St., Eureka Springs, Ark. It's probably not politically correct to be plugging a tobacco emporium in this day and age, which should give you an insight into the workings of the typical Ozark mind. We'd endorse such an establishment just to be contrary, even if an awfully large percentage of us didn't love our tobacco (which we do; I personally smoke a corncob pipe). At White River you'll find not only a large selection of fine-tasting tobaccos, but also a nice selection of pipes and cigars as well. Smoke 'em if ya got 'em.

Dickson Street Bookshop (479-442-8182), 325 W. Dickson St., Fayetteville, Ark. The Dickson Street Bookshop has been around forever and a day, and you could spend almost that much time leafing through the 100,000-plus volumes in stock. If you're a fan of the written word, you have just found the mother lode of rare volumes, antique books, and out-of-print volumes.

✳ Special Events

Also see Towns and Villages.
February **Chocolate Lovers Festival** (1-800-809-5392; www.eureka chocfest.com), Best Western Inn of the Ozarks Convention Center, US 62 West, Eureka Springs, Ark. Taking place on Valentine's Day weekend, this dentist's dream festival features chocolate sculpting, a chocolate fountain, numerous chocolate competitions, entertainment, and an all-day chocolate feast. $10 adults, $6 ages 6 and younger. My guess is you could probably raise the price to $100 and the 6-and-under crowd would still come.

April **Carving in the Ozarks** (www .carvingintheozarks.com), US 62 East and Rockhouse Rd., Eureka Springs, Ark. Donatello and Michelangelo were OK, but you just wonder what those ol' boys could have accomplished if some wise soul had placed a chain saw in their hands. A reasonable facsimile of the answer to such a question can be found in late April at Carving in the Ozarks. Chain saw carvers from all over America show up to transform chunks of wood into bears, eagles, and such. Admission is free. After the carving is done, all the pieces are auctioned. A portion of the proceeds goes to the Eureka Springs High School skills class, the Eureka Springs Historical Museum, and Susan G. Komen for the Cure.

Ozark UFO Conference (479-354-2558; www.ozarkufo.com), Best Western Inn of the Ozarks, US 62 West and SR 23, Eureka Springs, Ark. Those seeking to relive the halcyon days of their intergalactic abduction can sate their need for things extraterrestrial at this little green man shindig in Eureka Springs. You'll come across three days' worth of speakers, audiovisual presentations, and discussions. I assume you'll also meet a few abductees who have come into contact with Elvis, Bigfoot, Mr. Spock, and nasty probing devices. Admission at the door is $70 for all three days.

May–October **Pickin' in the Park** (479-936-5487; www.mainstreetrogers .com), Frisco Park, Rogers, Ark. For the best in bluegrass, country, and gospel, just drop by Rogers's Frisco Park any Saturday evening between Apr.–Oct. Folks show up from all over with their guitars, banjos, basses, and dulcimers to pick the tunes and jam with anyone who feels the urge. Or you can simply bring a lawn chair and listen. There is no alcohol allowed, and if you wish to do a bit of pickin' of your own, just keep in mind that this is strictly an acoustic gig.

May **War Eagle Fair** (see *October*).

Crawdad Days Music Festival (870-880-6265; www.crawdaddays .org), Harrison, Ark. The mid-May

Crawdad Days take place on the Main Street Square and Lake Harrison. The main entrée of the day is music, music, and more music. However, once your feet take to bouncing, you can enjoy food, a cardboard boat race, volleyball, basketball, and (for the more enthusiastic among you) a 5K race. It should go without saying that one of the highlights of the event is a crawdad boil. Admission is free, as are the concerts and car show. You do have to pay for rides on the midway and food.

June **Mudtown Days** (479-770-2185; www.mudtowndays.lowellarkansas.gov), Ward Nail Park, Lowell, Ark. For more than 30 years the annual Mudtown Days festival has taken place over Memorial Day weekend. You'll find a parade, fireworks, softball and baseball tournaments, lawn mower and wheelbarrow races, and an infinite amount of food and music. The commemoration of Lowell (originally named Mudtown, given how many stagecoaches seemed to get stuck here) even includes a Civil War reenactment and a tractor pulling contest (for you coastal folks, that would be where tractors pull heavy weights, not where people try to pull tractors).

Rusty Wheels Tractor Show (see *October*).

August **Frisco Festival** (479-936-5487; www.friscofestival.com), downtown Rogers, Ark. Taking place on the last weekend of August, the two-day Frisco Festival is a celebration of the now defunct Frisco Railroad. There's a chili cook-off and a very elaborate cardboard train race. There's also live music, rides galore, not to mention a chicken BBQ, an old-fashioned ice cream social, and a pancake breakfast. Admission is free (in that you can wander all over the place), but specific events, shows, train rides, and amusements may charge a fee.

Northwest Arkansas Bluegrass Festival, Harrison, Ark. Taking place in mid-August at Harrison's Beacon Park 5 miles north of town, this is the oldest three-day bluegrass festival in the state of Arkansas. There are jam sessions galore, stage performances, and endless gospel and bluegrass. Of course, no bluegrass festival would be complete without a wide selection of food. Camping is available, and alcohol is not permitted on the fairgrounds. $10 Thurs. and Fri., $12 Sat. A three-day pass is $25. The music starts at 6:30 each evening of the festival. Saturday's pickin' and grinnin' begins at 1:30.

September **Bikes, Blues and BBQ** (479-527-9993; www.bikesbluesand bbq.org), Fayetteville, Ark. This biker rally is quickly becoming one of the most popular in the U.S., drawing more than 250,000 people and 75,000 bikes on the last weekend in September. You'll see 15 or more free bands (music from country to rock to blues to jazz), and the food found along Fayetteville's eclectic Dickson Street could keep you occupied for hours. Still, you might not want to gorge yourself too much . . . at least not until after the BBQ cook-off is over. And as you no doubt suspected, no

bike rally is complete without a variety of "biker babe" competitions.

October **War Eagle Fair** (479-789-5398; www.wareaglefair.com), 11036 High Sky Inn Rd., Rogers, Ark. Taking place both in May and mid-October, the War Eagle Fair dates from 1954 and showcases the very best of arts, crafts, and handmade items (you won't find mass-produced trash here) at hundreds and hundreds of vendor booths. Admission and parking are free, and of course there is plenty of food available. Gates open at 8 AM and close at 5 PM Thurs.–Sat. during the event. On Sun. the gates close at 4 PM. For the finest products from weavers, woodworkers, painters, sculptors, stained-glass artists, and much more, War Eagle is the best-known craft fair in Northwest Arkansas.

Rusty Wheels Tractor Show (870-743-1511; www.rustywheels.com), 5772 Hwy. US 65 South, Harrison, Ark. For the finest in old tractors, old engines, and old guys who really like old tractors and old engines, don't miss this show. It's held on the second weekend of October (and the second weekend of June) at the tractor club's showground 6 miles south of Harrison on US 65. Show hours are 6 AM–7 PM, and you can stock up on good country food such as biscuits and gravy.

THE WHITE AND THE BUFFALO

A s I wrote this chapter, several Ozarkian friends suggested that perhaps I shouldn't heavily broadcast the majesty and charm this region exudes. They do not want it to change, to become overpopulated, to alter in form, style, or grace by a single iota. They love the quiet peace found in secret places not commonly frequented by visitors or tourists. They revel in the sheer beauty of locales that still look and feel like centuries past. In good conscience I could of course never fully abide by such a request; after all, this guide is meant to serve as a complete road map to the reader. It is meant to lift the veil and reveal the indescribable magic that is the Ozarks.

On the other hand, in some simple way, my friends are inadvertently granted their wish. The truth is that neither words nor pictures can do justice to the intangible allure of the White and Buffalo Rivers. You have to see it, taste it, touch it, hear it. Only then can you honestly discover what makes the locals cherish this area so deeply. You have to float the rivers or walk their banks. You have to breathe deep the crisp air as you gaze at towering bluffs. You have to stroll the forest, allowing the silence to permeate your soul. You need to feel the primeval tug of that trout on the line, watch the bass leap, regress to a more primitive state of mind as an elk pushes its way through briars and limbs. To know it, to really know it, the icy chill of spring-born whitewater must splash on your face, carrying you away to the nesting ground of dreams unborn.

And it's not just about the great outdoors. Yes, the fishing in the White, Buffalo, and Little Red Rivers is excellent. Streams that produce world-record trout—a 40-pound, 4-ounce brown was taken from the Little Red in 1992—are not something at which one scoffs. Bull Shoals, Norfork, and Greers Ferry Lakes offer visitors and natives alike a water wonderland. Being Army Corps of Engineers projects, these huge bodies of water are surrounded by the type of wooded campsites that make lodging under the stars a pure pleasure. In the populated havens along their borders you will find restaurants, museums, bed & breakfasts, and entertainment galore.

But still there is more. This is an area that virtually dispels unhappiness; it is not tolerant of brooding minds or downturned lips. Just try to keep your toe from tapping when you visit Mountain View, the Folk Music Capital of the World. When you hear the joyous strains of banjo, bass, fiddle, and guitar at

The White & the Buffalo

© The Countryman Press

MISSOURI
ARKANSAS

34 · 49
Pocahontas
412 · 63
Walnut Ridge
Newport
167
Batesville
14
67
9
56 · 69
Heber Springs
Norfolk Lake
14
Greers Ferry Lake
OZARK NAT'L FOREST
Clinton
Mountain Home
5
27 · Marshall
16
235
14 · BUFFALO NAT'L RIVER
Harrison
1
27
7
62 · 412
OZARK NAT'L FOREST
Clarksville
21 · 40

N

Point of Interest
Camping
Visitor Center
Unpaved Road

Miles
0   5   10

Bear Creek
65
412
Crooked Cr.
62
Western Grove
Harrison
206
Bellefonte
123
Davis Cr.
65
Dogpatch
7
206
Buffalo R.
Hasty
Carver
Gene Rush Wildlife Management Area
Cave Cr.
74
Piercetown
Mount Judea
Ozark
Erbie
Jasper
7
Little Buffalo R.
Kyles Landing
Steel Creek
74
Compton
Ponca Wilderness Area
Ponca
Lost Valley
21
Upper Buffalo Wilderness Area
43
412

Buffalo City
Leatherwood Wilderness Area
OZARK NATIONAL FOREST
14
Lower Buffalo Wilderness Area
Big Cr.
Rush Landing
Buffalo Point Ranger Station
Spring Creek
Maumee II South
Buffalo R.
Bear Cr.
St. Joe
65
374
Woolum
Richland Cr.
Pindall
Marshall
65

every turn, when you see musicians jamming for the pure fun of it on the town square, a smile will rise to your face unbidden. You might go to Heber Springs and watch the World Championship Cardboard Boat Races, just another of the countless festivals that illustrate the endless humor of the Ozarks and its people. You will begin to understand the type of personality that has perfected the art of self-amusement, that has mastered the ability to create laughter from thin air.

Some things just have to be seen to be believed. Some things just have to be felt. Some places are like that, too. They're rare as hen's teeth, granted, but they do exist.

This is one of those places.

AREA CODES This region of Arkansas wanders a bit, containing all three of the state's area codes. The vast majority of the towns here utilize the **870** code. Near Greers Ferry Lake and Heber Springs, the code is **501.** A few towns in this region used the **479** code.

GUIDANCE While you won't want to misplace the invaluable, multipurpose resource put out by the **Arkansas Department of Parks and Tourism** (501-682-7777 or 1-800-NATURAL; www.arkansas.com), 1 Capitol Mall, Little Rock, Ark., another fantastic general vacation site can be found under the name of **Ozark Mountain Region** (870-404-2741; www.ozarkmountainregion.com), P.O. Box 1080, Flippin, AR 72634.

When traveling near Batesville, Ark., hints and tips are available from both the **Batesville Area Chamber of Commerce** (870-793-2378; www.mybatesville .org), 409 Vine St, Batesville, Ark., and the **Ozark Gateway Tourist Council** (870-793-9316 or 1-800-264-0316; www.ozarkgateway.com), 1652 White Dr., P.O. Box 4049, Batesville, AR 72503.

In the southern part of the region, details on the many recreational opportunities available in the Greers Ferry Lake district can be found at the **Greers Ferry Lake & Little Red River Association** (www.greersferrylake.org), P.O. Box 1170, Fairfield Bay, AR 72088, or the **Fairfield Bay Area Chamber of Commerce** (1-888-244-4386; www.ffbchamber.org), P.O. Box 1159, Fairfield Bay, AR 72088. Also at Greers Ferry, check out the **Heber Springs Area Chamber of Commerce** (501-362-2444; www.heber-springs.com), 1001 W. Main, Heber Springs, Ark.

Two other chambers of note are the **Jasper–Newton County Chamber of Commerce** (1-800-670-7792; www.theozarkmountains.com), P.O. Box 250, Jasper, AR 72641, and the **Clinton Chamber of Commerce** (501-745-6500; www.clintonarchamber.com), 290 Main St., Clinton, Ark. The former is a prime source for those who wish to float the Buffalo National River, while the latter will provide the detail you need to enjoy the National Championship Chuck-wagon Races.

For more fun on the water, a rundown of activities in and around Bull Shoals and Norfork Lakes (as well as the White and Buffalo National Rivers) are as close as the **Mountain Home Chamber of Commerce** (870-425-5111 or 1-800-822-3536; www.enjoymountainhome.com), P.O. Box 488, Mountain Home,

AR 72654. Another "mountain" town that should not be missed is Mountain View, Ark., home to the amazing Ozark Folk Center State Park. Find out more via the **Mountain View Chamber of Commerce** (870-269-8068 or 1-888-679-2859; www.ozarkgetaways.com), 107 N. Peabody Ave., Mountain View, Ark.

GETTING THERE *By car:* On the eastern side of this region, US 65 is your quickest route to the general vicinity of both the Buffalo National River and Greers Ferry Lake. More to the west, US 63 crosses the Missouri-Arkansas border at Thayer, Mo., and runs south through Batesville. Traversing the northern edge of the section is best accomplished on US 62. For a more scenic excursion and a slower pace, opt for SR 5, SR 9, and SR 14.

By air: Once again, your best bet for travel in the northern section of the Arkansas Ozarks is **Northwest Arkansas Regional Airport** (479-205-1000; www.nwara.com), 1 Airport Blvd., Bentonville, Ark. The airport is serviced by Allegiant, American Eagle, Continental, Delta, US Airways Express, and United. For even more flight opportunities, albeit requiring a bit more travel by auto, you can fly to or from the **Branson Airport** (1-888-359-2541; http://flybranson .com), 4000 Branson Airport Blvd., Hollister, Mo. This facility, which opened in May 2009, holds the distinction of being the only privately owned, privately operated, commercial service airport in the United States. The airport offers direct, nonstop flights to a number of cities, and is serviced by AirTran, Frontier, and Branson Air Express. The **Little Rock National Airport** (501-372-3439; www.lrn-airport.com), 1 Airport Dr., Little Rock, Ark., is serviced by Delta, Southwest, American, American Eagle, United, Vision, Continental, and US Airways. At the far southwest edge of this region, **Fort Smith Regional Airport** (479-452-7000; www.fortsmithairport.com), 6700 McKennon Blvd., Fort Smith, Ark., is serviced by American Airlines and Delta.

MEDICAL EMERGENCIES The Buffalo River country has several large hospitals that can handle any medical needs or emergencies. Also keep in mind that many small towns have local hospitals or medical clinics. In Batesville you will find the **White River Medical Center** (870-262-1200; www.wrmc.com), 1710 Harrison St., Batesville, Ark. This regional hospital has 199 beds and 80 physicians covering a full range of services. The **Ozark Health Center** in Clinton (501-745-7000; www.myozarkhealth.com), 2500 US 65 South, Clinton, Ark., moved into its new facility in 2004. Services at Ozark Health include 24-hour emergency care, surgery, labs, radiology, respiratory, and outpatient care. Considering that Clinton hosts the Chuckwagon Races, which inevitably result in some nasty accidents, you can presume that the emergency room docs here know their stuff.

Should you suffer injury or illness while playing around on Greers Ferry Lake or the Little Red River, you would be well served to drive on down to the **White County Medical Center** in Searcy (501-268-6121; www.wcmc.org), 3214 E. Race Ave., Searcy, Ark. This 438-bed acute care hospital boasts more than 1,300 employees and better than 150 physicians. It's a state-of-the-art health center, handling virtually every procedure and nearly every test you could ever require.

A much smaller hospital, **Stone County Medical Center** (870-269-4361; www .wrmc.com), SR 14 East, Mountain View, Ark., is a 25-bed critical access facility offering emergency room service, surgery, diagnostic imaging, respiratory care, rehab, and lab work. Last but not least, the **Baxter Regional Medical Center** in Mountain Home (870-508-1000; www.baxterregional.org), 624 Hospital Dr., Mountain Home, Ark., is a 268-bed hospital with 100 physicians on staff. As a large regional facility, Baxter Regional's menu of services is as long as your arm (which the folks here will happily fix if you break it).

✳ Wandering Around

EXPLORING BY CAR Sylamore Scenic Byway (479-964-7200; www.fs.fed .us/oonf/ozark/recreation/byways.htm), Ozark–St. Francis National Forests, 605 W. Main, Russellville, Ark. If you head south on SR 5 at Calico Rock, Ark., you will be traveling on the 26.5-mile Sylamore Scenic Byway. This is a particularly gorgeous drive in fall, what with all the changing colors of the oak-hickory forest, but you will also experience high limestone cliffs and a number of panoramic vistas. Continuing on your route through the Ozark National Forest, turn west onto SR 14 (at the town of Allison) and then north onto FR 1110. This road takes you to **Blanchard Springs Caverns,** and you really have to see this hole in the ground to appreciate why it has attracted millions of visitors since 1973. Blanchard is a living cave, still in formation, and the Forest Service offers both mild and difficult tours. You can also fish in Mirror Lake (where the spring emerges) or take a short walk to a glorious waterfall. From Blanchard, you may continue on FR 1110 back to SR 14, or you can just stay a while. Camping is available at Blanchard Springs as well as the nearby Gunner Pool and the Barkshed Recreation Area.

EXPLORING BY FOOT ♿ **Mossy Bluff Trail** (501-362-2416; www.swl.usace .army.mil/parks/greersferry), 700 Heber Springs Rd. North, Heber Springs, Ark. Located at Greers Ferry Lake, Mossy Bluff is a 1.6-mile trail that wanders up a wooded bluff and looks down upon both Greers Ferry Dam and the Little Red River. Along the way you will spy Balanced Rock, which should be arrested for breaking the laws of gravity; the Double Tree (sort of an interdeciduous marriage—two healthy trees of differing species that have somehow grown together); and the Weeping Rocks. This last is a bluff face that often seems be shedding tears as groundwater percolates through the earth and emerges through tiny cracks in the stone. For those who are either handicapped or less than ambulatory, the 660-foot **Buckeye Trail** is wheelchair accessible and offers picnic tables and some pretty views. Trailheads for both Mossy Creek and Buckeye can be found at the William Carl Garner Visitor Center.

EXPLORING BY RIVER Buffalo National River (870-439-2502; www.nps .gov/buff), 402 N. Walnut, Suite 136, Harrison, Ark. The Buffalo was the first river in America to receive the title "National," achieving that designation via a 1972 Act of Congress. Beginning in the Boston Mountains to the west, the Buffalo is nearly 150 miles in length and features limestone bluffs in excess of 500 feet high, whitewater, tranquil floating, horseback and hiking trails, wilderness areas, gravel and sandbars, and infinite opportunities to take photos of wildlife, including a growing elk population. Smallmouth bass are the fish of choice along this river, although you may catch any of about 50 different species, and more than 135 miles are floatable. You will find plenty of outfitters throughout the area, and camping is available year-round at most access points. Better yet, because this area is under the jurisdiction of the National Park Service, you can set up your primitive campsite anywhere along the length of the Buffalo. For those who might want to learn more about the river before embarking, stop by the **Tyler Bend Visitor Center** near Marshall, Ark., just off US 65.

This is seriously one of the most beautiful rivers in America, and both the middle and lower sections can be floated by anyone who can tell the difference between a canoe and a calliope. In other words, it's mellow from midpoint all the way to the spot where it joins the White River. There are any number of little towns close to these sections, so both access and acquisition of supplies are a breeze.

The upper sections of the river are a somewhat different story. The Buffalo's upper reaches feature a number of white-water rapids of varying difficulty; you'd be wise to know your level of expertise before putting paddle to stream. On the other hand, should you float the Upper Buffalo, you can pull your canoe to the bank, take a 1-mile walk, and visit Hemmed-In Hollow. This box canyon features a 200-foot waterfall, the highest in the heartland.

There is one other section of the Buffalo, but it should be reserved solely for aficionados of whitewater. Found in the headwaters section between the towns of Boxley and Fallsville, this stretch of the Buffalo is known locally as the Hailstone River. You'll encounter whitewater in the Class III range, not to mention boulders, undercut banks and ledges, twists, turns, and drops. Again, not for the faint of heart, and not recommended for any but the most proficient.

White River (501-682-7777; www.arkansas.com/lakes-rivers/river.aspx?id=17). When discussing the White River below Bull Shoals Dam, you're discussing the quest for monster trout. Yes, the scenery is gorgeous, and there are resorts and access points aplenty. But the 90-mile stretch of river downstream from Bull Shoals (basically to the town of Guion, a little blip of a place in Izard County) has produced brown trout over 30 pounds and rainbows over 19. The fish are fat and plentiful for a couple of reasons. First, the discharge from the Bull Shoals hydro plant comes from the cold water deep in the lake. It's just the right temperature for trout. Second, Arkansas Game and Fish annually dumps untold thousands of trout in the river. This combination of factors makes for the type of angling experiences that are the stuff of dreams. True, you may not catch a 33-pound brown, but trout in the 5- to-10-pound range are extremely common (and people catch a few 20-pounders nearly every year). Oh, and there is also the possibility of catching cutthroat and brook trout.

As a general rule, most folks like to float fish the White in a jon boat (a flat-bottomed aluminum craft—one of which can be seen at the side of almost any house in the Ozarks) equipped with a fairly small outboard, comfy chairs, and a

BULL SHOALS DAM

well-stocked cooler. While fly-fishing is extremely popular, Ozarkers aren't picky about bait. Crawdads are very popular, but so are worms, corn, and marshmallows. This might offend the sensibilities of fishing purists, but then again, your garden-variety Ozarker has never really cared too much about such politically correct nonsense. We fish with what they're biting on, be it a Woolly Bugger fly, a Bass Buster Beetle Spin, or a fat ol' night crawler. Fishing is about catching fish, after all, not what the neighbors think of your equipment.

The beauty of the White River, with its high bluffs and deep forests, cannot be overstated. However, again, it is the fishing that draws the crowds. That, and the White River Monster.

Indeed. From Guion south, the White starts warming up, and you will catch your regular river fish. But, near the town of Newport, locals have reported seeing a 30-foot, spiny-backed, snaky sort of critter for the past 100 years. They call him "Whitey," and he supposedly bellows and (when not swimming) walks the muddy banks on three-toed feet. A fellow snapped a good picture of Whitey in the early 1970s, and in 1973 the Arkansas General Assembly created the White River Monster Refuge next to Jacksonport State Park. The resolution put in the record by the legislators deemed it a crime to "molest, kill, trample, or harm the White River Monster while he is in the retreat."

I've said it before and I'll say it again: If you want to be amused, you'd best learn to amuse yourself. Ozarkers are real good at that.

Little Red River (501-362-2416; www.swl.usace.army.mil/parks/greersferry /visitorscenter.htm), P.O. Box 1088, Heber Springs, AR 72543. The Little Red begins its trek around the town of Scotland, Ark., and meanders to the west until dumping into Greers Ferry Lake. It is below Greers Ferry Dam where things start to get interesting. Stocking of trout in the Little Red began in 1966, and the downstream good-fishin' stretch of 35 miles has since become a favorite of those seeking browns, rainbows, and cutthroats. Just how popular is this river? In 1992 the late "Rip" Collins pulled a 40-pound, 4-ounce brown from the river, setting a new world record (incredibly, he caught the monster on ultralight tackle). You'll find numerous outfitters, access points, marinas, and camping along the Little Red, and at Greers Ferry's **Carl Garner/Army Corps of Engineers Visitor Center** you can hike trails overlooking the river and find more specific details.

Below the dam, the Little Red's flow is dependent upon the release of waters from the hydro plant. The river may be lower or higher, but it's floatable at all times. If you want a river that has fast sections and not a lot of boulders and snags, this is a great choice. The scenery is classic, and as a basic rule, the farther you get from the dam, the more placid the waters become. Of course, the farther downstream you go, the greater the risk that the water is low. No matter. The fishing is fine and you can't beat the surroundings.

Spring River (870-856-3210; www.arkansas.com/lakes-rivers/river.aspx?id=15), Hardy, Ark. The fact of that matter is that some folks prefer a natural spring over those that are aided or assisted by human-made dams. I personally don't see the difference—water is just water after you're a few miles downstream—but the Spring River is about as natural as they get. The massive Mammoth Spring, which pumps out more than 9 million gallons of 58-degree water per hour, is the fountain from which the Spring springs. Trout fishing is good, fly-fishermen love it here, and the floating is superb. Outfitters abound, and canoe rental is always right around the corner. Floaters will not be disappointed in the least by the high bluffs or the forests that line the banks of the Spring. One nice thing about this

MAMMOTH SPRING

river is that its waters are clear as glass (and cold—just get splashed by the guy in the front of the canoe if you don't believe me). The Spring is all sorts of gorgeous. Bring your camera for shots of wildlife and the occasional (small) whitewater waterfall.

✳ Towns and Villages

Batesville, Ark. This is the second oldest city in Arkansas, ceded to the U.S. by an 1808 treaty. Trading outposts appeared here along the White River around 1810. Today the "City of Hospitality" lives up to its name. The town of nearly 10,000 is also known for Lyon College, home of the annual Arkansas Scottish Festival, and the renowned Old Independence Regional Museum.

Clinton, Ark. Located on the Little Red River and just a stone's throw from Greers Ferry Lake, this seat of Van Buren County holds an annual event that cannot be duplicated anywhere in America. Though the National Championship Chuckwagon Races began as just an excuse for a Labor Day party among a few friends, they didn't stay that way for long. Today more than 20,000 people show up to watch not only chuckwagon racing, but also bronc fanning and a "Snowy River Race." And yes, just like the movie of the same name, that last event involves downhill runs and a dive into the river. This town of 2,598 does it right.

Fairfield Bay, Ark. A new town by any standard of dating, Fairfield Bay can be found on the western shoreline of Greers Ferry Lake. Established in 1966 as something of a retirement village, Fairfield is called home by approximately 2,459 full-time residents. One of the many reasons visitors stop here is for golf, with the famous Mountain Ranch (usually named the Top Public Course in Arkansas by *Golf Digest* magazine) and challenging Indian Hills golf courses. Fairfield Bay also offers activities such as trail riding, cruises, camping, and fishing.

Hardy, Ark. With only 597 residents, Hardy may not be the biggest town around. It is, however, loaded with things to do. Mammoth Springs is located just a few miles north, and the river it feeds (the Spring) offers year-round floating and excellent fishing for rainbow trout. In the warmer south fork of the river, you can try your luck for bass, walleye, or even a muskie. Originally settled in the late 1800s and a getaway for the wealthy of Memphis during the Roaring '20s, the Hardy downtown of today is full of quaint shops offering the wares of local artisans. In addition, you can check out three museums, enjoy summer musical shows and festivals, and stay in a number of bed & breakfasts.

Heber Springs, Ark. The seat of Cleburne County, Heber Springs is regarded as the epicenter of activity for both the 31,000-acre Greers Ferry Lake and the Little Red River. Originally known as Sugar Loaf, the town today boasts nearly 7,307 residents. Since 1963 particularly, when the lake was completed, Heber Springs has drawn visitors from around the country for a variety of water sports, fishing, and resort opportunities. Even better for anglers, the Little Red holds the distinction of being the site where the world's largest brown trout (40 pounds, 4 ounces) was landed in 1992. Greers Ferry Lake also holds the world angling record for walleye and hybrid striped bass. In Heber Springs you'll find a wealth of places to dine, stay, and shop, not to mention the annual World Championship Cardboard Boat Races.

Jasper, Ark. This is a small but gorgeous area, and the 484 residents of Jasper are nestled in the midst of lands protected and owned by either the state or federal government. The most popular spot to float on the Buffalo National River is just north of Jasper (a 25-mile section between the towns of Ponca and Pruitt); it offers huge bluffs, campgrounds, and Hemmed-In Hollow, the highest waterfall in the heartland. Each June, Jasper plays host to the Buffalo River Elk Festival. This shindig honors the large-racked herbivores that are making a comeback in the region, not the fraternal organization with a secret handshake.

Mountain Home, Ark. This town of 12,485 is virtually surrounded by the 22,000-acre Norfork Lake and the 45,000-acre Bull Shoals Lake. Just a few miles south of Mountain Home, the Buffalo National River flows into the White. If this information doesn't give you a good impression of what goes on in these parts, then it might be helpful to add that the state-record striped bass taken from Bull Shoals weighed in at 53 pounds. Brown trout of more than 30 pounds and rainbows topping 19 pounds have been landed on rod and reel out of the White. Canoeing, camping, and water sports of all sorts rule the day in Mountain Home, not to mention the glorious beauty of Bull Shoals–White River State Park. Restaurants, resorts, golf courses, and historic venues are plentiful. You could easily spend a couple weeks around Mountain Home and not even come close to being bored.

Mountain View, Ark. This town of 3,101, seat of Stone County, is widely known as the Folk Music Capital of the World. Such a lofty claim can easily be backed up should you happen to drop by the Ozark Folk Center. This state park, really the only one of its kind, has as its mission the task of preserving the traditional music, crafts, heritage, and traditions of the Ozarks. In Mountain View you will find a plethora of music festivals, such as the Arkansas Folk Festival in April and the Mountain View Bluegrass Festivals in March and November. Then again, you could also attend the Arkansas Bean Fest and the Great Championship Outhouse Races on the last weekend of October. During the warmer months you'll find all sorts of folks pickin' and grinnin' on the town square, and if you tire of the music, there's always the phenomenal fishing on the White River. Indeed, it's a little place, but during some of its festivals the town population may expand to upward of 100,000.

Pocahontas, Ark. It is only fitting that a woman named Cinderella was involved in the naming of Pocahontas. Dr. Ransom Bettis, father of the aforementioned girl, is listed as the first settler in the area that would later become the Randolph County seat. Thomas Drew married young Cindy and, apparently fond of lyrical names, Drew and Bettis joined forces to found Pocahontas. It's good they focused on the female protagonist of the Pocahontas tale, as a town named Captain John Smithburg would be less than pleasing to the ear. At any rate, this town of nearly 6,616 souls is the site of Old Davidsonville State Park (Davidsonville having been the oldest settlement in Arkansas). Good fishing and floating abound here, and in fact there are five waterways (the Fourche, Current, Eleven Point, Black, and Spring) that can keep any worm-drowner occupied for days.

MUSEUMS ✿ ✐ ⚹ **Mark Martin Museum** (870-793-4461; www.markmartin museum.com), 1601 Batesville Blvd., Batesville, Ark. NASCAR fans will be well acquainted with the name Mark Martin. During his long racing career Martin has racked up an impressive number of wins (he's finished second in the Sprint Cup Series standings five times, and in 2005 brought home nearly $6 million in prize money). Now, at his Ford/Mercury dealership in Batesville, Martin has created a museum dedicated to his legendary career and the sport of racing. You'll see the Batesville native's Viagra/Coca-Cola car, his 1990 Folgers Thunderbird, and the 2005 IROC car that he drove to his fifth championship. For racing fans, this is a must-see. You can buy Mark Martin merchandise on the premises, or even drive away in a new car.

✿ ✐ ⚹ **Old Independence Regional Museum** (870-793-2121; www.oirm.org), 380 S. Ninth St., Batesville, Ark. Open Tues.–Sat. 9–4:30, Sun. 1:30–4. $3 adults, $2 for those over 55, $1 for kids over the age of 6. Housed in an impressive 1936 WPA structure constructed of locally quarried sandstone, the Old Independence is on the National Register of Historic Places. Open since its restoration in 1998, the museum is a living legacy to the 12 counties that were at one time part of the huge Independence County (Baxter, Cleburne, Fulton, Independence, Izard, Jackson, Marion, Poinsett, Sharp, Stone, White, and Woodruff). Exhibits date from the days of the Shawnee Indians to more modern times.

✿ ✐ **Van Buren County Historical Society Museum** (501-745-4066; www .arkansas.com/attractions/attr_detail.aspx?id=18751), 1123 Third St., Clinton, Ark. Open weekdays 10–4. No admission fee. The Van Buren County Museum traces the history of Van Buren County, with a priority placed on family histories and displays.

✿ ✐ **Log Cabin Museum** (501-884-4899), 335 Snead Dr., Fairfield Bay, Ark. Open Mon. 2–5, Tues.–Sat. 1–4. Admission is free. For a look at how Arkansawyers lived in the 19th century, drop by this 1850 log cabin, which was dismantled, moved to its current site, and re-created in painstaking detail. All items found within the cabin would have been used in a home of the 1880s.

✿ ✐ **Veteran's Military Museum** (870-856-4133 or 870-856-3677), 738 Main St., Hardy, Ark. Open Sat. 10–5, Sun. 11–5. Admission is just $1. There are thousands of items crammed into this little museum, military memorabilia ranging from the Revolutionary War to the Gulf War, including a nice selection of the virtually indestructible Willys Jeeps.

✐ ⚹ **Vintage Motorcar Museum** (870-856-4884), 301 W. Main S., Hardy, Ark. Open Mon.–Sat. 9:30–4:30, Sun. noon–4:30. $6 adults, $3 for kids under 12. This private collection features 50 cars ranging from a 1908 Sears Runabout to a 1981 DeLorean (gotta love that stainless steel and those gull-wing doors). Some of the exhibits are a little odd (car jacks?), but all in all this is a pretty amusing place.

✿ ✐ ⚹ **Hilary Jones Wildlife Museum & Elk Information Center** (870-446-6180; www.arkansaselkcenter.com), SR 7 North, Jasper, Ark. Open daily 9–5. Free admission. This museum is named for Newton County native Hilary Jones, who made a repopulated Arkansas elk herd his main priority when he was on the Arkansas Game and Fish Commission. In fact, the herd itself bears his name. This museum features elk information, aquariums, and a plethora of information on rivers, hunting, fishing, and outdoor recreation. A gift shop features carved wooden toys and all sorts of interesting gewgaws and gimcracks fashioned from elk antlers.

🦌 ✎ ♿ **Olmstead Museum** (501-362-2422; www.olmstead.cc), 108 S. Fourth St., Heber Springs, Ark. Open weekdays. Sometimes it's a good thing to be able to say that business is dead. The Olmstead Museum, found in the Olmstead Funeral Home, traces the history of the postmortem biz. Established in 1896, this is the oldest business in town, and it's on the National Register of Historic Places. You will find the obligatory horse-drawn hearse, funeral artifacts, and many photos of early Heber Springs. As you'll soon discover, people are dying to come to the Ozarks. Guided tours are offered by appointment.

E. Bob Jackson Memorial Museum of Funeral Service (870-523-5822), 1900 Malcolm Ave., Newport, Ark. Just in case you didn't get enough funeral fun and inhumation hijinks while you were back in Heber Springs, the E. Bob Jackson Memorial Museum of Funeral Service can help you top off your tanks. On hand is yet another 19th-century, horse-drawn death wagon, as well as a chapel and all sorts of memorabilia. Guided tours are offered by appointment, because you just can't drop into a funeral home any old time you'd like.

CULTURAL SITES 🦌 ✎ ♿ **Batesville Confederate Monument** (870-793-2378), 192 E. Main St. (Independence County Courthouse), Batesville, Ark. Maybe the South won't rise again, but the soldiers of the Confederacy are never truly forgotten in Batesville. On the lawn of the courthouse square you will find the Batesville Confederate Memorial, a remembrance of the local men and units that served in the War Between the States.

✎ ♿ **Top O' the Ozarks Tower** (870-445-4302; www.topotheozarks.com), Tower Road off SR 178 (2 miles west of Bull Shoals Dam), Bull Shoals, Ark. Open seasonally every day (usually from mid-Mar.–Dec.), this 180-foot tower on top of Bull Mountain affords a view of more than 50 miles on a clear day. The panorama of Bull Shoals Lake and the White River is very nice as well. The tower is elevator equipped (you don't have to walk the entire 240 steps, but you do have to walk some to reach the uppermost deck) and has been the site of 34 weddings since 1964. Admission is $5.50 for those 13 and up, $2.50 for those ages 7–12.

🦌 ✎ **Mountain Village 1890** (870-445-7177; www.1890village.com/index.htm), 1011 C. S. Woods Blvd., Bull Shoals, Ark. Open Mar. 15–May 15, Wed.–Sun. 10–5; May 15–Labor Day, daily 9–6; Labor Day–Oct. 31, Thurs.–Mon. 10–5. $5 adults, $3 children. Mountain Village 1890, located next to Bull Shoals Caverns, is a collection of 11 authentic houses and businesses that have been restored to 1890s perfection. There's a jail, blacksmith and coffin shop, church, doctor's office, general store, and much more. Around the re-created village you'll see plenty of livestock (ducks, rabbits, and miniature horses and donkeys), and of course you don't want to miss the Ozark moonshine still. This one is the real

deal, discovered in Bull Shoals Caverns in 1958. It allegedly belonged to a ridge
runner named Manfred Long. Should you wish to get hitched among stills and
miniature donkeys, the church at Mountain Village 1890 is available for the service, as is the Crystal Altar Room in Bull Shoals Caverns.

🦐 🐚 ♿ **Cotter Rainbow Bridge** (870-435-2663), US 62-B, Cotter, Ark. Spanning the White River at the little town of Cotter is the famous Rainbow Arch
Bridge. One of the most photographed bridges in the Ozarks, this one was built
in 1930 and is listed on the National Register of Historic Places. The old bridge
was getting to be in sad shape, so the Arkansas Highway Department began an
extensive renovation in 2002. Work was completed in 2004 (to the tune of $6
million), so now you won't feel you are going to plunge into the river when you
drive across the thing.

🦐 🐚 **Indian Rock House** (501-884-4899), 337 Snead Dr., Fairfield Bay, Ark.
OK, kids, it's unsubstantiated rumor time again. The Indian Rock House, a sandstone grotto residing under a hillside on Fairfield Bay's Indian Hills Golf Course,
was for certain the home of Bluff Dweller Natives. A more dubious story that
consistently makes the rounds is that Hernando de Soto met with Indians at this
site in 1542 while searching for the Fountain of Youth. My bet is that he probably met with Jerry Lee Lewis, Bigfoot, Judge Crater, and the ghost of Jim Morri-
son while he was there, too. At any rate, the grotto is sort of cool, if you're into
grottoes, and is conveniently located close to the Log Cabin Museum.

🦐 🐚 ♿ **Greers Ferry National Fish Hatchery** (501-362-3615; www.fws.gov
/greersferry), 349 Hatchery Rd., Heber Springs, Ark. Open daily 7–3. Admission
is free Established in 1965 by the U.S. Fish and Wildlife Service, the Greers

THE MUCH-PHOTOGRAPHED RAINBOW ARCH BRIDGE

Ferry hatchery breeds and stocks more than 203,000 pounds of trout each year, placing them to a large degree in the very cold tailwaters of dams such as Greers Ferry. (Just in case you wondered, 203,000 pounds of trout translates to more than 1 million fish). More than 50,000 visitors tour this facility each year, and a visitors center features an aquarium and guided tours.

🍴 ⚲ ♿ **William Carl Garner Visitor Center** (501-362-9067; www.swl.usace .army.mil/parks/greersferry/visitorscenter.htm), 7000 Heber Springs Rd. North, Heber Springs, Ark. Hours (though they vary) are generally Apr. and Oct., Thurs.–Mon. 10–6; May–Sept., daily 10–6. The center is usually closed Nov.–Mar. Admission is free. The official Army Corps visitors center for Greers Ferry Lake, the Garner Center offers general information on the lake and dam, an exhibit area and auditorium, an audiovisual presentation on the Little Red River region, and a replica of the 40-pound, 4-ounce, world-record brown trout caught by Rip Collins in the Little Red in 1992.

🍴 ⚲ ♿ **Old Mill** (870-269-5337; http://oldmillcountrystore.com), 306 W. Main St., Mountain View, Ark. This old mill, aptly named "Old Mill," was in operation 1914–1969. A large-scale restoration was undertaken in 1983, and today visitors may view the original equipment and peruse photos and memorabilia from the very cool town of Mountain View, Folk Music Capital of the World.

Wolf House (870-425-2755; www.baxtercounty.org/wolfhouse.php), SR 5, Norfork, Ark. The oldest house in Arkansas (built sometime between 1809 and 1825), the Wolf House resides in its original location at the confluence of the White and Big North Fork Rivers. Owned by the city of Norfork and staffed by volunteers, the renovated old home is full of nearly 500 items dating from the 18th and 19th centuries. The 1870 "hanging mousetrap" and "glass parlor flytrap" indicate that keeping up with pesky and pestilent vermin was a full-time

WOLF HOUSE

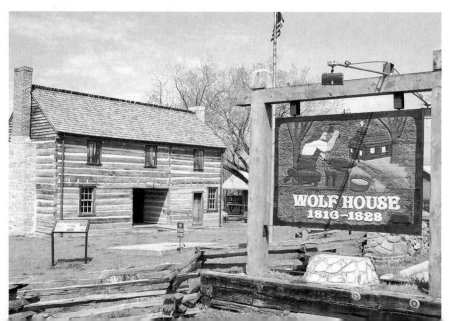

job in years past. (Now we just worry about computer spam, politicians, and the supplicants of political correctness . . . somehow the vermin of then seems preferable to the vermin of now). For a step back in history, this is the place. Call ahead for hours and fees.

HISTORIC SITE Natural Bridge (501-745-2357), Clinton, Ark. Just travel 4 miles north of Clinton on US 65 and you'll find a natural 100-foot sandstone bridge. The Natural Bridge took millions of years to form, and in fact was often used as a bridge by the pioneers. A small museum and gift shop near the site is open mid-Mar.–late Oct.

ELEPHANTS ✍ ♿ **Riddle's Elephant and Wildlife Sanctuary** (501-589-3291; www.elephantsanctuary.org), Greenbrier, Ark. I've always wondered if an elephant with skin problems has to visit a pachydermatologist. No matter, if you want to see elephants up close and personal, you must absolutely visit Riddle's. Granted, this 330-acre preserve is just a tad outside of the Ozark borders (a few miles north of the town of Conway off US 65), but it's also just different enough that a few miles shouldn't prevent inclusion in this book. This sanctuary, founded in 1990, houses and cares for all breeds of elephants obtained from zoos, circuses, and even private owners. If you're really, really into elephants, the sanctuary offers numerous "Elephant Experience Weekends." From Friday night through Sunday you'll take part in feeding, watering, bathing, toenail trimming, and (one imagines) filling up the peanut trough. The price is $700 and includes all meals (the human type) and lodging in a dorm. You must be 18 or older to participate.

✷ To Do

FISHING 🎣 ✍ ♿ **Collins Creek** (501-362-2416 or 1-877-470-3309; www.swl .usace.army.mil/parks/greersferry/hiking.htm). Located off SR 25, Heber Springs, Ark. Near the Greers Ferry National Fish Hatchery and adjacent to Greers Ferry Dam, this seasonal stream was converted to a year-round trout fishery by the Arkansas Game and Fish Commission. Named for the late Rip Collins, who caught the world's largest brown trout from the Little Red River, the project required the building of a cold-water supply line from the base of the dam to the creek and took eight years to complete. Now the creek is home to rainbow and brook trout and three special fishing platforms for the handicapped. This is a catch-and-release-only stream, and children under 16 may fish anywhere for free. Adults who have licenses are permitted to fish the lower stretches when accompanied by a child under 16.

GOLF 🎣 ⛳ **The Course at Eagle Mountain** (870-612-8000; www.thecourse ateaglemountain.com), 800 Gap Rd., Batesville, Ark. This relatively new course in Batesville is an 18-hole, 7,009-yard semiprivate challenge complete with pro shop, bar, and grill. Greens fees for 18 holes are $50 (which includes a cart and range balls) Fri.–Sun. and $40 Tues.–Thurs., Apr. 1–Oct. 31. Rates are $10 cheaper in the off-season. Nine-hole fees are $35 Fri.–Sun. and $30 Tues.–Thurs., Apr. 1–Oct. 31.

❧ ❧ **Cooper's Hawk Golf Course** (870-368-3280; www.coopershawkgolf.com), SR 69 Spur, Melbourne, Ark. Another recently built facility, this 18-hole, 7,011-yard public course features a fully stocked pro shop, full bar and grill, and very affordable rates. With cart included, greens fees for 18 holes are $38 Mon.–Thurs. and $48 Fri.–Sat.

❧ ❧ ❧ ❧ **Mountain Ranch Golf Club** (501-362-5577; www.tboxgolf.net/content), 820 Lost Creek Pkwy., Fairfield Bay, Ark. The awards are many for this course. The *Arkansas Democrat-Gazette* gives it a number one ranking, and *Golf Digest* says it's the best public course in the state. That renowned authority and *Golf Week* magazine rank Mountain Ranch as one of the top 500 courses in the nation. This very challenging par-72, 18-hole course features a well-stocked pro shop, practice range, and clinics by PGA experts. **Bogie's** restaurant is also on-site for your after-round enjoyment. There are various fees at Mountain Ranch, depending on whether you have purchased a golfing package. However, for the general public, rates run $45 Mon.–Thurs. with cart included. Rates are $55 Fri.–Sun. Play after 2 PM and rates drop to $35 and $40, respectively. That is a phenomenal deal for a course of this quality.

❧ ❧ ❧ **Tannenbaum Golf Resort** (501-362-5577 or 1-866-876-8269; www.tbox golf.net), 5 Kustin Dr., Drasco, Ark. This golfing community/resort offers another par-72, 18-hole course rated highly by *Golf Digest.* The joy or the curse here, depending upon your perspective and golf proficiency, is the wide change in elevation from hole to hole and tee to green. The facility also offers a driving range, putting and chipping green, and practice bunker. Also, if you tire of golf, you are close to the incredible fishing of Greers Ferry Lake and the Little Red River. Greens fees run $45 Mon.–Thurs. with cart included. Rates are $55 Fri.–Sun. Play after 2 PM and rates drop to $35 and $40, respectively.

❧ ❧ ❧ **Big Creek Golf and Country Club** (870-425-8815; www.bigcreekgolf .com), 452 Country Club Dr., Mountain Home, Ark. Seeing as how *Golf Digest* gave Big Creek five out of five stars and in 2001 called it "the best new course in America," the magazine obviously thinks it's a doozie of a place to play. Sitting on 200 acres, the 7,320-yard, 18-hole course features a three-tiered driving range, practice putting and chipping greens, and a practice bunker. Also on-site is a well-regarded restaurant with a full bar. Summer rates for the general public are $55 on weekdays and $65 on weekends, Apr.–mid-Oct. This includes a cart rental; winter rates are lower. You can't wear blue jeans or tank tops on this course, and the management will be right unhappy if you try to tote along your own cooler of Budweiser.

TRAIL RIDES ❧ ❧ **Horseshoe Canyon Guest Ranch** (870-446-2577 or 1-800-480-9635; http://horseshoecanyonduderanch.com), SR 74 West, Jasper, Ark. An all-inclusive, 350-acre dude ranch located 7.5 miles west of Jasper, Horseshoe Canyon is high in the sky at 2,100 feet. Offering a horsy type of vacation for the entire family, it charges a single rate that covers cabin, meals, maid service, kids' programs, canoeing, horseback riding, rock climbing, skeet shooting, swimming, riding a zipline, and any other ranch activities. Summer rates begin at $205 per night for adults, $160 for ages 8–16, and $110 for ages 3–7.

During summer there is a three-night minimum stay; in fall and spring (when rates are lower), a two-night minimum. This is an interesting ranch featuring knowledgeable staff and a herd of very well-trained horses. Rides generally last from 1½ to 4 hours (primarily in the morning and afternoon), and any number of social gatherings take place after dinner. The ranch offers satellite Internet access for guests, but pets are not accepted. Also, should you wish a swallow of hooch while sitting around the campground, you'll need to bring your own. Newton County, where Horseshoe Canyon ranch is located, is drier than an Amish joke book.

✳ Wild Places

🐾 ☠ ♂ ♿ **Ozark National Forest, Sylamore District** (870-269-3228; www .fs.fed.us/oonf/ozark), 1001 E. Main St., Mountain View, Ark. Part of the 1.2-million-acre Ozark National Forest, the 133,000-acre Sylamore District consists of deep forests and beautiful streams, bluffs, meadows, and rivers. It also holds such treasures as Blanchard Springs Caverns. There are campgrounds set up at such places as Blanchard, but since this is national forest, you can pitch your tent almost anywhere. Hiking, hunting, fishing, and horseback riding are all equally popular in the Sylamore District. If you're really into hiking, a 31-mile stretch of the Ozark Highlands Trail travels close to SR 342 north of Mountain View.

For the **Buffalo National River** and the **White River,** see *Exploring by River.*

PARKS 🐾 ☠ ♂ ♿ **Bull Shoals–White River State Park** (870-445-3629; www .arkansasstateparks.com/bullshoalswhiteriver), 153 Dam Overlook Ln., Bull Shoals, Ark. Consisting of 45,440 acres of water straddling the Missouri-Arkansas border, Bull Shoals Lake and the White River offer one of the greatest combinations for water sports and monster-trout fishing in the U.S. The Bull Shoals–White River State Park, at 732 acres, is located at the spot where Bull Shoals Dam crosses the White River. The park, established in 1955, in fact stretches along the banks of the White; over the years it has become one of the most popular fishing/camping destinations in Arkansas. Featuring 105 campsites along the river, the park offers interpretive programs Apr.–Jan., picnic areas, playgrounds, trails, and a marina. The latest addition to Bull Shoals–White River is a $4.8 million, nearly 16,000-square-foot visitors center. The center, named after longtime Arkansas resort owner Jim Gaston, includes interpretive exhibits, a theater, gift shop, and exhibit hall. Campsites run from $11 per night for a primitive tent spot to $80 per night for "Rent-An-RV" units. At the marina/dock, 20-foot jon boats with a 15-horse motor begin at $107 per day plus fuel, and kayak rental begins at $25 per day (or $8 per hour). Rental of a canoe or kayak with haul-back services is $55 per day.

🐾 ☠ ♂ ♿ **Mammoth Spring State Park** (870-625-7364; www.arkansasstate parks.com/mammothspring), SR 9 and US 63 North, Mammoth Spring, Ark. Spewing out 9 million gallons of water per hour, Mammoth Spring forms a 10-acre lake and serves as the headwaters of the Spring River. You can't actually see this spring (it's 80 feet under the lake), so you'll just have to trust me that it's there. However, this park features much more than simply its giant natural spigot. A tourist information center offers exhibits, basic services, and a gift shop, and a walking trail leads to a restored 1886 Frisco railroad depot. The depot and its grounds not only hold a caboose and historical artifacts, but are also near the remains of an early mill and hydroelectric plant. Picnic tables and a playground, set amid large oak trees, overlook the lake. The 1886 Frisco Depot museum and caboose are open Tues.–Sun. 8–5; admission is $2.25 adults, $1.25

🏛 🏕 ✒ ♿ **Ozark Folk Center State Park** (870-269-3851; www.ozarkfolkcenter .com), SR 382 (1 mile north of Mountain View). Turn left onto Jimmy Driftwood Pkwy., which is also SR 382. It dead-ends at the folk center parking lot. Let's put it this way: If you can visit only one place in the Arkansas Ozarks, this should be it. In a word, the Ozark Folk Center State Park is amazing, not to mention one-of-a-kind. An 80-acre complex within the 640-acre park is dedicated to preserving the old Ozark heritage through traditional music, dance, pioneer skills, stories, and native crafts. More than anything else, it is this park that makes Mountain View the Folk Music Capital of the World. In the park's Crafts Village (open Apr.–Nov., Wed.–Sat. 10–5), you'll find a plethora of local artisans demonstrating the art of the old homestead and creating Ozark crafts. During this same season, the park's 1,025-seat music theater offers concerts Tues.–Sat. at 7 PM, and frequent Sunday gospel sings. There's a gift shop (open daily 10–5:30 during the season) offering everything from corn husk brooms, pottery, and oak baskets to knives, quilts, and real fruit preserves. You may stay in the park's 60-room Dry Creek Lodge any time of year or enjoy a uniquely southern Ozark meal (no possum, though) at the Skillet Restaurant. The restaurant is only open during the season, daily 7 AM–8 PM. You'll find a smokehouse, herb garden, tram service, and music, music, and more music. It seems everywhere you venture in this park you will trip across musicians playing either solo or in groups; strumming fiddles, dobros, and dulcimers; picking at guitars, banjos, bass, and autoharp.

In addition, the Ozark Folk Center holds a celebrity concert series every season (call or check the park's website for details and prices), along with myriad classes, workshops, and festivals. Workshop topics run the gamut from medicinal herbs and botanicals to pottery techniques to dulcimer playing. And this is just a tiny sample.

Admission to the Crafts Village or music auditorium alone is $10 for adults, $6 for ages 6–12. A combination admission for both the Crafts Village and music auditorium is $17.50 for adults, $8.25 for kids. Tickets for the celebrity concert series vary by performer. Family passes, three-day passes, and season passes are also available.

ages 6–12. Both pedal boats and single kayaks can be rented for $6 per hour, and a tandem kayak is $8 per hour. You should note that there is no camping at Mammoth Spring.

🦐 🐾 ✎ ♿ **Jacksonport State Park** (870-523-2143; www.arkansasstateparks.com /jacksonport), 205 Avenue St., Newport, Ark. Marking the border of the Delta and the Ozarks is Newport, Ark., home of Jacksonport State Park. Thanks to the steamboat trade, Jacksonport was a busy and rollicking place in the 1800s. During the Civil War, the area was nearly always in a tug-of-war between the Gray and Blue, and at one time or another it was occupied by both. Today the centerpiece of the park is the old 1872 **Courthouse Museum.** Also on the site are picnic tables, a playground, a swimming beach on the White River, and 20 campsites with water and 50-amp electric service. Campsite fees are $22 per day for a campsite with water and power. Admission to the Courthouse Museum is $3 for adults, $1.50 for ages 6–12.

🦐 🐾 ✎ ♿ **Old Davidsonville State Park** (870-892-4708; www.arkansasstate parks.com/olddavidsonville), 7953 SR 166 South, Pocahontas, Ark. Davidsonville, near the town of Pocahontas, was the site of the first post office, courthouse, and land office in Arkansas. This town is so old that, by the 1830s, it was already approaching ghost status. Today the 180-acre park contains trails, exhibits, picnic tables, and interpretive tours, but the real reason most folks come to Old Davidsonville is to fish. The park is bordered by the Black River, has a 12-acre fishing lake (handicapped accessible in places), and rents fishing boats, pedal boats, and canoes. Of the 49 campsites, 23 offer water and electricity ($18 per night), 25 are tent sites ($11), and one offers water and 50-amp service ($22). A 14-foot

OLD DAVIDSONVILLE STATE PARK

fishing boat (human-powered) is just $15 per day, and either a canoe or pedal boat is $5 per hour. A canoe trip with hauling included is $30. There is also the chance to take an interpretive/historical canoe trip ($35 per canoe) or an interpretive tour by foot of the old Davidsonville town site ($6.50 adults, $3.50 kids).

LAKES Greers Ferry Lake (501-362-2416; www.swl.usace.army.mil/parks /greersferry/index.htm), 700 Heber Springs Rd. N., Heber Springs, Ark. Consisting of nearly 40,000 acres of water surface, Greers Ferry Dam was dedicated in 1963 by President John Kennedy; in fact, this was Kennedy's last dedication before his assassination in Dallas. Around the lake you'll find 18 Army Corps of Engineers campgrounds, not to mention nearly infinite private campgrounds, B&Bs, hotels and motels, marinas, restaurants, and entertainment. Because of the mild winter climate, this area is becoming increasingly popular as a retirement spot. This means that local businesses cater heavily to some of the more passive types of recreation, such as golf, fishing, shopping, and eating. The Little Red River below the dam is renowned for its monster trout, and (as if I haven't mentioned it enough in this chapter) the 40-pound, 4-ounce brown caught by Rip Collins still holds the world title.

Norfork Lake (870-425-2700; www.swl.usace.army.mil/parks/norfork/index.htm), 324 W. Seventh St., Mountain Home, Ark. I was straddling a sailboard about half a mile out on Norfork Lake (I never have learned how to tack correctly; sailing is an evil sport) when a freak storm dropped rain, lightning, and 50 mph winds on my head. My old friend, Edward T. Boys, was stuck out there as well, graciously trying to help fix the twisted rudder on my board. As I recall, with lightning blasting all around us, Ed and I were forced to lie flat in the water and hold onto those stupid hunks of plastic polymer for near an hour. Bobbing and freezing, I finally looked at him and said, "Well, here's another fine mess I've gotten us into." Ed and I have inadvertently gotten each other practically killed, deafened, humiliated, or maimed a few hundred times over the course of our lives (driving, sailing, blowing things up, accidentally dropping cars on each other), but that's another story.

Finally a brave soul in a motorized jon boat cruised out through the crashing waves, tossed us a rope, and saved Ed and me from hypothermia and/or becoming popcorn salesmen at the Pearly Gates. It was a highly embarrassing situation, and I'm glad we survived, as dying via an inability to paddle a modified surfboard on a normally placid lake is simply pathetic.

That said, in no way, shape, or form do I blame such a mishap on Norfork Lake itself. With its 550 miles of shoreline and 22,000 surface acres of water, this is one of the most popular weekend spots in the Ozarks. Created in 1944 by the Army Corps, a dam (built for both flood control and hydropower) crosses the North Fork River a few miles from the little town of Norfork, where the North Fork joins the White River. Around the lake you will find 19 developed parks either managed or subbed out by the corps, and camping is nearly as popular as fishing and boating. The numerous commercial docks offer guides, boats, and equipment of all sorts, and there is a plethora of lodging and dining options. Norfork Lake is loaded with catfish, bass, walleye, bluegill, and crappie, and it's not terribly uncommon for someone to catch a 30-pound striped bass. Moreover, because of the lake's water clarity, scuba is a hot ticket. Last but not least, the 25,000 acres of corps land around the lake allow for great hiking.

Bull Shoals Lake (870-425-2700; www.swl.usace.army.mil/parks/bullshoals), 324 W. Seventh St., Mountain Home, Ark. Featuring 45,000 surface acres of water and surrounded by 60,000 acres of Army Corps of Engineers land, Bull Shoals has been a haven for vacationers and retirees since the 1950s. The White River was dammed for both flood control and hydropower in the late 1940s (the dam itself is about 7 miles north of Cotter, Ark.), and the fishery below Bull Shoals has long been known for containing some of the largest trout in the U.S. Within the lake itself, though, the usual suspects of fish (catfish, bass, walleye, and all sorts of panfish) are plentiful for the talented (or just patient) angler. Between the corps, the state of Arkansas, and local entities, there are 19 separate parks around Bull Shoals. In total these parks encompass 18 boat ramps, 11 campgrounds, 13 picnic shelters, 11 marinas, seven designated swimming areas, and much more. As you would imagine, private enterprises such as lodges, resorts, motels, restaurants, and bed & breakfasts are more than plentiful. With little or no effort you can locate any number of places that will sell or rent you boats and equipment, provide guides, or meet any other need you might imagine.

CAVES ♂ 🦐 ✎ **Bull Shoals Caverns** (870-445-7177; www.bullshoalscaverns .com), 1011 C. S. Woods Blvd., Bull Shoals, Ark. Open Mar. 15–May 15, Wed.– Sun. 10–5; May 16–May 31, daily 9–5; June 1–Aug. 15, daily 9–6; Aug. 16–Labor Day, daily 9–5; Labor Day–Oct. 31, Thurs.–Mon. 10–5. Call for rates. If you are in the dark about the personality of your spouse-to-be, it might be appropriate to get hitched in the Crystal Altar Room deep within Bull Shoals Caverns. Then again, for something less permanent (and in some cases less rocky), you might just want to tour the sights in this living cave. Owned by the same folks who own the Mountain Village 1890, the cave features such geological nifties as a rotunda, cave drapes, stalactite and stalagmite gardens, soda straws, and boxwork.

🦐 ✎ ♿ **Blanchard Springs Caverns & Recreation Area** (1-888-757-2246; www.fs.fed.us/oonf/ozark/recreation/caverns.html), SR 14 West, Mountain View, Ark. Caves administered by the U.S. Forest Service often feature much better tours and sights than their commercial counterparts. This scenario is especially evident at Blanchard Springs Caverns, one of the most interesting holes in the ground you'll ever discover. A three-level cave (two levels are open for guided tours), Blanchard offers several options for exploring. The Dripstone Trail Tour requires about an hour and is accessible to strollers and wheelchairs if you have helpers with some muscle. Tours leave frequently and are available year-round; $10 adults, $5 ages 6–15. The price is the same for the Discovery Trail Tour, although this path is more arduous. There are 700 steps, so you need to be in decent shape. The Discovery Trail Tour is only available Memorial Day–Labor Day. Lastly, if you really want to get down and dirty (with emphasis on both— literally), take the Wild Cave Tour. This trip, which is about four hours long and requires reservations, takes you through parts of the cave's undeveloped middle

BLANCHARD SPRINGS CAVERNS

level. You need to be in good shape, as there is much climbing and crawling involved. Also, children under 10 are not allowed, and parents must accompany children ages 10–12. The price for the Wild Cave Tour is $75 per person, and for this tour you need a minimum of 3 people and a maximum of 12. Tours take place Apr.–Oct.

❦ ♂ **Hurricane River Cave** (870-429-6200; www.hurricanerivercaverns.com), US 65 South, Pindall, Ark. Located north of Conway off US 65 (or about an hour due south of Branson, Mo.), the cave's tour follows an ancient subterranean riverbed. Of course the usual stalactites, stalagmites, columns, and soda straws are both evident and prevalent. One interesting aspect of Hurricane River is that it's been a prime spot for skeletons. Saber-toothed tigers, prehistoric bears, and a complete Indian skeleton have been found within this hole. No surprise on the human bones, as those who share space with lions and bears tend to have a shortened life span. There's a neat waterfall at the entrance to this cave, and the grounds are quite pretty. Hurricane River opens at 9 AM Mar. 1–Oct. 31; tours take about 45 minutes and cover roughly a quarter mile. There aren't a lot of steps (fewer than 40 total), so you don't need to be an Olympic athlete to wander about under the ground. Admission is $8.50 for adults, $4.50 for ages 5–12. In addition, a Wild Cave Tour—which includes a boat ride on an underground river followed by climbing and crawling—is available. This option is by reservation only and limited to parties of six with everyone above the age of 12. Call for pricing.

✳ Lodging

The number of inns, resorts, B&Bs, and cabins located in this section of the Ozarks is truly astounding. Catering to the millions who visit the White and Little Red Rivers, as well as Bull Shoals, Norfork, and Greers Ferry Lakes, innkeepers offer accommodations to suit every taste, style, and thickness of wallet. Should you wish to peruse further than the recommended establishments listed here, I suggest you check out the website provided by the **Bed and Breakfast Association of Arkansas** (www.bed andbreakfastarkansas.com). This site will provide you with further possibilities (as well as some dandy recipes) and more than a few photos of individual guest rooms.

BED & BREAKFASTS Ashley House Bed & Breakfast (870-368-4577; www.ashleyhouse.net), 618 E. Main St., Melbourne, Ark. Reputed to be the oldest home in Melbourne, the Ashley House was transformed via a 1999 renovation from antiques store to B&B. The home's original flagstones nicely set off the front porch and white picket fence, and Ashley's seven guest rooms are loaded with antiques. Four of these rooms feature king-sized beds, three have queens, and there are also two private guest houses and two river cabins on the property (the cabins are $198 per night with a two-night minimum). All rooms have a private bath and, in a bow to technology, wireless Internet. Located within close proximity to both the Cooper's Hawk Golf Course and the White River, Ashley House also handles weddings, meetings, and conferences, and it offers both antiques and original artwork for sale.

Call to inquire about rates, kids, and pets.

☕ The Cedars Bed and Breakfast (870-297-4197; www.thecedarsbnb .net), Old Dolph Rd., Calico Rock, Ark. For a stay in the country, it would be hard to beat the setting or hospitality of The Cedars. You can stay in one of two private cabins. The huge, two-story, 10-bed cabin runs anywhere from $65–$150 per night (depending upon the time of year and how many rooms you want). The smaller cabin (which does not accept kids under 10) is $75 per night. This is a well-designed establishment set in a 240-acre stretch of woods, and the management will be happy to set you up with area fishing guides.

⚓ River View Hotel Bed & Breakfast (870-297-8208; www.ozarksriver view.com), 100 Rodman, Calico Rock, Ark. Open through the summer season until mid-Oct. With a view of the White River and a spot on the National Register of Historic Places, this 1923 hotel is a simple sort of place for those who wish to get away from it all. Nice touches that help accomplish this goal are rooms without telephones, cotton sheets dried on a clothesline, and a spacious front porch with a swing looking down at the White. All rooms have a private bath. There are TVs in all the rooms, and in the past few years the old black-and-white sets have been upgraded to color. Kids are welcome here, and though you can smoke outside, don't puff in your room. The River View gives you a bit of the feel of being in the 1950s, and the rates for any of the eight rooms range $65–75. If you have an urge to be an innkeeper, The River View was for sale at the time of this writing (July

LUXURIOUS BOMB SHELTERS

✇ ♿ Beckham Creek Cave Lodge (1-888-446-6043: www.ozarkcave.com), HC 72, west on SR 327 from Parthenon, Ark. For what may be the strangest and most luxurious lodging in the entire Ozarks, you need to go underground. This cave house, residing amid a 280-acre estate, was originally built by the co-founder of the Celestial Seasonings Tea Company. Apparently, after viewing the 1980s end-of-the-world movie "The Day After," the gentleman decided to build himself a little post-apocalyptic haven in Arkansas. When the end of the world failed to appear on schedule, his wife insisted he sell it. The current owners now allow travelers the chance to spend a night or a week in a lodging that's been featured on *Lifestyles of the Rich and Famous*, HGTV, *NBC Nightly News, People* magazine, *National Geographic, Four States Living,* and *The Barefoot Traveler.*

Though the chopper pad, blast-proof concrete walls, and private water system fed by an underground spring still exist, such is just the beginning. The great room alone measures 2,000 square feet, and there's a huge window that allows light in from outdoors. The room comes in handy if you want to watch the satellite TV or enjoy the professional sound system. The kitchen is of chef quality, coming with all appliances and utensils, and between the kitchen and great room is a long bar with stools and a breakfast nook. Upstairs is a game room and recreation area with pool table and gaming table. Five bedrooms feature private baths, and each is themed (in the vein of presidential or honeymoon suites). Central air and heat, as well as humidifiers, will keep you both cozy and dry. Beckham Creek Cave Haven can accommodate parties from 2 to 20 at one time, and there is a two-night minimum. The management of Beckham Creek prefers that you call for a rate quote.

2011). Just call the owners if you've got a bunch of money burning a hole in your pocket.

✇ **The White River Inn Bed & Breakfast** (870-430-2233; www.the whiteriverinn.com), 924 CR 174, Cotter, Ark. The White River Inn offers more than a touch of luxury for those vacationing on the White River. Five individual guest suites feature 14-foot ceilings, custom-made Mission furniture, fireplace, and Jacuzzi. You'll sleep on 600 thread count sheets and under hand-fashioned quilts. In addition, for a kicked-back evening you can enjoy satellite TV and wireless Internet. You may relax on overstuffed leather couches and chairs, watch the big screen, or play any number of board games in the lodge's great room. A wall of 8-foot windows looks down upon the White River Valley, which also makes this room a wonderful spot to enjoy a leisurely breakfast of locally picked berries, cereals, sausage or bacon, juices, coffee, and homemade biscuits. There is also an outdoor hot tub and a trophy room with mounted big game from around the globe. Rates at White River Inn are $225–375 per night for either double or single occupancy. Add $100 for each additional adult and $50 for each child. The cost is $1,525 per night if you'd care to rent the entire lodge. This facility is more than happy to set you up with fishing guides and spa services, but smoking and pets are not permitted. Kids under 15 are OK, if well behaved, at the owner's discretion.

🦌 ♦ ♿ **Biggers Bed & Breakfast** (870-856-4718 or 1-866-856-4718; www.biggersbnb.com), 20 Bluff Rd., Hardy, Ark. Looking down on the Spring River, Biggers B&B is often the choice for weddings, honeymoons, anniversaries, and (of course) fishermen. An outdoor pool and hot tub are on-site, and the facility prides itself upon arranging such services as fishing guides, massages, and spa treatments. Three luxury suites ($150–175) include a king-sized bed, gas fireplace, two-person hot tub, microwave, refrigerator, coffeemaker, digital cable TV, private bath, and wireless Internet. Three deluxe guest rooms range from $90–125. Two smaller, standard rooms can be had for $70 and $85. Kids are welcome (assuming they aren't wild heathens), but this place changed hands in 2011 and pets are no longer accepted. Smoking is only permitted outside, at the pool area, or on the balconies of suites. Breakfast is included in your room price, and the property is also home to the well-regarded **Bluff Steak House,** open Thurs.–Sat. evenings.

♿ 🍴 **Abbe House Inn & Sports Resort** (501-250-2223 or 1-877-250-2223; www.abbehouse.com), 3144 Riverbend, Heber Springs, Ark. You will find no shortage of space in this 12,000-square-foot inn. A home of the "Tara" genre, it features giant white columns and three verandas totaling 1,700 square feet. It comes as little surprise that Abbe House was voted 2004's number one bed & breakfast for outdoor sports enthusiasts by *Inn Traveler* magazine. Situated on 12 meticulously cared-for acres, this inn also backs onto the Lost Creek Golf Course and is close to the Little Red River, Fairfield Bay, and Greers Ferry Lake. Each of 11 guest rooms features a queen-sized bed and whirlpool bath, and rates include a true southern breakfast served family-style. For those who wish to eat dinner on the premises, the Louisiana-born owners can provide delicious entrées in the $15–25 range. Also, beer and wine are available with your meal. Rates for individual rooms run $85–105 per night, but a variety of packages are offered. One very good option is a guided fishing trip for two on the Little Red River. All tackle and equipment is provided, as are accommodations and breakfast, lunch, and dinner. The cost is $430 plus tax for two people ($330 for one person), and the only thing that isn't guaranteed is that you'll catch fish. The Abbe House is also well known for its weddings. Full or partial planning is available, and price quotes are happily provided.

♦ **Anderson House Inn Bed & Breakfast** (501-362-5266; www.andersonhouseinn.com), 201 E. Main St., Heber Springs, Ark. With 14 guest rooms, a private club, and a world-class restaurant, Anderson House is another establishment that is in the heart of fishing utopia. Under new management since the first edition of this book, Anderson House features rooms with antiques and handmade quilts. The great room of the Anderson offers a fireplace of natural Arkansas fieldstone, a giant-screen TV, and free WiFi. The restaurant features a four-star chef from California who has successfully merged the tastes of the Golden State's wine country with the best aspects of southern cuisine. Kids are OK, but dogs will have to find their own accommodations. Use of the devil weed (that would be tobacco, for you city folks) is relegated to porches and balconies. This facility prefers that you call for room rates.

🐾 🦴 🐕 **Barn on the Buffalo** (870-446-6121; www.barnonthebuffalo .com), SR 74 East, Jasper, Ark. After observing some of my more eccentric housekeeping habits (so the dogs have their own couches and easy chairs—big deal), visitors have occasionally been moved to comment, "Boy . . . you musta' been born in a barn." Seeing as how I've seen some pretty spiffy barns in my life, such criticisms don't rile me a whit. A perfect example of fine barn living would be the Barn on the Buffalo. Located near Jasper, Ark., the peaceful haven on 8.5 acres is located just 300 feet from the Little Buffalo River. Walking trails, beaver dams, fishing, swimming, and canoeing are just out your door. The barn itself, fully renovated, features a complete kitchen, full bath, air-conditioning, TV and DVD with movies and DirecTV, and three bedrooms. It sleeps up to nine people and includes all utensils, dishes, and linens. The best part of the Barn is its affordability. You can rent one bedroom for $75 per night, or all three for $95 a night. There's a one-time fee of $25 if you bring along Fido, but no charge for extra folks in your room (this is the only B&B I've ever seen that offers that option). Nice touches here; don't forget to look down and take note of the hand-painted floors. Last but not least, the Barn's "Spring Break" special allows you to rent the entire barn for $900 a week. Groups won't find a better deal anywhere in the Ozarks.

Country Oaks Bed & Breakfast (1-800-455-2704; www.countryoaksbb .com), 17221 SR 9, Mountain View, Ark. It's pretty hard to go wrong in Mountain View. Country Oaks is located just a mile from the town's famous square, and all that music floating around in the air just makes a body feel perky and bright. Situated on 69 acres, a newly built, Victorian-style farmhouse holds five guest rooms, while a separate carriage house holds three more. The property includes a 7-acre lake noted for producing bass as large as 10 pounds, and you'll greet the morning with a full breakfast. As is consistent with many B&Bs in this region, the unspoken theme here is simplicity and fun. Relax on the porch or one of the many benches scattered about the property. Play horseshoes, read a book, or take a walk. Rates run $65–125, and neither pets nor children under 12 are permitted. A dog and a cat or two reside here, so if you want canine companionship, the house hound will likely be glad to oblige. Smoking is outside only, and since this is a dry county, you'll either have to bring your own firewater or learn how to build a still.

🦴 **Wildflower Bed & Breakfast on the Square** (870-269-4383 or 1-800-591-4879; www.wildflowerbb.com),

100 Washington St., Mountain View, Ark. In summers some of the greatest bluegrass and folk musicians imaginable congregate on the town square and play until their fingers wear out. For those of a musical bent, the Wildflower's location cannot be beat—it's located right on that same square, so you can pick, grin, sing, or just listen to your heart's content. Of course you're also close to some great fishing, hiking, and shopping. This inn, built in 1918 and on the National Register of Historic Places, features rooms with king- or queen-sized bed, cable TV and a CD player, private bath, WiFi, ceiling fans, central heat and air, bathrobes, fresh cookies, and a huge buffet breakfast. Rates are $69–139 per night. Kids are OK, but pets are not. Also, Wildflower is pretty strict about its no-smoking policy. Get caught smoking inside the building and you'll have a $200 clean-ing fee added to your credit card. That's fair, because there are plenty of ashtrays on the porch. Call and inquire about weekend packages.

✎ **Inn at Mountain View, 1886** (870-269-4200; www.innatmountainview .com), 307 Washington, Mountain View, Ark. Built in 1886 (hence the name) and on the National Register of Historic Places, the inn offers 11 guest rooms and suites. Frankly, there's not a square inch of this place that could be described as anything other than friendly and charming. Rates run $98–145 per night, with the $145 Garden Suite including a Jacuzzi for two, fireplace, shower, kitchenette, and lace curtains. Amenities in the other rooms are private bath, king- or queen-sized bed, central heat and air, ceiling fan, cable TV, and wireless Internet. The common room holds a big-screen TV with DirecTV and pay-per-view, DVD and VCR, PlayStation 2, video library,

INN AT MOUNTAIN VIEW, 1886

books, and popcorn. There are water gardens in the backyard, and you stay (literally) right next to the fire rings and square where all the local musicians gather for acoustic jams.

RESORTS ✐ Esta's White River Retreat

(808-896-5662; www.estas whiteriverretreat.com), 280 Sloan Ln., Locust Grove, Ark. Relaxing and off the beaten path (about half an hour from either Mountain View or Batesville), Esta's offers eight log-and-cedar cabins with stunning views of the White River. The grounds themselves feature a pool, boat ramp, and sports field with volleyball, basketball, and horseshoes. A two-night stay is required, and it includes a river-view cabin with Jacuzzi and full breakfast. Esta's can also provide full wedding services; those interested in nuptials on the White should call for a quote. This is another spot that is located in a dry county, so if you want a drink (and don't want to have to drive 40 miles), it is advised that you BYOB. Call or email the innkeepers to receive a rate quote or to ask about special packages.

🦞 🐾 ✐ 🚹 Bull Mountain Resort

(1-800-530-5647; www.bullmountain -resort.com), 2224 Central Blvd., Bull Shoals, Ark. Your pet is welcome here so long as you pay a partially refundable deposit. In addition to liking the pups, Bull Mountain offers 10 one- and two-bedroom cottages with heat and air-conditioning, cable TV, coffeemaker, microwave, linens, and dishes. You're close to Bull Shoals Lake, but for those evenings when you wish to stay in, the facility features a pool, fire pits, horseshoes, and volleyball. Rates are $65–99 per night, $390–594 per week. Please note that smoking is not permitted inside the cottages.

✐ 🚹 Calico Rock Cabins

(901-299-4952; www.bbonline.com/ar/crcabins), 500 Calico St., Calico Rock, Ark. If you seek a little more privacy than you'll find at the resorts or B&Bs, these two cabins—both sitting on a high bluff above the White River—offer it in spades. You'll love the view, the glowing wood interior, and the stone fireplace. The cabins offer a full kitchen with dishwasher and microwave, wraparound deck, gas grill, Jacuzzi, and all linens and towels. The price for the cabin at 500 Calico St. is $150 per night or $850 per week. The second cabin, located at 406 Calico St., runs $175 a night or $950 a week. Neither smoking nor pets are allowed.

🦞 ✐ Rainbow Bridge Lodge

(870-435-6666; www.rainbowbridgelodge .com), Second St. and McLean Ave., Cotter, Ark. Located in downtown Cotter on the second story of a historic building, this 3,400-square-foot space comes with a full kitchen and cable TV, and offers access to a dock, pier, and boat launch. Cotter is at the heart of great trout fishing in the White River, and the real draw here is Rainbow's guided fly-fishing service. Owner and guide George Peters has been fly-fishing for more than 50 years and guiding in Arkansas since 2002. The entire lodge can be rented, but you'll need to call ahead and inquire about lodging and guide rates.

🦞 🐾 ✐ 🚹 Sportsman's Resort on the White River

(1-800-626-3474; www.sportsmans-resort.com), 458 Marion County Road 7004, Flippin, Ark. A well-known resort on the White River, Sportsman's offers 22 cabins located on 5.5 park-pretty acres. All the cabins (newly renovated in 2003) come with kitchens, satellite TV, microwave, coffeemaker, cookware, and utensils. Daily maid service is available for a small additional fee. Conveniently, a small grocery store on the premises carries almost every staple you will need. Lodging rates range from $79 per night for an efficiency to $349 for a chalet that sleeps 12 and boasts a 48-foot outdoor deck. Amenities include a playground for the kids, swimming pool, basketball court, and horseshoe area, but in truth most people are here for the fishing. Rental boats—20-foot jon boats with 9.9 horsepower motors and accessories—run $99 for a full day and $60 for a half. Many guests opt to hire an experienced guide; prices range from $170 for a half day to $327 for a full day.

Sportsman's is one of the few places around that is truly dog-friendly, something exemplified by the fact that it doesn't charge an extra fee for Rover. This is a very gracious gesture, as dog owners know how hard it is to find accommodations that will (a) accept a pet at all and (b) not charge you an exorbitant extra fee for hypothetical damages. That said, it is the responsibility of Rover's owner to not abuse the pet policy this establishment offers (i.e., don't screw it up for the rest of us). Keep pup off the bed, and don't let him trash the joint. You will have to sign a damage-responsibility form stating that you'll pay up if your dog breaks something.

🦐 🐈 ✏ ♿ **Gaston's White River Resort & Restaurant** (870-431-5202; www.gastons.com), 1777 River Rd., Lakeview, Ark. Without doubt the best-known resort on the White River, Gaston's has been serving customers since 1958. What started as six cottages and six boats on a 20-acre plot is now 400 acres, 2 miles of riverfront property, and 79 cottages that

cover the spectrum from an economy model with two beds to a two-story lodge with 10 bedrooms. There's an airstrip on the property for those who wish to fly in, more than 70 rental boats, a very nice restaurant, club, gift shop, tennis court, playground, game room, swimming pool, and nature trails. And if you're looking for a ringing endorsement, Gaston's has been written up by (take a deep breath here), the *Arkansas Times, Better Homes and Gardens, Woman's Day, Midwest Living, Outside* magazine, *Southern Living, Field & Stream,* and many other publications. There is no additional fee for bringing your pets, but the resort does ask that they not have fleas and that they stay on a leash if outdoors.

Cottage amenities include cable TV, phone, voicemail, and high-speed Internet. A two-bed unit with a bath (more of a hotel room) is $85 per night for two people. The standard cottage, which comes with king-sized and double bed, bath, and kitchen, is $138. Two-bedroom cottages are $169–227, and prices go up from there. Four-bedroom cabins are $387–765, and the 10-bedroom River Villa, which sleeps 20 people, rents for $1,240 per night. Prices for a two-person guided float trip (18 miles) begin at $326 per day. The long float is best for those who want to sightsee and just do a little bit of fishing. Serious anglers will want to opt for a local trip, which covers far fewer miles and is intended to help you hook a lunker. The price for a full day is $280 for two people, or $326 with lunch. Note that you need to bring your own equipment, bait, and fishing license. You can also rent boats, motors, fishing tackle, chairs, rods, and reels at the dock. Keep in mind that the fee is $900 if you accidentally sink one of the resort's boats. Gaston's calls itself "America's Number One Trout Fishing Resort." Judging by its longevity and repeat business, more than a few folks agree.

CANOE OUTFITTERS, CAMPING, AND RVS ✪ ❀ ♿ Sylamore Creek Camp & Cabins

(870-585-2326 or 1-877-475-4223; www.sylamorecreek .com), 214 Sylamore Creek Rd., Mountain View, Ark. Located on Sylamore Creek on the site of an old Indian village, and with the White River just a few hundred yards downstream, this facility is but 5 miles north of Mountain View. Fishing and swimming are at your disposal—there is a boat ramp on the creek—and cabins, tent sites, and RV spaces are available. A "lodge"-style camp store carries all sorts of groceries, drinks, ice, and fishing supplies. Though off-season rates are less expensive, Mar. 1–Nov. 1 cabins cost $70–140 per night or $420–840 weekly. Kids under 12 stay free, and all the cabins are nonsmoking. RV sites come with water, electricity, picnic table, grill, and fire rings. For basic water and electric the price is $18 per night, $108 per week. A full hook-up is $22 a night, $132 per week. If you'd like cable TV, there's an additional fee of $3 per night, $14 per week. Wireless Internet is also available. Last but not least, both primitive tent sites and those with services are available. A site with electricity and water is $18 per night, $108 per week, and a primitive site goes from $12 per night or $72 per week. Pets on a leash are permitted.

✪ ❀ ✪ ♿ Bull Shoals–White River State Park

(870-445-3629; www .arkansasstateparks.com/bullshoals whiteriver/camping), 153 Dam Overlook Ln., Bull Shoals, Ark. (see *Parks*). To make reservations, either call the number above or make online reservations at www.accessarkansasparks .com/servlet/WebresResDesk?6006.

✪ ❀ ✪ ♿ Jacksonport State Park

(870-523-2143; www.arkansasstate parks.com/jacksonport), 205 Avenue St., Newport, Ark. (see *Parks*). To make reservations, either call the number above or make online reservations at www.accessarkansasparks .com/servlet/WebresResDesk?6022.

Old Davidsonville State Park (870-892-4708; www.arkansasstateparks .com/olddavidsonville), 7953 SR 166 South, Pocahontas, Ark. (see *Parks*). To make reservations, either call the number above or make online reservations at www.accessarkansasparks .com/servlet/WebresResDesk?6037.

Greers Ferry Lake (501-362-2416; www.swl.usace.army.mil/parks/greers ferry or www.greersferrylake.org), 700 Heber Springs Rd. N., Heber Springs, Ark. The Army Corps of Engineers manages 13 campgrounds around Greers Ferry containing more than 1,200 individual campsites. Most are open Apr./May–Oct./Nov., though the John F. Kennedy Park (which also offers access to the Little Red River) is open year-round. Campsites are $12 at the Mill Creek campground, while other areas run $10–18, depending the availability of water and electricity. Spots may be reserved by calling 1-877-444-6777 or visiting www .recreation.gov.

Bull Shoals Lake (870-425-2700; www.swl.usace.army.mil/parks/bull shoals), 324 W. Seventh St., Mountain Home, Ark. At Bull Shoals Lake, 12 campgrounds containing 400 individual sites are managed by the Corps of Engineers. The range is from primitive tent clearings to spots with both water and electricity. The campgrounds are open Apr.–Oct., but call ahead; exact dates vary. Campground fees are $14–20. Spots may be reserved by calling 1-877-444-6777 or visiting www.recreation.gov.

Norfork Lake (870-425-2700 or 1-877-444-6777; www.swl.usace.army .mil/parks/norfork/index.htm), 324 W. Seventh. St., Mountain Home, Ark. At Norfork the Army Corps manages 11 campgrounds with 467 individual sites, as well as four primitive camping areas. As a rule the campgrounds are open Apr.–Oct., with prices $9–20 per night. Spots may be reserved by calling 1-877-444-6777 or visiting www.recreation.gov.

Ozark National Forest, Sylamore District (870-269-3228; www.fs.fed .us/oonf/ozark), 1001 E. Main St., Mountain View, Ark. You may camp almost anywhere for free in the Ozark National Forest, as long as you don't mind not having any services. There are a number of day-use areas and approved campgrounds in the forest—which sometimes include swimming beaches, boat ramps, and more—most of these have a $3-per-vehicle, per-day fee.

Buffalo National River (870-439-2502; www.nps.gov/buff), 402 N. Walnut St., Harrison, Ark. Camping opportunities are plentiful along the Buffalo National River. You can pitch a tent most anywhere so long as it's at least half a mile from any developed area. There are 13 separate campgrounds, with the Maumme South, Spring Creek, and Woolum sites being free and open year-round.

These sites are of a more primitive nature (as is the Carver site, which charges a fee) and are available on a first-come, first-served basis. Also, these sites are not handicapped accessible. The popular Buffalo Point campground offers both tent sites and drive-in sites with water and 20- or 30-amp service. To play it safe, you should reserve a site here by calling 1-877-444-6777 or by checking out www.recreation.gov. This campground offers 83 drive-in sites, 20 walk-in sites, and is handicapped accessible in spots. Fees vary; call or visit the reservation website for details. Campgrounds of a more modern variety, but that charge a fee Apr.–Oct. (they are open and free the rest of the year), are the Erbie, Kyles Landing, Lost Valley, Ozark, Steel Creek, and Tyler Bend sites. Some offer drive-in services, tent camping, or both. Most offer a few handicapped-accessible sites. Tent sites average $10 per day, drive-in sites $17.

✳ Where to Eat

EATING OUT 🍴 ♿ ✐ 🍷 **Josie's at the Lockhouse** (870-793-7000), 50 Riverbank Dr., Batesville, Ark. Open for lunch Tues.–Fri. 11–2, for dinner Thurs.–Sat. 4–11. Reservations are recommended for dinner. A family restaurant, Josie's is a big and airy establishment that overlooks the White River. The restaurant moved to this location in 2004 after many years in Waldenburg, Ark. Not only can you get a great steak or catfish fillet, but if so inclined you can also take the stage during frequent open-mike and karaoke nights. On weekends you'll find live music more often than not. Mondays offer all-you-can-eat catfish.

Thursday nights feature smoked ribs, and Saturday nights are known for prime rib.

🦟 🖋 ♿ **Sodie's Fountain & Grill** (870-453-7632; www.sodies.com), 109 N. First St., Flippin, Ark. It goes without saying that any restaurant that features large seating capacity (I'd estimate about 150 in this case) and a gift shop is gearing heavily toward tourists. That's not a bad thing as long as the food is decent, and Sodie's definitely gets a ranking of more than decent. OK, you can get breakfast, lunch, or dinner (a fairly standard menu), but that's not why I'm recommending you stop. The reason to come to Sodie's is for its reasonable facsimile of an old-fashioned drugstore soda fountain. The shakes and malts are hand dipped; the ever-trustworthy banana splits and sundaes are made while you watch. More than that, you have to like a place that fixes you a lime or cherry Coke by squirting (or "jerking"—hence the name soda jerk) a dollop of flavoring into your cola. It's a nice touch. In Flippin you're right on top of some pretty fine fishing holes—the White and the Buffalo Rivers, to name two. Better yet, in case you didn't know, this town was pretty much ground zero for Bill and Hillary Clinton's infamous Whitewater land-development fiasco. I couldn't tell you if the famous political power couple ever ate at Sodie's, and thus I will refrain from expounding on the ironic, hypothetical interplay that might have transpired when a soda jerk meets the other kind.

🖋 ♿ 🍷 **Gaston's White River Restaurant** (870-431-5202, ext. 206; www.gastons.com/restaurant.php), 1777 River Rd., Lakeview, Ark. Open daily from mid-Feb. until Thanksgiving weekend for breakfast, lunch, and dinner. Dec.–mid-Feb., the restaurant is open Fri. night–Sun. Brunch is served Sun. year-round. Judging by the number of the contraptions hanging from the ceiling, somebody at Gaston's likes bicycles. Then again, they also enjoy old-timey photos, farm tools, and antiques. Gaston's Resort itself has been around for more than five decades, and the restaurant features not only locally famous trout dishes, but also a full bar and wine list. The breakfast buffet includes the usual suspects of eggs, omelets, pancakes, French toast, bacon, sausage, and much more for $9.95. For lunch you can pig out on a massive chicken-fried steak for $12.50, or grab a barbecued pork sandwich for $10.50. Most sandwiches are in the $8.25–10.50 range. Dinner offers a host of appetizers (again, running at or around $10), and a full rack of hickory-smoked ribs for $29. A variety of trout dishes (of the amandine and hollandaise genre) are priced in the $25–28 ballpark, and a filet mignon is $39. Numerous seafood entrées are on the menu and a 12-ounce rib eye will set you back $34.

🦟 🖋 ♿ **Fred's Fish House** (870-625-7551), 207 Main St. (off US 63), Mammoth Spring, Ark. Sometimes less is more—more or less. Thus, the only thing you need to know about Fred's Fish House is that it's often cited as serving the best catfish in Arkansas. I'd say such a statement is partially incorrect; Fred's serves up the best catfish in the Western world. The cooks use cornmeal batter (not too heavy and not too light), and your meal arrives with hush puppies, coleslaw, and pickled green tomatoes. If ordering the all-you-can-eat deal,

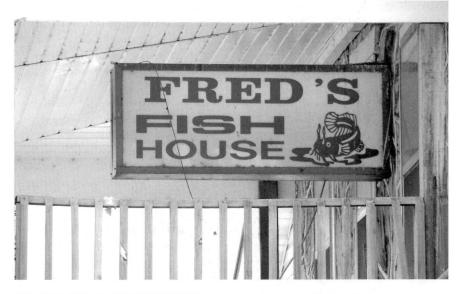

FIND YOUR WAY TO FRED'S FISH HOUSE

don't fill up too quickly on french fries or the puppies. Pace yourself and concentrate on the catfish. Best of all, you're not even going to come close to breaking the bank by eating here (expect to pay $15–20 tops). Listen closely . . . this place is legendary. Eating a ton of catfish at Fred's is something of an Ozark rite of passage.

DINING OUT ✍ ♿ ⚕ **178 Club Restaurant** (870-445-4949; www .178club.com), 2109 Central Blvd., Bull Shoals, Ark. Open Tues. 4–9; Wed.–Sat. 11–9; Sun. 9:30–8. In business since 1980, this well-known eatery at Bull Shoals has a menu that is roughly the size of the Reader's Digest condensed version of War and Peace. If you can't find something you like at 178, then you'd best just cook at home. Dinner appetizers include escargot for $7.99, or baked Brie for $9.99. The seafood menu runs the gamut from mahimahi to shrimp to walleye. But, in keeping with the in-depth catfish reports featured throughout the other chapters of this book, please note that 178's fillet, either fried, broiled, or blackened, is $14.29. For a better deal, not to mention more novelty, the seafood platter offers shrimp, clams, scallops, catfish, and frog legs for $21.99. Steaks are in the $17–23 range, and chicken entrées run $16–17. The Sunday brunch is pretty famous in these parts and runs $8.99. The 178 Club also offers a full bar, wine list, and beer.

✍ ♿ ⚕ **Café Klaser** (501-206-0688; www.cafeklaser.com), SR 110 East (across from the Swinging Bridge Resort), Heber Springs, Ark. Summer hours are Mon.–Wed. 4:30–8:30, Thurs.–Sun. 11–8:30. On Fri.–Sat. nights the restaurant is open until 10. Located right on the Little Red River, Café Klaser has a signature dish that everyone should try at least once. The crawdad-stuffed tenderloin, available in 5- and 10-ounce varieties, is that fine fillet of beef stuffed with crawdads and rice. The cost, from small to large, is $14.95 or $20.45. Other than that, you will find a number of Cajun-style dishes here, as well as plenty of seafood and steak. Frog legs are $11.95, and the catfish fillet is $10.95. Another specialty is the shrimp moutarde at $13.95, or you can have the tried-and-true 16-ounce rib-eye steak for $18.95. You'll find plenty of salads and burgers, and (happily) Café Klaser also offers the legendary oyster po'boy sandwich. It's $7.95, as are the equally delicious catfish, shrimp, or crawdad po'boys. The exterior of the café is a bit disconcerting—basically a very large green and white steel building—but don't let that stop you in the least. The inside is nice and the food is terrific. Liquor laws in Arkansas can be a bit dicey, but Café Klaser has a private club license, so you can get a beer or a drink. The law states that all members of the club (and their guests) can have a nip, and thus a year's membership is only $10 (you just fork it over at the front desk). It's a silly law that makes no sense, but then again an awful lot of laws are like that. More than a few parts of Arkansas are still whacky in regard to the consumption of alcohol, and I'm pretty sure the words written on the state seal read "Lips that touch liquor will never touch mine."

✳ Entertainment

✿ ✎ **Ozark Heritage Arts Center & Museum** (870-447-2500), 410 Oak St., Leslie, Ark. You might not think the old stone gym in Leslie (a 1938 WPA-built structure) would hold a 400-seat theater. As we say in the Ozarks, "That's what ya get for thinkin'." The auditorium features everything from local performers to

an open-mike night on Friday. Not only is there a theater in the facility, but there's also an art gallery, a museum full of artifacts from the Leslie of yesteryear, and all sorts of interesting remnants that came from what was once the world's largest whiskey barrel factory. This place is amazingly gorgeous inside; definitely worth a stop for nifty sights and good music. Hours change in winter and summer, so call ahead for this information and various admission prices.

LIVE MUSIC ✿ ✎ ♿ **John Taylor's Laid Back Pickin'** (870-269-9597), 16484 SR 9 South, Mountain View, Ark. The current John Taylor carries on the Mountain View music tradition pioneered by his father and grandfather. This music show of longstanding reputation features not only the old tunes of the Ozarks, but a number of newer pieces as well. Dancing is also part of the show, and visitors are invited to kick up their heels (but not during the gospel numbers—that would be viewed as rude in these parts). This is a family show, and everyone is welcome. While there is no set admission price, donations are expected (this can be whatever you think is fair and can afford). This is good mountain music the way it ought to be, and it's well worth any price you're willing to pay. Apr.–Oct., all shows begin at 7:30 on Mon., Tues., Fri., and Sat.

✿ ✎ ♿ **Jimmy Driftwood Barn** (870-269-8042), 19775 SR 5 North, Mountain View, Ark. If you aren't immediately acquainted with the name of the late Jimmy Driftwood, he was the man who wrote the classic tune, "Battle of New Orleans." In fact, he wrote it 18 years before it became famous, as a way for his high school history students to remember that the fight took place during the War of 1812. Driftwood is an Arkansas icon for his prolific recordings and compositions, and his barn is still a hot spot for music. Stop by at 7 PM Fri.–Sun. and you'll catch incredibly talented local musicians playing country, gospel, and bluegrass. Call ahead for information on special events and prices.

🍴 🎵 ♿ **Mountain View Folklore Society** (870-269-8215), 224 Franklin St., Mountain View, Ark. From 7–9 every Sat., drop by this Franklin Street address to hear local musicians playing traditional Ozark tunes. In summer bring a lawn chair, look at the stars, and watch the performers as they take the stage in front of the courthouse. There is no admission fee, but donations are always welcome if you feel like pitching a few bucks in the hat.

THEATER 🍴 🎵 ♿ **The Imperial Dinner Theatre** (870-892-0030 or 1-888-515-8218; www.imperialdinner theatre.com), 1401 SR 304 East, Pocahontas, Ark. When it opened in 1941, the Imperial was one of those grand old movie houses that featured nickel flicks, a neon marquee, and that newfangled air-conditioning. The theater closed in the mid-1970s and sat empty for two decades. Renovated in the 1990s by volunteers, the Imperial came to be known for educational classes, live plays, and musical presentations (along with full meals) approximately every other month. Then the floods of 2011 hit. The levee on the Black River busted wide open, and the Imperial was in the path of the raging floodwaters. The destruction to the old theater was immense. Volunteers are still restoring the building at the time of this writing. They're an unsinkable bunch, however, and performances should be under way again by the time this book sees print. Make sure to give them a call if you're traveling toward Pocahontas. This is a class act, and the group promises that shows in the reconstructed building will be as good or better than ever.

SPECTATOR SPORTS 🎵 **Batesville Speedway** (870-613-1337; www .batesvillemotorspeedway.net), 5090 Heber Springs Rd., Locust Grove, Ark. A ⅜-mile, red-clay oval track, the Batesville Speedway features stock

JIMMY DRIFTWOOD BARN

cars, modifieds, sprint cars, and even demolition derbies. For Fri. and Sat. races, the gates generally open at 5:30. Grandstand seating is $5 for adults, with kids 11 and under admitted free. Ticket prices are considerably higher for major races and special events.

 North Central Arkansas Speedway (870-449-5277; www.north centralarspeedway.com), US 62, Flippin, Ark. Located 4 miles west of Flippin on US 62, this speedway features a ⅜-mile dirt track, and hosts races every Fri. night. You'll see hobby stock cars and trucks, modifieds, pure stock and cruisers, mini stocks, and go-carts. The racing season runs mid-Mar.–Oct., with gates opening at 6 PM and racing beginning at 8 PM. General admission is $10 for adults, $8 for seniors, and $5 for kids ages 6–12.

✴ Selective Shopping

Serenity Farm Bread (870-447-2211; www.serenityfarmbread Serenity Farm Bread.us), Leslie, Ark. Open Mon.–Thurs. 8–5, Fri. 8–4, Sat. 9–4, Sun. 9–3. For some of the best sourdough bread you'll ever taste, stop by one of Serenity Farm's two locations in Leslie, about 50 miles south of Harrison, Ark. The first location is in the old Farmer's Bank Building; the second is about half a mile south of town in a 100-year-old Sears "kit" house. This operation uses only certified-organic flours, unrefined sea salt, filtered water, and natural sourdough starter. The company ships its tasty products all over the U.S.

The Dulcimer Shoppe (1-877-269-4422; www.mcspaddendulcimers .com), 104 Sylamore Ave., Mountain View, Ark. Mon.–Sat. 9–5. The dulcimer is one of those instruments that is incredibly easy to play—and much harder to master. The craftsmen at The Dulcimer Shoppe have nearly 150 years' combined experience in building these instruments by hand and will have you up and strumming in no time.

THE DULCIMER SHOPPE

Stone County Ironworks (870-269-8108 or 1-800-223-4722; www.stone iron.com), 408 Ironworks Dr., Mountain View, Ark. This place calls itself "America's Blacksmith Shop," which isn't bad considering that the operation began in 1979 in an abandoned gas station. For beds, furniture, garden accessories, or virtually anything else forged and crafted from iron, this is the place.

✳ Special Events

Also see Towns and Villages.
March **Bluegrass Music Show** (870-448-3665), Van Buren County Fairgrounds, Marshall, Ark. This mid-March show features numerous bands guaranteed to keep your toes tapping. $8 per day.

Main Street Hardy Spring Gun & Knife Show (870-856-3571; http://old hardytown.net), Hardy, Ark. Held in late March in the old Hardy gym (there's also a fall show in November), this is the place to be if you like things that go bang. There's plenty of buying, selling, and trading of both old and new guns, but you'll also find knives of every shape, size, and description, Civil War memorabilia, and a variety or doodads, gewgaws, gimcracks, and novelties. The show takes place Sat. 9–5, Sun. 10–4. $3 adults; children under 12 admitted free.

Ozark Folk School (870-269-3851; www.ozarkfolkcenter.com), 1032 Park Ave., Mountain View, Ark. Held for three and five days in mid-March, the Ozark Folk School affords you the opportunity to learn all the stuff your humorless, grammar-obsessed high school teachers ignored. You can take workshops in blacksmithing, stained

glass, pottery, or quilting. You can learn how to make lye soap, cook on a woodstove, or grow and tend an herb garden. You'll pick and grin as you attend workshops on mountain dulcimer, banjo, fiddle, or ukulele, and tone your voice on Ozark folk songs. Craft workshop fees vary, but planning on around $500 is a safe bet. As a rule, you can take only one class during the week, because classes are given at the same time. If you wish to stay on-site, check out the various lodging and meal programs. The Ozark Folk School is held at Ozark Folk Center State Park, located 1 mile north of Mountain View off SR 382, which is off SR 5, SR 9, and SR 14.

April **Arkansas Folk Festival** (870-269-8068), Mountain View, Ark. It would be something of a letdown if the Folk Music Capital of the World didn't have a folk festival. Fear not, for it takes place over three days in mid-April. Bring an instrument if you play; if you don't, just grab yourself some spoons, a kazoo, or a tambourine. People will be jamming all over town, particularly on the town square. In addition to nonstop music, the festival includes a parade; arts, crafts, and food vendors; and a variety of games and competitions.

Arkansas Scottish Festival (870-698-4298; www.lyon.edu/scotfest), Lyon College, 2300 Highland Rd., Batesville, Ark. Taking place for two days in late April, this festival celebrates the Scottish roots of Lyon College with piping, dancing, a parade of clans, and a traditional feast. There are also Scottish athletic events, most of which seem to revolve around tossing oddly shaped objects. Admission price varies from year to year, but it's generally less than $20 for adults

June **Hardy Homesteaders Day** (870-856-3811), Loburg City Park, Hardy, Ark. For one day in mid-June, Hardy celebrates the past with wagon rides, quilting and spinning demonstrations, blacksmithing, corn grinding, mule jumping, turtle races, and much more. Admission is free, though there are some minimal charges for food and drink.

Buffalo River Elk Festival (870-446-2455; www.theozarkmountains .com), Jasper, Ark. Taking place on the town square for two days in late June, this free event draws more than 100 artists, vendors, and artisans. The kids can take part in the fishing derby, and everyone loves the Dutch oven cook-off and horseshoe tournament. Live entertainment is a given. These are the Arkansas Ozarks, after all.

July ✍ **World Championship Cardboard Boat Races** (501-362-2444; www.heber-springs.com/world -championship-cardboard-boat-races), Heber Springs, Ark. If you always wanted to be a boatbuilder but lacked the time, knowledge, or funds, you can still sate your latent desire by entering the World Championship Cardboard Boat Races in Heber Springs. It's held on a single day at the end of July, and you can shoot for being the "pride of the fleet" (unless your boat happens to sink in spectacular fashion, in which case you receive the Titanic Award). In addition to the boat races, kids can take part in a sand-sculpting contest and dig for buried treasure. You won't want to miss the World Championship Watermelon Eating Contest, and at the end of the festival the Cardboard Boat Demolition Derby is a flat-out riot. For admission and parking you won't spend more than about $5.

August **White River Water Carnival** (870-793-2378; www.mybatesville .org/white-river-water-carnival-2011), Riverside Park, Batesville, Ark. It's not the oldest festival in Arkansas (that would be the Yellville Turkey Trot), but it is the oldest Arkansas festival on the water. The White River Carnival, nearly 70 years old, takes place for two days on the first weekend in August. You can expect a car and motorcycle show; arts, crafts, and food vendors; a huge parade; and the White River beauty pageant. As always, prepare yourself for great music.

September **National Championship Chuckwagon Races** (501-745-8407; http://chuckwagonraces.com), 2848 Shake Rag Rd., Clinton, Ark. Taking place Fri.–Sun. every Labor Day weekend, the Chuckwagon Races make a NASCAR event seem as tame as a game of Yahtzee. With a variety of races, this extravaganza's prime focus involves folks driving their carts and chuckwagons at full tilt around an oval track. It has to be seen to be believed, and there are plenty of ambulances on hand in case somebody flips, tips, or crashes. More than 20,000 people show up for the races, and if you want a motel room in Clinton, you'd best call months in advance. The ranch where the races are held does offer camping; reservations (yes, you'll need them if you want a spot) are accepted after July 5. Call 501-745-5250 or 501-745-8407 to reserve your spot. More than just races, the spectacle also includes clinics, concerts, BBQ, horse and mule sales, a barn dance, a trade show, and even a nondenominational church service. If you tire of the chuckwagon races themselves, which is virtually impossible, you can also watch a Snowy River Race. This flat-out horse race is straight out of the famous scene from the movie *Man from Snowy River.* Adult admission to the races is $25 Fri.–Sat. and $15 Sun. Kids 6–12 get in for half price.

White River Days (870-445-3629), Bull Shoals–White River State Park, 129 Bull Shoals Park, Lakeview, Ark. This Labor Day weekend event celebrates the history and majesty of the White River. Admission is free, but there is a charge if you wish to take either a lake or river cruise.

October **Turkey Trot** (870-449-4676; www.yellville.com), Yellville Area Chamber of Commerce, P.O. Box 369, Yellville, AR 72687. The oldest festival in Arkansas, the Turkey Trot has been held in mid-October every year since 1946. You'll hear turkey callers from all over America, watch the turkey parade in downtown Yellville, eat a turkey dinner, and enjoy innumerable food booths, vendor stands, live bands, and contests. There's even a turkey trot beauty pageant.

November **Mountain View Bluegrass Festival** (870-269-2542 or 870-269-2704; www.mountainview-bluegrass.com), Mountain View, Ark. One of the many productions hosted at the Ozark Folk Center State Park, this three-day event in mid-November features not only a plethora of great bands and solo artists, but also an infinite number of impromptu jams. A three-day pass is $55, with tickets for individual days being $20.

INDEX